DWIGHT MACDONALD ON MOVIES

Books by Dwight Macdonald

The Root Is Man
The Ford Foundation
Memoirs of a Revolutionist
Against the American Grain: Essays on the Effects of Mass Culture
Parodies: An Anthology (editor)
Poems of Edgar Allan Poe (editor)
Dwight Macdonald on Movies

DWIGHT MACDONALD ON MOVIES

by

DWIGHT MACDONALD

PRENTICE-HALL, INC., ENGLEWOOD CLIFFS, N.J.

PN
1994
M313

Second Printing.........November, 1969

We gratefully acknowledge permission to reprint articles from the following: *Film Heritage*, Fall 1967; reprinted by permission F. A. Macklin. *The Symposium;* reprinted with the permission of James Burnham, April 1933, pp. 159–177, and July 1933, pp. 280–300. *Partisan Review,* July and August–September 1938, Winter 1939; © 1938 and 1939 by *Partisan Review*. *Partisan Review,* November–December 1942; © 1942 by *Partisan Review*. *Esquire Magazine,* © by *Esquire, Inc.*

CONTENTS

FORENOTES

THIS is a selection from my writing on movies during the last forty years. I left out some pieces that seemed juvenile, dated, or—in the case of the monthly reviews I wrote for *Esquire* from 1960 to 1966—even more evanescent or "fugitive" than the ones I've included. I've done some cutting, most drastically in the *Miscellany* pieces and the *Partisan Review* history of Soviet Cinema, and very little rewriting. Everything is identified by name and date of publication, except for *Esquire* articles which are followed only by the date of the issue. Also, in the grab-bag of Part VI: "Trims & Clips"—my favorite section, where I advise casual, unserious readers to begin—I felt the year of publication was enough for such important trivia.

I KNOW something about cinema after forty years, and being a congenital critic, I know what I like and why. But I can't explain the *why* except in terms of the specific work under consideration, on which I'm copious enough. The general theory, the larger view, the gestalt—these have always eluded me. Whether this gap in my critical armor be called an idiosyncrasy or, less charitably, a personal failing, it has always been most definitely there.

But people, especially undergraduates hot for certainty, keep asking me what rules, principles or standards I judge movies by—a fair question to which I can never think of an answer. Years ago, some forgotten but evidently sharp stimulus spurred me to put some guidelines down on paper. The result, hitherto unprinted for reasons which will become clear, was:

(1) Are the characters consistent, and in fact are there characters at all?
(2) Is it true to life?
(3) Is the photography cliché, or is it adapted to the particular film and therefore original?
(4) Do the parts go together; do they add up to something; is there a rhythm established so that there is form, shape, climax, building up tension and exploding it?
(5) Is there a mind behind it; is there a feeling that a single intelligence has imposed his own view on the material?

The last two questions rough out some vague sort of meaning, and the third is sound, if truistic. But I can't account for the first two being there at all, let alone in the lead-off place. Many films I admire are not "true to life" unless that stretchable term is strained beyond normal usage: *Broken Blossoms, Children of Paradise, Zéro de Conduite, Caligari, On*

ix

Approval, Eisenstein's *Ivan the Terrible*. And some have no "characters" at all, consistent or no: *Potemkin, Arsenal, October, Intolerance, Marienbad, Orpheus, Olympia*. The comedies of Keaton, Chaplin, Lubitsch, the Marx Brothers and W. C. Fields occupy a middle ground. They have "consistent" characters all right, and they are also "true to life." But the consistency is always extreme and sometimes positively compulsive and obsessed (W. C., Groucho, Buster), and the truth is abstract. In short, they are so highly stylized (cf. "the Lubitsch touch") that they are constantly floating up from *terra firma* into the empyrean of art, right before my astonished and delighted eyes.

THE first half of Keaton's *Sherlock Junior*, for example, is one of those genre comedies of calf love that the more earthbound Harold Lloyd specialized in. It's set in a small town whose streets, houses, and interiors are photographed with that sharp realism common in our silent comedies (what an accurate, detailed family album of how America used to look!). It is populated by the commonplace types of the period (given the usual comic twist that exaggerates them into folk-mythical grotesques, just as the prosaic policeman was metamorphosed into the Mack Sennett cop). But the second half of *Sherlock Junior* cuts loose from these mooring strings and drifts free across magical country. By a great stroke of invention, the lovesick Buster is a movie projectionist, so that the medium becomes the artist's material—an advanced approach Keaton undoubtedly never heard of and wouldn't have understood if he had. He falls asleep in his projection booth, dreaming about his girl and his frustrated love. His *doppelganger* extracts itself from his sleeping body, takes off its hook the ghost of the Keaton pancake hat, literally a "lid" (the real lid still hanging there: a nice touch), claps it on his head, and walks down the aisle of the darkened theatre to climb up on the stage and step into the society-crook melodrama being projected on the screen. The characters become transformed into his girl, her parents, his rival, and himself, all of them dressed to the nines. As the great detective, Buster sports a soup-and-fish outfit, slightly baggy in the seat and gaping in the wing collar, but including a magnificently draped watch chain he twirls with uneasy insouciance.

The rest of the film—except for a brief and funny real-life coda—chronically violates every natural law except that of optics (movie optics, that is). In one sequence, the background keeps shifting arbitrarily, crossing up Buster who jumps into a ravine and lands on a rock in the midst of a choppy sea, into which he dives, only to sprawl on his face in the sands of a desert. In another, he escapes from gangsters who have him trapped in a dead-end street by taking a running dive through a large square aperture which, by raising her tray, a motherly old lady selling pencils opens up not only in her own midriff but also in the wall behind her. There's no explanation of this or any other *lapsus naturalis* in this 1924 film which makes later efforts by Dali, Buñuel, and Cocteau look pedestrian and a bit timid. They felt obliged to clarify matters by a symbolistic apparatus. Keaton never rose—or sunk—to that.

T. S. Eliot summed it all up long ago with his usual laconic authority: "The egregious merit of Chaplin is that he has escaped in his own way from the realm of the cinema and invented a *rhythm*. Of course, the unexplored possibilities of the cinema for eluding realism must be very great." (I especially like that offhand "of course.") This prophetic *aperçu* is one that recent explorations by Bergman, Fellini, Resnais, and other contemporary masters into the "possibilities for eluding realism" are beginning to illustrate two generations later.

GETTING back to general principles, I can think offhand (the only way I seem able to think about general principles) of two ways to judge the quality of a movie. They are mere rules of thumb, but they work—for me anyway:

(A) Did it change the way you look at things?
(B) Did you find more (or less) in it the second, third, *n*th time? (Also, how did it stand up over the years, after one or more "periods" of cinematic history?)

Both rules are *post facto* and so, while they may be helpful to critics and audiences, they aren't of the slightest use to those who make movies. This is as it should be. The critic's job doesn't include second-guessing the director by giving him helpful suggestions as to how he might have made a better film. If the director knows his business, such "constructive criticism" (as it's called by sincere philistines in the boondocks and by insincere philistines on Madison Avenue—which might be called a metropolitan boondock) is an impertinence.* If a director *doesn't* know his business, which is not uncommon, it's an irrelevance. Of all the sources from which he might get wised up—agents, girl friends, col-

---

* The director's business, of course, may not coincide with the critic's business. William Wyler, to take the first Hollywood veteran that comes to mind, knows by now (as he should) just how to make a slickly-machined, chromium-plated Hollywood movie. But his business has never come close to mine. Looking over the two inches of his film credits in Leslie Halliwell's useful reference book *The Film-goer's Companion* (Hill & Wang, 1967, $12.50) I find many pretentious middlebrow duds like *Wuthering Heights, Dead End, The Best Years of Our Lives, The Children's Hour,* and many films like *Ben-Hur* and *The Friendly Persuasion* that are unpretentious lowbrow duds.

leagues, observant cutters, perceptive grips, Mom, Dad, Billy Graham, Christian Science—the least likely is by reading the reviews of his still-born creations. The intelligent ones will mystify and depress him, and the dumb ones will tell him he's doing just fine.

Shifting the focus from the director to the critic (and paraphrasing Groucho), I wouldn't want to see a movie by a director who had to learn to make movies from my reviews. They say it's easy enough to be critical, or negative, or destructive, but it isn't really. To stick to serious, negative, unconstructive criticism takes a lot of thought and effort. In this country today, the undertow pulling the critic into the dangerous waters of positive, responsible thinking seems to be getting stronger every year. In forty years I can't recall anything I've written that has had a specific, definable effect on anybody connected with the making of movies. I've encouraged some directors to persist, but since all directors appear to persist unto death (and sometimes afterward, it seems) there's no way to tell. The only hard evidence would be the opposite: my success in encouraging directors and actors to get out of movies and into something better suited to their talents, like selling insurance or becoming the bursar of a small denominational college in upper Michigan. Some of them must have given up and slipped into something more comfortable during the six years I was writing for *Esquire,* but as far as I know, the two or three dozen I devoted myself to educating—tirelessly, selflessly, month after month—are still unpersuaded, still gnawing away like beavers at the roots of cinema. I used every resource in the critical lexicon: reason, ridicule, patient demonstration of their incompetence, impatient expostulation when they continued to inflict it on movie audiences, long parodies, short jeers, odious comparisons with their betters, appeals to the glorious past and the brilliant future of the art—in neither of which tenses I could see them cutting much of a figure.

My detachment was incredible, almost priggish. True, I met Joseph Losey at a London dinner party by unfortunate chance (unfortunate because I rather liked him personally). But I have never seen, let alone met, Elia Kazan, Tony Richardson, Jules Dassin, Stanley Kramer or Luchino Visconti, to name some of my regular parishioners to whom

---

In all this industrious manufacture, there's nothing except *Detective Story,* a sound melodrama, that I recall with even the mild pleasure evoked by four or five of the almost-as-many films of Billy Wilder—another old Hollywood hand (or hack) often confused with William Wilder, but more lively and talented. Not very much more—only enough to be visible on the Hollywood scale, where the local Doctor Johnsons don't disdain to settle the precedence between a flea and a louse. Quite the contrary, it's their main occupation.

xii

I strove to bring the simple message: *Give It Up!* But they haven't. Nor have—to name a few of the stars I tried to persuade to take up some occupation that would not require them to impersonate somebody else— Alain Delon, Elizabeth Taylor, Laurence Harvey, Kirk Douglas, Burt Lancaster, Anthony Perkins, Doris Day, Melina Mercouri, Yul Brynner, Audrey Hepburn, Richard Harris, Monica Vitti (the wrong actress disappeared at the beginning of *L'Avventura*) . . . but why go on? It's most discouraging. I can't even claim credit for Bosley Crowther's retirement as the *Times* movie critic. He was pretty old—sixty-two, my age.

THE lesser question is whether, after one has dazedly stumbled out of the movie theatre (Plato's cave inside which the reality outside is perceived only indirectly by its flickering reflection on the wall), the director has imposed his personal vision strongly enough while one was immured in his shadowy underworld to make it seem, for a while, more real than the common light of day. I experienced this after seeing *Children of Paradise,* and I was similarly affected when I first saw certain Soviet silent movies—also after re-viewing *Birth of a Nation* several years ago. *Grand Illusion* is another that gave me temporary astigmatism. The hallucination soon dissipates like a dream, but also like a dream, it may be significant. Perhaps such films make some change in one's subconscious that lasts long after the visual effect has vanished; certainly they have cast a temporary poetic spell on me that I don't often feel. In a larger sense, it seems obvious that the great directors and the great schools of cinema have changed our awareness of our environment as the impressionists and post-impressionists did: by showing us a new way of seeing the world—visual, not conceptual. Cinema, like music and painting—its closest, most incestuous relatives in the arts—is mute when it comes to expressing ideas (look at "tone poems" and Victorian moralizing paintings). But there are too many ideas around in this scientized age, and not enough sensory perception of what's right in front of our noses or eyes (as against our brains). That's one reason I like movies. It seems unnecessary, and therefore boring for you and me, to dredge up examples to support this point.

The second time I saw *8½,* two weeks after the first, I took more notes than I had the first time, so many beauties and subtleties and puzzles I had overlooked. The third and fourth times I saw it (in connection with courses on movie history I was giving at the University of Texas in 1966 and the Santa Cruz campus of the University of California in 1969), I didn't take notes, having written at some length what I had to say—see "Fellini's Obvious Masterpiece" in Part I. But I enjoyed it all over again each time. A masterpiece delights first by its originality and then by its familiarity. You don't get tired of Homer, or the Alice books.

I've seen *Citizen Kane* seven or eight times, and it's still fresh: the *March of Time* pastiche that summarizes Kane's career and parodically announces the themes to be developed; the breakfast-table dissolves telling us in five minutes of cinematic shorthand all we need to know about Kane's first marriage and why it failed; the opera scenes which successfully combine irony, pathos, realism and technical bravura, and the breaking-up of Kane's second marriage—its emotional climax: the cockatoo's sudden, unnerving screech that gives shocking tongue to Kane's mute despair as his most precious possession walks out on him and he begins to die. (He begs her not to leave him, and she wavers until he protests, "You can't do this to me." "Oh, yes I can!" she says, and does.) Herman Mankiewicz's script is one of the marvels of this marvelous film. Another is the sound track: released in 1941, *Citizen Kane* was the first movie to fully transcend the "talkies" stage, integrating sound with image in the abstract, non-literary way Eisenstein and Pudovkin had prophesied in their 1928 manifesto on the future of the sound film. The cockatoo's shriek is an instance. It is also notable because like *Kane*'s imagery in general, it is not one of those dragged-in symbols so fashionable in many "advanced" films and so dear to graduate students. Rather it's an unforced metaphor, arising naturally out of the action: that cockatoo was not imported to articulate Kane's agony; he was there because he was part of the zoo his master's collecting mania had assembled.

SOME movies don't wear well, of course. *Hiroshima, Mon Amour* and *Breathless* impressed me when I saw them first in 1960 because they were striking out along new paths (which were also the old ones of the silent period to which Resnais and Godard were returning, just as the post-impressionists went back to Renaissance and earlier traditions of painting to make their avantgarde-rearguard revolution). Five years later, both looked a little time-worn. This is a tribute, of course, to their success historically: their innovations have become common practice. Fellini's *I Vitelloni* (1953) is another pioneer—in anti-dramatic realism—that now looks dim to me. But there have been ground-breaking movies which have transcended the historical dimension: they have dated for the mind without fading to the eye. The last time I saw *Birth of a Nation,* for instance, I realized how completely Griffith's technical innovations have been assimilated. But I was also impressed by the power and originality with which he used them: the beauty of the close-ups, often poetic, romantic in an "old-fashioned" style (that I don't mind at all, myself), but always composed with a plastic authority that should please the most up-to-date eye; the carefully calculated design of individual shots; the laconic boldness with which he stylized a scene, leaving in the minimum to make his dramatic point and omitting the connective, explanatory clutter less confident directors throw in (under the illusion they are "building up" the scene when in fact they're tearing it down). I was even thrilled once more by the cross-cutting montage of the "Griffith ending," S.O.P. in such melodramas for generations. My reaction was not *déja vu,* but "how come?" Why did so much look so good after fifty years of imitation? Although I distrust that snob-word "genius," it's the only adequate term here.

RE-VISIBILITY can be a matter of decades, or of days. The most extreme instance of the latter is *Last Year at Marienbad* (1961) which is not a masterpiece (see my review in Part V), but which so curiously fascinated me I saw it three times in one week. On the one hand, it was one of the most technically interesting movies I've seen, using every device including such uncommon ones as stop motion and reverse printing with the greatest freedom and yet also with a control that kept the parts subordinate to the whole so that a harmonious tone was sustained throughout. On the other hand, what *was* the whole, expressed with such disciplined virtuosity? What did it all "mean"? I couldn't make sense out of the plot or the characters; everything kept changing like a kaleidescope—and was just as hard to remember one or two shakes later. So I went back, twice. I was no closer the last time than the first to understanding the relations between the husband, the wife, and the (perhaps) lover. But I did come to see what the director, M. Resnais, and the scenarist, M. Robbe-Grillet, meant when they insisted that *that* wasn't what they had had in mind at all. They disagree on what, if anything, did happen last year at Marienbad. I saw that the only point of their film is the affect of what impinges on the eye of the spectator. Like seeing music. Although I got no emotional affect, or kick, from my three *Marienbad* immersions as some friends did, I got plenty of visual ones each time. Perhaps my reasons for so compulsively returning to *Marienbad* were less conscientious than I thought. Rationalistic detection may have been a cover-story for a secret craving, a prurient itch for a low sensual experience of visual imagery that I didn't dare admit to myself. When a modern critic hears the word "beauty," he releases the safety catch on his fountain pen.

Some long term re-visitings have been disappointing. Two of my early enthusiasms were for Von Stroheim's *The Wedding March* (1927) and Von Sternberg's *The Case of Lena Smith* (1929) which co-starred in my first printed movie piece, "Imaginative Art in Some New Films," in the May 1929 issue of a very little "little" magazine aptly named *Out-*

siders. I haven't seen *Lena Smith* since then, and I'm told it's been lost or destroyed—negative and all prints—in some fit of Hollywood absent-mindedness (cinema is the most physically fragile of modern arts). But I did see *The Wedding March* recently at Lincoln Center. Its *longeurs* were more evident than its *grandeurs.* Stroheim's horseback flirtation with Fay Wray in the crowd, restricted to eye and lip movements plus a few tugs on the reins, was still a wonder of subtlety. For the first ten minutes, that is. But the realistic scenes in the brothel and the butcher-shop seemed too much so, the romantic ones among the apple blossoms not enough so—and he did take his time.

My passion for Cocteau's *Blood of a Poet* (1930) survived almost forty years. (I used to compare it, in style and montage, with Eisenstein's *October;* oh God! I was being brilliant, of course, but still, oh God!) It perished the other month when I screened it in my Santa Cruz movie course. It suddenly showed its age, looking mannered rather than stylized, more affected than affecting, terribly thin in content and slow in movement. The hero's dive through the mirror (which becomes a pool into which he splashes) was as magical a shock as ever, but his underwater progress along the hotel corridor took forever. His voyeuristic keyhole sights (which I used to think deeply symbolic, as perhaps they are) now looked just arbitrary, and, in another sense, all too predictable: what else would you expect to find going on in the rooms of a surrealist hotel?

Intellectually, I can still see what I admired in both films, but concretely (which is all that counts) they now look dated.

When I first saw *The Cabinet of Dr. Caligari* (1919) in the twenties, I respected but didn't enjoy it. Indeed, I couldn't really see it then, my eye being too strongly conditioned by the dynamic, *plein air* style of Griffith and the Russians. It has become increasingly visible in the sixties, and I now think it's a masterpiece—perhaps minor and certainly very special, but with a unity of atmospheric style (rare in movies) that reminds me of Poe's tales, to which it bears other resemblances. *Caligari* is a historical sport, a mule without cinematic progeny (though fertile and prophetic enough politically—see Siegfried Kracauer's *From Caligari to Hitler* for an interesting over-demonstration) which violates every received idea about the "true" nature of the medium. It is a photographed stage play when it isn't an art exhibition: the stills are superb expressionist pictures in themselves, and they give a remarkably complete idea of the film—an ominously complete idea, if it is assumed a movie should move. Cinematically, *Caligari* can hardly be said to move at all. It is static, frozen (with terror?), and claustrophobic, while most movies, because of their technology (the limitless, omnivorous camera

xvi

and the manipulative freedom in the cutting room) tend to be restless, extensive, and agoraphilic—also realistic. *Caligari* is completely artificial. The cast, grotesquely costumed and made up in a "sick" *commedia dell'arte* style, perform with operatically stylized gestures in sets that are carefully painted and sculpted so as to destroy the slightest illusion of reality. Even the outdoor scenes are psychologically indoors—perhaps literally; it's hard to imagine a real sky in *Caligari,* or a real anything. About the only movie techniques used are the close-up and the angle shot (plenty of the latter, the camera being as crookbacked as the sets). There may have been a few right-angles in *Caligari;* if so, I missed them. There's no trace of montage, although Griffith had introduced it a decade earlier. The sophisticated trio who made *Caligari*—and didn't or couldn't follow it up with another work despite its huge success (perhaps they were as baffled by it as everybody else)—must have known Griffith's work. But they had something else in mind, and they produced a unique anti-movie that came close to perfection by breaking all the rules—one reason I like it.

THIS is a fast century. A generation used to be twenty years, and is now closer to five—and even in the older, traditional arts, a lot has happened in the forty years since I began writing about films. In the raw young medium of cinema, which is only two years older than I am (dating its birth as an art form around 1908, when D. W. Griffith began to invent its basic vocabulary all by himself), the pace has been headlong. Movie "periods" are measured in decades rather than centuries, as in other art history. This doesn't make criticism any easier.

Three major periods might be defined:

CLASSIC SILENT (1908–1929), which subdivides into *American* (Griffith, Stroheim, and the makers of silent comedies); *Weimar German* (Murnau, Lang, Pabst, and *Caligari*); *NEP Russian* (Eisenstein, Pudovkin, Dovzhenko, *et al*).

EARLY, OR MEDIEVAL, SOUND (1930–1955), which could also be called *PRIMITIVE* if the comparison is to the later sound period, or *DECADENT* if to the earlier silent period. Complete eclipse of the German school (never to rise again) and almost complete of the Russian (exceptions: Donskoi's trilogy on the life of Gorky, and Eisenstein's two-part *Ivan the Terrible*), both of them killed by totalitarian politics. A regression elsewhere for technological reasons: the engineers invented the sound track; the masses demanded "talkies" (or more accurately, the money-men thought the masses demanded it—we'll never know, as always in the box-office game). The directors, who had learned how to make silent movies and were innocently refining and deepening their knowledge, suddenly found it antiquated, immaterial, and irrelevant; they had to learn a whole new technique overnight. Results: spotty. Some good American films by Hawks, Ford, and others, but only two masters—Lubitsch and Welles. In France, René Clair's early comedies, Vigo's *Zéro de Conduite*, Renoir's *Grand Illusion* and *Rules of the Game,* and Carné's *Children of Paradise* were on the old level, but none of them did much with the sound track. In post-war Italy, the neo-realist school of Desica (*Shoeshine, The Bicycle Thief*) and Rossellini (*Open City, Paisan*)—cinejournalism with a social commitment—opened up new subject matter but was less original in technique.

LATER, OR RENAISSANCE, SOUND (1956 to date) has by now produced a body of work that is, for the first time since 1930, comparable to that of the *CLASSIC SILENT* period. (See Part V for reviews of some of the masters—and some of the non-masters.) After the doldrums of the thirties and forties, an esthetic of the sound film is being developed. "Old" masters like Bergman, Fellini, Antonioni, Truffaut, Resnais, Buñuel, and Kurosawa have been joined by lesser and/or younger ones (especially in France and Italy) in experimenting with the sound track so as to make it a structural element and not just an ornamental gimmick pasted on by the engineers. Like its predecessor, the present cinematic renaissance advances by returning to the silent classics. It, too, is an international movement that seems to flourish everywhere except (by historical irony) in Germany, Soviet Russia, and the United States—the countries that produced the great schools of classic cinema.

THE foregoing mini-history may explain why in some of the earlier pieces here I make an assumption I no longer think is true: that silent cinema was intrinsically superior to sound. The superiority was there, all right, easily demonstrable in the Early Sound Period, and I didn't tire of demonstrating it. But when I began reviewing for *Esquire* in 1960, just as the renaissance was getting into full swing, I soon realized I was seeing a new kind of sound film, and I ceased to make nostalgic (and invidious) comparisons with the twenties—a natural change of mind when confronted with new evidence. What was not defensible was my view that silent cinema was *intrinsically* superior. The error is partly explained as extrapolation into the future the pattern of the past, a typical weakness of pragmatic thinkers like me. (I'm always being surprised, which has its uses and its charm, but also its drawbacks.) But it was mostly due to an uncharacteristic failing: for once in my checkered career I held fast to a general principle for a long time. I shan't make *that* mistake again!

The principle, of course, was montage. (Younger readers see "Eisenstein and Pudovkin in the Twenties," Part IV, for an explanation of this archaicism.) Under the influence of the Russians plus Rudolf Arnheim's clear, well-reasoned, and persuasively documented little book *Film** (1933) plus my own tastes and prejudices formed by exposure to the silent classics, I concluded that montage was *the* structural principle of cinema, forgetting that any generalization beginning with "the" should be looked on with suspicion ("a" is almost always more likely to be correct). Today when some of the greatest masters like Antonioni and Bergman use it very little and none of them use it very much, it's hard to understand, let alone sympathize with, how we old-line *cinéasts* could have clung to the dogma of montage with such grim Presbyterian narrowness that we came to resemble a more romantic Scotch type, the die-hard Jacobites who after 1745 ("the forty-five") loyally rallied to the Old Cause.

"WAS it only a dozen years ago," I wrote in 1942 "that many of us were writing on cinema as the great modern art form? [That "the" again —danger, thin ice!] Our enthusiasm was not misplaced, our theories were not unfounded. And yet the wonderful possibilities that lay before the cinema ten years ago have withered. . . . The potentialities, which really existed, which still exist and in even richer profusion, simply were not realized, and the cinema gave up its own idiom and technique to become once more what it was before Griffith: a mechanical device for recording stage plays. . . . It has been many years since, anywhere in the world, a film has been made which, aesthetically speaking, is cinema at all." I cite this lament partly for its period flavor; it may bring back a whiff of the funereal cerements in which, for too long, we wrapped the corpse of our dead love, slain by the engineers and money-men. But mostly it's here to make me wonder how I could have written the last sentence which excludes from true cinema ("aesthetically speaking") quite a lot of territory. Assuming "many years" means at least ten, or since 1932, a number of films had been released in that period which I should have thought even a Presbyterian-Jacobite would have to admit were real cinema and not "recorded stage plays": *Kane, Grand Illusion, Rules of the Game,* Donskoi's Gorky trilogy, *Zéro de Conduite,* plus a few of Lubitsch's comedies (notably *Trouble in Paradise,* which

---

* Revised and updated (to 1938) by the author and re-issued by the University of California Press as a paperback, *Film as Art,* it is one of the very few theoretical essays on movies I have found useful, or readable. Another is Irwin Panovsky's brilliant and suggestive "Style and Medium in the Motion Pictures" (1934), reprinted in Daniel Talbot's *Film: An Anthology,* also a University of California paperback.

I appreciated lengthily in 1933, ending: "It almost makes one believe in Hollywood again.") Also, on a more modest but still respectable level were Huston's *The Maltese Falcon,* Hawk's *Scarface* and *Bringing Up Baby,* John Ford's *The Informer* and *Stagecoach.* Could I have missed or forgotten all of them? Or did I decide on reflection that not one qualified as "a film which, aesthetically speaking . . ."? Criminal negligence or arty priggishness? Perhaps a bit of both, and I won't plead historical extenuation. It was a time of trouble for us faithful believers in the art of cinema, but it wasn't anywhere near that bad.

DWIGHT MACDONALD
April 1969

PART ONE

PERSPECTIVES

AGEE
AND
THE
MOVIES

TO ME, the great thing about the movies is that it's a brand new field," James Agee wrote me in the summer of 1927. "I don't see how much more can be done with writing or with the stage. In fact, every kind of recognized 'art' has been worked pretty nearly to the limit. Of course great things will undoubtedly be done in all of them, but, possibly excepting music, I don't see how they can avoid being at least in part imitations. As for the movies, however, their possibilities are infinite—that is, in so far as the possibilities of any art CAN be so. So far as I can see, all that's been done so far is to show that art is really possible on the screen. We've barely begun to stir the fringes of their possibilities, though. Some guy in *Theatre Arts Monthly* says that, because of the limitations set on the personalities of the actors, through the loss of voice and actual presence, and because of the like failure to set up actual scenery before the audience, realism is impossible in the movies. Rot! Did you see *Stark Love* or *Greed?* Then you know the ridiculousness of that! Can writing or drama hope to rub your nose in realism as the movies do? Could *Potemkin* have been staged or described to even approximate the realism of the movie itself? I don't see how.*

"But the screen needn't stop at realism. The moving camera can catch the beauty of swaying, blending lights and shadows, and by its own movement impart to it as definite a rhythm as poetry or music ever had. Von Sternberg did his damnedest in *Salvation Hunters* to 'photograph a thought'—so he calls it. He's never had such a chance since, and the idea has flopped, but why shouldn't it be exhumed? I suppose UFA tried philosophy in *Metropolis,* but from all I hear that was made unpalatable by being inextricably interlocked with a rancid brand of ham. Well—right there's a huge field in itself."

Agee was seventeen when he wrote this, and I was twenty-one when I received it. We had just missed each other at Exeter, but an English teacher there put us in touch, writing me that Agee was "a literary phenomenon," as he was. But we soon found that our liveliest common interest was not books or writing—though we had a lot to say to each other about them, too—but the movies, which we

* For comment on some of the points raised in this paragraph, see the Appendix to this essay on page 10.

4

both took seriously as *the* great, new twentieth-century art form. There weren't then so many cineasts on the campuses as there are now, and we felt we were lucky to have found each other. The next year he graduated from Exeter and went on to Harvard; I graduated from Yale and went on to a writing job with Luce's newborn *Fortune.* He joined me there, after graduating from Harvard in 1932.*

By seventeen, then, Agee had not only conceived the passion for cinema that never left him, becoming if anything more intense toward the end of his life, but was also able to formulate his reasons for this choice in terms that were clear and, for him, were to be permanent: cinema can do things the older arts can't do: it is "a brand new field," the only major art originated in our century, both characteristic of it and also uniquely able to express it fully; "the movies' possibilities are infinite." He even catches himself up, after his refutation of what sounds like a particularly silly carp by "some guy in *Theatre Arts Monthly*" has led him into a one-sided insistence on the cinema's realistic qualities, and adds a paragraph ("But the screen needn't stop at realism," etc.) on those abstract, formalistic, stylized possibilities which have been so extensively realized in the last fifteen years. Furthermore, he is already fascinated by cinema as an art he wants to practice himself, not only as was, and is, my own case—as a subject for criticism. The paragraph preceding the ones quoted above from his 1927 letter is about technical matters. "Why was my movie jargon puzzling?" he begins and proceeds to explain the "lap dissolve" (which I must confess it's taken me forty years to realize doesn't refer to holding the camera in the lap but to over*lapping;* should have read his letter more carefully) and concludes: "Another thing I'm quite hipped on is moving the camera about. In *The Last Laugh* the camera was almost incessantly in motion, except during close-ups. You can see by regulating the speed of the movement and the scope of its vision you can get indescribable effects—anything from long, sweeping 'strokes' to short jabs and spurts. By thus manipulating the camera you can achieve a marvelous pliance that no other art can hope to equal."

* See "Jim Agee: a Memoir" in my *Against the American Grain* for details and other letters, mostly on movies.

All in all, a remarkable and, considering how things turned out, rather sad letter. For Jim never got to make a movie, which was his own fault, of course, from one point of view, and, also of course, from another, the fault of the time and the place he lived in. My own view tends toward the second "of course." Granted he was a shameless inopportunist—that he accomplished as much as he did despite his heroic efforts to fail by all twentieth-century-American standards of success is evidence of his genius—still I think he was unlucky in his historical period, as in many other aspects of his career. A generation earlier or later might have suited him. Earlier he might have developed his literary talents without distraction from cinema; later he could have made movies like everybody else, On-Hollywood or Off-Hollywood. As it was, he had to settle for writing about movies instead of directing them. Not so bad for us but not so good for him.

Agee brought to film criticism some qualities not as common in the trade as they might be. The most distinctive one I have already mentioned: he fell in love with movies at an early age and the affair didn't cool off—on the contrary! Although he never actually brought her to bed (i.e., made a movie), love makes one observant of subtleties and nuances. Agee's reviews are suffused with intimate understanding. Most of the films he dealt with are not much—with his usual bad luck in timing, he dealt with cinema between 1943 and 1948, a period that was pretty much a blank (except for the Italian neo-realists) compared to the silent twenties or to the renascence of the sound film that began with Bergman in the mid-fifties. However, Agee's film criticism is still good, and important, reading. Who cares, after all, about the musical performances Corno di Bassetto, alias Bernard Shaw, covered so diligently and copiously in London from 1888 to 1894; and who can resist reading his critiques today? Nor does one read Max Beerbohm's reviews of the Edwardian theatre to find what he thought of the latest work of Pinero or Henry Arthur Jones or John Galsworthy but rather to find why, and how, he thought what he thought. So with *Agee on Film,* v. I.

Not that his infatuation with the movies didn't have its draw-

6

backs. A lover sees many aspects, mostly interesting ones, of his beloved that more objective observers miss, but he also sees many aspects, mostly interesting ones, that aren't there. Jim could always fill out the botched, meagre, banal outlines of what was actually projected on the screen with his own vision of what, to his sympathetic, imaginative eye, the director had clearly intended to be there—and what would, had he been the director, undoubtedly have been there. I remember more than once seeing some Hollywood mess on his recommendation, finding it a bore, complaining to him and being told either that it was so boring that it was exciting (an argument which impressed me then as much as it does now) or else being shaken by his interpretation of certain parts— he always looked at the parts, I always at the whole—which was so ingenious, concrete and convincing as to make me wonder how I could have missed such beauties. Convincing, that is, until I saw the film again, as with two of his favorites, Chaplin's *Monsieur Verdoux* and Wyler's *The Best Years of Our Lifes.*

His critiques, in short, are usually more interesting than their subjects. A fatal defect in a reviewer, whose job is the modest one of a tipster oriented toward the consumer: which book or play or movie will entertain not the reviewer but the customer? A venial sin, however, in a critic, whose scope is broader and whose conclusions, therefore, are not as important as the way he arrives at them—i.e., what one learns on the trip. Although I disagree, excepting a few splendid low-comedy scenes in the old Sennett tradition, with Agee's three-part *Nation* eulogy of *Verdoux,* the social, political and even some of the aesthetic arguments he develops in the course of arriving at his erroneous conclusion seem to me of the greatest interest. For, besides his lover's dedication, Agee brought to bear other qualities that are also rare in the field: intellectual power; a knowledge of books and music and other arts that I hate to call "a broad cultural background" but can think of no more concise term; a moral independence (sorry again, I mean I can't imagine him taking seriously the late *"auteur* theory" or the "in" inanities of the Mekas-Warhol high-fashion underground—he has some bleak remarks about the late Maya Deren, one of their *ur* culture-heroines). And he knew how to write, a knack not common in cinematic literature.

7

Agee was in fact the most copiously talented writer of my generation, ready, like the players in *Hamlet,* to take on anything: tragical, comical, historical, pastoral and, to bring Polonius's categories up to date, critical, polemical, analytical, factual, poetical and journalistical. An all-around, all-in professional word-slinger, the kind editors dream about. Also the kind that gives them nightmares, for this surface versatility and adaptability was cross-ripped by deeper tides—very private standards, commitments, reluctances, refusals so deep in his psyche as to appear to be quirks or, as we say now, hang-ups—which frustrated them. He was never able to get down on paper anywhere near as much of his prodigal gifts as some of his less prodigious but more practical contemporaries were. No sneer, intended at thrifty exploitation of one's talent—it's always been one of my strong points—nor do I mean to endorse the "mute, inglorious Miltons" line of romantic argument. If they're mute, they're not Miltons. A writer is judged by what he writes, not by what we (or he) think or hope he might have written if only . . . (As an idea cannot claim more meaning than can be deduced, without unreasonable strain, from its verbal expression: "thoughts too deep for words" are also too deep for thought.) But there are exceptions to every practical rule, or ought to be, because experience is varied—as against certain philosophical systems whose logic works smoothly because it is abstracted from the friction of imperfect reality—and I think the works Agee never got around to writing, or rather to finishing, may be such an exception. I can think of no other writer of my generation who could when he was in the vein, rise to a more powerful, original style, formally; or a style more flexibly adapted to express the particular subject. Agee was a "natural" writer, as Honus Wagner and Shoeless Joe Jackson were "natural" ballplayers. He also had something not common in American writers—a peculiar ability, again when he was going good, to combine emotion and thought, a mailer-bellow cameleopard. In his best writing the conventional antithesis between "feeling" and "intellect" disappears, merging into something beyond talent or craft, something which only the old-fashioned word "genius" adequately describes.*

* Cf. some of the poems; parts of *The Morning Watch* and *A Death in the Family* (especially in the latter the lovely six-page prelude, "Knox-

8

Although he made his living as a journalist and although he knew he was much more than that—they always do—my impression is that Jim didn't think of himself as primarily a writer. He had three loves, in ascending order, I'd guess: music—mostly as a consumer though he liked to play the piano; literature—mostly as a producer though his readings of *Ulysses* at parties in the small hours might be called a kind of interpretative criticism; and the greatest, his first and deepest: the movies. As a consumer or fan (derived from "fanatic") always. In his middle years as a critic for *Time* and *The Nation*.* In 1948 he gave up not only movie reviewing but also the security of Luce's "collective journalism" with, I imagine, some idea that time was running out on his dreams and he must at last, after so many years, leave this dead-end safety

ville: Summer 1915," a poem that happens to be in prose); "A Mother's Tale," the only allegory of the sickness of our age, from the Nazi death camps to our own Vietnam bombings, that can stand comparison with Kafka, partly because it is clearly not influenced by Kafka; and most of *Let Us Now Praise Famous Men,* a flawed, uneven masterpiece, beginning with the pretentious and undescriptive title, but still a masterpiece in the American style: a masterpiece in fits and starts that shifts awkwardly, embarrassingly between subjective and objective, confession and description, moralizing and research. Rather like *Moby Dick.*

* Luce talked grandly about "collective journalism"—which meant one felt no craftsman's responsibility for one's writing because one didn't sign it and because a hierarchy of editors, as enlivening as most hierarchies, were empowered to delete from or add to one's copy whatever they thought might make it more like their idea of Luce's idea of The Magazine, and, if they were acute enough to discern it, as they sometimes were, less like one's frail, cowering little notions which were by definition personal not collective and so in the "free kill" zone where anything that moved, in style or ideas, was shot down on sight. The destructive effects of this on a fine critic may be seen by comparing, in *Agee on Film* (*I*), his reviews for *Time* with those for *The Nation*. (When they are on the same film it is really depressing.) The latter are superior in every way: more serious and more witty; more sensible and more imaginative; more free and more disciplined. The stuff he ground out for the *Time* mill—the only excuse for including it was to show the contrast—is clever hack work, rhetorically shrill but muted as to his own thought: a gaudy, tightly confining uniform like a bandleader's whose jaunty vulgarity even Agee, with all his squirmings, couldn't make fit him.

and try to break out into the movies. He wrote scripts for movies made by others (Huston, Laughton) or not made at all, and he kept reaching for the great prize that had always eluded him: the privilege of making a movie all by himself. Some of these scripts—see *Agee on Film (II)*—are so needlessly specific in their visual and technical instructions as to suggest they are those of a frustrated director. Also a director who might have done something remarkable. He almost made it, his reputation in the business was growing, another year or two maybe. . . .

But he didn't have another year or two. He died prematurely at 45 of a heart attack long predicted by his doctors unless he moderated his immoderate style of living, which he was unable, or unwilling, to do. Also prematurely in another sense: Agee was never in harmony with the *zeitgeist*. He died in 1955, just as the post-war renascence of cinema was beginning, a movement which soon gathered momentum in Sweden, Japan, France, Italy (practically everywhere but in this country) and even enough aesthetic prestige, in this age of the culture boom, or explosion, maybe just pop, the *kulturpop*—to intimidate Hollywood, an easily frightened animal, into tolerating if not art at least its surface manifestations, the arty. Art or arty, whatever "they" expected of him, it is likely that, had he hung on another few years longer, Agee might have been tossed a movie to gnaw on, as John Cassavetes was after the *succès d'estime* of *Shadows* in 1960. That Cassavetes blew it—he seems to have reverted to acting of late, perhaps his natural level—doesn't mean Agee would have. If Hollywood hadn't worked out, and if he had survived into the sixties, Agee might have given us, at the ripe old age of 55, the first important "underground" movie, filling a long-felt gap that is still gapping. But he didn't, he died much too soon. He had "that talent which 'tis death to hide," and it killed him.

APPENDIX I

I originally wrote the following as an archaeological footnote to the first paragraph of Agee's 1927 letter that begins this memoir. But it got out of hand, even for archaeology, and interrupted too lengthily, so I think it's better here:

The point about the inferior realism of a possible stage *Potemkin* to the actual movie was sounder than Agee could have known at the time. Years later Marie Seton's biography of Eisenstein revealed that Eisenstein decided to leave the theatre for cinema precisely because of the former's realistic limitations. The last play he directed was Tretyakov's *Gas Masks,* in 1924, which he tried to make "real" by staging it in the Moscow Gas Factory. "What happened? Actuality knocked the dramatic fiction of *Gas Masks* on the head. The conflict between the play, which was supposedly 'life' rather than 'art' and the factory setting, which was part of actual life, appeared so sharp that in Eisenstein's words, 'the cart fell to pieces and the driver dropped into the cinema' . . . The real factory, and the audience of real workers, made *Gas Masks* look patently artificial."

Only exception I can think of to the general point about the stage being more limited than the cinema as to realistic effect is O'Neill's *Long Day's Journey Into Night,* a big one, since this is without question the greatest American play. It does show that the stage, if the playwright is obsessed enough with "telling it like it is," can be as realistic as cinema; but few dramatists are so obsessed.

I had seen both *Stark Love* and *Greed.* . . . Saw the latter again ten years ago, it still looks like a masterpiece, though an even clumsier one than O'Neill's *Journey* but with the same hypnotic, ancient-mariner power of an artist who insists on telling his tale in the tempo of what he thinks is "real life," without any concessions to conventional dramatic form or interest; integrity and seriousness of purpose can be enough, sometimes—at least if the artists, as here, are both experienced craftsmen; *Greed* and *Journey* were unique in their creators' works, statements they just *had* to get stated, for personal rather than aesthetic reasons. It is curious in both cases how carrying the realistic—in Stroheim's case, naturalistic—mode to its logical extreme produces an unexpected kind of stylization.

Stark Love I remember as an extraordinarily pure and "advanced" movie—the ghastly title was probably given it by the distributor: a semidocumentary, semifictional work whose undramatic photography, use of nonprofessional actors and uncompromisingly realistic picture of a social milieu—that of the poor-white Appalachian hillbillies—was very different from American movies

11

of the time (1927) and more like the films we were getting from Germany and Russia. It seems to have been lost forever, no print remaining, and all I know of the director, Karl Brown, is that he had been the cameraman on *The Covered Wagon* (1923); his career, if any, after *Stark Love,* has vanished with his one movie. I think it not impossible that *Stark Love,* with its severe, Brady-like camera work, also its locale and its theme of the life of the rural Southern poor, "the insulted and injured," may have been one of the memories that impelled Agee, with his photographer friend, Walker Evans, to take on the *Fortune* assignment of living with and reporting on the "three Southern tenant families" that are the subject—along with Agee's reactions to them and to other things—of *Let Us Now Praise Famous Men.* It may also well be that, after they got down there, Karl Brown's movie gave them a preliminary "fix," emotionally and visually, a *point d'appui.* (Or it may also well *not* be.)

No slur meant in ranking Agee's reactions as a subject that competes with the families. Quite the contrary. The families usually win out. And, more important, one of the virtues of the book, both as literature and as reportage, is that the author puts himself into it on every page. This allows him a freedom of expression and stylistic invention (of which he takes full advantage) that the Just-Give-The-News-Please or *New-Yorker*-Objective mode denied, for example, to Truman Capote, whose *In Cold Blood* is so deliberately, artfully bare of personal style or comment. The idea seems to be to achieve the impersonality of the Recording Angel—though it reads more like a blotter entry by one of his less imaginative desk sergeants. As for truth, it is odd that by pushing himself with both elbows and feet into the foreground, Agee gives if not a more accurate picture than Capote, a more truthful one (which is the point, after all) because the reader can allow for Agee's personality as a distortion of the picture (Evans' camera seems to have no personal distortion). But no such allowance is possible with a writer who calculatingly keeps himself out of the picture and insists he is telling not his truth but The Truth. It is possible, though sometimes difficult, to believe in the existence of a man named James Agee, but it is not possible to believe in a recording angel named Truman Capote. One meets so few angels. Tolstoy made the

12

best stab at it to date, but he enjoyed the inventive freedom of the old-style fiction novel, while *In Cold Blood* staggers, like an over-handicapped race horse, under the weighty limitations, for either writing or truth-telling, of Mr. Capote's invention, the non-fiction novel, which seemed more clever at the time than it does now.

—*Film Heritage,* Fall 1967

APPENDIX II

I've just come across, in my disorderly files, an earlier 1927 letter from Agee which supplements the one quoted from at the beginning of the preceding article, expressing his cinematic, and indeed directorial, sensibility in more detail:

Sunday, June 26, 1927

. . . I'm going in to Boston to see *Stark Love.* Have you seen it? Despite its godawful title, I image it's rather fine. At any rate, being of the southern mountains, it is of great interest to me. I saw both *Variety* and *Potemkin* and know of nothing to beat *Variety* for realism except Stroheim's *Greed.* Have you seen it? That man has real genius, I think. He's able to photograph the most unprepossessing things and to raise them to a symbolic significance. As for *Potemkin,* I think it was pretty messy on the whole but perfectly marvelous as a study in the orchestration of movement. The first shots in the picture—the repeated flashes, first of water sousing the rocks, then of the sea lying in a welter on a flat shining plane of concrete—gave me just what I've been looking for in the movie, a sort of keynote speech, a topic sentence as it were. *Variety* approached it in the fuzzy old man and the long dusty corridor. *The Last Laugh* made its first shot an occasion for a mere explosion of technique—but I know of no other picture which has tried it at all.

I have a wild desire to direct *Ethan Frome,* and the first thing I thought of was my first and final shots. Do you know the story? Mrs. Wharton compresses it into a very few days and builds her background into the story. I'd begin with the death of Ethan's mother—an oblique shot, from near the ground, of a coffin being lowered into a grave—a lap dissolve—becoming a shot from the coffin lid with rain blurring the lens and the light above telescoping

13

into a small rectangle. The four walls of the grave, rough-dug, slipping slowly upward with cut roots sprawling out. Camera moved upward, out of the grave, swings in behind the crowd, catching in profile the heads of Ethan and Zeena. Then the camera swings on up the hill—with the group at the grave crumbling away in the rain and snow—swerves over a semicircular sweep of New England country and comes to rest on the Frome farmhouse. . . . And at the end, Ethan, Zeena and Mattie in the kitchen on a winter night. Mattie sitting very straight, Zeena hunched near the fire, Ethan leaning against the fireplace. Make the composition obvious enough to be remembered. Then a lap dissolve into three gravestones—two crazily leaning, one straight between them. Night— snow sifting over them. Then a series of dissolves, 6 or 8 of them, first fast, then slowing down to a stop, with the gravestones half-buried in the snow. It seems to me this would have some of the symbolism I admire so in Von Stroheim.

Have you ever thought of trying to direct in the movies? I'd give anything if I had the guts to try it—to go within a year or so, too. I have one or two short stories which I've worked out much more carefully as movies than as writing—and I think they could be told entirely without subtitles. . . . It seems to me that *The Last Laugh* has opened almost a new field for us—that of psychology. . . . What couldn't be done with Freud in the movies!

8½ :
FELLINI'S
OBVIOUS
MASTERPIECE

I CAN'T say that Fellini has been one of my favorite directors. *The White Sheik* I thought crude compared to Antonioni's comparable tragicomedy about a similar milieu, *The Lady Without the Camellias*. For all its poetic realism, *La Strada* left a sentimental aftertaste, mostly because of the performance of Fellini's wife, Giulietta Masina, which was praised for just the quality that put me off: her miming, which recalled all too faithfully the original creators of the style—Langdon, Keaton and Chaplin. My favorite up to now has been *Cabiria* (1957), a Dickensian mixture of realism, pathos and comedy; Mrs. Fellini also played the lead, this time with more restraint. The much-admired *I Vitteloni* (1953) I've seen only on a tiny 16-millimeter screen; it looked good, but my eye isn't practiced enough to know how it would look full-size.* The also admired *La Dolce Vita* I thought sensationalized, inflated and cinematically conventional, despite some brilliant episodes which (like the unbrilliant ones) made their point before they were half over. And Fellini's episode in *Boccaccio 70* was even worse than De Sica's: a stertorous laboring of a theme—censors are secretly prurient—that was probably considered hackneyed by Menander. But now Fellini has made a movie that I can't see any way not to recognize as a masterpiece.

This portrait of the artist as a middle-aged man is the most brilliant, varied and entertaining movie I've seen since *Citizen Kane*. I saw it twice in as many weeks, and the second time I discovered many points that had escaped me in the first viewing, so headlong is its tempo, so fertile its invention. What I had found exciting the first time still seemed so, nor was I conscious of any *longueurs,* with two exceptions: the night visit to the tower (Guido's talk with Rosella merely verbalized what had already been shown to our eyes) and the scene in the car between Guido and Claudia (her "How big will

* I have seen it full-size since this was written and it *didn't* look good. I think it one of those historically important films like Visconti's *La Terra Trema,* Godard's *Breathless* and (possibly) Resnais' *Hiroshima, Mon Amour* which haven't worn well because their innovations have become commonplace—too successful, in a sense—while there isn't enough else in them to engage our interest today. The antidramatic naturalism which fifteen years ago was exciting in *I Vitelloni* has become so familiar that the film now looks pedestrian, faded.

16

my part be" would have been enough to make the point). A great deal is packed into every scene, like *Kane:* of well-observed detail; of visual pleasure; of fine acting in minor roles (Guido Alberti's The Producer, Edra's La Saraghina, Madeleine Lebeau's Actress). And finally, like *Kane,* it deals with large topics like art, society, sex, money, aging, pretense and hypocrisy—all that Trollope wrote about in *The Way We Live Now*—just the opposite of these cautious little (though not short) art films that lingeringly explore some tiny area of impingement between three undefined characters or, if the director feels in an epic mood, four.

The action, or Argument, is as simple as its development is complex. Guido (played by Marcello Mastroianni with style, humor and delicacy) is a famous director who has retreated to an Italian seaside health resort to avoid a breakdown and to finish the script of a spectacular of stupefying banality about the flight to another planet of the survivors of a nuclear war. The script is long overdue: a huge Canaveral-type launching tower has been erected on the beach—it cost a real $140,000 in the real film, we are told by the Joseph E. Levine handout which is also real, relatively—cast, producer, technicians, everybody is waiting around while costs tick along like a taxi meter as Guido tries to break through his Creative Block, and meanwhile to placate and if possible evade their persistent demands. His mistress arrives (a full-bodied, empty-headed soubrette right out of a Franz Lehar operetta—really wonderful performance by Sandra Milo) and is presently followed by his wife (Anouk Aimée manages to look astringent and attractive simultaneously), necessitating another series of evasions and placations that are all the more difficult because his relation to each is unsatisfactory since he is still, in middle age, trying to square the sexual circle: to possess without being possessed, to take without giving. His personal and professional lives are thus speeding toward catastrophe on parallel tracks. It happens. Mistress and wife finally clash in a scene of irretrievable social horror. The movie comes to smash at a huge publicity party the producer gives to force Guido's hand. Badgered by questions he can't answer, since the script is still hardly begun, Guido crawls under a buffet table and shoots himself. He springs back to life at once and begins to solve all his problems,

17

emotional as well as cinematic, in a happy ending that has been widely deplored.

There are three kinds of reality in *8½*, and the film proceeds with constant shifting of gears between them. (Like *Marienbad,* but a secular version of that hieratic mystery: quick, humorous, jazzy, direct—you always know what gear you're in.) There is Guido's real present, as outlined above. There are his memories of his boyhood and of his dead parents. And there are his Walter Mitty daydreams of a harmonious realm of *luxe, calme, et volupté* in which all his problems are magically solved: the artist's world of creative fantasy. Its symbol is a beautiful young girl in white who keeps materializing and fading away throughout the film, and seems to be a kind of Muse. After his wife and his mistress have disastrously collided, Guido leans back in his café chair, closes his eyes (behind dark glasses), and revises the scene so that the wife compliments the mistress on her dress, and the two are presently waltzing together; since this works so well, Guido's editing goes all the way, and we have the lovely, and witty, harem fantasy, which poeticizes Freudian ideas about the libido even as it parodies them.

Everything flows in this protean movie, constantly shifting between reality, memory, and fantasy. Free association is its structural principle. A description of just what happens in two sequences may give some idea; I make no claim for detailed accuracy for these notes taken in the dark; they are merely what one viewer saw, or thought he saw. The first comes early in the film; the second covers the last half hour or so.

(1) A bedroom in a shabby hotel. Guido asks Carla, his mistress, to make up like a whore and go out into the corridor and come into the room as if to an unknown client. Carla: "Oh, good—we've never tried *that* before!" But she keeps spoiling the mood by chattering about her husband. (She's always trying to get Guido to give him a job: "He's serious, not pushy at all, that's his tragedy," she says in an earlier scene. "He knows more about Roman history than anybody. You'd like him.") Also by remarking, as Guido makes her up: "just like one of your actresses"; and, as she goes out, wrapped in a sheet, "I don't think I'd like that kind of life, I'm a homebody, really." (Cf. Proust's Charlus trying to get the hard-

18

working youth he's hired to whip him in the male brothel to admit he's really a brutal criminal—the young man is shocked, he's the only support of an invalid mother, he insists, to Charlus's disgust.) She spoils it completely when she comes in, flourishing a bottle of mineral water—"The landlady gave it to me for my stomach." It's a hopeless anticlimax when she flings wide the sheet. . . . Guido sleeps while Carla reads a comic book; both sleep. . . . A black-robed woman, seen from behind, appears; Guido wakes; she gestures to him to follow. . . . He is in a great weedy cemetery bounded by two long lines of high crumbling walls in which are niches and tombs. He talks with his dead father and mother (the woman in black). His father complains, in a reasonable tone and with precise gestures, as one explains why a new flat won't do, that his tomb is uncomfortably cramped; Guido listens sympathetically. . . . The producer and his assistant appear and complain to his parents that Guido is lazy and irresponsible; the parents agree he has always been a problem. . . . Guido helps his father back into his grave, tenderly, a dutiful son. He kisses his mother goodbye, she suddenly embraces him passionately and kisses him on the mouth, turning into a younger woman (his wife, as we find later).

(2) Interior of a movie theatre, empty except for Guido, who is isolated with his contemptuous collaborator; lower down we see his wife with her sister and friends, and the producer with his entourage. Guido must at last choose the cast, from screen tests; no more stalling, the producer warns, I can make it tough for you if you force me to. Wife's party murmur approval, everybody glares at Guido. The critic-collaborator, sitting just behind him, begins again to tell him how stupid his ideas are. Guido listens courteously, as always, then (beginning of shortest fantasy-sequence) raises one finger. Two assistants take the critic by the arms, lead him into the aisle, put a black hood over his face, a rope around his neck, and hang him. Back to reality: shot of Guido with his collaborator, undamaged, still sitting behind him. Producer calls for projectionist to begin; screen is lit by a blazing rectangle of light that is switched off at once. Beginning of longest fantasy, which lasts to the end, with dreams inside dreams inside dreams; from now on, despite some misleading illusions of reality, we are inside Guido's head. The screen tests are not for parts in the science-fiction

19

movie Guido is supposed to be making, but for roles in his own story, i.e., in the movie we have been watching: wife, mistress, La Saraghina, etc. The producer sees nothing strange, since he's now in Guido's head too, and keeps demanding that a choice be made. But Guido says they're all bad. Only the originals will do, after all, since no matter how talented the massive actress who imitates La Saraghina, she isn't the real thing.

A man whispers to Guido, as he sits dejectedy watching the tests, that Claudia, whom he knew years ago as a young actress, wants to see him about a part. Guido follows him eagerly, is excited to find that Claudia (played by Claudia Cardinale) looks exactly like the Muse (also played by Cardinale) he has already encountered several times in mysterious and frustrating circumstances. He takes her for a night drive in his sports car to talk it over. The first thing she says is, "How big will my part be?" . . . Cut to a provincial town square, old houses facing each other, a baroque gateway closing one end, the whole giving the effect of an oblong room open to the sky: camera peers through the only window that is lit and we see Claudia the Muse, all in white, against white walls, setting a white table with fruit and wine—a lovely, poetic glimpse. (Gianni di Venanzo's photography alone would make *8½* worth seeing.) Guido and the other Claudia drive into the square, but now all the windows are dark—his Muse has fled before her earthly (and earthy) twin. Stopping the car, Guido tries to explain his troubles to Claudia. "It's because you don't know how to make love," she replies, with a smile implying she could teach him. No, you're wrong, he insists, a woman cannot change a man. "Then you brought me here, you cheated me, and there's no part for me?" "Yes, there's no part for you," he replies wearily, "and there's no movie." Suddenly they are blinded by the headlights of three cars that roar into the square, bearing the producer and his aides. The producer tells Guido he has decided to get things started with a big press conference and party at the launching tower tomorrow morning. They all get into the cars and drive off. . . .

The journalists and cast and guests are gathered at the tower on the beach; it is cold and windy. (Someone says, "You kept us waiting so long—look, it's almost winter.") Waiters behind long tables with elaborate foods and drinks. Guido arrives, tries to

20

escape, is seized by the arms and dragged to the speakers' table, past a lineup of reporters shouting questions in various languages. Everybody surges up to the table—more questions, pleas, insults—skirts and tablecloths billow in the wind, which is getting stronger —bedlam, babel, a Mad Hatter's press conference. Guido refuses to say anything since he has not even cast the movie yet. Producer, venomous aside: "I'll break you, I'll see that you never make another picture, you're ruining me." Guido dives under the table, crawls along on hands and knees, people reach down to grab him, he pulls out a pistol, puts it to his temple, a loud report. . . .

Guido alone on the beach except for some workmen on the towers. "Take it down," he shouts up at them, "all of it." Collaborator-critic appears, Guido explains he's decided not to make the picture. "You're absolutely right," says the critic, "I respect you." They get into Guido's car, the critic drones on congratulating Guido on having the courage not to make a mediocre film "that will leave a mark on the sands of time like the deformed footprint of a cripple." As Guido starts to drive away, the magician from an earlier scene—an old friend who seems to have occult powers—appears in front of the car in his top hat and tails, his face made up dead white with red lips and darkened eyes like a clown, smiling his professional smile (manic yet gentle) and pointing with his wand. Guido looks out of the car and sees his father and mother, who wave to him, then Claudia the Muse, smiling and beckoning, then the others from his past and present, all dressed in white. (The critic is still explaining why it's impossible to create in this age—he cannot see these people.) Guido gets out of the car, takes up his director's bullhorn and begins to arrange everybody; he has decided to make an entirely different movie, about himself—his memories, his women, his creative problems—in short, the movie we have just seen. Like Prospero in another drama with a most implausible happy ending, he summons them all: parents, wife, mistress, producer, technicians, actors, the Muse Claudia, even himself as a boy who leads a gay little parade of musical clowns. And they all come, walking up from the sea, pouring down from the steps of the launching tower, linking hands with Guido and his wife in a long line that dances along a seawall to the tinny blare of the circus band. The last shot is of the ten-year-old Guido, dressed in his

21

seminarian's uniform (now white instead of black), strutting along proudly in front of his band.

Most of the critics have objected to this finale as bogus, escapist, sentimental, a specious "solution" that is incongruous with what has gone before, a happy ending arbitrarily tacked on, etc. In a generally favorable review in *Sight and Sound,* for instance, Eric Rhode writes in solemn disapproval: "Both Guido and Fellini show themselves incapable of making a distinction between the truths of the mind and those of behavior. The self-reflective spirit can swiftly turn narcissistic, and although Guido may confront his inner world, he fails to confront his social obligations." Or, as a psychiatrist objected to me: "He has failed to integrate reality and fantasy." This is all true—no confronting of social obligations, no integration of the real and the unreal, and plenty of escapism. I didn't for a minute believe that Guido had changed: the reconciliation with his wife—he asks her if their marriage can't be "saved" and she replies, "I can try if you will help me"—was unintegrated fantasy, as was the affectionate kiss he gives his mistress. On the plane of real behavior, his wife will continue to be censorious, his mistress will continue to be vulgar, and he will continue to betray both of them and will still greedily try to get love without giving love. The most that has happened in the "real" world is that Guido has achieved some insight—"I am what I am and not what I want to be"—which may or may not influence his future behavior; probably not. But he has triumphed in the "unreal" world of fantasy, which for him is the real one, since it is there he creates. In the sphere of the imagination, he *has* faced up to his problems and resolved them, for there he has made a work of art that hangs together and is consistent with itself. (I could never understand why "art for art's sake" is usually sneered at—for what better sake?) All through *8½* Guido (and Fellini) are escaping from one kind of reality, but only in order to rush boldly and recklessly into another kind, the artist's kind. In this sense, the finale is consistent with what has gone before—and, in fact, its logical conclusion.

John Francis Lane wrote in a recent issue of *Sight and Sound:* "I'm afraid that however fond we may be of the director of *I*

22

Vitelloni we are not really deeply concerned about his intellectual and sexual fetishes. Fellini has been too honest, too courageous, too sincere. He has made a film director's notebook, and I am not surprised that directors everywhere (even those who usually hate Fellini's films) love this picture." I think the implication of self-indulgent narcissism in the first sentence is wrong. Granted that, as Fellini was the first to insist ("more than a confession . . . my testament"), Guido is himself and *8½* is his own Life and Hard Times, I think the miracle is how tough-minded his autobiography is, how he has been able to see himself at a distance, neither self-sparing nor self-flagellating, a wonderful Latin moderation throughout, realistic and ironic. Guido's hat, for instance, clerical black but worn at a lady-killing slant and with a worldly twist, is a perfect symbol of Fellini's own ambivalent feelings about the Church. Or there is the clowning he often uses to preserve his humanity in the movie jungle, such as kneeling between the marble lions at the foot of the hotel's grand stairway, salaaming and ululating gibberish salutations to the producer making his stately descent. Nothing duller than someone else's fetishes and neuroses, agreed, but I think in *8½* Fellini has found the objective forms in which to communicate his subjective explorations.

A major theme of the film is aging, which obviously worries Fellini. He expresses it not in Bergmanesque symbols or narcissistic musings, but in episodes that arise naturally out of the drama: the elderly patients lining up for the curative waters; the senile cardinal; Guido's friend, the aging diplomat (who looks very much like him, with a decade or two added) who is divorcing his wife to marry one of his daughter's school friends and whom we see, doggedly jaunty, doing the twist with his nymphet fiancée, sweat pouring from a face set in an agonized grin; the aging actress who desperately cries out to Guido as he tries to escape politely: "I am a very passionate woman—you'll see!"; the magician reading the dowager's thoughts: "You would like to live another hundred years." One of the most sympathetic traits of Guido is the patience, gentleness, humor—the good manners of an old and tolerant culture—with which he responds to the reproaches of everybody around him, reproaches all the more irritating because they are justified. He is less patient, however, when the nerve of old age is

23

touched. He encourages an old stagehand with acting ambitions to do a soft-shoe dance and croak out a song, then dismisses him brutally. *Memento mori.* So with the half dozen dignified old men his assistant has rounded up for extra parts: "How old are you?" he asks each. "Seventy-one," "sixty-three," "eighty-four," etc. You're not old enough," he says, turning away contemptuously. The theme is stated most fully in a scene in the corridor outside the production office (where everybody has been working in a Kafka-esque-bureaucratic frenzy at three in the morning) when Guido is waylaid by his elderly assistant director, Conocchia, who begins by weeping into his handkerchief ("You don't trust me, you won't let me help you, you tell me nothing, I was once your friend"), and works himself up into a rage: "I've been in movies thirty years—we used to do things you'd never dare!" Guido, who has been listening with his usual ironical patience, like a man waiting for a thunderstorm to pass, suddenly explodes: "Get out, leave me alone, you . . . old man!" (Two young men from the production office poke their heads out: *"Vecchio? Vecchio?"*) But Conocchia has the last word. "You're not the man you used to be!" he shouts as Guido walks away.

I hazard that *8½* is Fellini's masterpiece precisely because it is about the two subjects he knows the most about: himself and the making of movies. He doesn't have to labor his points, he can move freely, quickly, with the ease of a man walking about his own home. And so much can be suggested in so little footage! That tall, aristocratic blonde, for instance, Guido glimpses several times in the hotel. She fascinates him because she looks like the heroine of an international spy thriller; he never meets her (the closest he comes is to put her into his dream harem), but he does overhear her end of a long-distance telephone conversation, which sounds like a bad movie script but which vastly intrigues him. Several kinds of parody are intertwined in this tiny episode: of movie clichés, of Guido's romantic eroticism, and—a feedback—of a man whose job it is to fabricate these glamorous stereotypes, himself falling for them. Successful parody is possible only when the parodist feels "at home with" (significant phrase) his subject. This familiarity also means that Fellini is able to keep *8½* right down to earth, so that what might have been one more labored exercise in fantasy—like De

24

Sica's *Miracle in Milan,* for instance—is spontaneous, lifelike and often very funny. I think Fellini has become the greatest master of social comedy since Lubitsch.

8½ takes us further inside the peculiar world of movie-making than any other film I know. I once asked the Argentine director, Torre Nilsson, why important movie directors seem to lose their creative powers so much more often—and completely—than major artists in other fields. (I was thinking of Welles and Hitchcock.) He replied: "In movies, once you make a success, you become public property; you are overwhelmed with fame, money, women, admirers, promoters, and you can never get away from it. A painter or writer or composer creates by himself, but directors have to have hundreds of other people around all the time. So they burn themselves out early." When I saw *8½*, I saw what he meant. Guido is distracted in the literal sense: "to divide [the mind, attention, etc.] between objects." They're all here: the highbrow journalist who asks about his philosophy, and also the lowbrow one—"Couldn't you tell me something about your love life?"; the producer who bullies him about the production schedule and the accountants who nag him about costs; the property man who begs Guido to take on as extras his giggling teen-age "nieces"; the playboy who wants him to sit up all night drinking; the man who waylays him in the lobby, waving a script: "It shows the necessity of universal disarmament; only a man of your courage and integrity could do it"; the press agents and tourists and mistresses, including his own. All there, and each wants a slice of him.

The reviews of *8½* in the newspapers and in magazines like *Newsweek* and *The New Yorker* have been enthusiastic. The public likes it, too. But the "little-magazine" critics have been cool and wary, as though they felt they were being conned. Their objections, remarkably uniform, suggest to me that the trouble with serious film criticism today is that it is too serious.

> All these sequences are so magnificently filmed that the breath is hardly left to voice a query as to what they mean. Gianni di Venanzo's black-and-white photography and Piero Gherardi's sets and costumes provide such visual magic that it seems pointless to make philosophical reservations on the film's content. Yet the

25

sheer beauty of Fellini's film . . . is deceiving us. (John Francis
Lane in *Sight and Sound*.)

He goes on to complain of "pretentiousness of subject matter" and
"artistic inflation." It's true, beauty and art are deceivers ever. The
pea is never under the shell Fellini has given us every reason to believe contains it. In James and Conrad this is called ambiguity.

> The trouble seems to come from another quarter—moral and
> intellectual content. Fellini's last three films seem to me to rank in
> merit according to the amount of "meaning" in each. *La Dolce
> Vita* fairly reeked of "meaning," with its Christ symbols, parallels
> to Dante, moral indictment of a contemporary life style, and what
> not. [This is not ironical—D.M.] The *Boccaccio '70* episode had
> its little fabulated moral. But *8½* has little or no intellectual con-
> tent. The difference shows in the very titles. *La Dolce Vita* evokes
> a moral tradition of some kind. *The Temptation of Dr. Antonio*
> (with its echo of "The Temptation of St. Anthony") prepares us
> for religious allegory. But *8½* drives us right back into Fellini's
> biography. . . . The artist's promise of a moral or intellectual
> "point" bribes us (me) to take part in his (my) illicit fantasies.
> Without an intellectual superstructure, his personal fantasy fails
> to engage other persons. (Norman N. Holland in *Hudson Review*.)

It would be needlessly cruel to comment on these stiff-jointed lucu-
brations, though I can't help wondering what the quotes around
meaning mean. Does he "mean" it? In addition to his other burdens,
Mr. Holland groans under a massive load of primitive Freudian-
ism. Maybe this explains why he dares to express openly a puritan
nervousness when confronted by useless beauty that his colleagues
express more discreetly.

> Since *La Dolce Vita,* Fellini's films have been following a trend
> that certainly culminates in *8½*. [Briefest trend in cultural history
> since the only Fellini film between *Vita* and *8½* was the half-hour
> episode in *Boccaccio 70*—D.M.] It is the triumph of style over
> content. At the end of *8½* we are excited not because Fellini has
> told us something significant about the artistic process, but because
> he has found such a visually exciting metaphor for his idea that it
> does not matter if this idea is not quite first-rate. . . . Nothing
> very significant is said about illusion and reality, dream and art.
> (Gary Carey in *The Seventh Art*.)

26

True that when it comes to making significant statements about illusion and reality and other high topics, Fellini is "not quite first-rate" compared to, say, Dr. Erwin Panofsky, of the (Princeton) Institute of Advanced Studies, whose 1934 essay, "Style and Medium in the Moving Pictures," is a classic. But I doubt that Dr. Panofsky, a modest and sensible man, would claim he could have made *8½*, any more than Fellini, also sensible if not modest, would aspire to a professorship of, say, Cinematic Philosophy. Mr. Carey ends his review on the usual sub-puritan note: "*8½* is really a visual experience, its only profundity resting there." And what better resting place?

> Fellini's latest "autobiographical" oddity. . . . The nicest possible thing one could say is that he had had the guts to try and shove this particular form of lachrymose sexuality into the environs of art. . . . Of course, the result is horrendously pretentious. . . . She [Anouk Aimée as the wife] is where Fellini's vulgarity positively beckons us into attention and in so doing ruins a fantasy. He just can't deal with the grown-up issues she incarnates. But as a cinematic outlet for the imagination—the sort of stuff a director like Fellini *can* cope with . . . the film is extraordinary. . . . *8½* looks marvelous and doesn't matter much of a damn. (John Coleman in the London *New Statesman.*)

No comment.

> The tone is never sure, but falters between irony and self-pity, between shamefaced poeticism and tongue-tied self-mockery. . . . The second failure . . . [is] ignorance. . . . *8½* piles problem upon problem, which is permissible; but sheds no light, which is not. . . . Fellini, apparently afraid of becoming a self-repeater with diminishing returns as so many famous Italian directors have become, tries for something new: symbolism, metaphysics, solid intellectual content. . . . What made Fellini's early films great . . . was their almost total avoidance of intellectualizing. (John Simon in *The New Leader.*)

The first sentence seems to me about as obtuse or perverse or both as you could get in eighteen words: I detected no self-pity, but on the contrary was impressed by the objectivity with which Fellini presented himself and his most personal worries; the poeticism was

27

real poetry, and it was far from shamefaced, in fact it was blatant, exuberant; and any critic who could apply the adjective "tongue-tied" to Fellini, always fluent to the point of garrulity, must have an ax to grind. Mr. Simon's was a polemical one: his review is unique in finding nothing to praise in *8½*. The closest he comes is: "Despite two or three good scenes [not specified] it is a disheartening fiasco." (It pains me to write thus, or should anyway, since I respect Mr. Simon's critical acumen so much that I wrote an introduction to his recent collection of essays, *Acid Test*.) Why "ignorance" is a fault in an artist I don't see, nor why he has to solve any problems except those of constructing a work of art, which are difficult enough. Shakespeare was a bit of an ignoramous—"little Latin and less Greek"—nor do we expect *King Lear* to "shed light" on geriatrics. I agree that Fellini is no thinker, and that he is at his worst when he intellectualizes. I also agree that "all the principal characters . . . are sublimely dichotomous," that "the dialogue bulges with antinomies," and that Fellini isn't in the same league as "the great masters of ambiguity—Pirandello, Brecht, Valéry, Eliot." Compared to that Yankee lineup, he's a busher. But all this is beside the point since, at least as I read *8½*, Fellini is *not* trying for "symbolism, metaphysics [or] solid intellectual content."

This brings me to the crux of my quarrel with the all-too-serious critics (an exception was Jack Hirschman's jazzy paean in *Film Quarterly*) and indeed to what I see as the crux of the film itself. Because it is technically sophisticated, and because it deals with major areas of experience, these critics look for philosophical depths in a movie which is superficial—I think deliberately—in every way except as a work of art. They call Fellini a phony for not delivering the goods, but I don't see his signature on their bill of lading. On the contrary, some of the best comedy in his film is provided by intellectuals: the affected young beauty who has written a treatise on "The Solitude of Modern Man in the Contemporary Theater"; the highbrow British reporter who pesters Guido with questions like, "Is it that you cannot communicate? Or is that merely a mask?" And above all the collaborator who has been assigned to help Guido complete his script—an eye-glassed, beak-nosed superintellectual whose lean face is fixed in lines of alert, sour suspicion. This personage—listed in the cast credits as The Writer, and played with waspish authority by Jean Rougeul—is endlessly articulate about the script; it's narcissistic ("just another film about your childhood"), romantic, pretentious, tasteless, and mindless: "Your main problem is the film lacks ideas, it has no philosophical base. It's merely a series of senseless episodes. . . . It has none of the merits of the avant-garde film and all the drawbacks." How can a director make more explicit his rationale? Life imitated art, as elsewhere in this strange film* and the actual highbrow critics reacted to *8½* much as The Writer did to Guido's script. Several people I've talked to—and I must admit there is as much conversational as printed opposition to *8½*—have suggested that The Writer is merely a ploy by Fellini to disarm his critics by making all their points in advance; they might have added the American woman who at the end shouts, "He's lost. He hasn't anything to say." Maybe. But he was a good prophet. For the "serious" critics have by now become habituated to profound, difficult films that must be "interpreted" from the language of art (what's on the screen) into the language of philosophy (what what's on the screen "really means"). It began with Bergman (whom I've always thought strongest at his shallowest) and reached a comic climax in the recent efforts of Franco-American *auteur* critics to read *The Birds* as a morality play about Modern Civilization, and a pathetic one in the efforts of almost everybody to make sense out of that triumph of non- and indeed anti-sense, *Last Year at Marienbad*—everybody except its creators, who said they themselves disagreed on what it "meant."

The off-putting quality of *8½* for all but the less intellectualized critics (and the public) is that it is nothing but a pleasurable work of art which might have been directed by Mozart—and there were

* Fellini found himself embarked, with costly sets built and stars under contract, on a kind of explanatory sequel to *La Dolce Vita*," reports *The New Statesman*. When he found this didn't work, he did what Guido did—switched to a film about himself, that is, about a famous director who finds himself blocked on a film. Reality came as close to overwhelming Fellini as it did Guido. According to *Sight and Sound:* "Two weeks before *8½* opened in Rome he still hadn't made up his mind how to end it."

no doubt pundits in his day who deplored the frivolous way he played around with Masonic symbolism in *The Magic Flute*. It is a worldly film, all on the surface: humorous, rhetorical, sensuous, lyrical, witty, satiric, full of sharply realistic detail and also of fantastic scenes like the great one in the steam bath. The essence of *8½* is here: the visual panache of the movie-makers making their way down the stairs, swathed in sheets like Roman senators and wreathed in smoky steam like the damned going down to hell, terrific but also just a touch burlesque on Biblical spectaculars—the loudspeaker, "Guido, Guido. His Eminence will see you now"—the burlesque becoming strident as Guido's colleagues push around him, warning, "Don't hold anything back from His Eminence," while they ask him to put in a word for them, and then turning to satire, as Guido stands before the aged Cardinal (also wrapped in a sheet, bony neck and chest bare, mist swirling about him like God's mantle) and complains, "I'm not happy, Your Eminence." "Why should you be, my son?" the Cardinal replies with unexpected vigor. "That's not your job in life. . . . *Nulla salvatio extra ecclesiasm.* . . . That which is not of God is of the Devil." The scene closes with an exterior shot of a small cellar window that swings slowly shut as if excluding the sinner (*extra ecclesiam*) from the heaven within. There is plenty of symbolism here, indeed every shot is a metaphor, but they are all as obvious as the closing window. This is perhaps the difficulty; nothing for the interpretative tooth to mumble, no Antonionian *angst,* no Bergmanesque Godhead, no Truffaut-style existential Absurd to perplex us. Like Baroque art, of which it is a belated golden ray, *8½* is complicated but not obscure. It is more Handel than Beethoven—objective and classical in spirit as against the romantic subjectivism we are accustomed to. It's all there, right on the surface, like a Veronese or a Tiepolo.

One could drop still another name, the greatest of all. Is there not something Shakespearean in this range of human experience expressed in every mode from high lyric to low comic, from the most formal rhetoric to the most personal impressionism? And don't the critics remind one of those all-too-serious students who try to discover "Shakespeare's philosophy" and always fail because Shakespeare hadn't any; his "ideas" were all *ad hoc;* their function was to solve dramatic rather than philosophical problems. As Jack

30

Hirschman writes: "Fellini has . . . come free of that awful psy-cho-philosophical air which pervades *La Dolce Vita.* . . . In *8½* people are on earth not because they are destined to be trapped by cultural despair, but because they are destined to play out the roles of their individual realities."

Finally, in *8½* Fellini steals from everybody, just like Shake-speare. "Theft" on this scale becomes synthesis: *8½* is an epitome of the history of cinema. His thefts are creative because they are really borrowings, which are returned with the fingerprints of the thief all over them. The childhood episodes are Bergmanesque chiaroscuro, as the great scene on the beach when La Saraghina dances for the schoolboys, which echoes, right down to the brutal beat of the music, an even greater beach scene, that between the soldiers and the clown's wife at the beginning of *Naked Night:* but this is a Latin Bergman, sensuous and dramatic and in no way profound. When Guido and his wife quarrel in the hotel bedroom, the bleak failure to make contact (and the austere photography) recall Antonioni, but *this* alienated couple don't suffer in silence, they yell at each other. The early scene in the rest-cure garden is full of heroic close-ups à la Eisenstein, but they are used (like "The Ride of the Valkyries" thundered out by the hotel band) for satiric counterpoint to the aging, prosaic faces of the invalids. The general structure—a montage of tenses, a mosaic of time blocks—recalls *Intolerance, Kane,* and *Marienbad,* but in Fellini's hands it be-comes light, fluid, evanescent. And delightfully obvious.

The above text, revised slightly and expanded considerably from the original review in the January, 1964, *Esquire,* is that of my Afterword to Deena Boyer's *The Two Hundred Days* of *8½* (Macmillan, 1964).

ANTONIONI:
A
POSITION
PAPER

EVERYWHERE I go people begin talking about one film—
Antonioni's *L'Avventura.* Their feeling about it is intense
and personal: they have discovered a movie that is unlike any other
they have seen, one that comments on modern life in the intimate,
subjective terms that hitherto have been found only in books. They
—that is, we—compare notes on each scene, argue about the significance of details. I know of no movie that has stimulated so
much interesting talk. A kind of Antonioni underground is forming,
analogous to the early devotees of Joyce and Eliot.

This phenomenon, the most encouraging mutation in taste since
I began this column, is fairly recent. When *L'Avventura* was shown
at Cannes in 1960, that elegant and philistine audience hissed and
booed and the jury, which gave the *palme d'or* to the more showy
Dolce Vita, fobbed off *L'Avventura* with a "special award." It did
take the grand prize at that fall's British Film Festival, but its first
run over here was only moderately successful. Bosley Crowther of
the *New York Times,* whose imprimatur alas is essential to most
foreign films, was warily hostile: "Frankly, we do not gather what
Signor Antonioni is trying to prove. . . . This business of being
deliberately and even boastfully obscure in art not only is ostentatious but it also leads one to suspect the artist is not clear in his own
mind and lacks self-discipline. . . . In contrast to *L'Avventura* is
the brilliant new British film, *Saturday Night and Sunday Morning.*" (I must confess "brilliant" is the last adjective I should have
applied to *Saturday Night.*) However, despite Mr. Crowther, the
Antonioni underground has been making headway. In the British
Film Institute's international poll of critics on the ten best films of
all time, *L'Avventura* placed second. And a half-dozen Brandt
neighborhood theatres here in New York have recently revived it
with great success.

I think Antonioni as a director has four special qualities.

His photography is severe and classical. In a recent *Horizon,*
John Simon remarks on "the highly charged use of black and white
in *L'Avventura,*" continuing: "This is not the chiaroscuro, the
gradual intermingling of light and dark, that seventeenth-century
painters were so fond of [one might add Bergman]; this is a
juxtaposition of the sharpest whites and blacks, that, for all their
jostling each other, remain achingly distinct." Distinct and yet

harmonious, for the blacks, whites and grays are tonally related, so that the foreground is not detached from the background as in the usual overlighted Hollywood photography.

He is the Veronese of films, a master of calculated composition. His groupings are, like Veronese's, both austere and luxurious, classical in design but baroque in surface and texture. He is able to present a complicated scene without any cluttered effect, as in the fashion show in *Le Amiche* or the lobby of the hotel in *L'Avventura*.

He is also a master of what might be called film choreography, bringing out the emotional meaning of a scene by the interacting lines of motion of the actors. So we get both a static formal composition in each shot and also a beautifully controlled movement before the camera, as if a painting came to life.

Finally, he can explore character with novelistic subtlety. His people are related to each other in scenes which are not determined by the necessities of advancing the story—the Hollywood "plot line"—but rather by the author's search for cinematic expressions of their human essence. (It is significant that he writes his own screenplays.) This results, as it does in the better novelists, in a loose, sprawling kind of plot that presents a series of what James Joyce called "epiphanies"—in his words "the sudden revelation of the whatness of a thing . . . the moment in which the soul of the commonest object seems to us radiant." In his biography of Joyce, Richard Ellmann writes of this technique: "It seeks a presentation so sharp that comment by the author would be an interference. It leaves off the veneer of gracious intimacy with the reader, of concern that he should be taken into the author's confidence, and instead makes reader feel uneasy and culpable if he misses the intended but always unstated meaning, as if he were being arraigned rather than entertained. The artist detaches himself from his material so as to push the reader into it." Joyce once remarked, only half-joking, that he expected the reader of *Finnegans Wake* to give his whole life to it, and Antonioni says: "I want the audience to work. I ask them to see the film from the beginning and devote their full attention to it, treating it with the same respect they would give a painting, a symphony or any other work of art. I treat them with the same respect by inviting them to search for their own

35

meanings instead of insulting their intelligence with obvious explanations." No wonder Mr. Crowther was indignant.

Making the audience work has never been popular in Hollywood, whose directors are trained to make everything very clear, nudging us to the proper response. That "mood music" forever moaning and throbbing in the background, for example; a blind man could follow a film by Kazan or Kramer or Wyler. Antonioni's sound tracks, on the contrary, are miracles of understatement, mostly using natural sounds, including the human voice, and often reversing the Hollywood pattern and stepping the sound *down,* or even eliminating it completely, during the "big scenes." He doesn't nudge, he states. The odd thing is that some of us in the movie audience, an increasing number of late years, rather enjoy doing some work, perhaps because we are used to books and music and paintings that require some effort from the consumer. This is incomprehensible to the successful Hollywood director—I've talked with a few—who invariably attributes my preference for Resnais, Kurosawa, Godard, Visconti, Bergman, Antonioni, et al., to a combination of perversity and snobbishness. He cannot understand why one wants to pay for bread when one can get stones for nothing.

—May 1962

THE
AMERICAN
STASIS

WHY can't we make movies anymore? Our silent cinema ranked with that of pre-Hitler Germany and pre-Stalin Russia. We still had the knack in the thirties and early forties, those doldrum years between the end of the silent film, its technical advances cut short abruptly, and the development of a sophisticated use of sound. No masterpieces except for *Citizen Kane* but a richness of lively, virile pictures in many genres—gangster, Western, musical, satire, muckraking, and all those comedies. Only France, with Clair, Renoir, Vigo, Cocteau, Carné rivaled us then. But after 1945 we lost our touch. None of the important postwar schools or directors have been American, from the neorealism of De Sica, Visconti and Rosselini through Bergman and Kurosawa to the French *nouvelle vague* of Truffaut, Godard and Resnais and the later Italians led by Fellini and Antonioni. New ways have been discovered of using sound as a formal device comparable to the way the silent directors used images, and in the last fifteen years there has been an international renaissance. Everywhere except here.

When I began to write this column in 1960, there was still hopeful talk about the artistic liberation of Hollywood through the "revolution of the independents." But nobody talks about it anymore. The growth of production companies owned by actors or directors and independent of the old-line big studios has been a great success in reducing taxes but hasn't made much difference in the quality of our movies. The "independents," bold enough as businessmen, are not very independent as artists; they have been too well drilled in the old Hollywood school to take advantage of their economic freedom. Nor is there much to be hoped, judging by their recent work, from such once-promising younger directors as Lumet, Penn, Mulligan and Frankenheimer.* They were educated in an even worse school than Hollywood, namely, TV, from which they have acquired bad habits like addiction to the close-up (that TV screen is so tiny) and chronic over-emphasis (every minute of TV has to "grab" the viewer lest he turn that little knob—it takes

* Two years later, I'd say this still stands. True, Penn made a good film at last, *Bonnie and Clyde,* but also true Kubrick, the one great hope of the younger Americans, spent three years on perfecting the photographic effects of an over-long and over-blown space fantasy called *2001*.

38

more effort, as well as a financial sacrifice, to walk out on a movie).

Our off-Hollywood cinema hasn't been doing very well either. I remember some films of interest years ago: *Shadows, Pull My Daisy, The Connection, Jazz on a Summer's Day*. But most of those involved have shown a decided falling-off in their recent films— really spectacular in the case of Cassavetes. As for the "underground" school, formerly the New American Cinema, centering around Jonas Mekas and *Film Culture,* they are appealing as rebels against bourgeois respectability (though not very original, the bourgeoisie has been having a rough time for several generations now) and impressive as publicity experts, especially now that Andy Warhol has thrown in with Mekas, like P.T. Barnum joining forces with Brann The Iconoclast. But as moviemakers they don't seem any more talented today, judging by some recent films I've seen by Warhol, Smith, Markopoulos, Marie Menken and Kenneth Anger, than they did several years ago when I used to criticize at length such works as *Guns of the Trees* and *The Sin of Jesus* under the naïve impression I was pricking a bubble when in fact I was inflating it, every knock being a boost in Mekasland. (My reference to Anger, I should explain, is not to his excellent 1964 film, *Scorpio Rising,* but to his 1966 *Inauguration of the Pleasure Dome,* a fancy-dress camping expedition into "the abyss between man and God" which makes great play with double and triple exposure—I've often wondered why multiple exposure is so rarely used in movies, now I know—and builds up a monumental tedium in forty minutes.)

While I was in Texas,* I caught up on my movies, avant-garde and rear-guard. *The Sound of Music* was playing right across from the campus for the whole four months I was there and when it won those Oscars, I thought it my duty to inspect it. The same week, such is the porosity of our culture, I was able to see for the first time some films by Warhol and Anger, both programs being put on by Cinema 40, a student film club operated with great enterprise by a senior named Gregory Barrios. Perhaps because I happened to see *The Sound of Music* the day after I saw Andy Warhol's *Harlot,*

* At the University, in Austin, spring of 1966, teaching a course in History & Criticism of Cinema.

they seemed to me to be connected, in one way antithetical, in another complementary.

THE SOUND OF MUSIC

. . . has grossed over sixty million dollars in its first year and will probably replace *Gone with the Wind* as the most profitable movie ever made. I can see why, also why it won five Oscars. The only puzzle is why it grossed only sixty million and didn't win all the Oscars.

They must often wonder Out There whether some elaborately expensive bit of nothing will draw at the box office, but they must have been sure about this one. It has everything:

Nuns: the gutsy, going-my-way kind, full of beans under those great costumes (only sea gulls can upstage nuns as camera material) like Debbie Reynolds and Roz Russell in two current movies I shall probably not get around to seeing. . . . Saint Teresa crossed with the Wife of Bath. . . . There is the obligatory wise old Mother Superior: "My child, I have found that when the Lord closes a door, He opens a window."

Children: seven, from six to sixteen, assorted sexes, each cute as a little red wagon, cute enough to make your heart ache, or your teeth. . . . Carefully varied as to their personalities and each in his or her way craftily appealing, they go through their routines with the docility of a troupe of trained dogs. Their "good-bye" song, rendered twice, is recommended to all who hate cute children. Fields! Thou should be living at this hour!

Family drama, TV style: Dad is a stiff-necked Austrian baron who huffs and puffs but never blows the house down because he is always defeated by mom and the kids since he is always wrong (but lovable—he welcomes defeat in good American paternal style). Mom isn't literally mom—she died before the film begins—but a sprightly young novice the wise old Mother Superior sends to the baron as a governess. She at once becomes supermom, organizing the kids to revolt against stuffy old dad, introducing the Sound of Music into his house (and heart) and finally becoming super-step-mom after the baron's elegant blonde fiancée gives up—she is prettier, richer, and cleverer, but she Can't Do Anything With Those Children. Dad is played uneasily—it's the fattest bit part in movie history—by Christopher Plummer, a former actor who has

40

become a Hollywood leading man. Mom is Julie Andrews, who has never been more wholesome or energetic; she throws herself into her part, literally.

Nazis: The manufacturers were shrewd enough to realize that the milk of human kindness needs to be cut with a little acid, for dramatic purposes, also to make the villains Nazis, which doesn't hurt at the box office. So the baron is a staunch anti-Nazi, unlike most Austrian barons of the period, or most Austrians for that matter, for reasons as unexplained as those which led the frolicsome Miss Andrews to think she wanted to become a nun, and when the local Nazis try to move in on him after the Anschluss, he outwits them with ease—they are paper-tiger Nazis—and the whole family walks over a sunny mountain meadow to the nearest border and Freedom under the personal management of Sol Hurok.

Salzburg: Many picturesque shots of the baroque architecture of Salzburg, also of the pretty countryside and quaint costumes. Everything except what is generally associated with Salzburg: music. I am told that the actual Trapps often sang Bach and other real music. The Hollywood Trapps are limited to the compositions of Mr. Richard Rodgers. The Sound of Muzak.

The entrepreneurs left nothing to chance. With all the above going for them, they added a belt to their suspenders. Their movie is a reprise of three consumer-tested properties: *Life with Father,* the record-run play by Lindsay and Crouse which first exploited in a big way the poor-dad-clever-mom theme; *The King and I,* by Rodgers and Hammerstein, which successfully transplanted the theme to Siam; and the stage version of *The Sound of Music,* also by Rodgers and Hammerstein, the book being by Lindsay and Crouse. The producers did venture outside this incestuous circle of pretested success when they chose Robert Wise to direct their movie. But although Mr. Wise once worked with Orson Welles on *Citizen Kane,* his later career, after he became a director, was reassuring, from *Mademoiselle Fifi* (1944) to *So Big* (1953) and *Two for the Seesaw* (1962). He also is credited with the direction of *West Side Story,* which some admired more than I did. Once again the entrepreneurs were right: Mr. Wise got an Oscar for "best direction" and his movie got the supreme Oscar from his fellow craftsmen, namely, "best movie" of 1965. Doubtless Mr. Rodgers' tunes and Mr. Hammerstein's lyrics also played a part. The latter

41

were, as usual, simple, warm, full of feeling and doggerel: "The hills are alive with the sound of music," "How do you hold a moonbeam in your hand?" The former were pleasant, bland and immemorable, a comedown from those jaunty, extra-dry tunes Mr. Rodgers used to write for *Pal Joey* and other musicals he did when his lyricist was Lorenz Hart. But just right for Mr. Hammerstein and The Sound of Muzak.

I must now admit that I was not as bored as I had expected to be by *The Sound of Music*. There is something interesting about any man-made product that approaches perfection of its kind, also about any exercise of supreme professional skill, and this was both: pure, unadulterated kitsch, not a false note, not a whiff of reality; and every detail so carefully worked out, all moving along so smoothly in the familiar tracks, sparing one the slightest effort, all the seeing and feeling and hearing done for one by competent, highly paid professionals. I came out full of goodwill toward all humanity, even Dean Rusk, feeling it was a pretty good old world after all. A moral massage—the glow must have lasted at least ten minutes. So no wonder it's pulling them in.

There's one little puzzle, however: how can both *Psycho* and *The Sound of Music* make box-office records? Is it possible to enjoy both the Marquis de Sade and *Rebecca of Sunnybrook Farm?* Perhaps we have *two* mass audiences, like the offensive and the defensive teams football coaches alternate, each of them patronizing only its own kind of movie.

Or perhaps the American public is even more schizoid than I had thought.

HARLOT

Andy Warhol's first sound film lasts two hours. The first shot— and the last and also all the ones in between—shows two young women (or rather what appear to be such), a blonde and a brunette, in thirties-type evening gowns, seated on a sofa behind which two young men, in tuxedoes, are standing; all four are posed in stiff, elegant attitudes, like a still from an old movie. The blonde has a handbag in her lap, the brunette holds a white Persian kitten. All four are motionless, staring into space or at the camera. Presently, no rush, a dialogue between two male voices begins on the sound track; it continues throughout the film; whether by design or

42

accident, it is three-quarters unintelligible; from what I could make out, a man was explaining to a friend why his marriage with a screen star had collapsed. (Harlow's marriage with Paul Bern maybe—the blonde vaguely suggests Harlow and the only reason for the title, except as audience bait, is the Harlow-Harlot echo.) After another leisurely interval, we get the first movement: the blonde takes out a cigarette and the man directly behind her leans over and lights it. Five or ten minutes later, the blonde slowly opens her handbag, slowly takes out a banana which she peels (slowly) and begins to eat. After this had gone on quite a while with the banana not getting visibly shorter, I went out and refreshed myself by looking at the university tower for fifteen minutes. It didn't move either, but I hadn't expected it to. Returning, I found the scene exactly as before with the blonde beginning to extract another banana (slowly) from her handbag. I left immediately, walked across the campus and—our porous culture—slipped into the first act of a very good production of *Julius Caesar*. Someone who stayed the course told me that about three-quarters of the audience stuck it out, perhaps hoping the title would be justified, perhaps assuming "he must have *something* in mind." My informant said there was some real action toward the end of the hour: the blonde pulled her skirt up and revealed a pair of masculine legs, and one of the men poured some water on her (his) head.

I forgot to mention one bit of action in the part I saw: the kitten got loose. Cats are smart.

Harlot is thus the antithesis of *The Sound of Music* in every way except artistic success. It's Hobson's choice there. How do you prefer to be bored? Elaborately or simply? Professionally or amateurishly? Hollywood or camp? Hanging or shooting? To any audience but an educated one, it would instantly be obvious that *Harlot* is a mystification like such other Warhol "movies" as *Sleep* (the camera records the head and hairy chest of a man who sleeps for the normal eight hours; the trick is to catch it when he turns over on the other side) or *Empire* (a motionless camera fixed for eight hours—so I'm told—on the Empire State Building) or *Haircut* (shows a man getting a haircut, lasts thirty minutes as does the haircut). Warhol is the Ponzi of the movie world, a comparison he would probably enjoy if he knew who Ponzi was, the deadpan master of put-on, as clever a cultural huckster as Truman Capote,

43

more so indeed, since Capote has a product to sell while Warhol has only himself, his personal style and mystique; his products are nonexistent, salable only because he has already "sold" himself, like the old-time high-pressure insurance men, to a public educated beyond its cultural means which is afraid to be laughed at if it doesn't respond to an exact silk-screen replica of a Rinso carton at $300 or a movie called *Haircut* that simply shows . . . a haircut. I must be missing something, the earnest consumer of advanced art thinks.

And yet, and yet—Warhol may be a Ponzi as an artist and his "movies" may be, indeed are, boring mystifications, but he is interesting as a sort of aesthetic philosopher, a practical critic so to speak, and his "movies" make sense not in themselves but as a deliberate reaction against movies like *The Sound of Music*. The Hollywood movie has become so technically proficient and so rigidly fixed in cliché convention that it has lost contact with the world outside and also with its own medium, like such nineteenth-century French academic painters as Bouguereau. And as Manet and later the Impressionists tried to get back to visual reality and to the feeling of paint and canvas by new techniques that made the academics accuse Manet, and later Cézanne, of not "finishing" their canvases—a Bouguereau seems not painted but thrown per-fect and complete on the canvas in one act of creation by some angelic creature who didn't have to mess around with brushes—so the rough-and-ready school of "underground" moviemakers like Warhol and Jack Smith (*Flaming Creatures*) tries to break out of the Hollywood technical slickness by shaky hand-held cameras, blurred sound recording, under-exposing or over-exposing film without bothering much about it, sloppy framing of shots, careless cutting, and endless repetition.

The difference is that the Impressionists negated *salon* painting as a necessary first step toward a positive new style, so that Manet is enjoyable even to those who have never heard of Bouguereau, while Warhol doesn't go beyond negation. It would never occur to one, from these "underground" movies, that cinema could be an interesting medium.

—August 1966

COSA
NOSTRA

I'M not looking forward to the movie version of *In Cold Blood*. Mr. Capote has constructed, with enormous pains and skill, an artifact that works efficiently in its own terms, appealing to the whole range of the mass audience, from the most to the least sophisticated. He invested six years of his life on the research and writing and he deserves his millions as much as John D. Rockefeller, Henry Luce, Somerset Maugham and other hard-working, hardheaded entrepreneurs deserved theirs. But let's not exaggerate. Mr. Capote talks grandly about "the nonfiction novel." In spite of the dedication with which he collected his massive research—"My files would almost fill a whole small room, right up to the ceiling"— and the cleverness with which he has deployed it for maximum effect, including such movie techniques as the Griffith cross-cutting in the first chapter between the Clutter family and the steadily approaching death car, the "establishing" long shots of the Kansas milieu, the psychological close-ups of the killers, the death-row prison background, with the other condemned killers playing bit grotesques counterpointed against the decent, normal home life of the chief detective and his wife—despite all this craftsmanship he has achieved not a breakthrough but rather a *tour de force* whose limitations are not apparent because it is *cosa nostra*. Our thing.

With the unerring touch of a bad dentist Capote hits and keeps hitting a sensitive nerve of our time, as is obvious from the response—instant best-sellerdom, the four issues of *The New Yorker* in which it appeared selling out on the stands faster than any issues in the magazine's forty-year history, the *New York Times* Sunday book section giving six pages to an interview with him by George Plimpton, an absorbing document because of the skill of the questions and the frankness of the answers, plus a less fascinating front-page review by Conrad Knickerbocker: "[Capote] broods with the austerity of a Greek or an Elizabethan. . . . *In Cold Blood* presents the metaphysics of anti-realism through a total evocation of reality." (Earlier he observed, "The tragedy was existential.") "Not the least of the book's merits is that it manages a major moral judgment without the author's appearance once on stage. . . . Mr. Capote has restored dignity to the event. His book is also a grieving testament of faith in what used to be called the soul."

Mr. Knickerbocker's "total evocation of reality" puzzles me

because what seems most dubious to me about Capote's "nonfiction novel" is its claim to documentary truth. I don't doubt every fact in it can be found somewhere in that small room full of data, though I wish he had given some indications of where he got what, nor am I reassured by his remark to Plimpton: "I think I may burn it all. The book is what's important. It exists in its own right. . . . I don't really want people poking around in the material of six years' work and research." But facts can lie as much as the camera can: they are part of the truth but they are not the truth. It makes a difference which facts are chosen ("One must be a 'literary photographer,' though an exceedingly selective one"), and also how they are arranged: "In the nonfiction novel one can also manipulate: if I put something in which I don't agree about I can always set it in a context of qualification. . . ."

The very qualities that make the book such a remarkable *tour de force*—the author's intelligence, his sense of form and the strength of his personality—play an ambiguous role. The answers he got to his questions, which constitute the bulk of his data, were to some extent shaped by the questions and by his relation to the respondents. In the case of Perry Smith, this was extremely close and lasted for years right up to the day Perry left him, with a kiss, to go out to be hanged. The quote every reviewer includes is Perry's remark about Mr. Clutter: "I thought he was a very nice gentleman. Soft-spoken. I thought so right up to the moment I cut his throat." This is indeed terrific, summing up the dark side of our age, but may not Perry Smith, in that long intimacy with his fascinating and dominating literary friend, have become a Truman Capote character? Interviewing someone many times over a period of years—and Smith wasn't the only informant of which this was true—may set up a feedback, a ventriloquial effect. "He was a really talented boy, in a limited way," Capote told Plimpton, "he had a genuine sensitivity [and] when he talked about himself as an artist, he wasn't really joking at all." He added that when Perry asked him, "Why are you writing this book?", he said he had "no moral reasons worthy of calling them such, it was just that I had a strictly aesthetic theory about creating a book which could result in a work of art. . . . And Perry would . . . laugh and say, 'What an irony!' . . . And he'd tell me that all he ever wanted to do in

47

his life was to produce a work of art. 'That's all I ever wanted in my whole life,' he said. 'And now what has happened? . . . I kill four people and *you're* going to produce a work of art.' " Capote adds, with that detachment that is one of his most admirable traits, "Well, I'd have to agree with him. It was a pretty ironic situation." Admirable, but kind of creepy too, as when one reads in *Newsweek:* "[The book] will have a fantastically wide readership—cutting across all levels, from thriller fans to pundits concerned about the future of man, criminology and art. In the meantime, Capote speeds from interview to interview, from a thousand-copy book-signing to the making of a documentary movie. 'A boy has to hustle his book,' he chortles. At the moment his prime concern is decorating his new Manhattan apartment."

The other puzzling thing about Mr. Knickerbocker's peroration is that "moral judgment," restoring "dignity to the event," and "a grieving testament of faith" in "the soul" are precisely what I don't find in the book. I agree with the author that he wrote it for artistic and not moral reasons—to such an extent that a serious artistic flaw is its failure to present any moral attitude, indeed any attitude, to the terrible events it so effectively narrates. The title cuts two ways, as I think the admirably frank author has noted somewhere. The kind of coldblooded detachment requisite to his conception of "the nonfiction novel" limits its artistic scope, as may be seen by comparing *In Cold Blood* with two fictional novels about neurotically motivated murders: *Crime and Punishment* and *The Stranger.* Capote has just enough freedom of selection and manipulation to make the result not quite truthful, but not enough to make it a work of art. He is hobbled by his self-imposed limitation to "the facts" he can extract from other people ("My feeling is that for the nonfictional novel to be entirely successful, the author should not appear in the work"). Since Dostoevsky and Camus could invent what they needed, they could express their ideas about the meaning of their fictions, could make their own moral judgments and give some human relevance, thus dignity, to "the event." The former created characters who talk much, and expressively, to his purpose—there are plenty of remarks as memorable as Perry Smith's in *Crime and Punishment.* The latter used a different method: a deliberate sparseness, almost banality, of description and dialogue that ren-

48

ders his sense of the hero's alienation and anomie better than any transcript, however shrewdly edited, of sloppy, garrulous contradictory reality.

Coming at last to the movie, I think *In Cold Blood* is a "natural" for filming today for the same reasons that it is an instant, one might say a pre-frozen, best seller. Namely, and roughly, (1) its subject is an atrocious crime which found the victims helpless, and (2) the motor of the action is abnormal psychology.

(1) It's become unfashionable to object to subject matter and with some reason when one remembers that *Madame Bovary, Ulysses* and *Sister Carrie* were once attacked as "sordid," "unpleasant," etc. But I think Capote's subject may be objected to on the same grounds that a cat playing with a mouse may be: that it is morally unedifying—prurient might be a more up-to-date term—and not interesting dramatically. It is a one-way business, no conflict: the Clutters didn't have a chance; their human qualities, the husband's strength (which might have prevailed) or the wife's weakness (which might have aroused pity) didn't and couldn't, given the circumstances and the psychology of the killers, make any difference. Although Capote takes pains to describe them as individuals, the Clutters were depersonalized by the event that overwhelmed them. This is not tragedy, where the conflict of character determines the catastrophe, but more like a traffic accident. Homer could make an epic of the bloody, barbarous Trojan war because there was enough equality in the opposing forces for their human qualities to make a difference; the gods intervened, but they had conflicting loyalties. An *Iliad* in which all the gods were on one side would have been like what happened to the Clutter family—not a very interesting *Iliad*. For the same reason, the Nazi death camps, or our atomization of Hiroshima and Nagasaki, are horrors beyond tragedy, unsuitable to art because the victims were helpless before a catastrophe that had no more relation to their characters, motives or actions than an earthquake.

(2) The depersonalization of the victims is matched by that of their executioners, who kill for reasons of abnormal psychology so removed from rationality as to be unpredictable and almost accidental. (The psychotic motives behind the Nazis' massacre of the

Jews is obvious, but our government's decision to obliterate the two Japanese cities seems to me to also have its peculiar aspects.) These depersonalizations are in terms of plot, of why what happens that does happen. Capote goes to much greater, and more successful, efforts to describe the contrasting personalities of the two murderers than he gives to their four victims—the material was, of course, much more extensive, also the actor is in general a more interesting subject than those he acts upon—and each of the six, killers and killed, does emerge (to some extent) as an individual. But this individuality, this humanity played no part in determining the fate of the Clutters and very little in deciding the actions of Perry Smith and Dick Hickock. The objection to introducing a mentally disturbed person into a drama, whether as criminal or as victim, is that he or she is by definition a "wild" card in the deck, unfair artistically, since anything can happen, also severely limiting the meaning, since madness is eccentric, in the literal sense of being outside the central human experience as well as being impenetrable to all but psychiatric specialists. Also, contrary to popular belief, the madder, the duller.

In practical, or box-office, terms, however, I must admit the above views are in the minority. Today a little touch of sado-masochism makes the whole world kin. *Cosa nostra.* Alfred Hitchcock, as skilled and cold-blooded a craftsman as Truman Capote, a dealer in shock, as another might go in for dry goods, who is constantly experimenting on the nerves of his audience like a mad scientist in the kind of film he has always been too sophisticated to make—Hitchcock began the present cycle with *Psycho.* Like *In Cold Blood,* it had an immediate and enormous success with both the public and the critics.* And like Capote's book, it fits neatly

* Though not with this critic. I reviewed it in the October, 1960, *Esquire* as follows:

They won't seat anyone after *Psycho* has begun. But since the only interest is the denouement—except for a rather nice bit in which a pretty girl taking a shower is stabbed to death with lots of nudity and blood—one is confronted with a dilemma which can perhaps best be resolved by staying home. For this is third-rate Hitchcock, a Grand Guignol drama in which the customers hang around just for the tiny thrill at the end; like a strip tease; and one feels as one comes out, as in both these cases, that one has been into the sado-masochistic genre described above. The victims are completely at the mercy of the killer because, like the audience, they don't realize he is crazy, and so the hard-boiled detective is as helplessly surprised when Tony Perkins swoops down on him in drag as Janet Leigh had been in her shower. At the end, Hitchcock made a halfhearted stab at explaining how Tony had gotten that way, but his psychiatrist sounded as peculiar as his patient. The customers didn't care they had gotten the two nasty little shock-thrills they had come for, one of them especially delicious: a pretty, naked—thus *really* helpless—young woman stabbed to death in two orgiastic minutes of powerfully cut, angled, lit and photo-

---

had; bad taste in the mouth. I think the film is a reflection of a most unpleasant mind, a mean, sly, sadistic little mind. But there used to be humor and romance in his films as well—I am thinking of *The Thirty-Nine Steps* and *The Lady Vanishes*. These larger qualities have been leached out by his years in Hollywood, and there now remains only the ingenuity and the meanness.

Every Sunday evening on television Hitchcock used to put on a half-hour drama; some were silly, some merely disgusting, some admirably ingenious, but almost all were well-cast and tightly directed. If one wanted Grand Guignol with an O. Henry twist—and I confess I looked at the show regularly—this was the way to get it. There is an automatic discipline in having only half an hour, as in having only fourteen lines for a sonnet. But *Psycho* is merely one of those television shows padded out two hours by adding pointless subplots and realistic detail. (Hitchcock still has his Sunday TV show, but it is twice as long and half as good, since all he has to say could be said in half an hour.) Also in this longer length, the people come out more as individuals and so the sadism, which is a mere convention in the half-hour show, becomes real and disgusting. One has got to know quite a lot about the girl who is knifed in the shower and her fate affects one the more strongly (not to mention the gloating way her butchery is pictured). All in all, a nasty little film.

I'm against censorship on principle, but this killing in the shower makes me wonder. And not because of the nudity. I favor more nudity in films; also more eroticism and sensuality. It is the sadism that bothers me. Our censors have the opposite view. They see nothing wrong in showing with intimate, suggestive detail a helpless woman being stabbed to death, but had Mr. Hitchcock ventured to show one of Janet Leigh's nipples, that would have been a serious offense against morals and decency.

51

graphed film, and involving no human passion or motives; she chanced to stop at a motel run by a homicidal maniac, could happen to anybody, just one of those things. Later Hitchcock carried the genre to its nuttiest limit with *The Birds,* which showed man, the hitherto unchallenged grand champion of predators, as the helpless victim of . . . birds, and not even birds of prey but law-abiding species like gulls and starlings and sparrows which suddenly, for unexplained reasons attack *Homo sapiens* and definitely have the upper hand by the time the movie ends. It was an ultimate, the heavies were even less predictable and harder to reason with than psychotics.

The purest exercise in homicidal mania yet made, and the most singleminded, is Roman Polanski's *Repulsion. Psycho* begins with a deliberately misleading half-hour of everyday life, or what passes for such in Hitchcock's world, in this case adultery and embezzlement, and he keeps bringing us back to the prosaic so his little shocks will be more unexpected. But in *Repulsion* there is no compromise: the note is struck at once and is held all through the film. Made by the clever young Polish director who gave us *Knife in the Water,* financed by an English company, shot in London and acted by an English cast except for the young French actress, Catherine Deneuve, who is excellent in the leading part, *Repulsion* shows that our thing, *cosa nostra,* is international. For two and a half hours, Mr. Polanski takes us step by step through Miss Deneuve's descent into madness, and with so subtle a mastery of detail that I should think it might make a good training film for classes in abnormal psychology. The first hint, for instance, that more was wrong than a tendency to daydream comes during a chat with her older sister in their sunny morning kitchen; the camera moves up close behind her blonde mane as she talks, then abruptly, with no relation to the dialogue, her hand darts up and begins to scratch greedily, and somehow insanely, at her shoulder.

An interesting film for specialists, but why do the rest of us want to see it and why did Polanski want to make it? He keeps himself out of *Repulsion* as antiseptically as Capote and Hitchcock detach themselves from their products, which, as in their case, diminishes the meaning of his work. Is he trying to tell us something more than the brutal "facts" in the case, and if so what, and why? Perhaps he was intrigued by the technical challenge of making something out of a limited subject, perhaps he felt some secret, unacknowledged attraction to the theme, perhaps he wanted to make an "entertainment" film—the quotes are intentional—in the West that would be successful enough to get him other jobs in the richer, greener, freer pastures this side of the Iron Curtain. If the last, it seems to have worked at the box office; if the middle, I hope his id enjoyed itself (mine didn't); if the first, he does make mental disease as dramatic as it can be made, which is not very.

The first hour of *Repulsion* is as brilliant, fluent, inventive and beautifully controlled cinema as I've seen since Bergman's *The Silence*—another example of the genre, come to think of it, a milder one, with neurosis instead of psychosis, and sexual instead of physical violence. Also, while Bergman's symbolism of a society whose people can't communicate with each other didn't work very well, at least he tried for a larger meaning; Polanski doesn't try. The note of repulsion—for once a movie is perfectly titled—that is, of the threatening ugliness of life as it looks to the girl, is masterfully struck in the opening shot, perhaps a trifle too masterfully: a withered, be-ringed hand hangs down to be clasped by a smooth young hand, camera moves up the scrawny arm dangling limply (operating table? morgue?) to a frightening African witch doctor's mask in white clay with two sodden pads over the eyes, another young hand lifts one pad off, an eye glares at us from a wrinkled face, the camera pulls back and we realize we are in nothing more ominous than a beauty parlor. For the next hour, as the girl's psychosis deepens, we see her dislike of her sister's lover, compounded of distaste for his coarseness (and also, perhaps, envy of her sister's enjoyment of his virility), slowly change into a horror of sex, of males, including her own romantic—and platonic—young admirer, and of life itself. Repulsion. It is all done with style and economy: the sister's sighs and moans, in bed with her lover in the next room, that keep the girl awake at night; ribald cries after her of some street workmen cut to a close-up of the tired food on her plate in a cheap restaurant; metaphors that are part of the story, not dragged in, like the skinned rabbit, as gruesome when it is first taken out of the fridge, curled in on itself like an embryo and

53

horribly glistening, as when it later hardens and crusts in decay; or the neglected potatoes on the drainboard sprouting ever more disgustingly—really shocking close-ups—or the street band of three old men shuffling along, one of them bent almost double and perpetually walking backward—which makes it for some reason very depressing; her face distorted into grossness and lunacy by the round bulge of a polished teakettle; a quarrel with her sister while a brutal all-in wrestling match pounds away on the telly.

The ominous squalor of everyday life has not been photographed with more loving care since *Greed*. But Stroheim was making a comment on existence, not giving us a case history; Trina and McTeague drive each other close to madness but not over the edge; at their most obsessed, they move us because they are not fundamentally different from us. In the first hour of *Repulsion,* the girl is still in some contact with reality and so we can at least be interested, even though the director's extreme detachment makes it hard to feel much for her. But after the older sister leaves her alone in the flat to go on a trip to Italy with her man, she loses contact, her world shrinks physically to the flat she dares not leave and psychologically to the narrow, repetitive, tedious world of madness, and Polanski begins to be stifled by the eccentricity of his theme. Although she murders first her young admirer and then her landlord in gruesome and well-acted scenes (the English supporting cast is very good), somehow the last hour-plus drags more and more. Some of Polanski's ideas for showing her mental state are very good: the sudden widening of cracks in the walls (with shivery music); her first hallucination of being raped—she sees a door blocked by a wardrobe pushed open, the light from the hall growing as the wardrobe topples noiselessly and a shadowy man (who looked to me like her sister's lover) runs in, grinning and hairy, seizes her, and pushes her face down on the bed while she screams silently—the hallucination being indicated by the absence of sound. But then it happens again, and again, and I felt the director was getting as desperate as his heroine, especially when he has her flee down a long hallway while male hands thrust through the walls to grab her. Okay for Cocteau, but a discord in Polanski's realistic style, a lapse of taste, what the trade calls too "indicative," also corny. As was the denouement, the discovery by the sister and her

54

man, when they get back from Italy, of what's happened in the flat. A delicate moment because only the most precise under-keyed direction could have avoided giggles from the audience as they see the reactions to one body submerged in the bathtub and the other lying under an overturned sofa with his feet sticking out. But Polanski loses his cool and begins to direct like Kazan or Visconti. The sister glimpses the body in the bath, begins screaming and pointing toward the bathroom; her man comes in with the bags, tells her to shut up and when she doesn't cuffs her around. Kazan-esque. He's a tough guy but I think he might have noticed that wildly stabbing finger and taken a peek into the bathroom before hitting her. Then he rushes out to phone the police and she collapses, enabling Elia Kazanski to heighten a scene that needed lowering by bringing in a horde of neighbors, attracted by the noise, who carry on like an operatic chorus. One of them, an aged man in a bathrobe, totters into the living room, sees the feet of the other corpse, and totters out, registering shock so violently the scene got a laugh that could not have been the director's intention. The last shot is of the sister's man picking up Miss Deneuve, whom somebody discovered under a bed, and bearing off her limp body with the same kind of grin her hallucinator ravisher had had.

The genre is now so well established that it has begun to parody itself, like the James Bond movies. The pop *Psycho* was Aldrich's *Whatever Happened to Baby Jane?*, which was camp to the cognoscenti and Grand Guignol to the ignoscenti and so made a lot of money. *Hush, Hush, Sweet Charlotte* followed, by the same director and with two aging stars again making monkeys out of themselves, well-paid, psychoneurotic monkeys. There was also *Strait-Jacket* ("from the author of *Psycho,* the director of *Homicide* and the costar of *Baby Jane"*) whose ads began: "WARNING! *Strait-Jacket* vividly depicts ax murders."

—April 1966

One of the most tasteless (and sensible) of the drama criticisms Bernard Shaw wrote for *The Saturday Review* was an obituary in the issue of March 2, 1895. "Mr. E. F. Smyth Pigott, for twenty years examiner of stage plays to the Lord Chamberlain's department, has joined the majority," he began. "The justification of the Censorship is to be found in the assumption . . . that, if the stage were freed, managers would immediately produce licentious plays; actresses would leave off clothing themselves decently; and the public would sit nightly wallowing in the obscenity which the Censor now sternly withholds from them. This assumption evidently involves the further one that the Examiner of Plays is so much better than his neighbors as to be untainted by their assumed love of filth. This is where the theory of the Censorship breaks down in practice." Shaw then demonstrated that the late departed had been in no way superior to his neighbors, describing him as "a walking compendium of vulgar insular prejudice . . . [whose] official career in relation to the higher drama was one long folly and panic in which the only thing definitely discernible in a welter of intellectual confusion was his conception of the English people rushing toward an abyss of national degeneration in morals and only held back on the edge of the precipice by the grasp of his strong hand." Shaw went on to make a point that is to my present purpose: the late unlamented had denied licenses to serious plays and granted them to trivial ones, "encouraging lewd farce at the expense of fine drama." He had banned Shelley's *The Cenci* because it involved incest, but he had not objected to certain "blue" (by 1895 standards) plays of a routine commercial kind. He did license Ibsen's plays but only because he thought "they were too absurd to do any harm," according to Shaw, who backs up his paraphrase by some direct quotations—Shaw always supports generalizations with evidence, an old-fashioned habit I find refreshing.

We have our Smyth Pigotts today. I thought of Shaw's remarks when I saw two current films of exceptional nastiness which have had no difficulty with the censors, while *Lolita,* de-erotized though it is, has had to make a pretense of excluding those under eighteen, and Shirley Clarke's excellent film version of *The Connection* is still denied—at this writing—a New York opening. For some peculiar reason, this state is one of the few that applies to movies the worst kind of censorship: precensorship. Here a license in advance of public showing is necessary, just as in Czarist (or Communist) Russia, and this the New York Board of Regents has denied to *The Connection* because Miss Clarke and her co-producer, Lewis Allen, insisted on retaining the word "shit" as junkie slang for heroin. Last July, the Appellate Division of the New York Supreme Court agreed with them: "In most instances the word is not used in its usual connotation but as a definitive expression of the language of the narcotic. At most, the word may be classified as vulgar but it is not obscene." The Appellate Division therefore ruled that the film might be shown. (Jack Gelber's original play, nowise different as to That Word, had a long run in New York without any trouble with the censors, since there aren't any for plays. It is only movies that are subject to precensorship, except for the normal exercise of police powers—and cops are usually more hesitant than censors, perhaps because they aren't so "secure" either as intellectuals or as moralists.) The Board of Regents did not accept this ruling and has now carried the case to the highest state tribunal, which means another long and costly delay. One is tempted to exclaim "Shit!"—a word, incidentally, that may be printed in this magazine without any legal fuss, since books, magazines, newspapers, plays and such media are protected by the U. S. Supreme Court under the First or free-speech Amendment to the Constitution.

Experiment in Terror was directed by Blake Edwards, who botched up *Breakfast at Tiffany's* and who here actually succeeds in getting less out of Glenn Ford and Lee Remick than they have to give. *Cape Fear* is better artistically and therefore worse morally, since its director, J. Lee Thompson, actually puts across what Mr. Edwards just fumbles around with. The two films are identical twins, with the same basic theme—the stalking of helpless females by a near-psychotic male criminal—and the same Cat v. Canary plot line.

Experiment opens with a young bank teller (Lee Remick) being grabbed from behind by an unidentified male who whispers in a glutinous voice that she must steal and deliver to him $100,000, or else. It's quite a long scene, about five times as long as is needed to establish the dramatic point, but it has some very nice close-ups of Miss Remick's fear-contorted face and also some interesting suggestions of rape as she hangs, helpless, in his grasp, one gloved hand over her mouth and the other—where? The "or-else" turns out to mean Death for herself and Worse for her virginal kid sister. The subsequent events are mostly just silly—Mr. Edwards is a really ungifted director, even by Hollywood standards—because his Good People behave with such unerring stupidity in every crisis that one cannot summon up the sympathy necessary for emotional involvement. Mr. Ford is supposed to be an F.B.I. agent, and there are several "placing" scenes at local headquarters, but he and his superiors are even greater bunglers than the real article. The criminal takes advantage of the moronic level of his F.B.I. opponents to capture the kid sister. He takes her to his hideout and commands her to undress. She does, down to panties and bra, and then, though she seemed to me most attractive, he loses interest; the Hays-Breen Code has been riddled but still there are limits. But the suggestion of nudity and rape has been made, and the prurient are appeased (if not satisfied) while the Puritans—which today means the Catholic Legion of Decency rather than such antiquated Protestant enterprises as The Society for the Suppression of Vice—are also appeased (if not satisfied).

Cape Fear is a different and more pungent kettle of fish. Not only is the direction better, but also Robert Mitchum is really terrifying as the psychopath; it's the best performance of his I've seen since his tough and weary captain in Lester Cowan's *Story of G.I. Joe* back in 1945. Here he has the same kind of sleepy authority Jackie Gleason had in *The Hustler*. Gregory Peck as the "hero" (he is as much a duffer at protecting the womenfolk as F.B.I. agent Ford) is his usual vapid self—how did Henry King get that superb performance out of him in *The Gunfighter?* Mitchum is really *too* good: with the casual relaxation of Bing Crosby he breaches all the defenses of Mr. Peck and his nice but slightly stupid wife and daughter. It's no contest, really, and the final scenes in the remote bayou country to which Mr. Peck, for reasons clear only to the script writers, has sent his two females for safety—he is hovering in the swamp too, with a deputy sheriff, but of course they louse it up—are close to pornography. I have nothing against pornography when it's good, clean sex, but I don't enjoy watching a cat play with a mouse, and I got no pleasure from seeing Mr. Mitchum—huge, brawny and sweatily bare-chested—toy first with the frantically terrified ten-year-old daughter and then move on to conquer her shrinking, pleading mother. I wonder what the Board of Regents thought of those scenes; probably too busy protecting the public from That Word to take any notice; at any rate, *Cape Fear* may be viewed by any one tall enough to shove his or her dollar through the ticket window. I also wonder about the effect on children of that last half hour, with Mr. Mitchum killing the deputy sheriff by holding his head under water (and almost dispatching Mr. Peck by the same method) and then raping the helpless mother and child. He didn't, of course, but the suggestion, putting it mildly, was there. I think it reasonable to assume that the makers of *Cape Fear* were restrained by prudence rather than morality. There are legal limits, after all.

I should not resist an argument that, for adults, there should be no such limits. But I think children should be legally barred from films like *Cape Fear* and *Experiment in Terror,* both for their own sake and for ours, so that we may see grown-up films without worrying about some ridiculous Board of Regents. The British system is more sensible: "X" films for adults only; "U" films for everybody; and "A" films for adults and children accompanied by adults. The last is silly, but the other categories make sense. *The Connection,* for example, was given an "X" certificate and was shown in London last year; it has so far been shown, in the country in which it was made, only in Scottsdale, Arizona. If moral lines are to be drawn, then I don't see the logic of allowing *Cape Fear* to be shown to everybody while *The Connection* is denied to everybody. This seems to me to be Smyth-Pigottism.

—November 1962

PART TWO

REVIVALS

OUR
ELIZABETHAN
MOVIES

THIS century, so indifferent to the poet and the painter, so warped and feeble in creative power, has strangely given birth to a new form of art that has already produced its masterpieces. If our writers are uninspired and our musicians impotent, at least the directors of our moving pictures have done work comparable to that of the past in emotional power and in beauty of form. On them has fallen the mantle of those great magicians of the Renaissance who called into being the thousand and one shapes of human passion and destiny. Our movie directors, some of them at least, seem to possess the touch that makes their creations both moving and beautiful, existing both as a thing in nature and as a formal expression of art. Their movies live as the paintings of Leonardo, the dramas of Shakespeare live—though perhaps not in the same degree—because they are deeply concerned with human life. This does not make them aesthetically good: as will be shown in a later essay, the degenerate theatre of our times is also concerned with life—too much so, indeed. But when extreme beauty of form blends with this interest in the emotions and destinies of men, there result such masterpieces as *Greed, The Cruiser Potemkin, The Lash of the Czar, Stark Love, The Wedding March, The Case of Lena Smith,* and *The End of St. Petersburg.*

Historically, it is to be expected that the movies should give us our highest type of aesthetic expression. Long ago the other arts reached, and passed, their climaxes in respect to technique: letters and the plastic arts in the Renaissance, music in the late eighteenth century. Their possibilities have long been known, their remoter provinces explored more and more intensely. A new departure in technique must today appear somewhat forced, as, for example, in the modern theatre the expressionist drama of Germany and the experiments of O'Neill in *The Great God Brown* and *Strange Interlude.* So thoroughly have the main technical resources of painting, drama, and the rest been developed that he who would discover new ones must travel far into the regions of the eccentric and the unnatural. In a word, the modern painter or musician arrives on the scene a century or two after the major battles in his art have been fought. Not so the movie director. Fifty years ago his medium did not exist; twenty-five years ago it was in the crudest state imaginable. And films only five years old can easily be detected from their now antiquated technique. The talkies, of course, have been in existence scarcely a year, bringing with them new problems and possibilities in technique before those of the silent film have been half exhausted. The movie director is in the happy position of a man who has come into a fortune and whose chief concern is how to spend it. A wealth of untouched and unexploited means of expression lies at hand. He has but to take advantage of this new material with all his ingenuity and imagination.

In being a young art, the movies are fortunate in a subtler way as well: in their relation to the public. Like the plays of Elizabeth's reign, our movies are not generally considered "art" at all. Often, indeed, pedants consider them the very antithesis of art, just as Elizabethan-latinists contemned the popular drama of their time. Movies are created for the enjoyment of the people, not the delectation of the connoisseur or the dilettante. It is well known that the greatest Elizabethan dramatists did not consider their plays of permanent value enough to see them through the press—Ben Jonson, of course, was a striking exception. Today a movie has the same ephemeral life: once it is played, it exists no longer, to the public at least. It may reappear as a "revival" a year later but only those strange persons who haunt the small "art" theatres will be interested. There is the same vast production—hundreds of plays, hundreds of movies a year—and the same confusion, or rather complete chaos of good, bad, and mediocre. Shakespeare was highly regarded by the public of his time, and so were several gentlemen whose very names are long forgotten. Though Von Sternberg's *Underworld*, a remarkable film, was the greatest box-office success in the year it appeared, who knows what piece of folly and stupidity pleased the customers the next year? On the same program at a cheap movie house I once saw a Tom Mix "Western," one of the most vapid and infantile forms of art ever conceived even by the brain of a Hollywood movie producer, and *The Lash of the Czar,* a Russian film of the greatest subtlety and sophistication. That such a combination was incongruous probably occurred to no one in the theatre. A movie is a movie, and people cannot be

65

bothered about aesthetic distinctions when they are in search of enjoyment.

Nor, indeed, can they be so bothered any other time. Painful as it may be, it is a fact that not one person in a thousand understands, or is even interested in, aesthetic values. They read novels, look at paintings, hear music, but they are seeking to be excited, instructed, distracted from their troubles, anything except aesthetically moved. And yet, though the public taste is not impeccable, and though the people do not understand, or even perceive, many of his finest effects, the artist seems to draw strength from contact with his fellow men as Antaeus was refreshed by touching his mother earth. It is better that the public should respond to work of genius though it may respond equally to the charlatan—better for the man of genius. In other fields of art today the distinction is only too rigidly drawn between what is good and what is popular. A great source of strength for the movies lies in the fact that this distinction has not yet come to be made in that field. Therefore the movie director communicates his creations to a public as broad and inclusive as that of the modern painter, for instance, is small, narrow, special-ized. The soil is deep enough to nourish the highest trunks, the most abundantly spreading branches. Some such communication, or at least the feeling of it, would seem almost essential to the develop-ment of the highest artistic productions. Religion, the ancient immemorial meeting place of the great and the small, the powerful and the weak, has also long served as common ground for the artist and the layman. Through this medium the Greek tragedians, Dante, Milton, Bach, and the painters, sculptors, architects of almost every age reached their fellow men. Entertainment is an-other such meeting place: Homer, the Elizabethans, Molière, and now the motion-picture directors, approach the public through that channel. These last are the fortunate creators in this age, since they feel that connection with their fellows without which no creative work can grow rounded and full-bodied.

There are other interesting parallels between our movies and the plays of Elizabeth's reign. Both have achieved masterpieces within a few decades of their birth; from *Gorboduc* (1561) to *Tambur-laine the Great* (1587) and *Dr. Faustus* (1588) is about the same

66

stretch as from *The Great Train Robbery* (1904) to *The Cruiser Potemkin* (1926). Incidentally, the two earliest masters, Christopher Marlowe and Serge Eisenstein, are curiously alike. The inhuman brilliance of their technique quite dominates the slight philosophical content of their work. Compared to the mature appreciation of human values that marks a Shakespeare, a Chaucer, or a Protozanov, they are gifted barbarians. Not only does Eisenstein resemble Marlowe in the fact that his technique dominates but also in the nature of this technique. The same vigorous, pulsating rhythm driving without hesitation towards its climax can be felt in the speeches of Tamburlaine, the conqueror, and in the film sequence showing the "Potemkin" preparing for the approaching battle. The movement of later, more mature works is not so direct. In *Macbeth* and in *The Lash of the Czar* there is more hesitation to the blank verse and to the sequences, the hesitation of the mature artist who must qualify, explain, and analyze the actions of his people. The powerful rhythms of Marlowe and Eisenstein are unbroken by this need for philosophical reflection.

* * * * *

That the movies should be distinguished by great beauty of form is all the more striking in that precisely this element is weakest in the modern theatre. While the plays of our time have degenerated into an infantile mimicking of reality, the movies have more and more tended to express reality in terms of art, which is quite another thing. That nine out of ten movies are cheap, banal, drearily shallow means nothing except that, as every one knows, nine out of ten attempts at artistic creation are failures. The tenth film justifies the rest. This is important: that the general background out of which the movies come makes it at least *possible* for the tenth film to be produced, just as the general state of the English theatre made it possible for *The Duchess of Malfi* and a few score of other masterpieces to be produced. The modern theatre, however, is in such a condition that it is not even *possible* for anything artistically good to come out of it. As my essay in the next issue will demonstrate, the writers of plays for some time have ceased to use words artistically, that is, as units that can be combined to achieve formal

67

beauty as well as to express a meaning. Hence, our plays have degenerated until they scarcely remain within the province of art. This analysis of the theatre will make clearer, by contrast, the nature of the movies.

—The Miscellany, December 1929*

* Of this, my second published piece of writing on movies, I've reprinted the first five paragraphs and the last, enough to give an idea of the general line of argument, which, forty years later, seems to me ingenious, overstated, and on the whole valid. The above excerpts also give some idea of the rhetoric, which is not valid. When "emotional power and beauty of form" is followed by an even more embarrassing formulation, one reaches for the editorial scissors. I found, however, that the moment I tried to edit, the whole sleazy fabric began to unravel. So I have altered nothing. Furthermore, any such fixing up as of 1969 would have adulterated the article's chief interest today, as a period piece redolent of that innocent missionary enthusiasm in which we early cineasts lived and had our critical being—so little yet written! so many yet to be converted!

The Miscellany was a really little "little magazine"—600 circulation. Four of us, just out of Yale (F. W. Dupee, George L. K. Morris, Geoffrey T. Hellman, and myself) put out half a dozen numbers from 1929 to 1931.

D. W. GRIFFITH,
OR
GENIUS
AMERICAN
STYLE

D AVID Wark Griffith is the great pioneer of the cinema who, years before any other director, realized the possibilities of his medium. Intuitively, he grasped those essentials of cinematography which the Russians developed systematically a decade later. The typical finale he developed for his pictures, so invariable that it is called "the Griffith ending," is a crude but effective use of montage: the camera shuttling back and forth between the whites besieged in the cabin and the galloping Klansmen (*The Birth of a Nation*) or between the girl drifting toward the falls and her lover coming to her rescue (*Way Down East*) creates a rhythm that is purely cinematic. Griffith was also the first to make extensive use of the close-up, another basic element in modern technique, as well as of many lesser devices such as fade-outs and fade-ins. These devices are today such commonplaces that one notes chiefly the crudity with which Griffith employs them, but in his time they represented an advance into unexplored territory. Marlowe's development of blank verse was no more revolutionary.

If Griffith foreshadows the Russians in technique, he anticipates them even more strikingly in the subject matter he chooses and the way he treats it. His *Birth of a Nation* (1915) and *Intolerance* (1916) are the first movies to make use of the *extensive* powers of the cinema. They are the first movies conceived on such a scale that the individuals are less important than the vast background of time and space against which they move. Griffith treats his epic subjects as Eisenstein does, not as historical narratives running through time but as cinematizations in space of abstract themes. He shapes them primarily to express an *idea* ("War is terrible," "Through the ages love and intolerance have been at strife") to which the story is subordinated as a mere allegory. Hence the point of view of *The Birth of a Nation* is as one-sided as is that of *Ten Days that Shook the World*. Both films are propaganda, with Negroes as the villains and southerners as the heroes in one as against the same relationship between bourgeois and workers in the other. This agreement between Griffith and the Russians on the essentials of cinematography is all the more impressive when one considers the difference in environment as well as in time, between the U.S.A. of 1915 and the U.S.S.R. of 1925.* Griffith would seem to have hit upon a

* Griffith's influence on the modern Russian cinema was probably small compared to that of the Constructivist Theatre, Pavlov's theories

70

universally valid approach to the cinema. The phrase "hit upon" is accurate.

Temperamentally Griffith is of the theatre. His is the lantern jaw, the aquiline nose, the gleaming eye of the old-style Shakespearean actor. He began life as a stage actor (he must have been a good one) and he has most of the actor's traits of character. When he is making a picture, he is said to have no sense of money and little concern for what is "practical." Like Von Stroheim he will go to any lengths to get the effect he wants. Like all able directors, he insists on dominating his productions and treating his actors merely as so much cinematic material. The better to do this he sometimes intentionally misleads his players about the plot, telling them only what he wants them to express in each scene and taking on himself the entire responsibility for fitting their performances into the whole structure. His theatrical temperament gives him a sense of the dramatic whether in acting or in montage and shot-composition. An even more important gift is a certain emotional facility. The censoring of *Intolerance* moved him to write and publish "The Rise and Fall of Free Speech in America," a pamphlet which describes the late Mayor Gaynor of New York as "that great jurist who stood out from the ordinary, gallery-playing, hypocritical type of politician as a white rose stands out from a field of sewer-fed weeds." Strong language, but the Mayor was on Griffith's side of the argument. The moral earnestness of this is repeated in the subtitles of *The Birth of a Nation,* which equal the loftiest flights of Daniel Webster. An emotional conviction of the importance and rightness of whatever idea possesses him at the moment is the driving force of his movies. It sweeps them to triumph or dashes them to disaster according to the artistry with which Griffith handles it. I doubt if

---

of reflex action, and, above all, the experiments of Kuleshov in cinematic theory. Though Pudovkin cites many examples from Griffith films in his book *On Film Technique* and though he says that Griffith's *Intolerance* opened his eyes to the possibilities of the cinema, his association with Kuleshov must have been the prime formative influence on his art. Pudovkin's turning from epics like *Storm Over Asia* to the domestic drama of *Life is Good* is curiously parallel to Griffith's progression from the epical *Intolerance* to the intimate human drama of *Broken Blossoms* and *Isn't Life Wonderful?* Let us hope Pudovkin's artistry suffers as little by the change as Griffith's did. (As of 1968, or 1938, we are disappointed.—D.M.)

71

Griffith knows when he succeeds; I am sure he does not know *how* he succeeds. His genius seems to be purely instinctive. The work of no other director presents such violent contrasts between emotional power and bathetic sentimentality. His people act according to the conventions of the popular novel—yet what superb cinema he gets out of their actions. From any point of view except a cinematic one, his pictures are absurdities.

Griffith is a typically American product. He is to the cinema what Edison is to science: a practical genius who can make things work but who is not interested in "theory,"i.e., the general laws that govern his achievements. Although his intuitive sense of cinema grasped the essentials of movie technique long before the Russians, he never really understood what he had discovered—which accounts for his not developing montage beyond the see-saw stage used in his finales, and for the fact that his latest picture, *Lincoln,* is less interesting technically than *The Birth of a Nation.* A few years of analysis, of comparing notes, of thinking about cinematic theory, and the Russians carried Griffith's discoveries far beyond anything he himself has done. During the past ten years Griffith has gone to seed with a thoroughness possible only to the American artist. The process has been all the more complete because Griffith, as seems inevitable for the man of talent in this country, has always been an isolated figure, one who grew up in no school and who leaves none behind him, a self-made genius. Unaware of his own powers, without the intelligent communication with his fellow directors that gives Eisenstein and Pudovkin perspective on their work, guided only by his extraordinary flair for the cinema, Griffith pioneered into virgin lands whose richness he only half suspected.

—The Miscellany, March 1931

Goethe said of Byron that as a poet he was a genius, "but when he thinks he is a child." I would put it the other way round: the "poetic" side of Byron seems dated and stagey now, while *Don Juan* and the letters reveal a surprisingly mature mind, tough, humorous, masculine. But Goethe's epigram applies very well to the three great masters of the American silent film—Griffith, Stroheim, and Chaplin—each of whom combined an instinctive mastery of cinematic effects with a naive unconsciousness of the meaning of their films. I once spent an evening with Griffith; it was in the thirties, years after he had made any films; he looked and behaved like an old-style ham actor of the Walter Hampden school, hawk-nosed, dramatic in gesture and voice. He was quite drunk and kept putting in long-distance calls to Hollywood stars who always seemed to be "on the lot"; this didn't discourage him—"Just tell her it's Mr. Griffith calling; she'll come." But she never did. Later he had a print of *Intolerance* run off for us. As we followed the monumental architectonics of the film, the most ambitious use of montage ever attempted, with its four stories in different historical epochs counterpointed one against the other, with the fantastic Babylonian scenes and the stark gray newsreel realism of the modern strike and prison scenes—as we dedicated cineasts followed, or tried to, his masterpiece, Griffith kept up a running stream of comment. "That's Jack Barrymore," he would say as a super emerged briefly from the mob around Christ (H. B. Warren) on the cross. "His first screen appearance." "See that girl with the plate of grapes? That's Joan Crawford [or some such]; I gave her her first part." We couldn't get him talking on the magnificent technique; what evidently impressed him, and what he thought would impress us, was his prowess as a "star-maker." What we thought his badge of honor—that Hollywood couldn't use him—he was ashamed of; his comments, like his long-distance calls, were to show he wasn't a back-number, a has-been. Griffith was the inventor, and to this day remains, except for Eisenstein, the most creative user of the two basic elements in cinematic technique, montage and the close-up; but when he thought, he was a child. It was a comically frustrating evening—like meeting Titian and getting from him only gossip about the dukes he had painted.

—*Encounter*, January 1957

NOTES
ON
HOLLYWOOD
DIRECTORS
(as of 1933)

A GOOD Ph.D. thesis," commented Eisenstein after he had seen what many consider the finest American talkie: Milestone's *All Quiet on the Western Front*. The remark is significant. It sums up the American movie. What Eisenstein meant is that *All Quiet* shows that Milestone understands his medium, that his technical proficiency entitles him to a Ph.D. in cinematics. But, also that the film is not a creative effort. "Now that you've shown that you know how to make a movie, let's see you make one," is what Eisenstein in effect was saying. As we shall presently see, neither Milestone nor any of his contemporaries in Hollywood have been able to carry out Eisenstein's injunction. For all its technical proficiency, Hollywood gives birth to perhaps one movie a year that is not aesthetically stillborn.

The explanation is simply that the Hollywood director has nothing to say. For the artist to create, however lamely, he must believe in something—realism, romanticism, Communism, his own importance, it doesn't matter what. He must have standards of some sort, and feel a certain pride in maintaining them. He may let himself be bent by outside pressure to a greater or lesser extent, depending on his temperament, but his sense of integrity must draw the line somewhere. None of these things is true of even the most talented Hollywood directors. They are not artists. They are craftsmen, specialists, technicians who turn out, perhaps with stifled boredom or indignation, whatever the industry requires of them. Sometimes a talented director gets a good scenario to work with, and the result is a film that is at least superficially interesting. More often, able directors waste themselves on hopeless scenarios. Whether the material is congenial or not, the Hollywood director accepts it without protest and dutifully sets to work on it.

Chairs can be made this way but not works of art. There is something lacking in American movies, even the best of them, and that is a sense of personal conviction. In my opinion, Hollywood has produced only two directors whose work is comparable to that of the greatest foreign directors. There may be more competent technicians in Hollywood than Von Stroheim and Griffith (though, making allowances for time, I doubt it), but there is no one with Griffith's ardent belief in abstract ideas, no one with Stroheim's passion for realism. That belief and that passion supply the driving force behind *Greed* and *Intolerance* and *The Birth of a Nation*. In

76

such films one feels the director actually had something to say and that he was going to say it if the heavens fell and Mr. Zukor frowned. Furthermore, both Stroheim and Griffith were extreme egoists, who insisted on making their movies just as they thought they should be made and who didn't hesitate to kick over the traces to get their own way.

But the Hollywood director of our day is neither an egoist nor an idealist. He is a good little boy who swallows, perhaps with a wry face, whatever the Zukors and the Laemmles ladle out to him. This prevailing attitude makes it difficult to evaluate the American cinema of today in terms of its directors. For the same individual's work varies widely according to the quality of the scenario. There are able directors who have made dozens of utterly insignificant films. And there are quite undistinguished directors who have, by some fluke or other, managed to produce a single excellent film in the course of a misspent life. There is, furthermore, the matter of actors. The Hollywood rule seems to be that the best directors never get the best actors. Thus James Cagney's genius for portraying the Irish mick is usually hampered by mediocre direction. John Barrymore gives distinction to many a commonplace film, and Garbo has only once in her Hollywood career had a first-rate director— Feyder, who made *The Kiss.* And so, with good directors making poor pictures and poor directors making good ones, with the actors often taking over a film entirely, it becomes difficult to write about American movies in terms of their directors. Perhaps the twenty-first-century critic will consider the Hollywood cinema as an impersonal, or rather multipersonal, engineering product similar to the automobile. For the present, however, it is easier to think in the old terms and to regard the director as the decisive factor in the creation of even a Hollywood moving picture.

DAVID WARK GRIFFITH at 53 is the dean of the world's movie directors. He started out as an actor (he still affects the high striped collars, pearl-gray derby, and British accent of old-school Broadway) and took up directing under protest. Almost from the beginning of the movies, when he was making two-reelers such as *The Lonely Villa* and *One Avenging Conscience,* he was recognized (and rightly) as The Great American Director. In 1914 he made his first important picture, *The Birth of a Nation,* one of the sensa-

77

tional hits of all time. Two years later he produced an equally sensational box-office failure: *Intolerance,* a lengthy and lavish super-spectacle which remains his peak achievement. (Both Eisenstein and Pudovkin testify to its influence on their work.) Important works followed: *Broken Blossoms* (1919), *Way Down East* (1921), *Isn't Life Wonderful?, One Exciting Night* (1923). Of late years his work has been consistently mediocre—*The Battle of the Sexes, The Sorrows of Satan, Abraham Lincoln,* et al. Since the dismal failure of *The Struggle* last year, he has done no directing. He has been speaking on the radio this winter on a program advertising Pond's Face Cream.

Unhappily D. W. Griffith has no place in a survey of American directors who are doing current work of interest. The utter collapse of Griffith, indeed, is one of the most tragic spectacles the American cinema has to offer. His historical importance can hardly be overstated. He was the first director to build a movie in terms of cutting, or montage, which he used with magnificent effect in *Intolerance* and which was later adopted by the Russians as the cornerstone of their cinema. To Griffith goes the credit for the close-up, the fade-in, the fade-out, the "masked shot" and many other technical devices that have long been commonplaces. And, most remarkable of all, a few of his films, despite their archaic photography and moth-eaten sentimentality, still have cinematic vitality. But it seems hopeless to expect anything more from him. At 51 he is "through." He has simply not grown into the present and has nothing to say to it. For Griffith is a profoundly unreflective artist. He shows no understanding of his own work, and the fact that George V liked *Intolerance* obviously pleases him more than the chorus of critical acclaim that still salutes that masterpiece. Lacking the intelligence to understand either himself or the world he lives in, Griffith's equipment for aesthetic survival consists only of an instinctive mastery of technique and a few intensely-felt moral ideas. Today his technique is obsolete and his ideas outmoded. There is nothing left for him except to reminisce twice a week, from 10:00 till 10:15 over WJZ.

KING VIDOR, once the brightest of Hollywood's bright young directors, will celebrate his fortieth birthday next year. Perhaps it is

78

old age creeping on him, perhaps some subtler cause, but in any case he has done nothing of interest since 1929. He began directing in 1912, at the age of eighteen, and has been steadily at it ever since. His most celebrated silent movie is *The Big Parade* (1925), "America's war epic,"—though an intelligent minority prefers his *Wild Oranges* (1924), from the Hergesheimer novel. He also directed Marion Davies, whose talents as a comedienne have never been properly exploited, in two excellent satirical comedies, *The Politic Flapper* and *Show People*. His talkie career began impressively enough with *The Crowd* (1928) and *Hallelujah* (1929), but has petered out into potboilers since then.

It is a peculiar condition of Hollywood cinema that even the most gifted directors make an appalling number of second-rate films. The only American director who has never turned out a mediocre production is Von Stroheim, who has made a scant dozen movies in his long career, who insists on getting his own way in all matters, and who scoffs: "Turning out pictures with the regularity of a sausage-machine is bound to make them as alike as sausages." The gibe goes directly home to King Vidor, who for two decades has been grinding out movies with sausage-machine regularity. By 1923 he had produced a long string of completely forgotten works —*The Sky Pilot, Love Never Dies, Peg O' My Heart,* and so on. His later silent productions include *His Hour, La Boheme, Proud Flesh,* and *Bardylys the Magnificent*. As for his talkie career, consider such recent efforts as *The Champ,* sentimental hocum of the worst sort, the routine *Cynara, Billy the Kid,* which wasn't good even for a Western, and the sloppy, antiquated *Bird of Paradise*. It is the privilege of the American director, working against time for unsympathetic masters, to descend into mediocrity. But Vidor abuses the privilege.

Even the best of Vidor's productions have been overrated by the critics. *The Big Parade* was exciting enough in its day—though credit for the "epic" scope which was its most impressive quality goes to Irving Thalberg, M-G-M's boy production genius. It was Mr. Thalberg, according to the story, who saw a chance to make the super-super movie of the Great War and who had Vidor shoot the whole thing over again on a bigger scale. But *The Big Parade* has been completely overshadowed by Milestone's *All Quiet on the*

79

Western Front. Only a few sequences are alive today: the transformation of the rookie material in the training camp; the girl's figure against the background of trucks and guns moving up to the front, the line of soldiers advancing through the woods. In *The Crowd* Vidor had a fruitful theme: the submergence of the individual in the masses of a big city. But the film soon turned into a pathetic little story of a young married couple who haven't enough money and whose child is killed by a truck. The theme is lost in a mass of human interest, and the picture is destroyed as an organic whole. While Vidor shows some personal conviction in the early parts of the film, he was spineless enough to make three endings—happy, ambiguous, unhappy—which were tacked on according to the type of audience. Perhaps Vidor's essential weakness is that he has enough imagination to choose significant themes, but not enough to sustain them. Thus in both *The Crowd* and *The Big Parade* he bit deeply into American life, but chewing what he had bitten off was another matter. It was the same with *Hallelujah,* the most ambitious film of Negro life that has yet been made. Here, certainly, was the chance of a century, and Vidor made every effort to rise to it. But his conception of the Negro was banal. Just as one met in *The Big Parade* the stock war characters—the vivacious French girl, the hard-boiled sergeant, the lanky company humorist— so in *Hallelujah* one finds the routine slices of Negro life: revival meeting, cabaret, cabin in the cotton. And these elements are handled in the routine way—as, for example, the scene in the Church with its uplifted hands, Tuskegee-choir voices, and arty lighting. There is also a technical inadequacy in the directing. The movement is too slow. The chase through the swamp, effectively photographed as it is, lasts twice as long as it should. Structurally, the film tends to break up into episodes, for Vidor has neither the Griffith sense of construction nor Sternberg's rhythmic drive.

There is no point in discussing Vidor's more recent productions. Of late he has divorced his wife, left Metro-Goldwyn-Mayer, and turned independent. Perhaps all these shocks will shake something good out of him in the future.

ROUBEN MAMOULIAN was born in Armenia in 1898, the son of a banker and an actress. Educated in Moscow and Paris as a lawyer,

80

he drifted into directing plays in London. There he was discovered by the late George (Kodak) Eastman, who brought him to Rochester, N.Y., as director of the American Opera Company. After three years of this Mamoulian began to direct plays in Manhattan: *Porgy, Marco Millions, A Farewell to Arms* and others. Paramount brought him to Hollywood in 1931 to make *Applause,* starring Helen Morgan. There he has remained ever since. He has made *City Streets,* whose scenario is said to be considered a model in Russia, *Dr. Jekyll and Mr. Hyde, Love Me Tonight,* and is currently directing Marlene Dietrich in *Song of Songs.*

Like Michael Arlen, Mamoulian is a bright young Armenian. Also similarly, his productions are glib, imitative, chic, with a fake elegance, a pseudo-wit and a suggestion of Oriental greasiness. They are marked with that vulgarity which is continually straining for effect, which cannot express a simple thing simply. A Mamoulian production can be depended on to overstress the note, whether pitched to lyricism, melodrama, fantasy. Thus his *City Streets,* a gangster melodrama, is directed as heavily and pretentiously as if it were *Greed* or *Sunrise.* There are brooding shadows, shots of pigeons flying beyond prison bars (freedom—get it?), weird angle shots of sculpture. Thus, too, in *Applause,* a sentimental little backstage tragedy, he put Helen Morgan through her extremely limited paces with all the solemnity due a Sarah Bernhardt. The trashy emotionalism of the story, which a more honest director would have restrained, Mamoulian plays up for all it is worth. His *Dr. Jekyll and Mr. Hyde* is a cheaply sensational affair compared to the silent Barrymore version. The brutal exaggeration of Hyde's make-up, physically so much more revolting than Barrymore's, spiritually so much less so, is a typical Mamoulian touch.

To Mamoulian's other cinematic crimes must be added that of plagiarism. *City Streets* is almost pure Von Sternberg. And his latest film, *Love Me Tonight,* is a René Clair film plus some Lubitschisms and minus Clair's freshness, wit, and charm. To make up for Clair's wit, Mamoulian has gone in for bigness. His country house is an enormous castle in the most opulent Hollywood tradition, with swarms of aristocratic inmates, long lines of servants, acres of sparkling polished floors. There is not one comic old spinster—there are three, which of course makes it three times as

81

amusing. (Mamoulian, by the way, has more of Cecil B. De Mille in him than his admirers suspect.) For Clair's freshness, Mamoulian substitutes a hectic experimentation with trick effects. Sometimes this is pleasing enough, as the use of slow motion in the hunting scene. But Mamoulian uses his tricks unintelligently, without taste. The shot of the horn-blowing huntsman, for example, taken from an Eisenstein angle, strikes a heroic note that is absurdly out of key in a musical comedy featuring Jeannette MacDonald and Maurice Chevalier. For Clair's casual charm Mamoulian can make no substitution. To be light and casual is simply not in him. The opening sequence, in which Chevalier's impromptu morning song is caught up by one person after another, and the closing episode, when the princess gallops after her lover's train and stops it by planting herself, on horseback, across the tracks—such things cry out to be treated lightly. Alas, the Mamoulian touch, too heavy even for melodrama, quite crushes the life out of such frail little blooms of fantasy.

The only reason for considering Mamoulian's work at such length is that he is taken seriously by many otherwise intelligent persons.

ERNST LUBITSCH is the only director in Hollywood with his own complete staff, which works with him on every picture he makes. They are mostly Germans, for although Lubitsch has been working in this country for nine years he is still more Teutonic than American. The son of a Berlin shopkeeper, he progressed from a job with Max Reinhardt to acting in movie comedies to directing comedies himself. But the films that made his reputation were two big-scale heavily wrought historical dramas: *Passion,* with Pola Negri as la Pompadour, and *Deception* with Jannings as Henry VIII. On the strength of these (together with his *The Flame* and *Sumurun*), he was brought to this country in 1924 and, with characteristic Hollywood intelligence, put to work directing Mary Pickford ("America's Sweetheart") in *Rosita.* Luckily, he came under the influence of Chaplin's *A Woman of Paris.* Stimulated by this pioneer film, he made a series of subtle, witty, smoothly made boudoir farces, all of them with a distinct "Lubitsch" quality. *The Marriage Circle* (1924), *Kiss Me Again,* and *So This Is Paris* were

82

the most notable. He also made what Paul Rotha (whose book, *The Film Till Now,* is an invaluable mine of facts about the movies) considers his most brilliant film: a satire on the Hollywood movie called *Forbidden Paradise* (1924). In his last silent film, *The Patriot* (1928), with Jannings as the mad Czar Paul, Lubitsch went back to heavy "costume" drama. His talkies have been disappointing—perhaps because he insists on tinkering with the spoken lines, despite his sketchy knowledge of English. Also, just as Sternberg has gotten into a rut with Marlene Dietrich, so Lubitsch repeated himself tiresomely in his Maurice Chevalier-Jeannette MacDonald series: *The Love Parade, The Smiling Lieutenant,* and *One Hour with You.* It is significant that his two best talkies, *Monte Carlo* and the current *Trouble in Paradise,* are not Chevalier films.

There are, in a sense, two Lubitsches. There is the Lubitsch who began as one of Germany's most popular screen comedians and who has developed as a highly individual director of boudoir comedies, with precisely the witty, sophisticated, deft, ironic touch needed for those delicious little affairs. And there is the Lubitsch who began as Reinhardt's assistant and who had always had a hankering for pretentious dramas with plenty of emotional fireworks and historical background. This second Lubitsch seems to me inferior to the first. A film like *The Patriot,* for all the impressive trappings of technique in which it is swathed, has something static, cumbersome and *dead* about it. As a "serious" artist, Lubitsch has nothing to say. The moral earnestness of a Griffith, the emotional drive of a Stroheim, Murnau's psychological insight, Sternberg's shadowy, somewhat "arty" lyricism with the camera—Lubitsch has none of these. His vital qualities are called into play only in comedy. When he takes himself seriously, it is as if an excellent vaudeville star should insist on appearing in Shakespearean tragedy.

About once a year—sometimes not so often—Hollywood turns out a movie that can be accepted without innumerable reservations. In 1931 it was *Little Caesar.* Last year it was Lubitsch's *Trouble in Paradise.* That this should have been so excellent a production is more than a little strange. It is true that Lubitsch enjoys the greatest reputation of any director now active in Hollywood. But this is based largely on his silent films. Of late he has made *The Man I*

Killed, a dismally slow-paced Teutonic tear-jerker, in which he indulged his weakness for being taken seriously and which he therefore considers his chef-d'oeuvre; *One Hour with You,* a routine Chevalier film; and *The Smiling Lieutenant,* another Chevalier film, which was a vulgarized, heavy-footed version of that charming German production: *The Waltz Dream.* There was therefore no reason to suppose that *Trouble in Paradise* would be anything more than just another movie.

It is, with all qualifications, superb. Within the admittedly drastic limitations of its genre, it comes as close to perfection as anything I have ever seen in the movies. The opening shot of the Venetian garbage barge with its discordant gondolier strikes the note of sophisticated burlesque that is held throughout. The pace is fast, as it should be: each shot is held just long enough to make its point, and the point is never hammered in. "Lubitschisms," those touches of wit that no other director quite captures, are scattered everywhere with a prodigal hand. There is enough "camera interest" for a dozen movies. When the lovers embrace, for instance, they are pictured rapidly (1) in the flesh, (2) in a mirror, (3) as shadows on a satin coverlet. As always, Lubitsch makes great play with the swinging camera, but he also gets some very nice effects with rapid cutting. Sound is used with especial brilliance. There are no "songs" arbitrarily set into the narrative like plums in a pudding. Instead, the action is accompanied by a running commentary of music. Like the old movie-organ pieces (still the best solution to the problem of movie music) this makes no attempt to be "good" in itself and is quite satisfied to serve as a background for what happens on the screen. Finally the decor, by Hans Dreier, is the best "moderne" job I have yet seen on stage or screen. Most cinematic excursions into modernism are either grotesque or tasteless, but Dreier's clocks, staircases, windows and chaise-longues are original, delicate and even refined.

Only Lubitsch, who works out every detail on paper before he shoots a single scene, could master all these sound and cinematic devices and put them smoothly to work in a single film. Varied and brilliant as is the technique, it never becomes obtrusive. It is always used to carry on and give point to the narrative. (Which, by the way, is banal—and quite unimportant.) Consider the climax of the

84

movie, certainly one of the classic scenes in film comedy, when Filibo suddenly remembers where he has seen the mysterious Duval before. Here the crashing chorus of mock-dramatic music, the excited jumping up and sitting down of Filibo, and the mad gyrations of the camera to follow him—all these elements come together with shattering effect. There is also the fact that Filibo is played by a master of light comedy, Edward Everett Horton. This suggests another of the film's excellences—the acting of Herbert Marshall, Charles Ruggles, and Kay Francis. But the list of virtues is endless. Enough to say that *Trouble in Paradise* almost makes one believe in Hollywood again.

HARRY D'ABBADIE D'ARRAST, according to an acquaintance, is "nervous, somber, ugly, continually making faces and slightly hysterical." He was born of a good French family in the Argentine in 1897. He learned his cinema abroad and came to Hollywood in 1922. For three years he was one of Chaplin's assistants, notably on *A Woman of Paris* (1923) and *The Gold Rush*. Later he made a series of sparkling Menjou comedies: *Serenade, Service for Ladies, A Gentleman of Paris*. In 1930 he collaborated with Donald Ogden Stewart on the story for *Laughter,* which he directed. After a lapse of over a year, RKO-Radio set him to work on a film version of the French comedy, *Topaze*. This is currently running and appears to have re-established his reputation.

It was d'Arrast's work with Chaplin on *A Woman of Paris* that bent his twig in the direction it has held ever since. When Chaplin undertook his only experiment in directing a serious movie, he could never have foreseen the enormous influence his effort was to have on the Hollywood cinema. Superficially, *A Woman of Paris* was an unpretentious little story of a *boulevardier* (Adolph Menjou) and his mistress (Edna Purviance, leading lady in most of Chaplin's comedies). But in a quiet moving way it brought to the screen for the first time a sophisticated analysis of human relations. There was subtlety in it and psychological penetration. Hollywood took over Chaplin's discovery, but with a difference. The film's witty, gay, ironic, deftly sophisticated note was at once appropriated, but the sensitive feeling for human realities, the pathos and the irony, were never recaptured. The comedies of Lubitsch and his

85

followers, more numerous today than ever, all stem from Chaplin's film. Menjou, whose flair for sophisticated comedy Chaplin discovered, has been playing a cheapened, externalized version of his *Woman of Paris* ever since.

But the most faithful disciple has been d'Arrast. Most of his comedies have the glitter of *A Woman of Paris* with none of its human warmth. The demand for sleek Parisian *roués* and satin-walled boudoirs is apparently inexhautible. Every now and then, however, d'Arrast makes a movie that cuts beneath the surface. In the silent days it was his significantly titled *A Gentleman of Paris,* a sort of Maupassant novelette done with lots of cold style. And he has made two talkies of exceptional interest. *Laughter* is memorable because it attempts (not entirely successfully but with a bitterness unusual in the movies) to satirize this money-built civilization, because it has some brilliantly insane dialogue by Donald Ogden Stewart, and because of fine performances by Glenn Anders, Frank Morgan, Frederick March, and Nancy Carroll. The current d'Arrast production, *Topaze,* is smoothly and intelligently directed. In it John Barrymore gives the finest performance of his screen career. Why an actor with such a sense of high comedy should be consistently given heavy romantic parts is one of the trade secrets of Hollywood. Also to be noted is Myrna Loy, in my opinion the most attractive, intelligent, and charming of present-day movie actresses. It is also a mystery why for years she has had to get along on "vampire" parts in Fu Manchu thrillers.

HENRY KING, born and raised on a Virginia plantation, began his career as a blackface song-and-dance man. After ten years in "legitimate" (vaudeville, burlesque, circus, stock) he went into the movies as an actor. His main achievements in this line seem to have been appearances opposite Lillian Lorraine in *My Lady of Perfume* and Baby Mary Osborn, first of the infant stars, in a series of films directed by himself. He has made every sort of movie, from archaic Pathé serials to the once famous Ronald Colman-Vilma Banky affairs, but his reputation rests entirely on two silent films: *Tola'ble David* (1922) and *Stella Dallas* (1925). While I was disappointed in his current *State Fair,* it is better than anything he has done for some time and at least has revived interest in his work.

86

"I rehearse my pictures just like a play," King once remarked, "and during the rehearsals I build up my continuity." This approach, diametrically opposed to that of Griffith, Eisenstein, and all who understand the movies most deeply, does not make for great cinema. And King is important neither for his photography nor his filmic structure. But he has a quality that is rare in Hollywood: a delicate, sure human sympathy. At his best he can make his people real and can induce one to follow their doings with emotional intensity. His feeling for people shows in the casting of *Tola'ble David*. His selection of Richard Barthelmess to play David was sheer genius. It was the first time Barthelmess played this type of part, and he has been playing it ever since, most lately in *Cabin in the Cotton*. King also took a Scotch musical-show comedian, Ernest Torrence, and made him into a really terrifying villain. "Torrence was so vehement," he explains later, "so full of needful expression, so intelligent at grasping what was wanted of him, that I found myself building on his part and curtailing the business of another."

Most Hollywood movies are about the very poor or the very rich because social extremes are always dramatic. Such movies as do not fall into these categories—films about gangsters, for instance, or actresses—usually deal with some picturesque minor social group. The epic of the externally undramatic middle classes has yet to be screened. The nearest we have come to it is King's *Stella Dallas*. There is no question that *Tola'ble David* is a more successful work, is indeed one of the most *perfect* movies ever made. But *Stella Dallas,* in my opinion, was a more remarkable film. The theme was Mother Love, a temptation for any director. But King presented it not as shrilly sensational melodrama but as a deeply felt drama of a middle-class mother and her middle-class daughter. The mother (Belle Bennett) is just a bit "common" according to bourgeois standards, and the daughter (Lois Moran) realizes that her mother is the chief bar to her marrying the "nice" young man of her choice (Ronald Colman). This the mother learns by chance (for her daughter is too fond of her to say anything) and to insure her daughter's happiness, steps out of her life. For Hollywood this plot is a triumph of originality, for the castastrophe is precipitated by nothing more sensational than the bourgeois idea of some people being "nice" and others being "common." That this conception has, in real life, given rise to more drama than all the gangsters in Chicago—this is beside the point as far as Hollywood is concerned. The scene is mostly a summer resort and here again King admirably re-creates, entirely without satire, the tone of such fortresses of the American bourgeoisie—the tennis, the wicker chairs on the porch, the flashy roadsters, the white flannels and the 9-to-12 dances at the Lake House. Now there have been summer resorts and, God knows, mothers enough in the movies. The only difference is that King's direction, warmly and delicately sympathetic, makes them seem true—"realizes" them in Cézanne's pregnant phrase. The greatest distinction of *Stella Dallas* is that it presents a mother-and-daughter relationship in which one believes and which is therefore intensely moving.

About King's latest work, *State Fair,* I find it hard to write with the proper critical restraint. I am not one who insists that a work of art shall be judged by its social implications, or lack of them. But there is a limit to the detachment of art from present-day realities. At a time when the American farmer is faced with ruin, when the whole Midwest is seething with bitterness and economic discontent, a movie like *State Fair* is an insulting "let them eat cake" gesture. The vaudeville rusticity of millionaire Will Rogers, the "cute" little-doll face of Janet Gaynor—thus Hollywood embodies the farmer! There was no excuse for the cheerfully trivial tone of the whole thing, the studied avoidance of anything more serious in the life of the farmer than whether his hog will win the state championship. And the slick, marshmallow-sweet Hollywood photography was in itself just cause for a national farmer's strike. What a chance for a realistic, documentary film of American farm life in these times! And Hollywood gives us a movie about as earthy as the gingham overalls in a musical comedy number. In spite of his scenario and a flagrantly inappropriate cast (what has become of King's flair for casting?) King manages to get in a few nice touches—the night ride to the fair and the rain at the end, for example. But the whole fabric was rotten with evasion of reality, and no amount of good directing (which King didn't give it anyway) would have been any use.

ERICH OSWALD HANS CARL MARIE STROHEIM VON NORDENWALD was born in Vienna in 1885, the son of a colonel on the Austrian general staff. He was graduated from the Imperial Military Academy in 1906, badly wounded in the head (only his protruding frontal ridge saved his eyesight) in the trouble with Bosnia-Herzogovina in 1908, cashiered for quarreling with his commanding officer. In 1909 he landed, penniless, in the United States. For five years he knocked around as a fashion correspondent, soldier, boatman, section hand, dishwasher, stable man, vaudeville actor and fly-paper salesman. In 1914 his knowledge of European military and court etiquette got him a job on a movie called *Old Heidelberg.* The war brought Stroheim suddenly into demand to play villainous Prussian officers in such pro-ally films as *For France* and *The Unbeliever.* He became known as "The Man You Love To Hate." Griffith gave him a mob part in the biblical episodes of *Intolerance* ("He's one of those guys yelling 'Crucify him!' " explains Griffith) and used him as art director in some later films. When the war ended, so did the demand for Stroheim. After months of starvation, he showed Carl Laemmle a scenario he had written and managed to get Laemmle to get him to make a movie from it. The maximum cost would be $25,000. The result was *Blind Husbands,* a melodrama of amorous intrigue done in the continental manner. It cost $85,000, but it was a box-office success. It was followed by *The Devil's Passkey,* a $75,000 production that somehow cost Mr. Laemmle $185,000 before it was finished. Stroheim now embarked on his masterpiece in this genre: *Foolish Wives* (1922) which he wrote, directed, played the lead in, and which was positively not to cost over $250,000. After he had shot 200,000 feet of film and spent over $1,000,000 the frantic Laemmle induced him to bring the picture to an abrupt end with a subtitle. But *Foolish Wives* was a great success. He was working on *The Merry-Go-Round* when Irving Thalberg, the curly-haired, cold-eyed Boy Wonder of Hollywood movie executives, took charge of Universal's production end. Thalberg has the keenest nose for box-office values in all Hollywood. Shrewdly he sensed that Stroheim was a deadbeat and forthwith fired him. Stroheim now went over to Metro which, in reckless disregard of Thalberg's judgment, gave him carte blanche to make a super-special movie from Frank Norris's novel *McTeague.* It is said that Stroheim had wanted to make the film ever since he had found the book, years before coming to Hollywood, in a cheap boardinghouse room. After he had run far over his allotted time and money, Stroheim presented Metro with a brutally realistic movie, completely lacking in sex and box-office appeal, that took ten hours to show. They cut its forty-two reels down to ten reels, called it *Greed,* and sent it out to the theatres. It was a complete failure. Those who have seen *Greed* in its entirety (no one seems to know just what has become of it now) pronounce it one of the greatest American films. In spite of everything, Stroheim was given *The Merry Widow* to direct. He turned out a frothy, sophisticated film that was a commercial success. In June 1926, Stroheim began making a movie for Paramount to be called *The Wedding March.* He took a year to make it, another year to edit it, and finally suggested that it be run in two sections, with an intermission for dinner. Over Stroheim's protests, Paramount cut the first half to ten reels and released it in 1928. So resoundingly did it flop that the second half, *The Honeymoon,* was never released. Next he wrote, directed, and acted in a white-men-in-the-tropics film starring Goria Swanson and called *Queen Kelly.* But something happened—the talkies came in or Miss Swanson wasn't pleased—and *Queen Kelly* was never shown in public. Since the talkies, Stroheim has been forced to fall back on acting. He has played, and well, in *The Great Gabbo, Three Faces East, The Lost Squadron,* and *As You Desire Me.* Recently Fox set him to work directing an affair called *Walking Down Broadway,* but called him off when he had taken 26 reels without any commercially tangible result.

The career of Stroheim presents in an intensified form the dilemma of every serious artist in Hollywood. His conflicts with the commercial end of the industry are those of his colleagues, and his frustration is theirs. But whereas they all compromise, more or less successfully, between Art and Mammon, such compromise is temperamentally impossible to Stroheim. He is a remarkable example, the only one Hollywood has to offer, of an artist who subordinates everything to what he considers his art. When he makes a movie, he loses all sense of time, of money, of human endurance. He keeps his actors at work until four in the morning, and he sees no reason why an audience should not be willing to sit through ten hours of a movie—if it takes ten hours to adequately express his idea. He is, in

90

fact, as indifferent to the reactions of the public as he is to the interests of the producers. "I never go to see my pictures in the theatres," he once declared. The amazing thing is not that Stroheim has been thwarted at every turn of his career but that the producers have let such a lunatic spend as much of their money as they have. Stroheim obviously has no place in Hollywood. To me, he is the most interesting director out there.

Greed is generally considered Von Stroheim's masterpiece, but the only one of his films with which I am very familiar is *The Wedding March*. My estimate of his ability is therefore based chiefly on that remarkable film. Since, as we have seen, it has been released only in a mutilated version, there is no point in criticizing it as a whole. Looking at the parts, one is impressed most of all by their great variation in tone. With the flexibility and resource of a virtuoso, Von Stroheim adapts his style to the particular mood or emotion he wants to convey. His love scenes are lyrical with moonlight, apple blossoms and soft-focus effects. His butcher shop and his brothel are presented with the most realistic insistence on the sordid and physical. The beginning of the film is in still another key: it is cool, deft analysis of social situations—a prodigal son asking his parents for money, a flirtation in a crowd. This flirtation is a lengthy episode in which, by a directorial *tour de force,* one's interest is held with only the slightest instruments of expression—a raising of the eyebrow, a glance, a discreet smile. To heighten the effect of this scene Von Stroheim places it against a background of an entirely different tone: the pomp and circumstance of the Corpus Christi procession. This same principle of dramatic counterpoint is followed in the treatment of the characters. The minor actors are not suppressed to form a neutral background to the "stars" as in most American movies, but on the contrary their personalities are strongly underlined. Thus when they come into contact with the principals or with each other, situations are created that are rich in the complexity of varying motives and emotions. The final wedding sequence, which assembles all the characters of the film, is built up wholly on this sort of counterpoint. *The Wedding March* is a most ambitious picture, as vast in emotional scope as *The Birth of a Nation* is vast in physical scope. Its greatness rests in the fact that it is ambitious without being heavy, serious without being dull, at once deeply felt and expressed in effective cinematic terms.

With Stroheim realism is a religion. His favorite author is Zola. There seems to be no limit to his appetite for reality. When he was a boy, he used to compete with his brother in picking out military insignia. "There were 106 infantry regiments in Austria with special markings and stripes. Yet I knew them all," he boasts. And again: "Somewhere in my subconscious mind I have a sort of photographic place. I see everything in the form of a scene for a picture." Innumerable legends have grown up around his attention to detail: how he spent two weeks teaching a squad of extras to salute in the Austrian manner; how he insists that cinematic grand dukes shall wear crests on their silk underwear and cinematic beggars shall wear tattered underclothes; how he blackened the hooves of a squadron of cavalry horses with shoe polish. The triumph of Stroheim's realism is *Greed*, which is pure Zola from the opening shots of the cheap dentist's office to the dead mule and salt-caked faces in the Death Valley sequence at the end. If *Greed* is Zolaesque, *Foolish Wives* and *The Wedding March* are Balzacian mixtures of melodrama, passion, and sophistication. Balzac would appreciate the worldly penetration of their analysis of personality, the richness of detail with which they define a social atmosphere, and the passion with which their characters pursue their ends. One recoils in amazement at the emotional intensity Stroheim can put into the melodramatic situations of such films.

"If I can dominate a player," Stroheim once remarked, "I can get anything I want from her." Actors to him are mere tools of his craft. They express *him,* not themselves. This was also the attitude of Griffith, who used to keep his actors in ignorance about the plot in order to keep the control more completely in his own hands. If they insisted on knowing something, he would purposely mislead them. No director gets more out of his actors than Stroheim. The doll-faced Mae Murray detested him when he directed her in *The Merry Widow,* but he forced her to really act for the first and last time in her career. He picked Zasu Pitts out of comedies and made her the tragic heroine of *Greed.* She has gone back to comedies, but Stroheim, and many of those who saw *Greed* call her the greatest tragic actress in Hollywood. (Milestone had her play the mother in *All Quiet,* but the executives couldn't take her seriously, and he had to re-take her scenes with Beryl Mercer in her place.) He found Fay Wray in Westerns and gave her the lead in *The Wedding March*. Stroheim himself is an actor of extraordinary power. His playing, like his directing, combines meticulousness with emotional intensity. With the utmost economy of means—a raised eyebrow, a slight motion of the lips—he gets terrific effects. His friend James Cruze, who directed him in *The Great Gabbo*, declares, "Von can steal any scene with the back of his fat neck."

In the twenty years Stroheim has been in Hollywood, he has made just seven pictures. Some directors—and able ones, too—turn out almost that many in a single year. LeRoy made six last year, Wellman made five. To such men a movie is merely a technical problem: how can this banal situation be dressed up to the best advantage, what directorial tricks will inject the greatest amount of synthetic vitality into it? But to Stroheim making a movie is an intensely personal experience. He takes it all much too seriously. He doesn't understand that Hollywood exists to make money and that it is the business of the director to turn out, as cheaply and speedily as possible, a picture that people will pay to see. But then Stroheim has never had any sense of money. He has worked a year without salary just to get a movie finished the way he wanted it. Stroheim is a foolish fellow indeed compared to a director like the high-powered Clarence ("Never Made a Flop") Brown, who gets $300,000 a year for putting Joan Crawford and Greta Garbo through their paces. He is stubborn, naive, conceited, wrong-headed, quixotic. Inevitably he has made an utter mess out of his career: only one movie in the last five years, and that never completed; his wife reduced most of the time to one dress; he himself forced to play small parts under directors who don't know a tenth what he does. But Stroheim has one quality which the slick, facile technicians now dominant in Hollywood somehow don't seem to develop: a sense of personal integrity. No pressure can make him do what he doesn't believe in. He stands up for his own ideas in spite of everything. He has guts. His career is a warning to most young directors, an inspiration to a few.

JOSEF VON STERNBERG, according to Paramount's handout, was born in Vienna in 1894 and was graduated from the University of Vienna "with several degrees." Furthermore—"He has sandy

93

brown hair, and blue eyes that give the impression of being dull. That is when he is brooding." Sternberg spurns as a canard the rumor that he was born Joe Stern of Brooklyn. Like everyone else in Hollywood, he has a "gag" whereby he calls attention to himself. His particular gag is that he is an artist—aloof, temperamental, not to be imposed on by mere $150,000-a-year studio executives. Strangely enough, there is a certain amount of sincerity behind this gag of Sternberg's. In its interest he had unhesitatingly shattered to bits his Hollywood career, and not once but several times. After a decade of apprentice work as film cutter, cameraman, scenarist, and so on, Sternberg entered on his career in 1924 by getting someone to put up $5,000 for a picture he wanted to make. This was *The Salvation Hunters,* a grimly realistic drama acted mostly by amateurs and photographed mostly against a mud scow in San Pedro Harbor. Chaplin saw the film and was impressed enough to give Sternberg $20,000 for a half interest. But when a Hollywood audience snickered at the preview, Chaplin pretended it was all a big joke—on Sternberg. The film was never released for a public showing. Perhaps as another joke, Chaplin had United Artists hire Sternberg to direct Mary Pickford. The film was never made: America's Sweetheart just didn't get along with Sternberg. He next went over to Metro-Goldwyn-Mayer, made two potboilers, and then broke his contract ("by mutual consent"). Once more Chaplin took him up. He directed Edna Purviance, Chaplin's leading lady in the older comedies, in *The Sea Gull.* "Beautiful but not human," was Hollywood's reaction. The film was never released. It began to seem as if Sternberg was temperamentally incapable of making a commercial movie. When, in 1926, Paramount gave him a contract, no one was very much excited. Sternberg surprised everyone, Paramount included, by turning out *Underworld,* a high-powered melodrama that is the ancestor of all gangster films. It was the biggest box-office success of 1927 and won Sternberg a bonus of $10,000 from Paramount. He has been with Paramount ever since then. Notable among his silent productions were *The Dragnet, The Last Command, The Docks of New York,* and *The Case of Lena Smith.* His first talkie he made in Germany for UFA: *The Blue Angel,* starring Emil Jannings. To play opposite Jannings he picked an obscure German musical comedy actress named Marlene

94

Dietrich. The story is that he chose her after hearing her say her one and only line in the show: "Hurray for the gentleman who has won the grand prize!" When he returned to this country, Dietrich came with him. His direction plus Paramount's astute publicity made Dietrich into a star of the first magnitude, the pretender to Garbo's crown. Except for *An American Tragedy,* every picture Sternberg has made since *The Blue Angel* has been built around Dietrich. There was *Morocco* in 1930, *Dishonored* in 1931, *Shanghai Express* and *The Blonde Venus* last year. His contract with Paramount expired several months ago and has not been renewed —largely because of a bitter quarrel over *The Blonde Venus.* He sailed for Germany in February—to work for UFA, was the report. But the Nazi revolution barred him (despite the "von") from a UFA job—as it is said to have also caused UFA to fire its most talented director, G. W. Pabst—and he sailed back to this country. There are rumors he is joining a new production company.

Perhaps the best approach to Sternberg is through Stroheim. The two are linked together in many ways. The "von" in Sternberg's name may well be a furtive tribute to the man who taught him the use of significant detail. From Stroheim he also acquired his taste for realism, his meticulous attention to lighting and composition. His first movie, *The Salvation Hunters,* which he still considers his best, was made soon after Stroheim's *Greed* appeared. Its brutal heavy-handed realism was precisely that of *Greed,* which Sternberg is said to have studied closely. Some interesting parallels can be drawn between Sternberg's *The Case of Lena Smith* and Stroheim's *The Wedding March.* Each was released in 1928; each was the last silent film by its creator; the setting of each was pre-war Vienna; each centered around a love affair between a young officer and a girl of the people; the full-scale reproduction of the facade of Corpus Christi church, one of the triumphs of Hollywood realism, was used in both films; and, finally, *Lena Smith* was dedicated to the mothers of the world, *The Wedding March* to the lovers of the world. Even Sternberg's well-known "signature," the black cat which appears in each of his films, may be traced to Stroheim. A black cat figured prominently and effectively in the climactic murder scene in *Greed.*

Sternberg presents that mixture of temperament and affectation

95

which marks the man of talent—as contrasted with the man of genius. Stroheim is far more *outré,* and at the same time less affected. He has the passionate sincerity, the naive directness of genius. But there is always something small and self-conscious about Sternberg's gestures. Stroheim is believable when he shaves his head and wears a silver bracelet. Sternberg is suspect even in so innocent a matter as the cane he carries. There is more than a little of the "art" director about Sternberg, and his films often have a slick "artiness" about them. Both men have fought for their aesthetic integrity, both are known in Hollywood as "difficult," which means "honest." But one feels that Stroheim is irreconcilable because it is in his nature to be so, Sternberg because he wants to keep in character as an "artist." A case in point was the uproar with Paramount over *The Blonde Venus.* Sternberg had written the scenario himself (it is notable how many of the directors considered are also skilled scenario writers) and he resented certain proposed changes—including, of course, a happy ending. When Paramount insisted, Sternberg took the train for New York. Paramount threatened to sue for $100,000 damages for breach of contract. ("One hundred thousand dollars? Is that all? I think they are trying to humiliate me," observed Sternberg, unimpressed.) Things were finally patched up, however, and Sternberg completed the picture. After seeing it, I wonder what all the shooting was for. There is nothing in it that makes the slightest difference, one way or another. It puts Sternberg in the ridiculous position of defending bad art against the onslaughts of commercialism. The pity of it is that there is a good deal of sincerity mixed up with Sternberg's faking and posing. And, of course, a great deal of talent. The talkie career of Von Sternberg is a study in degeneration. For him Marlene Dietrich has been far more of a *femme fatale* than for any of her cinematic victims. Each of her films has been just a little worse than its predecessor.

In his silent films Sternberg was as interesting a director as Hollywood had to offer. They were cut so smoothly, with such a delicate sense of rhythm, that they had that finished, complete quality which few American films possess. Their photography was the best in Hollywood: luminous gray tones, rich dramatic chiaroscuro, with each shot a well-thought-out composition in itself. A

96

scenarist himself, Sternberg knew how to tell a story, how to keep it moving and give it suspense. His films moved along smoothly and swiftly, with the minimum of waste motion. Skillfully he kaleidoscoped the narrative so as to get pace and avoid wearisome exposition, as in *Underworld* when the murder is followed immediately by the judge pronouncing sentence of death.

All of these gifts Sternberg had—and still has. But they have degenerated into the hollowest, most patent kind of technical trickery. His latest movie, *The Blonde Venus,* is perhaps the worst ever made. In it all Sternberg's gifts have turned sour. The photography is definitely "arty"—a nauseating blend of hazy light, soft focus, over-blacks and over-whites, with each shot so obviously "composed" as to be painful. Sternberg's rhythm has declined to a senseless, see-saw pattern. And his kaleidoscopic cutting has reached such a point that the film is all pace and nothing else. The scene changes often, simply because Sternberg didn't have the vitality to get anything much out of any one scene. Therefore his camera flits restlessly, and fruitlessly, from New York to New Orleans to Berlin to Buenos Aires. The whole thing reminded me of the galvanic twitching of a corpse. As for the story, the characterizations, and the cast—never has there been anything more naive, more absurdly artificial and Hollywoodish. To survive in the hostile atmosphere of Hollywood, it would seem, the artist must have something more than talent.

MERVYN LEROY is the current Boy Wonder among Hollywood directors. He is short, slight, and looks much younger than he is. When he went to a Manhattan theatre recently to see a play he was going to direct, he was unable to convince the man in the box office that he wasn't his own office boy. To lend himself dignity, he puffs solemnly on a large cigar. It is rumored that his real name is Lasky and that he is a nephew of Jesse Lasky, the producer. He was born in 1900 in San Francisco, and in 1920 he got a job as a cameraman at First National. He has stayed there ever since, which is something of a record in Hollywood. From playing bit parts and writing "gags" for Colleen Moore pictures, he progressed to directing Mlle. Moore (said to have had the largest fan mail any star ever received) in several of her innocent little diversions. Thence he rose

97

to directing less innocent but equally ephemeral productions: *Hot Stuff, Showgirl in Hollywood, Broadway Babies, Ritzy Rosie,* and so on. In 1931 he surprised everyone by turning out *Little Caesar,* a gangster melodrama that was an enormous success at the box office and with the critics. Since then he has made a vast number of films, most of them mediocre, a few worth recording. Notable are: *Five Star Final,* which had a moral and emotional force rare in the American cinema; *Gentleman's Fate,* an excellent gangster picture in which LeRoy extracted from John Gilbert his first decent talkie performance; a fast-paced farce called *High Pressure; Local Boy Makes Good,* wherein LeRoy managed to restrain the appalling antics of Joe E. Brown enough to make him human and amusing for the first and last time; the somber *I Am a Fugitive* and the trivial, smartly directed *Tonight or Never.* When his wife divorced him last summer, his salary was $91,000.

I should not hesitate to call *Little Caesar* the most successful talkie that has yet been made in this country. The credit goes chiefly, though not entirely, to LeRoy. He gave it a dynamic, driving pace which carried through to the very end. By skillful cutting he carried the rhythm of his episodes and related them so closely that, unlike most American talkies, *Little Caesar* seems to be an organic whole. He adroitly modulated the tone from tense melodrama (as in the gangsters' inner sanctum scenes) to satire (as in the superb banquet episode) to the bleakest realism (as in the last reel). And he precisely caught the atmosphere of his night club, of his cheap flophouse, of his lunch counters and hideaways. But there was also the performance of Edward G. Robinson (whom, to be sure, LeRoy picked, more or less out of the air, to play the part) which would have triumphed over any direction. And there was an excellent script and a plot which was both dramatically and psychologically effective. It was a remarkably fine touch in the grand tragic manner, to have Caesar's ruin brought about by his one human feeling, which is also his one weakness: his friendship for Joe Massara.

According to Hollywood legend, LeRoy had long been eager to make a movie out of W. R. Burnett's novel, *Little Caesar.* When he learned that First National had bought the rights, he determined to get the assignment. Afire with enthusiasm, he spent weeks wander-

98

ing about the Los Angeles waterfront, closely observing the way real gangsters acted and talked. His bosses were so impressed by his underworld erudition that they let him make the picture, which would normally have been assigned to a more eminent director. (LeRoy at the time had nothing to his credit except *Broadway Babies* and the like.) To avoid any possible interference from company executives, LeRoy refused to show them a single foot of the film until it was all taken, cut, and assembled. Then when it was beyond their power to tinker or tone down, he ran off the completed film—and knocked them out of their chairs. They released it just as he had made it, and predicted a big success at the box office. For once, they were right.

I have yet to see a dull movie by LeRoy. Whatever his movies fail to do, they always *move*. He knows how to give speed and pace to a film. His recent picture, *Hard to Handle*, for example, is a commonplace affair as to plot and dialogue, just another press-agent story. But LeRoy keeps the mechanism purring along at such a smooth, swift pace that one is not bored—until after it is all over and one has time to reflect. He makes his actors talk and move rapidly. He gets impetus every now and then by a quick succession of short shots dissolving into each other every five seconds or so. Above all, he doesn't dot his i's. Once his point is made, he moves on at once. Essentially, it is the vaudeville black-out technique.

LeRoy is perhaps the most efficient director in Hollywood. He is prolific, as the five full-length pictures he made last year testify. And he is versatile. Melodrama (*Little Caesar*), human document (*Two Seconds*), social propaganda (*Five Star Final*), farce (*High Pressure*), comedy of character (*Local Boy Makes Good*), sophisticated "drawing-room" comedy (*Tonight or Never*)—all are grist to his mill. LeRoy, in a word, is the answer to every producer's prayer: a director who has talent but who will do what he is told. It might be better if he had some of Stroheim's egotism and personal conviction, if he were a little more the individual artist and a little less the merely clever technician. But LeRoy makes no pretensions to being an artist. He is just a nice, modest, well-liked youngster, the boyfriend of Ginger Rogers, the intimate of Jack Dempsey and "Junior" Laemmle. "Mervyn," gushes a Hearst writer, "Mervyn is known as 'a great little guy' on both coasts. He doesn't pose as a prodigy, a genius, a 'von' LeRoy. He's just a young feller trying to get along." Which is precisely the trouble.

LEWIS MILESTONE, whose actual name is said to be Milstein, is stoutly built, ruddy, blue-eyed. He has a nice sense of humor and it is rumored about in Hollywood that he reads books. He was born in Russia in 1895. Sent to school in Germany by his father, a well-to-do manufacturer, he ran away to the United States. He worked in a photographer's studio and, on the outbreak of the war, entered the photographic division of the Signal Corps. After the war he went to Hollywood as a film cutter at $20 a week, met a director named Milton Seiter, and collaborated with him on a series of piffling productions: *Daddies, The Little Church Around the Corner, The Foolish Age* and so on. In 1924 he got a job as director with Warner Brothers. He proved to be so useful that he was constantly being lent to other companies to help out with pictures that were not going well. This worked until the day he discovered that Warner Brothers was paying him $400 a week and charging other companies a minimum of $1,000 a week for his services. He revolted, broke his contract, and went through bankruptcy to satisfy the judgment Warner Brothers won against him. A free man once more, he signed a four-year contract with Howard Hughes, who was just beginning his high-powered career as an independent producer. He made two excellent pictures for Hughes: the picaresque *Two Arabian Knights,* a rowdy, vulgar, and very funny comedy, and a gangster melodrama called *The Racket.* But Hughes, too, kept farming him out, which usually meant that he had to work on second-rate pictures. Milestone finally bought up the rest of his contract and once more regained his freedom. When Carl Laemmle in 1929 bought the screen rights to *All Quiet on the Western Front,* he sent for Milestone, already known as a director of ability and integrity, and had him make the movie. In 1931 he joined United Artists. He has made three films for them: *The Front Page,* which was widely considered the best movie of 1931, *Rain,* a very poor picture indeed, and *Hallelujah, I'm a Bum,* which is even more painful. He seems to be through with United Artists—perhaps wisely, considering his last two pictures—and to be pondering his

100

next move. There was a rumor last fall that he was to go to Spain with Sidney Franklin and Ernest Hemingway to make a movie about bullfighting. And a few months ago the papers printed an even more fantastic report: Milestone is to join forces with Lubitsch, Vidor and Sternberg in an entirely new producing company: Eastern Service Studios, Inc. Behind the new company is mysterious Captain Baynes. Behind Captain Baynes is the Electrical Research Products Corporation, which makes talkies equipment. And behind the Electrical Research Products Corporation is Western Electric. Captain Baynes is reported to have already leased the Paramount Long Island studio, idle for many months, and to have made practically sure of his four directors. The present moment is a propitious one for getting them together. Milestone is at loose ends. Vidor has been working on his own for several years. And Paramount's contracts with both Lubitsch and Sternberg are reported to have expired without being renewed. If Captain Baynes gets all four directors into his company, it will amount to a corner on Hollywood's best directorial talent.

To executives who grow worried when he is in the middle of a movie, Milestone quotes scripture: "O ye of little faith!" He will brook no interference once he has begun to work, and he insists on doing all his own cutting. His attitude is scrupulously, absurdly (from a Hollywood viewpoint) conscientious. Thus his break with Selznick two years ago, which killed the newborn Selznick-Milestone Pictures Corporation, came about because Selznick wanted him to assume responsibility for seven pictures a year. Milestone didn't think he could satisfactorily oversee so many pictures, and so he gave up an excellent chance to become an independent producer. When he was making *All Quiet,* he was continually pestered by the producers' insistence on a "happy ending"—which he didn't give them, by the way. Finally he called them on the phone and said: "I've got your happy ending. We'll let the Germans win the war."

An enormous amount of praise has been heaped on *All Quiet on the Western Front*—more, I suspect, for its obvious sincerity and emotional integrity than for its cinematic qualities. It is a very fine movie, but I am inclined to think it has been overestimated. There is much talk of the picture's realism, but I found the sets extremely artificial and the lighting very much in the overdramatic, glossy slick Hollywood manner. The French cottage had a property cow and a property cart posed in just the right place before it, the whole forming a composition reminiscent of a Royal Academy landscape. The daylit battle scenes were reeking with California sunlight (compare the grim gray tone of Russian war films), and the night tableaux were full of calcium star shells, melodramatic shadows, and fake moonlight. There were too many dugout scenes, and they were too full of confusion and squalor. Hollywood dugouts are always phony looking, anyway. Furthermore, the film is monotonous. Milestone is said to have cut it from 18,000 to 12,000 feet, but another 2,000 feet could easily have been taken out. The classroom scene was much too long: the effect of the teacher's patriotic monologue on his students could have been suggested in half the time. Another example is the scene where the boys look at the girl on the poster. This took several minutes, much too long in view of the minor point made by the episode. Milestone's use of the close-up seemed to me excessive. His trick of showing five or six faces in rhythmical succession, while effective as a means of presenting the boy soldiers as a group of individuals, became an annoying mannerism. He has a way of shoving his camera into the face of the speaker—a trick he repeats in *The Front Page*. This gives a powerful drive to the spoken lines, but it gets tiresome. Also, the lines aren't worth so much emphasis most of the time.

The limitations of *All Quiet* are most apparent when it is compared to a war film like Dovzhenko's *Arsenal*. Whereas the Russian has an inexhaustible variety of attack on his material, getting all sorts of contrasts and harmonies of scale, angle, distance, lighting, tempo and film texture, Milestone repeats himself tiresomely, his close-ups (even the infantry charges are done in close-up), his pearly gray lighting, his sluggish rhythm. Nor are there any such moments of intense imagination in *All Quiet* as occur in every reel of *Arsenal*. Even so absurd a war film as Griffith's *Hearts of the World* contains passages better than anything in *All Quiet*. I refer to certain panoramic shots, mostly at the beginning of reel five, epic in their sense of mass and distance and God's-eye scope. This is pure cinema—a matter of visual values entirely—and this is where

102

Milestone is weakest. His flair is for human, not abstract, drama. One is moved by his characters, whom he presents with sensitive awareness, but their cinematic realization leaves one cold.

Of what might be called the "younger generation" of Hollywood directors, Milestone and LeRoy are perhaps the most talented. Their work differs greatly. Milestone's movies tend to be slow-paced, brooding, emotional, Teutonic, while LeRoy's are speedy, hard-boiled, nervous, American. But they are significantly alike in one essential. I have already commented on LeRoy's extraordinary diversified output. And the writer who called Milestone "an efficient chameleon" was just about right. What is the common denominator of the rowdy slapstick of *Two Arabian Knights,* the dogged, bitter realism of *All Quiet,* the noisy melodrama of *The Front Page,* the gentle whimsicality of *Hallelujah, I'm a Bum,* and the cheap theatrics of *Rain?* To make for the last time a point I have already suggested several times before: the type of director now in the saddle in Hollywood is technically competent, clever, even intelligent but somehow lacking in individuality. It is not precisely a matter of "integrity," in Milestone's case at least. As we have seen, he compromises very little with his ideals and has suffered considerably through his insistence on making movies his own way. Rather it is a matter of personality. There is a certain individual quality to the work of the best of the older generation— Griffith, Lubitsch, Sternberg, Stroheim. Their movies may be very poor indeed, but they are unmistakably *theirs.* No such personal note exists in the work of the younger generation. They have, it seems, nothing to say.

—*The Symposium,* April and July 1933

Author's Note: The late Theodore Huff and I went to school together at Phillips Exeter Academy in the early twenties; I remember him as a tall, mild-mannered aesthete, one of a group of schoolboy intellectuals which was remarkably large and self-confident (not self-assertive, but one could hardly expect that in a boarding-school). Recently I came across a letter he wrote me in 1934 pointing out some inaccuracies in my "Notes on Hollywood Directors." Partly to keep the record straight, partly because it is an interesting document in itself, full of the scholarly devotion and excitement of the early *cineasts,* I reproduce it below, with cuts.

97 Engle Street,
Englewood, N.J.

Dear Dwight:

While looking about for the October issue of "Spicy Parisian Nights" in one of those back number stores, I came upon a magazine called "Symposium" with your article on Hollywood directors. Imagine my surprise! I never knew that you were such a student of the cinema. In the old days, I never heard you discuss pictures seriously and my impression was that you looked down on them as all the intellegensia [*sic*] of the time did (including Lincoln Kerstein [*sic*]). To be very frank, I am very jealous of you and Kerstein being such authorities and critics today. It's my proudest boast that I didn't have to wait for Eisenstein, Pudovkin and Clair. I considered movies an art years before and I have seen everything from "Cabiria" on. If you never heard me discuss films, it was because of the general attitude of the aestheits [*sic*] of the day. Fort Lee, near Englewood, was the first Hollywood, as you know, so I was brought up in the atmosphere. . . . Some of my earliest memories are watching Mary Pickford and others "on location" in Englewood with their yellow faces and purple eyelids. Did I ever tell you how (before Exeter days) I used to bicycle to Mammaroneck (32 miles round trip) on Saturdays to visit Griffith's studio and to watch (from afar) "Way Down East" and "Orphans of the Storm" in the making?

But what I started out to say was that I was very much impressed by your Notes. . . . Why don't you go on, list the foreign directors in the same way? . . . I could be of help as I have hundreds and hundreds of stills. . . . also I have the scenarios of many of the pictures you mention ("Woman of Paris," "Intolerance," for instance). I used to take them down in shorthand.

Just between ourselves, it seemed to me that many of the early pictures you discuss you hadn't actually seen but had done research on them. [*True, true—D.M.*] This criticism below of minor mistakes is only to show off what a "book of knowledge" I am on the subject when it comes to *facts*—even tho I can't write like you.

GRIFFITH: "The Avenging Conscience" was a five-reeler Mutual picture, 1913–14, and not one of the old Biograph two-reelers.

104

"Intolerance" was not produced two years later than "The Birth"; it was made the same year (though the Babylonian part wasn't made till 1915) and *released* in 1916.

Under "Important works followed," it was a mistake to list "One Exciting Night," a frank program picture, and to leave out "Hearts of the World" (1918), "Orphans of the Storm" (1921), and "America" (1924).

I don't like "archaic" photography either. Remember in an old picture you are apt to see a dupe or a dupe print. I consider parts of "Intolerance," for instance, far superior to the murky, artificial photography of today. And "Way Down East" is the high-water mark of photography for me. [*I now agree wholly about the "archaic" photography, especially after seeing "The Birth of a Nation" this summer for the fourth or fifth time; the photography, in its clarity and harmony of tones, seemed miraculous—far better than anything one has seen on the screen for decades.—D.M.*]

VIDOR: He first attracted attention with "Jack-Knife Man" (1920), a story of great simplicity and *no love interest*. It made his reputation.

"The Crowd" was not a talkie—it was made in the late silent era.

MAMOULIAN: I'm glad you don't like him. He certainly is a great imitator.

LUBITSCH: You pulled a great boner in saying Negri was La Pompadour. It was DuBarry of course. . . . He came to this country not in 1924 as "Rosita" was made early in 1923 (during our Upper-Middle year at Exeter). . . . And here is the remark I don't like: "With characteristic Hollywood intelligence, put to work directing Mary Pickford (America's Sweetheart)." It sounds too much like Seymour Stern, Harry Alan Potamkin or some other "highbrow" critic. Mary *brought* him over to direct her. . . .

HENRY KING: You left out "The White Sister" (1923) in his reputation-resting films. Surely this was one of the most beautiful pictorially ever made—taken in Italy before the days of "process" shots. Also his rehearsing like a play is not "diametrically opposed" to Griffith as D.W. used to rehearse for weeks in advance & work out things before going before the cameras.

105

VON STROHEIM: "Foolish Wives" was released in 1921, not 1922. I saw it at Exeter on a Wednesday, disguised in old clothes as a townie. [*Friday night was student night at the local movie house, the Ioka; Huff risked expulsion to gratify his scholarly passion.—D.M.*] If I had known you were interested, what fun we would have had seeing it. It really was, tho, an absurd mess even tho it is often spoken of today. . . . but it did give the feeling that the director was an individual of "driving force." . . .

VON STERNBERG: I don't agree that his films move swiftly and have pace. I think his films are very slow & languid. Who else ever uses such . . . slow dissolves (10 or 15 seconds) and general sluggishness? Also his annoying trick of always having something in the way! His characters are always obscured by palms, vines, gratings or shadows.

I hope you haven't minded these criticisms. . . . I really got a big kick out of the Notes. You took the words right out of my mouth when you said that the directors of today do not stand out as individuals; they are all on a competent dead level. . . . By the way, I had a job as cameraman and assistant last summer on a 16mm film made by a Yale man—John Flory '32. He got a seven-year contract with Paramount on the strength of it ("Mr. Motorboat's Last Stand"). He certainly was lucky. It's almost never happened before. . . . Well, I must stop.

Sincerely yours,
Ted Huff

PART THREE

AMERICAN THEMES

THE
DORIS
DAY
SYNDROME

ORIS DAY has become Betty Grable's successor as a sex symbol that offends no one and so does well at the box office. She is as wholesome as a bowl of cornflakes and at least as sexy. She has the standard American figure: long-legged, tallish (everything is on the -ish side) with highish, smallish breasts and no hips or buttocks to speak of. And the standard American (female) face, speaking in terms of aspirations rather than of realities: Nordic blonde, features regular, nose shortish and straightish, lips thinnish, Good Bone Structure. Miss Grable's chief physical asset was her legs, but Miss Day's is her face, showing the increasing timidity of our mass eroticism, from Theda Bara to Grable to Day. It is a face unmarked by experience, thus titillating the American male's Lolita complex, while at the same time, in contrast to Miss Grable's blank prettiness, it is full of Character, or maybe just Niceishness, so that it also appeals to the ladies. No wonder Doris Day is Hollywood's No. 1 box-office property. I suspect most American mothers would be pleased, and relieved, if their daughters grew up to resemble Doris Day. She has the healthy, antiseptic Good Looks and the Good Sport personality that the American middle class—that is, practically everybody—admires as a matter of duty. Especially the females. No competition.

Off duty, the American male has admired other kinds of femininity: the fine-drawn beauty of Garbo in which sex is spiritualized; the late Marilyn Monroe who defied classification, combining Lolita with the Dumb Blonde with a gay parody of both. One reason for her suicide may have been her inability to decide who she was, sex goddess or comedienne or serious actress. There are also such physiological grotesques as Jayne Mansfield, Jane Russell and the late Carole Landis (also a suicide) who, somebody once said, reminded him of a bureau with the top drawer pulled out; tough vamps like Jean Harlow, also a Dumb Blonde but she played it straight; and above all Carole Lombard, who kidded the Dumb Blonde (*Nothing Sacred, Twentieth Century*) with a style and wit no other screen actress has approached.

Doris Day, to return to our *moutons,* an appropriate cliché, after having served her apprenticeship in the kind of good-clean-fun shows, mostly musicals, in which Betty Grable and Esther Williams (underwater division) toiled all their lives, has now been promoted

110

to Sophisticated Sex Comedies. This was a shrewd move box-office-wise, but not so wise in other wises. Miss Day has only one expression beside her usual pleasantly bovine one: she opens her eyes wide. This must do for surprise, indignation, delight, shock, etc. It is inadequate, even though occasionally she *narrows* her eyes and sometimes goes so far as to pull down her mouth. Her European opposite number, Jeanne Moreau, has a figure somewhere between Miss Day's and Miss Mansfield's, i.e., womanly without being excessive about it. She also has a number of quite different expressions each of which conveys a specific emotion at a specific time. But this realistic virtuosity is precisely what is not wanted in the enormously successful series of Doris Day sex comedies. I was abroad when the first, *Pillow Talk,* was released, but I have seen the other two: *Lover, Come Back* and *That Touch of Mink.* Delbert Mann directed both and Stanley Shapiro co-authored the scripts. They have tried for a standardized product in which any touch of reality, spontaneity or artistry would be distracting.

Lover, Come Back was often good fun largely because of Shapiro's—and Paul Henning's—script, fertile in not-bad gags and comic situations. Mr. Mann's direction, however, was flaccid, without form or pace. I kept thinking how our old comedy directors, such as Lubitsch, Hawks, or the now-forgotten H. D'Abbadie D'Arrast, would have treated the script. But of course they would have imposed a style, and stylization today is as off-putting to the American mass audience as realism—an interesting study in cultural history would be why the masses in the twenties accepted Griffith, Chaplin, Keaton and Von Stroheim, but in the forties rejected *Citizen Kane.* By now, Hollywood, like TV, has managed to find a formula that combines the worst of both approaches, its products being both artificial and lacking in style.

The rest of the fun in *Lover, Come Back* is Tony Randall's performance as a neurotic advertising executive who tries to be the Napoleon of the agency he has inherited, but is constantly reduced to Colonel Blimp by his really Napoleonic subordinate, Rock Hudson, who isn't bad at all, by the way. As I have noted here before, although Mr. Randall is one of the best comedians in Hollywood, he has for the most part frittered away his talent in small routine parts. He is obviously a clever fellow—brains are

111

often an advantage even in movie acting—and his timing, the comedian's one essential, is perfect. Perhaps all a comedian needs is timing. What I remember most about George M. Cohan in *The Tavern* is his timing, which was enough to convince me he was a great performer, even though George Jean Nathan observed that if Mr. Cohan had delivered his lines straight, without pauses, double takes, counter-questions, and other delaying tactics, everybody could have gone home by ten o'clock. In England comedians like Alastair Sim and Terry-Thomas are given fat parts, but here Mr. Randall is minced up in that great blender-mixer which reduces everything to pap.

That Touch of Mink is a blurred copy of *Lover, Come Back,* cranked out on the Hollywood multigraphing machine. Cary Grant replaces Rock Hudson as the masterful, womanizing executive who often causes Doris Day to open, or narrow, her eyes. Gig Young replaces Tony Randall as his neurotic colleague, and not unworthily, perhaps because Mr. Shapiro—with Nate Monaster—has invented an amusing new subplot involving Mr. Young and his analyst. But this is all he has invented; for the rest, he has simply repeated, on the theory that if a gag was good once it will be even better the second time.

If *Lover, Come Back* was for the junior-high crowd, its successor is for the sixth grade. Perhaps this is why the usually reliable Cary Grant turns in a performance actually inferior to Rock Hudson's. He walks, or rather ambles, through the part, looking vaguely embarrassed by the lines he has to deliver and by the necessity to treat Miss Day as a sex object. Somehow he gives the impression he's not really there at all; at best, he seems to have just dropped in for a moment on his way somewhere else. I've never seen a more *invisible* performance. One of the lines that made Mr. Grant dematerialize occurs when he throws open the window of the hotel room in Bermuda to which he has lured Miss Day for immoral purposes (which are thwarted, on *two* trips to Bermuda, by as comical a series of imbroglios as we've seen since *Hellzapoppin;* they do go to bed at last but only after The Ring has been firmly attached to Miss Day). Anyway, Mr. Grant's first remarks to his intended prey, after the bellboy has departed, are: "Look at that view. Isn't it beautiful? This is the only place in the world where they have pink beaches."

He then gets down to a seduction that is considerably more perfunctory than the above tribute to the Bermuda Chamber of Commerce. The film is riddled with commercials: Miss Day takes a bus and as it starts GREYHOUND BUS LINES moves along in extreme close-up; the lovers emplane for Bermuda and PAN AMERICAN AIRLINES majestically marches across the screen as the plane begins to roll; they go to a ball game and there is no doubt one of the teams is the NEW YORK YANKEES (they sit in a dugout with Yogi Berra, Roger Maris and Mickey Mantle, also clearly identified); he buys her an expensive wardrobe, with much fanfare and parading of models, at BERGDORF GOODMAN (coy credit: "Our thanks to Bergdorf Goodman for being Bergdorf Goodman").

My only complaint is that the lovers didn't have a meal at Twenty One—I can see those jockey hitching posts drifting by in a pan close-up—and what a chance to have them conversing on equal terms with the Kriendler brothers! *Lover, Come Back* is mildly satirical, though the parody TV commercials fall flat because it is impossible to parody what is already a parody; but *That Touch of Mink* takes the consumer's paradise with complete seriousness. On second thought, perhaps the Twenty One ambience is too *recherché*. Maybe a scene in one of those Playboy Clubs; they might have been married there, with Bunnies for bridesmaids. I like to think it was proposed and that Mr. Grant vetoed the idea. There are limits to what even a professional actor will submit to, after all.

—November 1962

THE
CASE
OF
M. VERDOUX

THE Broadway premiere of *Monsieur Verdoux,* Chaplin's first talkie, took place in 1947. It was not a success: the audience was unsympathetic, at times audibly, and the daily reviewers were hostile, except for Archer Winsten of the New York *Post* and, less expectable and more important, Bosley Crowther of the *Times.* It was taken off after six weeks and, a few months later, was also withdrawn from national distribution. It didn't reappear on American screens until last summer [1966], when it was the popular hit of the Plaza Theatre's Chaplin revival series. For here at last the serious movie public, which has grown so rapidly of late, could see this "banned masterpiece" which the late Robert Warshow had celebrated in an essay in *Partisan Review* (reprinted in his posthumous collection, *The Immediate Experience*) as "a great work of irony," comparing it to Swift, and the late James Agee, in a three-part review in *The Nation* (reprinted in *Agee on Film,* v. 1), had called "one of the best movies ever made," saluting "this great poet and this great poem," and later adding, after six months' reflection: "Beside it every movie since *Zéro de Conduite* and *Modern Times* is so much child's play." Since these were made in 1933 and 1936, Agee's blurb took in a lot of territory. So no wonder the lines at the Plaza stretched around the block, and the re-reviews were enthusiastic or, at worst, respectful. You can't fight City Hall. Or the Cultural Establishment.

There was something else working for *Verdoux* last summer. While "banned" was mythical (since it was Chaplin's decision, from no more lofty a motive than pique, that had denied *Verdoux* to American distributors for seventeen years), it was true that its failure in 1947 was in large part due to certain pressures. Chaplin was unpopular because of the Joan Barry paternity suit (which he won, but only after the public had seen that their beloved Charlie, the "little man," was a libertine) and, more important, because of his alleged Communist sympathies. As Chaplin's *Autobiography* makes clear, and all the more since he is—as throughout that remarkable exercise in self-concealment—obviously trying to explain away things rather than to explain them, his fellow-traveling was prompted by nothing more sinister than vanity and a sentimental feeling for what he, like many others in Hollywood then, thought was the cause of the underdog. It was a case for Freud, not

116

Marx: a symbolic compensation for guilt feelings about his wealth rather than any wish to subvert the capitalist system that protected it. Groups like the American Legion, however, as simpleminded as he, picketed *Verdoux* (which, in a simpleminded way, satirized capitalism, war, and religion—so that the film was as objectionable as its creator) and, supported by the usual pack of moralistic wowsers, intimidated exhibitors.

But I wonder if the coolness of the 1947 audiences toward *Verdoux* can be explained wholly by the pressure of wowsers and patrioteers. Maybe moviegoers just didn't like *Verdoux* and maybe they had some good reasons not to. Looked at simply as another movie seen in the dark privacy of a theatre without either highbrow critics or lowbrow Legionnaires breathing down the back of one's neck, how does *Verdoux* strike one? That is, me.

I've seen it twice: in 1956 at the National Film Theatre in London, and in 1964 at New York's closest replica of that useful institution, except for the Thalia seven blocks farther up Broadway, Daniel Talbot's New Yorker Theatre. My 1956 reactions were published in *Encounter:*

> *Monsieur Verdoux* is really two films, one a sentimental melodrama, the other a comedy in the old Chaplin style that burlesques the melodrama. What makes it confusing is that Chaplin shifts gears between the two without apparently knowing he is doing so. He will be strutting around in a comic scene with Martha Raye, flourishing his moustaches in an exquisitely shaded parody of the stock-company notion of a boulevardier, and in the next scene, with a pretty street waif as his foil, he will be playing the part straight, hamming it up with innocent relish. It is unsettling to see an actor brilliantly taking off the conventional rhetoric of his trade one moment and the next employing it seriously, especially since Chaplin's serious rhetoric expresses a vain and foolish concept of himself—as the tragic man-of-the-world, disenchanted, elegant, sensitive, the gallant protector of the weak who, to make the bogus diamond shine all the more brilliantly, are usually crippled or blind. In the film after *Verdoux,* the disastrous *Limelight,* this mawkish exhibitionism goes right over the edge [and, as of 1965, his *Autobiography* shows us what was at the bottom of the abyss: not much one likes to see].

117

There is even a third film here, that bursts into the last part with shattering banality, a "message" drama, the message being that a man is a hero if he kills wholesale (like Napoleon or Hitler), but a murderer if he does it retail, an irony that was probably first observed by some ur-Montaigne of the time of Belshazzar. It was a sad day for Chaplin when the intellectuals convinced him he was the Tragic Clown, the Little Man. From a parodist he graduated into a philosopher, but since his epistemology was all instinctive, even physical (his eyebrows, fingers, teeth "know" precisely, instantaneously, how to behave in order to mimic a clergyman, a banker, a dandy, a tramp), it didn't help him in his new role. The nature of reality, which he understood intuitively as a mime, became opaque to him when he tried to think about it, and where he once danced lightly he now stumbles into bathos and sentimentality.

Rereading the above, after seeing *Verdoux* again last year, I think it on the whole accurate. The comic parts were as good as ever: Verdoux counting one widow's stack of bank notes with light-fingered professional speed; his amorous lunges at another as they sip tea on her sofa, upsetting her and himself but never his cup and saucer which, like a mad gyroscope, he keeps on the same level no matter where the rest of him is; the acrobatics at the wedding to keep out of sight of Martha Raye. And how could I have omitted *her,* the indestructible widow whose raucous sprawling vulgarity is the perfect foil to Chaplin's desiccated gentlemanliness, the messy life principle winning out over the neat little merchant of death? It is Chaplin's one triumph in casting, script and direction. But the rest! (And it should be remembered that "the rest" is more than half the film, closer to two-thirds, and that it is the distinctive part—the slapstick and pantomime are good but no better than Chaplin had been giving us since his first Keystone comedies in 1913—and also the part that the critics admire especially.) The rest looked even worse than it had eight years ago. The banality and pretentiousness of the script, as in the two long scenes with the waif-girl-of-the-streets (who for once isn't blind or crippled, except as an actress) with lines, delivered tremolo by Chaplin-Verdoux, like, "Is a little kindness such a rare thing?" and "In the sunset of our lives, we need love." The first of these scenes may be read in the

Autobiography. Apparently Chaplin is proud of it. One exchange may give the flavor:

"GIRL (*quizzingly*): You don't like women, do you?

"VERDOUX: On the contrary, I love women . . . but I don't admire them.

"GIRL: Why?

"VERDOUX: Women are of the earth . . . realistic, dominated by physical facts.

"GIRL: (*incredulously*): What nonsense!"

Her last comment may be explained by the fact, established earlier, that she has been reading Schopenhauer. "Do you like him?" asks Verdoux. "So-so." "Have you read his treatise on suicide?" It seems she hasn't. He's one up.

He's always one up. His wife is a paralytic, his boy is six, not big enough to worry about, his closest friends are a little chemist and his mountainous wife, both of them, for some reason, aggressively ugly, the women he preys on are (except for Miss Raye) easy game, the police are so stupid that he has trouble giving himself up to them, and in his final not at all *mauvais quart d'heure* in the death cell he scores off everybody, the jailer, the priest, even his own lawyer. He gives the priest a specially hard time. "I've come to ask you to make your peace with God." "I am at peace with God, my conflict is with man." "Have you no remorse for your sins?" "Who knows what sin is, born as it was from Heaven, from God's fallen angel, who knows what mysterious destiny it serves?" The priest doesn't know, so Verdoux tops his own line: "What would you be doing without sin?" Chaplin records all this, and more, in the pages of his *Aubobiogaphy* concerning his interview at the Breen Office, which made many foolish objections to the script—all of which Chaplin parries with ease—and one sensible one, "That's a lot of pseudo-philosophizing," which he disdains to answer. They ask him why he didn't give the priest "some worthwhile answer" to the "What-would-you-be-doing-without-sin?" topper, and he indulgently promises to "think up something for the priest to answer." If he did, I don't remember it. That priest just doesn't shine when he's up against Chaplin-Verdoux. He can't even get away with what one would think a puncture-proof exit line: "May the Lord have mercy on your soul." "Why not?" Verdoux shoots back quicker than Bob Hope. "It belongs to Him." (When a Breen official fatuously complained, "You don't talk to a priest like that," Chaplin, or Verdoux, upstaged him: "That line is said introspectively. You must wait until you see the film." I've seen the film and I don't understand how an actor can say a line "introspectively"; Chaplin didn't succeed anyway.) No wonder they instantly hustle Chaplin, I mean Verdoux, out to the guillotine. They were afraid he'd write his autobiography: *God Is My Straight Man.* One heaves a sigh of relief as that proud little figure walks slowly up the fatal courtyard to his destiny, erect, defiant, and smug to the end, and the camera draws back and back and those blessed words, surcease and anodyne, dawn radiantly on the screen,

"THE END."

Chaplin's direction is no better than his script. The photography is by an old Hollywood hand named Roland Totheroh, and looks it. Except for Miss Raye, the actors seem to have been selected by taking the first candidates sent up from Central Casting; they're not good even as extras, nor are there any of those familiar bit-part players that are often in Hollywood movies better than the principals; there are, in short, no faces that were familiar up to 1947 or that have become familiar since then, for obvious reasons in both cases. It must have been a cheap film to cast. The opening scene gives it to you right in the eye: a family group—they are beginning to wonder what has become of Aunt Mathilde—of stiffly nervous actors who walk around and overplay without making connection with each other, or with the spectator; clumsily directed and tritely photographed. Neither realistic nor stylized, *Verdoux* is amateurish without freshness, Hollywoodish without technique. It comes to life only when Chaplin is onstage, and even then only when he is parodying his boulevardier and not in the longer stretches when he is trying to impress us as a philosopher ("Have you read Schopenhauer's treatise on suicide? . . . It's the approach of death that terrifies"). As Chaplin's script is only a device to show him off (and not so much as an actor but, worse, as an actor's narcissistic dream of his "real" self), so his direction reduces all the other performers to stooges—no wonder he didn't bother much with casting—except for the indestructible Miss Raye. His directorial eye finds nothing

120

interesting in the inanimate world either, which is reduced to a conventional background for his own performance. I can recall few films in which there was so little to *see*. Since it is a movie, Chaplin thinks he has to show us realistic interiors and real landscapes and cityscapes, but they are botched in so routinely, with so little sense of what they look like, that they might as well be those painted backdrops of a park or a street, bordered with local advertisements, in front of which vaudevillians used to do their turns. In fact, *Verdoux* would have been better, not good but better, if Chaplin had had the imaginative daring to realize that a series of such backdrops was all he needed for his drama; it would at least have had an original, and appropriate, style—and I daresay some pop scenic designer will steal the idea if he hasn't already thought of it himself. (Think what a wrench would be given to Albee's *Tiny Alice*—and any wrench would be an improvement—if it were played against such appropriately flimsy specimens of the sign-painter's art, complete with ads for painless dentists, discothèques and psychoanalytic parlors, instead of expiring under the weight of that massive Belasco-type set!)

The closest *Verdoux* comes to visual style is a shot of the Eiffel Tower (to show us we are in Paris), supplemented, as a transitional device, by close-ups of revolving locomotive wheels (to show us we are leaving, or returning to, Paris). Economical but a little familiar. "Vorkapich Effects" they used to call them in the old, innocent Hollywood of the thirties, after a Yugoslav technician named Slavko Vorkapich who was rumored to have worked with Eisenstein. A modest Prometheus, Mr. Vorkapich brought to the hinterland this small spark of montage—other Vorkapich Effects included calendar leaves blowing off one by one to indicate the passage of time, shots of frenzied brokers intercut with newspaper headlines to indicate the 1929 market crash, and a series of quick-cut newsreel shots of soldiers going over the top, huge guns firing, mines exploding in No Man's Land, etc., to indicate that World War I had occurred. At this very moment, Mr. Vorkapich is in full course at the Museum of Modern Art, an institution that keeps abreast of the times, especially in its Film Department, with a series of ten weekly illustrated lectures under the general title, *The Visual Nature of the Film Medium,* with subtitles ranging from "To Hold,

121

As't Were, a Moving Mirror up to Nature" (camera movement), up to the grand finale: "Aesthetics of Film Content" (. . . transcending the literal meaning of the shot. . . . The objective correlative . . . dynamic images on the screen suddenly come to life in their own ineffable way).

To get back to *Monsieur Verdoux:* why did, and do, many intelligent critics evaluate it in terms that make unrecognizable the account I have given above? Who is right on the main point—is it a good movie?—cannot be settled definitively here, or anywhere, or ever, since it's an argument about values, not facts; each viewer must decide for himself which evaluation best explains what he saw on the screen. But some peripheral answers to the problem are possible. An editorial in the Summer 1964, issue of *The Seventh Art* takes an historical view. The editors think better of *Verdoux* than I, though not much. After describing "the brain-washing effects of reputation—Chaplin's . . . Agee's, Warshow's and The New York *Times'* " on the 1964 audiences as "merely the reverse of what occurred in 1947," they suggest that, whether or not *Verdoux* failed in 1947 because it was ahead of its time, as has been argued, it "has come to us now five years too late." (I doubt it would ever have arrived on schedule by my timetable, but let it pass.) "The objections raised initially," they continue, meaning the cinematic, not the moral or political ones, "which Agee refutes brilliantly if not convincingly, stand. The film's strong points—its gallows humor, its acerbic cynicism—these virtues have been exploited and possibly exhausted by the theatre of the absurd and its progeny. Not only does much of the technique seem dated now, the humor of the film has also passed its prime and has become, in one way or another, banal."

This seems reasonable, as far as it goes. But I think something simpler, and more fundamental, than period and fashion may also be involved: that the appeal of *Verdoux* may be political rather than cinematic, that those who find it important may be reacting to it more as a tract for the times, an indictment of the hypocrisies of capitalism than as a work of art. Robert Warshow, for instance, writes of it almost entirely in psychological and sociological terms, as was his custom. (Anyone interested in movies or popular culture will find *The Immediate Experience* brilliant and original, but he mustn't expect much aesthetic criticism, or much interest in it.) James Agee was, of course, a professional critic, but in the twelve pages devoted to *Verdoux* in his collection (Huston's *The Treasure of the Sierra Madre* is a poor second, with six pages) it is notable how defensive and often equivocal he is about it as a movie and how enthusiastic when he analyzes, as he does at length and with subtlety, its social and political meanings—or what he says they are; I found his glosses much richer than the text. He does defend on page 254 the casting, the script, the direction and even "the production," by which he seems to mean that perfunctory *mise-en-scène* I objected to above, but briefly, vaguely, evasively. The scrupulous honesty that was one of his most admirable traits makes him add, under *New Techniques:* "They are on the whole weakened derivations from styles developed before sound came, in Russia, Germany and this country, by Chaplin among others; virtually nothing has been done with sound." (And this was 1947, fifteen years after Clair and six years after *Citizen Kane*.) He also defends Chaplin's routine use of the camera and even those locomotive wheels, the former thusly: "Chaplin . . . obviously believes that if you can invent something worth watching, the camera should hold still and clear, so that you can watch it. That is still, and will always be, one of the best possible ways to use a camera: Chaplin is the one great man who stands up for it"; and the latter thusly: ". . . we sneer at Chaplin's frequent use of locomotive wheels, charging ever more desperately across the screen. . . . But in fact these wheels do a lot at once. They are in the best sense economical; they are cumulatively funny; they cumulatively express Verdoux's ever more frantic busyness; and they wind up the film like a tight spring." The defense of Chaplin's static camera reminds me of the paradoxical reflex by which Miss Susan Sontag defends bad movies (by, say, Godard or the Smiths) precisely on the grounds they *are* so courageously boring, so defiantly sloppy; as to those wheels, I saw no increasing desperation in their revolutions (in fact I thought Chaplin, with his usual economy—financial, not artistic —had simply used the same shot over and over), and I suspect that Agee's response is an example of his chief weakness as a critic: his directorial imagination which sometimes remade the movie inside his head as he watched it, so that what came out on his page was often more exciting than what had appeared on the screen.

Why is Agee so unconvincing about *Verdoux* as cinema and so persuasive about it as satire? I think the film struck home to him emotionally because of its anti-bourgeois "black" humor and because of his admiration for Chaplin and his generous indignation at the 1947 campaign of calumny.

"I love and revere the film as deeply as any I have seen," he wrote in *The Nation,* "and believe that it is high among the great works of this century. I wish I might discuss at proper length its weaknesses as a work of art and of moral understanding." I should have thought a three-part review might have been enough.

A great strain must have been put on Agee's fine intelligence by the pressure of his personal feeling for *Verdoux,* his love and reverence (not critical categories), and the contrary pull of his perception of its artistic defects. He was too honest, too serious, to gloss over the conflict by omitting either term. In his *Time* review, positive thesis and negative antithesis seesaw back and forth, as in the following excerpts, in which I have italicized the negative antithesis.

"Monsieur Verdoux *has serious shortcomings both as popular entertainment and as a work of art. But whatever its shortcomings,* it is one of the most notable films in years. . . . *It has its blurs and failures.* Finely cut and paced as it is, *the picture goes on so long . . .* that the lazier-minded type of cinemagoers will *probably get tired. Chaplin overexerts, and apparently overestimates, a writing talent which,* though vigorous and unconventional, *weighs light beside his acting gifts. As a result, a good deal of the verbal and philosophic straining seems inadequate, muddled and highly arguable*—too highbrow for general audiences, and *too naïve for the highbrows.*"

One sentence in Agee's review, however, is not antithetical: "At a time when many people have regained their faith in war under certain conditions and in free enterprise under any conditions, he has ventured to insist, as bitterly as he knows how, that there are considerable elements of criminality in both." That this is one of Chaplin's intentions I grant, and a noble one it is. But wasn't it Herbert Hoover who once described Prohibition as "an experiment

124

noble in purpose"? That Agee, and others whom I respect, take the will for the deed in *Verdoux* is a lapse that is explicable in such intelligent persons—for to call a badly flawed movie great because of its theme and its creator's intentions is like saying an orator is eloquent but inarticulate—only on the hypothesis that they are really interested in something else, something outside my province as a film critic, something that doesn't appear on the screen.

—April 1965

MR. GOLDWYN
AND
MR. LEVINE

SAMUEL GOLDWYN'S eightieth birthday was celebrated by a Hollywood banquet to which greetings were sent by practically everybody, including three men who are or have been Presidents of this country. The present incumbent, who misses no opportunity to demonstrate a love for Culture that verges on lust, wired (in part): *"The integrity of your work and your steadfast dedication to the highest standards of film production are a monument to your desire to serve and entertain your fellow-Americans."* Hoover and Eisenhower also telegraphed their encomiums which, since they are not cultural types, were more restrained. Truman, whose one great quality is common sense, didn't wire anything.

The *New York Times* paid its tribute with a Sunday double spread of stills from old Goldwyn films. "High points from his long pursuit of the best in movies" was the billing, but in my own cinematic landscape these peaks are barely visible: *The Squaw Man* (a 1913 Cecil B. De Mille absurdity), *The Little Foxes* (dramatic only insofar as Lillian Hellman's play was), *The Secret Life of Walter Mitty* (mildly amusing Danny Kaye impersonations), *Guys and Dolls* (the usual overproduced Hollywood musical based on Damon Runyon's synthetic folkery-fakery—cf. Ring Lardner for the real thing), *The Best Years of Our Lives* (I saw this recently and, *pace* Jim Agee, thought it middlebrow kitsch both as cinema and as social comment), *Wuthering Heights* (any one who could cast Merle Oberon as Cathy will get no telegram from me), and *Porgy and Bess* (more folkery-fakery—a patronizing caricature of Negro life). The *Times* titled this withered bouquet *The Best of Goldwyn* and so it may well be. "He has been a resolutely independent figure," the *Times* rumbled on, "largely financing his own films and making whatever stories suited him. By and large, these stories have also pleased a substantial public, eager to respond to intelligent movies of high artistic calibre." That is, by and large, nonsense. That Mr. Goldwyn has been "resolutely independent" is true enough—"I make my pictures to please myself," he once observed. But the embarrassing fact is that his films, like those of the current generation of Hollywood "independents," are only microscopically distinguishable from the rest. For what pleased Samuel Goldwyn was not very different from what pleased that "substantial public." There is no evidence he encouraged, or even tolerated, the live talents of our cinema, from Griffith to Welles.

128

Although I realize that criticizing an eminent American octogenarian is as risky as hanging the flag upside down—who would dare say that Carl Sandburg's address on Lincoln, intoned before a joint session of Congress in 1959, was sentimental, or that Robert Frost's recent *conversazioni* in Moscow were a mite trite?—still I must confess remembering with affection Edmund Wilson's 1937 review of Alva Johnston's biography, *The Great Goldwyn.* "I for one will be damned if I will feel patriotic about Sam Goldwyn's silver jubilee," Wilson wrote, apropros of the maestro's twenty-fifth anniversary in the movie business. "It is plain that today's producers, including The Great Goldwyn and the late lamented Irving Thalberg, are the same megalomaniac cloak-and-suit dealers that their predecessors were. You have only to look at their products." Amen. Hollywood's canonization of Thalberg—which bemused Fitzgerald into making him the sympathetic hero of *The Last Tycoon*—like the later hopes invested in Dore Schary after he had slain the Louis B. Mayer dragon, demonstrates merely that in the country of the blind etc. Because Schary and Thalberg were literate and civilized compared to the Mayers and Zukors and Laemmles and Cohns, they were taken to be veritable Goethes in that provincial jungle.

Thalberg's big chance came in 1924 when Von Stroheim made a masterpiece called *Greed* that in its original form ran for ten hours. Thalberg, then the "boy genius" production head of MGM, said *No.* Stroheim cut it to five hours, slightly longer than a later MGM product called *Gone with the Wind.* Thalberg said *No* again and commanded it be cut to under two hours. Stroheim refused and Thalberg fired him (doubtless with some *Schadenfreude* since, for obvious reasons, the two men had long detested each other) and somebody else trimmed it down to the present version, which is still impressive. One can only speculate on what the original was like before it was Thalbergized. A thalberger is to an actual movie what a hamburger is to an actual steak.

The Goldwyn myth is not based on literacy. His public image is that of an ignoramus who perpetrates such lovable "Goldwynisms," mostly concocted by press agents, as "in two words—impossible" and when told a script was too caustic, "To hell with the cost, we'll make it anyway!" The myth is that he is a movie genius, as intuitive as he is uncultured, who has defied Hollywood conformism to make pictures that are "different." But they don't seem different to me. The highest reach of his pioneering that my research has uncovered is importing into Hollywood in 1930 Busby Berkeley to do the dance routines for *Whoopee!,* starring Eddie Cantor (1962).

Cinema is the most ephemeral and fragile of the arts. Literature and music can last forever; sculpture and architecture can survive a long time. Paintings deteriorate, but not with the frightening speed of film stock: movies only thirty years old are lost because the prints have crumbled to bits, and many more would have perished except for the rescue operations of Eastman House in Rochester and The Museum of Modern Art Film Library. Cinema is fragile in another way. Suppose an art dealer cropped a few inches from his canvases, suppose a conductor omitted a movement of a symphony or played it without woodwinds, suppose Random House, after publishing a Faulkner novel, decided it was too long for maximum sales and reissued it with a hundred pages cut. And suppose the public was not even informed of such mutilations.

These suppositions are, of course, foolish since in the other arts such things aren't done. But they are in the movies. Bergman's *Through a Glass Darkly* is now being shown, outside New York, in a dubbed version. Visconti's *Rocco and His Brothers*—to cite the most scandalous of many such instances—lost a full hour somewhere between the time I saw it abroad and the time it was exhibited throughout this country; the one scene that might have been shortened to artistic advantage, the monotonous brutality of the rape-fight sequence, was left intact because the hucksters thought it was good box office. And now my son at Harvard sends me an A.P. story from The Boston *Globe:*

"Producer Joe Levine says he is going to cut an hour off Eugene O'Neill's *Long Day's Journey Into Night.* 'The O'Neill devotees are screaming their heads off,' says Levine, 'but wouldn't it be a greater crime if this classic were not commercially successful? It's a great picture in its entirety. It will be greater with an hour cut.' "

The answer to Mr. Levine's question—"wouldn't it be a greater crime if this classic were not commercially successful?"—is No. I'm glad he realizes that what he proposes *is* a crime, even though a lesser one than not giving O'Neill's masterpiece a chance to do well

130

at provincial box offices. It's too bad O'Neill wrote his play without benefit of Mr. Levine's advice; he could have made a great play into a greater one. I wonder what Sidney Lumet thinks of Mr. Levine's plan for improving his film version of *Long Day's Journey Into Night*. And what is the reaction of O'Neill's widow, who turned down higher offers and gave the play to him because she knew he would respect its integrity?

A few words on this Joseph E. Levine might be interesting. He is living proof they didn't break the mold when they made Louis B. Mayer. I first heard of him as the distributor of two fantastically profitable movies, *Hercules* and *Hercules Unchained,* quickie spectaculars that make *Ben-Hur* look like *Citizen Kane.* The formula was original: he bought the films, made by others, for peanuts: $100,000 or so. They were made abroad with inexpensive native actors (who were then crudely dubbed) and had for their closest approach to a star a heavily muscled young stalwart named Steve Reeves. But Levine spent lavishly—a million or so apiece—on promotion and publicity. This cynical tactic, which recognized that *selling* the product is the point, paid off handsomely in the hinterlands—the films were especially suitable for drive-ins. But Mr. Levine aspires to more than just profits; he wants to make the art scene too. His ambitions, nourished by the millions he made out of Hercules-Reeves, are now flowering like some exotic plant, say the Venus Fly Trap. Among the films that his Embassy Pictures has now in hand are: *Seven Capital Sins* (episodes directed by Godard, De Broca, Chabrol, among others); *Love at Twenty* (Truffaut and Wajda among others); *Boccaccio '70* (Fellini, Visconti, De Sica); a new version of the Brecht-Weill *Threepenny Opera;* and a movie based on Henry Miller's *Tropic of Cancer.* The last represents the high point to date of Mr. Levine's cultural climb. "We intend to maintain the spirit of the book and will not compromise Miller's work," his producers, Mr. Kastner and Mr. Shpetner, have grandly announced. "We will treat Miller's story with great respect and dignity, but without sacrificing the humor, anger, art and sex that made it internationally controversial." That "but" puzzles me as I imagine it may Mr. Miller. Are humor, anger, art and sex now considered undignified and disreputable? Some of them maybe, but *all?* The only clear points in the press release were that *Tropic of*

131

Cancer has a $2,000,000 budget and that "the book has sold more than a million seven hundred thousand copies to date in this country."*

I am also bewildered by Mr. Levine's decision to butcher O'Neill's masterpiece. The reason he gives sounds like his old, untutored *Hercules Unchained* self: the long version is all right for New York ("where there are O'Neill aficionados") but "on the road" it would appear "excessive" and "talky." (The whole play is "talky," and in fact that is its virtue.) How will the provinces smarten up about Culture, as Mr. Levine has, if they are fobbed off with a truncated road-show version? Is he kicking down the ladder by which he rose?

—March 1963

* 1968 footnote: No sign to date of this film.

GOOD BAD MOVIES,
BAD GOOD MOVIES
AND
THE
PAWNBROKER

THE good bad movie is a lively, authentic and, in its modest way, quite respectable product Hollywood used to make in the thirties and forties before it succumbed to the ravages of Culture, like a primitive tribe coming into contact with civilization and exchanging its simple folkways for Mother Hubbards, pidgin English and syphilis. Most of the Bogart and Cagney movies come under this head, also a lot of Western, gangster and horror-science films, plus a long line of "screwball" comedies like *Nothing Sacred, Twentieth Century, Bringing Up Baby* and such works of the late Preston Sturges (1898–1959) as *Sullivan's Travels, The Lady Eve, The Miracle of Morgan's Creek, The Great McGinty* and *Mad Wednesday,* also known as *The Sin of Harold Diddlebock.* In 1957 Manny Farber published a celebrated piece in *Commentary* on what he called "underground films"—not to be confused with a contemporary school that has appropriated the name but whose films are the opposite of those Farber was describing, being both uncommercial and untalented. Farber, as perverse and original a film critic as exists or can be imagined, celebrated such Hollywood directors as Howard Hawks and Raoul Walsh, the very titles of whose movies showed what he meant: *White Heat, The Crowd Roars, They Drive by Night, The Roaring Twenties.* His connoisseurship was so acute that, while he included in his underground pantheon John Ford and William Wellman, he excluded from the strict canon their more ambitious (and most generally admired) efforts, such as *The Informer* and *The Public Enemy.* He found them slightly bogus. To his impeccable taste, even Ford's *Stagecoach* was infected with Art—he reserved his enthusiasm for "the pre-*Stagecoach* Ford." Anticipating Harold Rosenberg's "action painting," Farber wrote of "action directors" whose "dry, economic, life-worn movie style . . . made their observations of the American he-man so rewarding." Like Rosenberg, he pushed his aesthetic far beyond the limits of what is usually considered art. The non-artist, indeed the anti-artist was his hero: "Hawks and his group are perfect examples of the anonymous artist who is seemingly afraid of the polishing, hypocrisy, bragging, fake educating that goes on in serious art." They "accept the role of hack" and work best "with material that is hopelessly worn-out and childish." There's something in this idea, especially as applied to the 1930–

134

1950 Hollywood, so long as it is not pushed too far. Like most ideas, however, it was pushed too far, first by the *Cahiers du Cinéma* group in Paris—independently of Farber, as far as I know—and then by their Anglo-American epigones who, after the most delicate calibrations on the *politique des auteurs* yardstick, concluded that Hitchcock's *The Birds* and Preminger's *The Cardinal* were masterpieces.

Of late, however, the *auteur* ideologues seem to be losing heart —what can one do with *Marnie* after all?—and the good bad movie is no longer a live issue. The problem today, with Culture booming and exploding everywhere and movies competing with novels and plays as okay subjects for critical exegesis, is rather the bad good movie, the movie with serious intentions and pretentions that turns its back haughtily on the box-office in order to make a Meaningful Statement about alienation, social injustice, the mechanization of modern life, the difficulty of communication, the impossibility of love, and other important matters, the movie that is directed up to the hilt, avant-garde-wise, the movie that lays it right on the line for the Browning Societies of our time, the audiences of the "art" movie houses—over six hundred now as against twelve in 1945—and the film clubs that are proliferating in our colleges. I intend no Philistine sneer, or at least not only a Philistine sneer: those grimly bluestocking Browning Societies awakened many a Victorian to the pleasures, and difficulties, of poetry; and our cinematic equivalents today are doing the same for the art of the movies, as well as making it economically possible, the American market being as big and rich as it is, for a dozen or so directors, all foreign, to create an international renaissance of the art. But seriousness is not enough; it needs to be adulterated with skepticism, common sense and even a little humor. Our cineasts, from ignorance or kultur-snobbism or both, tend to take the intention for the act and to accept as the genuine article such counterfeits, to name a few bad good movies that come to mind, as *Mickey One*, *The Servant*, *He Who Must Die*, *Sundays and Cybele*, *This Sporting Life*, *La Terra Trema*, *The Cool World*, *The Balcony*, *Hallelujah the Hills!*, *King and Country*, and *The Trial*, plus at least half the films shown at the 1965 Lincoln Center Film Festival and considerably more than half the movies that Jean-Luc Godard has

135

spawned since *Breathless.* Which brings me to Sidney Lumet's *The Pawnbroker,* the bad good film that has everything: alienation, anomie, neurosis, inability to love or communicate, the inhumanity of the metropolis, and the two great traumatic experiences of our age, the Jewish and the Negro, Harlem and the Nazi death camps. These themes are expressed with the most advanced technique: camera angles, extreme close-ups, jump cutting, subliminal flashbacks, bleakly sophisticated photography by Boris Kaufman (Vigo's cameraman in the thirties), art direction by the accomplished Richard Sylbert, and the lead played by Rod Steiger, a respected Method actor whose style, which generally strikes me as rather mannered in the over-under-acting tradition of his school, was well-suited to the catatonic character he was required to impersonate here. Yet *The Pawnbroker* seemed to me a bore and a phony, a vulgarization of a serious theme, an exploitation of cinematic "effects" used without taste or intelligence.

Was it perhaps the story? Steiger is a Jewish refugee who escaped from the death camp in which is wife and children perished, came to this country and established a modestly prosperous pawnshop in Harlem. To protect himself against his terrible memories, he has become an emotional zombie, refusing any human contacts, or reactions, beyond commercial ones, whether with his wife's family, with whom he lives in the suburbs, his clients, his young Puerto Rican shop assistant who admires him for unclear reasons, a Negro gang leader who uses his shop as a front, or a social worker (Geraldine Fitzgerald) who is lonely herself and tries in vain to break through his armor. His psychic stasis is shaken when a Negro whore, refused a loan, bares her breasts and offers herself to him, stimulating a flashback to a scene in the camp between his wife and some Nazi guards. When the whore tells him she works in a house controlled by the gangster chief, he calls on him in his luxurious apartment and breaks off relations, or tries to. He is then roughed up in his shop by the gang and, shortly after, is held up by some hoodlums, apparently operating independently, who have been tipped off by his hitherto devoted young assistant in a moment of pique (after all, his boss hardly gives him the time of day). A gun is pulled, the assistant, who seems a rather impulsive youth, has another change of heart and throws himself in front of Steiger, takes the bullet and dies. The hoodlums run away, Steiger holds the dying

136

boy in his arms, gives a great animal cry, like Olivier's famous Oedipus howl, which signified, I took it, the breakup of his emotional block, after which, to make it all very clear, he impales his hand on a letter spike and then staggers out into the street, bearing what it was difficult not to interpret as a stigmatum and pushes his way blindly through the curious, indifferent crowd as the picture ends.

Well, maybe it *was* the story. And also the way the agony was piled on, as if emphasis were needed. The picture begins, for instance, with an idyllic picnic scene with his wife and children before the war, all luminous and blurry, and—actually—in slow motion to make it even more idyllic; there follows immediately a sad contrast indeed, a drably photographed scene in the dismal backyard of the house in Queens he lives in with his wife's ghastly sister and her demanding, unattractive teen-age children. Some of the extras who came in to pawn things would melt a heart of stone (though not mine, or Steiger's): a young man offering a medal he got for scholarship (one dollar) and later a pair of bronzed baby shoes (one dollar), a dignified gray-haired Negro who longed for some conversation (which he didn't get), a smiling housewife who kept smiling, without return, when she got the usual dollar. (It occurred to me, after a number of these painful scenes, that a real pawnbroker who treated his customers that way would go broke in a few months.) The Negro gang chief was impossibly huge, menacing, evil, and he wore a silk dressing gown to boot. The Puerto Rican assistant kept insisting he wanted to learn the business but all he got from Steiger were cryptic lectures about what it meant to be Jewish: "All you have is a little brain." "Is that a secret society," the boy asks. "Yes." "What do I do to join?" "You learn to walk on water." The flashbacks often seemed contrived and overdone, as when a subway car that by New York standards wasn't terribly crowded reminds him of the freight car in which he was transported to the camp. But the real giveaway was the music which, in contrast to the sophisticated cutting and photography, moaned and blared and sobbed in shameless crescendos to back up the "big" moments. Mr. Lumet is a director who leaves no stone unturned, no bet unhedged.

—June 1966

137

KAZANISTAN,
INGELAND
AND
WILLIAMS,
TENN.

COMING back to this country after a year abroad, I immediately collided with the American press agent. "A CONTROVERSIAL NEW MOTION PICTURE HAS CAUSED AN EVENT UNPARALELLED IN THEATRE HISTORY." So Warner Bros. headlined a full-page ad for *Splendor in the Grass* in the *New York Times*. The text was equally dynamic:

> Elia Kazan's Boldest Production . . . An Original Screen Play by Noted Dramatist William Inge . . . already a contender for Academy Awards and possibly the most controversial film to come along in any year. [I like "possibly"—really sincere.] This has to do with its subject matter and the daring and forthright way director Kazan has put it on the screen. It is probable that certain members of the community will be shocked. . . . To allow time for the film to be discussed, to be highly praised or hotly attacked, a special showing has been arranged well in advance of the regular release. Those who attend it will be surveyed and their opinions noted.

Perhaps attracted by "bold" and "daring"—the burlesque-show vendors used to call it "broad-minded"—or perhaps by the prospect of being Surveyed and Noted, capacity audiences packed the two theatres where this forthright preview (as against the usual sneak kind) was held. Since I'd returned too late for the press shows, I was there.

Settling myself in my seat, dizzy from being thumped on the head by these promotional air-bladders, I looked forward to a lively evening. As the story unfolded, I tried to spot the "mature" and "controversial" theme that had forced Warner Bros. to take such elaborate precautionary measures. At one point the brother seemed to be taking an undue interest in his sister. Incest! I thought appreciatively. But nothing happened. Nothing continued to happen. No incest, no rape, no perversion, no adultery, no miscegenation, not even cannibalism. As I left the theatre, I was handed a questionnaire which deepened the mystery: "1. Assuming you have children, nephews or nieces aged sixteen or over, would you want them to see this picture?" (I thought the film should be seen only by children sixteen or under.) "2. Did you find anything censorable in this picture?" (No.) "3. Some people believe Hollywood should not

140

attempt themes such as this one. What is your feeling?" This merely raised again the question of what the theme *was*. I think I've now worked out the answer. The theme must be sexual since in Hollywood all morality is sexual. Barring some nuance of sin I'm too unsophisticated to get, I hazard that The Theme is: Should a Nice Girl Sleep with Him or Go to a Mental Hospital? And: Should a Clean-Living Boy Sleep with Her or Go to Yale? This seems to me an Emily Post problem, in the same class as Should Doilies or a Tablecloth Be Used for a Formal Tea?

It seems impossible that *Splendor in the Grass* could be contemporaneous with *L'Avventura*. Technically, it could have been made in 1930. As if Detroit should start turning out Stanley Steamers. Mr. Kazan is still basically a stage director; he knows about the close-up, he uses waterfalls as a background for sexy scenes (all that torrential noise), and he blurs the focus to indicate violence, but that is about the extent of his cinematic savvy. He is, furthermore, as vulgar a director as has come along since Cecil B. De Mille; in his movies—and in his direction of such plays as *J.B.* and *Sweet Bird of Youth*—the emotional pitch is always fortissimo, the hard sell is always in, and passions are torn to tatters to split the ears of the groundlings. Kazan is "forthright" the way a butcher is forthright when he slaps down a steak for the customer's inspection. His style is vulgar, or, as my dictionary puts it, "ostentatious and elaborate, marked by coarseness of expression, morally crude and flashy, congested or extravagant." But, in fact, he has no style, for style requires that certain effects be given up because they are incompatible with certain other effects. Kazan won't give up anything that can be exploited.

Nor is he a realist, though he probably thinks of himself as one. Superficially, Donskoi's Gorky trilogy and Eugene O'Neill's *Long Day's Journey into Night,* for examples, have no style; but considered more deeply, they have an anti-style style, that is, they give up the advantages of dramatic convention the better to render shapeless, jagged reality. Any person who is truly observed is interesting, if only because he is unique. What makes Hollywood's characters dull is that they are conventional types who are conventionally observed—and Kazan's up-to-date conventions are just as boring as those of Victorian melodrama, with which they have

141

much in common. Kazanistan is as mythical a country as Ruritania. So is Ingeland. The locale of *Splendor in the Grass* is given as Kansas in 1928. I've never been in Kansas, but I suspect that parents there even way back in 1928 were not stupid to the point of villainy and that their children were not sexually frustrated to the point of lunacy. I *have* been in the Yale of 1928 and I can testify that the deans I knew would not have allowed the father of a student about to be expelled either to shout at them or to pound their desks.

—December 1961

The reviews gave the impression *All Fall Down* is a daringly realistic study of middle-class family life. But in fact it is just another projection of William Inge's personal fantasies on that subject. The usual grotesques are on hand: the ineffectual, tippling father (a Karl Malden role and sure enough . . .); the doting, dotty, over-possessive mother (Angela Lansbury makes her almost believable); the rakish older brother, destructive to himself and to others (Warren Beatty is perhaps even less attractive than Mr. Inge intended); the sensitive kid brother (Brandon De Wilde, who else?); and the decent, inhibited beauty who is Mr. Beatty's predestined prey (Eva Marie Saint is clearly indicated).

One mark of a bad movie or play is that the characters exist only as functions of the plot, which means they have lots of Big Moments, but no small ones. Real people, however, exist all the time—this is known as the time-space continuum and is rigidly enforced everywhere except in Hollywood. Their small moments, or everyday life, count as much as the big ones and perhaps more, since there are many more of them. The relation of the rakish big brother to the rest of the family, on which the whole dramatic structure rests, is unconvincing for this reason. It is not believable that the parents (who are not morons, whatever their other Ingean weaknesses) and the kid brother (who keeps a journal and appears to be a reflective type) should not realize long before the film ends, and indeed before it begins, that Mr. Beatty is just a bum, and a dangerous one at that. As to how Miss Saint, who is represented as

142

a sensible career woman whatever her inhibitions, could become so overwhelmed by Mr. Beatty's raffish charms that she gets herself pregnant and could then decide on death rather than dishonor—such mysteries can only be explained by (a) Mr. Inge's very special ideas about family life, and (b) the plot line that ensues therefrom. But of course if the rest of the cast saw through Mr. Beatty—who hardly bothers to make himself opaque—as they would if they weren't so preoccupied with their Big Moments, then there would be no movie.

William Inge by now has established himself as a bush-league Tennessee Williams. He is a busher because he lacks the master's knack—"talent" would be too big a word—for diverting the audience's attention from the absurdity of his fables by means of poetic-dramatic showmanship. Art has often been created from the artist's neuroses, but only when he has been able to break through from *his* world to *the* world, from the personal to the public, and that takes more talent and psychic energy than either Mr. Inge or Mr. Williams possesses. Blake, James, Baudelaire, Joyce, to name a few, were able to impose their special worlds on us because they had new visions which were so powerful that they were obliged to create original forms, even new vocabularies, to express them. But the visions of Mr. Inge and Mr. Williams are not new but merely private, and they express them in the familiar conventions of modern playwriting, which are naturalistic. They are, therefore, often mistaken for uncompromising realists, while in fact their notion of reality is as bizarre as Edgar Allan Poe's. This odd combination of unrealistic content and realistic form has produced a great deal of misunderstanding and a great many bad plays and movies.

John Frankenheimer's direction might have stiffened the flimsiness of the screenplay by filling in some of the chinks with realism, real realism, that is. Instead, he has gone the other way. Not since certain German films of the twenties have I seen such overuse of camera angles, such cluttered sets, and such a profusion of props. He shoots wherever possible from behind lace curtains, hat racks or rubber plants—and his actors are almost invisible in the welter of baroque radio sets and Tiffany-glass chandeliers. His directorial eye is lavishly corny, as in the lakeside seduction, with willows, mist and swans yet! And must it be raining heavily when our betrayed heroine drives off to her suicide? Finally, it was his, or someone's, bounden duty to restrain Mr. Inge from his concluding Big Moment. Brandon De Wilde, at last enlightened as to the True Nature of his brother, walks out on him with a fat line: "You really hate life, don't you?" He keeps walking into a fruit-laden orchard aggressive with fertility in the morning light and, believe me, some contrast to his brother's crummy pad. The camera pans to his transfigured face which emits another fat line: "But *I* love life." Well, one gets the point.

—October 1962

The Topouzoglou family are simple folk. They live in Anatolia. They are Greeks. The Turks treat them badly, but not as badly as they treat the Armenians. This is the simple story of an especially simple Topouzoglou named Stavros. He is a handsome boy with big brown eyes and he looks sensitive but he is not a very good actor. He stares too much and his expression doesn't change enough. Maybe he really is not so sensitive after all. He will become the great-uncle of Elia Kazan.

Mr. Kazan has made a simple and insensitive movie called *America America* about how his ancestor was sent to Istanbul by his family and how he wanted to get to America and how he did get there at last. Mr. Kazan has also published a book also called *America America*. It appears to be the script of the movie. Orville Prescott says: "An astonishingly moving narrative." James Baldwin says: "A marvelous story." S. N. Behrman says: "Pure gold." S. N. Behrman also says: "There is scarcely a word in this text that is not irradiated with emotion . . . streams of harsh experience and hidden pools of desire." The present reviewer says: "Nonsense nonsense."

When great-uncle Stavros finally lands in America (America) every word is irradiated with emotion, not to say distilled like a sharp liquor from subterranean streams of etc. "Mr. Agnostis laughs. And now Stavros joins in, the first full, simple, free laugh heard from the boy since he left home. Now the others join in, all

144

laughing. Down the last gangplank come the eight boys and Mr. Agnostis. Stavros first. He falls on his knees and kisses the ground! Then he lifts up and releases a tremendous shout of joy." End of chapter six. Beginning of chapter seven: "The first thing we're aware of is an echo, many times magnified, of the shout that Stavros released on American soil. The Topouzoglou family, in Anatolia, is gathered around Isaac. The family has shouted as one." They have just received the first dollar remittance from Stavros and this is called match cutting and it is a bad way to write a book or to make a movie. *America America* goes on for three hours, which is too long. The characters are picturesque and predictable: Little People, or else Exploiters and Oppressors; but with a modern twist. *Cavalleria Rusticana* orchestrated by Lennie Bernstein. They sound dubbed and they speak the kind of good-earth basic English Pearl Buck inflicted on her Chinese peasants a long time ago. If I were a simple Greek boy living in "the land known as Anatolia," I would have been angry with my famous descendant for making me talk like that. It is good for the great-nephew that his grand-uncle finally made it. But is what is good for Elia Kazan what is good for America (America)? By Allah I do not think it! Truly, brother, that scamp of a Stavros has brought shame on our dramatic arts. May his soul rot in Lincoln Center.

—March 1964

In *Suddenly, Last Summer,* that crafty old bartender, Tennessee Williams, serves up a witch's broth of Venus Fly Traps, massacred baby turtles, cannibalism, voyeurism, homosexuality (just a pinch), near-rape by lunatics, a dowager who is sinister even by Tennesseean standards, and a mother who is willing to have her perfectly sane daughter lobotomized in order to get her hands on $100,000 cash. It is hard to know what to say about this misguided tour through the dank recesses of Mr. Williams' subconscious. It's all clearly nonsense: Victorian melodrama with a heavy villain, an innocent girl wronged, and a rescuing knight, updated with Freud, symbolism, and the kind of adolescent despair that passes in the Tennesseean world for philosophy. Yet it's also, just as clearly,

145

quite entertaining. Perhaps the answer is that Mr. Williams has a touch of the poet in him, not a very good poet but still a poet, and, more important, that he is willing to do anything, absolutely anything, for a dramatic effect. This makes his plays good theatre and bad art.

Similarly, one might complain that director Joseph L. Mankiewicz takes it in too high a key and underlines too heavily. If there's one thing a Tennessee Williams play would seem not to need, it's underlining. "Nature is cruel." "All poets, whatever age they seem to others, die young." ". . . lives of quiet desperation." ". . . the Venus Fly Trap, aptly named after the goddess of love." What can an actor do with such lines except hope they won't be overheard? Yet perhaps Mr. Mankiewicz was well-advised to use the sledge hammer, perhaps this approach best brings out the play's entertaining sensationalism. (Mr. Kazan has always used this method of Williams and who can deny the grosses have been—sensational?) He can score one directorial triumph: he has somehow extracted from Elizabeth Taylor a mediocre performance, which is a definite step up in her dramatic career. He was less successful with the other two principals: Katharine Hepburn camps around like an Oscar Wilde duchess played by Beatrice Lillie and Montgomery Clift is woebegone and inexpressive, as usual.

Glossily photographed, slickly directed, *Suddenly, Last Summer* is a well-tooled dramatic vehicle that has everything in it but a motor.

—April 1960

Mr. Williams is with us again, this time raised to the nth power. *The Fugitive Kind,* screenplay by Tennessee Williams and Meade Roberts from the former's *Orpheus Descending,* directed by Sidney Lumet, starring Marlon Brando, Anna Magnani, Joanne Woodward, Maureen Stapleton and Victor Jory, makes *Suddenly, Last Summer* look like *Rebecca of Sunnybrook Farm.* Why Mr. Williams is considered so "advanced" a playwright I have never understood. *The Fugitive Kind* is a combination of *East Lynne* and *The Curse of the Montressors* with a little Krafft-Ebing thrown in. The lines and situations are embarrassingly predictable. Thus when

146

Miss Woodward (the lost, drunken, rich nymphomaniac complete with sporty roadster) lures Mr. Brando (a golden heart beats in his splendidly animalistic breast) into the graveyard for her own purposes, she asks him if he knows the one word the dead are always saying. He doesn't—it takes him half a minute to remember his own name and, such is the languorous power of his acting, one is never sure he will make it—but I did. It was "life." Her reasoning is that Brando should therefore make love to her, but he refuses or perhaps just doesn't get her.

In *Orpheus Descending*—to which I'm told the film is faithful, indeed that it contains things cut out of the stage play doubtless for sensible reasons, any cutting would be an improvement—Williams unconsciously parodies himself much as Hemingway did in *Across the River and Into the Trees*. It is at once pretentious and frivolous, reaching for the largest meanings, but always short-circuiting them for melodramatic effect. The film version is also parodic. Brando has never been more Brandonian, Magnani never more Magnanesque. I've never taken to the latter because I think she overacts—and Italians *aren't* like that; I've been there; they often don't shout and they seldom scream. But perhaps overacting is all one can do in a Williams play. Similarly, Lumet's direction is meaninglessly overintense; lights and shadows play over the close-up faces underlining lines that are themselves in bold capitals; every situation is given end-of-the-world treatment.

It seems odd that a writer so addicted to big effects should not have learned that to have effects you must have contrast. If every line shrieks, all of them mumble. Overstimulation of the nerves finally produces the same narcotic effect as sedation. It is a moral as well as an aesthetic matter: there is no norm in Williams' recent plays, and so there is no human meaning to the action. They are documentaries made in a madhouse.

The Fugitive Kind contains one of the most remarkable job interviews in business history. After his rejection of Miss Woodward in the graveyard, Brando returns to the dry-goods store which Magnani is successfully running, though she seems hardly the merchandising type. It is about two a.m., surely a poor time to apply for a job, but he hammers at the door and Magnani appears in her wrapper and, since this is a Williams play, lets him in. All he wants is a chance, he says; he's a hard worker and would like to

learn the business. She states the pay and adds, "Please to understand, young man, you don't interest me no more than that
dummy." It is to be strictly business, one gathers. The interweaving
of merchandising and Williamsising throughout is fascinating. Customers are shown the door when they try to flirt with the virtuous
young salesclerk; the relocation of the shoe department is discussed
con brio; Magnani's sinister bedridden husband (face pouring
glycerine sweat) keeps questioning her business and sexual judgment, impotent jealousy getting all mixed up with accounts re-
ceivable. I can't imagine what the Harvard Business School would
make of it.

—June 1960

I wish that Tennessee Williams had written either fewer or better
plays. Having conscientiously wrestled with *Suddenly, Last Summer, The Fugitive Kind* and *Summer and Smoke,* I am now confronted with Richard Brooks' *Sweet Bird of Youth.* Mr. Brooks has
a considerable reputation, one of the many things I don't understand about movies. His *Elmer Gantry* I thought crude and over-
blown and so is this latest work. In *Gantry* he defused Sinclair
Lewis' satire by inventing a "good" side of a character Lewis
depicted as a lustful hypocrite and by having it win out in the usual
Hollywood upbeat ending. So here he bowdlerizes Mr. Williams'
play: Chance gave Heavenly not syphilis but a baby; Boss Finley,
her father, doesn't rant about white supremacy and his minions
don't emasculate Chance, they just mark up his face a little; and a
happy ending materializes in the last three minutes—contradicting
the logic of the preceding two hours—with Chance and Heavenly
driving off while the wicked father stamps around in impotent rage.
I don't object to any play of Mr. Williams' being dry-cleaned; it's
that the toning down was not from taste, but from cowardice in the
face of a mass audience (which will not accept, or so the box-office
pundits think, VD, castration, racism or sad endings); I deduce this
because the film is even more cheaply sensational than was the
play.
With one exception, the acting is atrocious. Ed Begley as Boss

148

Finley is so monstrously evil that one begins to giggle; Shirley Knight as Heavenly is out of Hollywood's ingenue stock bin; Mildred Dunnock (Aunt Nonnie) is out of the Mildred Dunnock stock bin, as she was in *Something Wild*—the decline of this once-interesting actress into a standardized spare part is another instance of the tendency of Hollywood to reduce its performers to clichés. As for Paul Newman (Chance), well, something will have to be done about Mr. Newman—they might deal with Laurence Harvey at the same time. He is simply not an actor and possibly not even alive; seems to be carved from wood, his movements stiff and jerky as a marionette, his one expression an agonized grimace as of wood trying to smile. His efforts to get the Princess to get him a starring part in Hollywood have a peculiar poignancy since one knows he can never make it.

The exception is Geraldine Page as the Princess, the aging movie star. Her role was the center of the stage play; Mr. Brooks, with his usual obtuseness, has tried to put Chance and the other Southern grotesques into the center, but Miss Page takes over the film as triumphantly as she did the play. Whenever she is on, one concentrates on her exclusively. She has all the attributes of a great actress—style, presence, wit, timing, emotional mobility, and beauty, or what is the important thing, the ability to give that effect to the audience. She is also able to imitate an actual person. Her triumph is all the greater because the Princess is an excessively unreal role. Miss Page is able to express the grandiose phoniness of the aging star and at the same time to let us glimpse the frightened person underneath, as Fredric March did in *A Star Is Born*. Something will also have to be done about the waste of Miss Page's vast talent in recent years on Westerns (*Hondo*), trivial plays (*Separate Tables*), and Mr. Williams' unsoaped operas. We can't expect her to do it—even the best performers seem to have no sense about their "vehicles," lending themselves to the first nonsense that comes down the pike. Perhaps some director in Rome or Paris will some day realize that here is an actress capable of meeting the highest demands in her art.

—June 1962

149

THE
PREMINGER
PROBLEM

OTTO Preminger's *The Cardinal* contrasts interestingly with two other American films released about the same time: Elia Kazan's *America America* and Carl Foreman's *The Victors*. They are subjectively sincere and objectively insincere—i.e., they are kitsch fabricated with the most "serious" intentions—while Mr. Preminger's latest non-effort is one-hundred percent insincere kitsch. Mr. Foreman thinks he has made a dissident political statement "in my own way," while in fact he has manufactured one more standard Hollywood product. Mr. Kazan has poured out his soul—spilled his guts in his language—to celebrate his own family history, but what appears on the screen is just another exercise in fake primitivism hopped up with one more corny invocation of The American Dream. "We all came here LOOKING FOR SOMETHING," his program note concludes. "What is the responsibility of the dream to the dreamers? This is the story of this country." I suppose Mr. Kazan means something, but I can't imagine what.*

Otto Preminger is intellectually the superior of such types; even morally, in a way: he has no illusions and few pretensions, he's a tough baby who never wanted to go straight, what's in it for me? Unfortunately his cynicism extends to technique. Billy Wilder, rather like him temperamentally, at least has a craftsman's curiosity and so sometimes gets some life into some of his movies. But I've never seen an interesting Preminger film. The *Cahiers du Cinéma* intellectuals and their Greenwich Village epigones have a high esteem for Preminger—I can imagine the sharkish grin with which he reads their tributes, he and Hitchcock must have many a hilarious session over *Cahiers* and *Film Culture*—but the fact is, whether recognized in Paris or not, that a Hollywood director can be slick, vulgar, and commercial and still turn out bad movies.

Otto Preminger is a great showman who has never bothered to learn anything about making a movie. His genius for publicity is obvious. No one is more skilled at giving the appearance of dealing with large "controversial" themes in a "bold" way without making the tactical error of doing so. *The Moon Is Blue* was an early rebel

* See page 144 for a review of *America America*. I've omitted my lengthy political, moral and aesthetic objections to *The Victors* as, in a book context, overkill. The prurient reader may consult the March, 1964, *Esquire* for the revolting details.

against the Hays-Breen Code; we got drug addiction in *The Man with the Golden Arm,* the Israeli bit in *Exodus,* the lowdown on national politics in *Advise and Consent,* and now *The Cardinal* takes us on a Guntheresque tour Inside Catholicism. But the *Moon* was baby blue, the golden arm was Sinatra's, and the political exposé dwindled to using New Frontiersmen (and Frontiers-women) as dress extras, shooting some scenes in the actual Senate Chamber, and trying, luckily without success, to induce Martin Luther King to play a Senator from Georgia. As for *The Cardinal,* we have John Huston cast as one—a gimmick analogous to Prem-inger's getting Joseph Welch to play the judge in *Anatomy of a Murder.* Plus much heavy-breathing publicity about authenticity: the costumes and decor seem accurate—there's even a complete 1910 locomotive and train that was hired at vast expense merely to transport the hero from Boston to his new parish—but *Tarzan of the Apes* takes us about as far into African anthropology as *The Cardinal* does into the inner workings of the Roman Catholic Church. A pity, since the theme might have made an interesting film. Mr. Preminger, like other publicists, is often convinced by his own press releases. He ventured to run off a preview in Rome—in the palace of the Holy Office, no less—for the real cardinals attending the second Vatican Council. The cardinals were not amused. "The Council fathers gave this film the reception it deserved," Henri Fesquet wrote in *Le Monde* (I owe this quote to the *New Yorker*'s "Xavier Rynne"). "But many were astonished their leisure time had been put to such bad use." I should add that M. Fesquet had earlier described *The Cardinal* as "not only stupid but also in dubious taste."

I agree with their eminences. The story, a Lanny Budd success saga, is neither plausible nor dramatic. Tom Tryon, a cowboy type without the light of thought, spirituality or emotion in his square-jawed pan, is a hero that must make everyone in the theatre feel if he can make it, why not me? John Huston is at least professional as a tough cigar-smoking Boston-Irish cardinal; he obviously enjoys every minute of ecclesiastical transvestism and it's not his fault if the part was a cliché before he was born—nor that his father would have done it better. Burgess Meredith was touching, as well as professional, as a failed priest, and the Austrian actor, Josef Mein-

153

rad, was excellent as Cardinal Innitzer. And that's about the case for the affirmative.

The script is so stilted it sounds dubbed: "Hasn't Darwin kind of put the skids to Genesis?" a Jewish chap asks our hero, who replies in kind. Coincidences swarm shamelessly. Returning from Europe, our hero boards a trolley car outside the dock and who is the conductor but his own father! A statue of the Virgin Mary begins to drip red fluid from the heart region; the Boston-Italian peasantry scream and carry on (might have yelled a little myself, in fact); our hero quiets them with a flow of impeccable Italian and later discovers it was all due to a leaky (and rusty) pipe; however, he argues, it really *was* a miracle since God had caused the leak, thus Premingerizing both believer and skeptic. (But what's the use of being God if you have to worry about plumbing?)

Their eminences must have squirmed a lot at that Vatican preview, from boredom. The trashy story is directed with little taste and less imagination. The extreme close-up seems to be Preminger's only method of emphasis. But even Romy Schneider's face is distractingly ugly when it has to fill that wide screen, while Huston's looks like a relief map of the Dakota badlands. One wants to know less about her pores and more about her other qualities, one wants the kind of data Truffaut conveys, by the most subtle and varied cinematic means, about Jeanne Moreau in *Jules and Jim*. The billboard view Mr. Preminger gives us of the area between Miss Schneider's chin and eyebrows is too much information—and not enough.

—March 1964

FILM CRITICISM: A NOTE ON METHOD

The defects of *The Cardinal* were so patent as to present a real problem to the *politique des auteurs* ideologues—since in their canon Otto Preminger is a very "in" director. I thought Andrew Sarris' solution, in *The Village Voice* (December 12, 1963) was bold and ingenious. He admitted everything and then, right before our eyes, like Betty Crocker making a cake on television, whipped

154

up a whole new aesthetic that took care of the admissions by making them irrelevant.

The first problem was to explain away Preminger's frank orientation toward the box office—there was a time when movie critics rather deplored this. Sarris meets it head on: "If the personality he exudes with the help of a corps of press agents is more that of a blustering impresario than of a brooding artist, the fact remains that the cinema, at its most introspective, has never been a fruitful calling for asthmatic aesthetes. As for Preminger's blatant commercialism, even the older and more respectable art forms have been infested with shrewd businessmen like Shakespeare, Dürer, Ibsen, Shaw, Brahms, Picasso." A nice try, though (1) from some personal knowledge of Preminger, whose brains I respect as much as I don't the uses to which he puts them, I'd say he's his own best publicity man and needs no press corps to project his public image; and (2) I should imagine those six nonaesthetic and nonasthmatic businessmen are remembered less for the shrewdness they share with Preminger than for the talent he does not share with them.

"The big merit of *The Cardinal*," Sarris continues, "is the sheer size and audacity of its conception. It has become fashionable in America to overlook the grandeur of Preminger's design so as to carp at the *gaffes* of his detail." He goes on to carp for a full column, making much the same carps I did in my review. Since he never explains just where he finds in *The Cardinal* either "audacity of conception" or "grandeur of design," I assume these are rhetorical rather than critical categories. That is to say, hot air. "The primarily visual critics will hail it and the primarily literary critics will deplore it," Sarris concludes. "If I side with the visual critics on Preminger, it is because we are in the midst of a visual revolution which the literary establishment is apparently ignoring if not actively resisting." From the fact that the written accounts of the funeral of President Kennedy were "pitifully inadequate" compared to what we saw on television he infers that writing is now obsolete: "At long last, the Image has made the Word superfluous."

But the word, as it has come down in written history, was precisely what made "the image of a riderless black horse possess a visual power" which Mr. Sarris thinks went "far beyond any literary meaning." For literary meaning was all that horse possessed. A vacant desk or a telephone off the hook would have been more meaningful symbols, in terms of the dead President's actual style of life, than those reversed boots dangling from the saddle—an anachronism that moves us today only because we have read in the history books of a time when the seat of power was the saddle rather than the swivel chair. As for the image making the word superfluous, I see no revolution. The Chinese sage who said "A picture is worth ten thousand words" said it a long time ago, and he meant nothing more profound or less obvious than that for certain subjects, such as state funerals, pictures are better than words. (The reverse is also true, of course—cf. the Works of that sharp man of business, William Shakespeare.)

As long as movies are the hybrid art they have been up to now, so long will they continue to share plot and dialogue with the novel, composition and tonal values with painting, and the rhythms of montage with music. The "visual-vs.-literary" antithesis is thus false to the nature of cinema. Also to the nature of art in general. For in Mr. Sarris' new aesthetic (his aesthetic, that is, as of now—who knows to what acrobatic feats of *ad hoc* theorizing he will be forced in order to defend Hitchcock's or Preminger's next clinker?) there is implicit a dichotomy between form ("visual") and content ("literary") which exists only in theory—and bad theory at that. In practice, the form *is* the content, while the content is so profoundly affected by the form in which it is expressed as not to be separable from it. One-sided judgments result from the Sarris approach, and which side is up isn't important. The Russian "socialist-realist" critics reach absurdity by considering only literary-political content, Sarris achieves it by overemphasizing visual form. In theory, that is, for in practice he is shrewd enough not even to try to tell us just where to look, in *The Cardinal,* for visual pleasure.

Finally, I object to the triumphant "at long last" with which we are told that words are now superfluous. Partly because I am a writer (as is he), but chiefly because it expresses an anti-intellectual, primitivistic tendency which seems to me affectation since the circles in which it is fashionable are—not wholly unexpectedly—intellectualistic and nonprimitive to the point of decadence. I agree with Edgar Allan Poe's objection to the similar romantic assumption by Rousseau and other *philosophes* that the natural state of

156

man is savagery: "What right have they to suppose this is his natural state? Man's chief idiosyncrasy being reason, it follows that his savage condition . . . is his *un*natural state. The more he reasons, the nearer he approaches the position to which his chief idiosyncrasy irresistibly impels him; and not until he attains this position with exactitude . . . not until he has stepped upon the highest pinnacle of civilization—will his *natural* state be ultimately reached."

Man has not attained a state of reason with any exactitude, nor has he yet stepped upon the highest pinnacle of civilization. Meanwhile, I am willing to settle for a little logic. And common sense. I promise to cease my resistance to the Visual Revolution, turn in my membership card in the Literary Establishment, and consider all future works of Mr. Preminger entirely in ocular terms—20/20 critical vision—as soon as he gives us a movie without plot or dialogue.

—October 1964

WHATEVER
HAPPENED
TO
HOLLYWOOD
COMEDY?

ONCE upon a time, long, long ago, Hollywood comedies were funny. First there was the classic age of Keaton, Chaplin, Harold Lloyd, Harry Langdon and some—though not as much as sentimental archaeologists now pretend—of the myriad spawn of Mack Sennett, the Diaghilev of slapstick. The tradition carried over into the talkies with W. C. Fields, Laurel and Hardy, and the Marx Brothers. It was dead by the forties, whether because the form had been worked out or historical change had made it archaic, but dead it was, and is, as recent attempts to revive it have demonstrated. With the coming of sound, another comic style developed, not so pure but funny enough for practical purposes: those fast-moving, tough-minded, jaunty social comedies of the thirties and forties that still bring an unwonted liveliness to our TV screens late at night: *Nothing Sacred, Twentieth Century, Bringing Up Baby, My Man Godfrey, The Front Page, Trouble in Paradise, The Thin Man, It Happened One Night, Bombshell, His Girl Friday, The Philadelphia Story,* and such works of the unjustly neglected Preston Sturges as *Hail the Conquering Hero, The Miracle of Morgan's Creek,* and *The Great McGinty.* They were often called screwball comedies—the Huston-Capote *Beat the Devil* was a belated example—and there was plenty of english on the ball. Patriotism, romance, motherhood, the mass media, civic virtue, Americanism were all given a satiric twist. Nothing sacred.

But in five years (1960–1965), I recall only two American comedies that made me laugh: Wilder's *One, Two, Three* and Kubrick's *Dr. Strangelove.* This is curious because in that period Hollywood has made an extraordinary number of movies that, in form and intention, must be classified as comedies. They are so relentlessly unamusing as to suggest not chance failures but a system. From five recent specimens—*How to Murder Your Wife, Bedtime Story, Kiss Me, Stupid, What a Way to Go!,* and *It's a Mad, Mad, Mad, Mad World*—I have deduced three basic rules of comedy they violate, systematically.

> Rule 1: Humor is like guerrilla warfare. Success depends on traveling light (a joke too long in the telling fails, the fun leaks out of a comic situation too elaborately set up); striking unexpectedly (the shock of incongruity makes us laugh, but a director who lets us anticipate it produces no shock, merely the expected congruity);

160

and getting away fast (reflection or elaboration may increase enjoyment in other forms of art but not in comedy, where he who lingers is lost).

Stanley Kramer's attempt to revive slapstick in *Mad World* fails for every possible reason, but one is that it is more like the battle of the Somme than a Vietcong raid. To watch on a Cinerama screen in full color a small army of actors—105 speaking roles—inflict mayhem on each other with cars, planes, explosives, and other devices for more than three hours with stereophonic sound effects is simply too much for the human eye and ear to respond to, let alone the funny bone. The permutations and combinations of hard-core slapstick are as severely limited as those of hard-core pornography, and for the same reason: they are entirely physical. Sennett's early comedies lasted one reel, or ten minutes; he thought Chaplin mad when he insisted on trying a two-reeler; both of them were right, for Chaplin, with his pantomime and his creation of a character, "the little tramp," was going beyond slapstick. Chaplin eventually went all the way to feature-length comedies—which were, still, only one hundred minutes as against Mr. Kramer's almost two hundred minutes—as did Keaton, Lloyd and Langdon; they were successful because each invented a comic personality whose imbroglios couldn't help being more varied, and unexpected, than the physics of custard pies and runaway automobiles. More amusing even than Mr. Kramer's grand climactic anticlimactic finale with a dozen "name" stars, male and female, being catapulted one by one from the wildly thrashing tip of a six-story fire ladder to soar through the air and crash-land in comic places like a fountain and a pet shop.

What a Way to Go! and *How to Murder Your Wife* are in the screwball tradition, but the old shack has been redecorated with solid-mahogany furniture, plush drapes and wall-to-wall carpeting. (The sheer material opulence and comfort of our society since the lean thirties and the nervous war years may be a factor: even a Lubitsch or a Hawks might have found it difficult to keep it fast and light with such massively lavish sets and costumes.) Betty Comden and Adolph Green wrote the script for the former, George Axelrod for the latter; all are highly regarded in Hollywood as purveyors of sophisticated wit, but they smother their comic ideas, none too

161

robust to begin with, under scripts which, like lethargic stagehands, take a long time setting up each situation and a long time dismantling it, spelling out each joke for the slow readers and then repeating it for those who can't read at all. The directors, J. Lee Thompson and Richard Quine respectively, cooperate by drawing out each scene with repetitive business and by encouraging such once-lively performers (now slowed down by too many unfunny comedies) as Jack Lemmon and Shirley MacLaine to take their time with their mugging. One of the many ways Mr. Quine puts across the comic point of *How to Murder Your Wife* (which is that Lemmon, a gay bachelor, is trapped into marrying, while drunk, the beautiful Virna Lisi, who proceeds to domesticate him) is to have Miss Lisi invade not only Mr. Lemmon's club but the steam room of Mr. Lemmon's club; one can imagine the uproar, the scandal, the naked males snatching up towels, the immediate arrival of the house committee, fully clad, the immediate expulsion of Mr. Lemmon, etc. It certainly makes the point, as also do the repeated views, throughout the film, of Mr. Lemmon's expanding paunch (point being Miss Lisi is a good Italian wife who stuffs him with pasta). I prefer the way they suggested, in *Nothing Sacred,* that a Vermont village was hostile to a reporter from the city: as he walked up the street from the station a small boy ran out of a yard and bit him in the leg.

Rule 2: The tragic or the realisic hero can be unattractive—Hedda Gabler was a bitch, Mother Courage one hardly warms up to, the Macbeths, as Max Beerbohm has noted, were deplorable hosts—and no one will object except those who complain that real life is sad enough without paying money. . . . But comedy is different. It cannot claim the license of either high seriousness or low realism. We sympathize with the situation of the tragic/realistic hero but it is with the comedian himself that we must sympathize, else it's not funny. He either must be positively attractive—the physical grace of a Chaplin, the social grace of a Cary Grant, the poetic ineptness of a Keaton or a Langdon or a Tati—or his unattractiveness must be so grotesque, so stylized that he transcends reality and wins our sympathy as a figure of wish fulfillment: W. C. Fields surreptitiously delivering a vicious kick to a bratty child, Groucho Marx flicking his cigar ash into Margaret Dumont's pretentious décolletage.

162

There are many unattractive comedians in these five movies. How Ray Walston and Cliff Osmond would strike me in more sympathetic parts and with a different director, I don't know; but in *Kiss Me, Stupid* they are as frantically unappealing a comedy team as I've seen since the Ritz Brothers. The people in *Mad World* are unattractive in two ways. They are all greedy, double-crossing crooks and bums; even Spencer Tracy, the honest cop, turns crooked at the end; one of Mr. Kramer's many bad ideas. And they don't look very good either: there's something depressing about seeing Tracy, Durante, Berle, Ethel Merman and other aging, or aged, stars—Mickey Rooney has gone from adolescence to puffy middle age with no transition—so wrinkled and flabby, trying to cavort around like Keystone cops; in the Sennett era, they who got slapsticked were younger. The most repulsive of all is Marlon Brando in *Bedtime Story*. He is an American soldier abroad who is a liar, swindler, blackmailer and—his specialty—a ruthless seducer (and impregnator) of women, his technique being to play on their sympathies as a lonely little soldier boy far from home. A better actor might have made this heel amusing—seducers and con men have their comic aspects—but Brando makes us detest him as a slob and bully; the pious smirk he puts on when he goes into the soldier-boy act is unappetizing, as well as being amateurishly "indicative" acting.

Rule 3: Comedy is sadistic, making fun of the misfortunes or miscalculations of others. The joke's on them, not us; we laugh at them. And even when we laugh with Falstaff, so witty at the expense of others, we also laugh at him because he has the misfortune to be fat. His corpulence corresponds to the ill-fitting clothes and grotesquely painted face of the clown—who, like him, is both subject and object, wit and butt. "Men of all sorts take a pride to gird at me," Falstaff explains to his page. "I am not only witty in myself, but the cause that wit is in other men. I do here walk before thee like a sow that hath overwhelmed all her litter but one." But there is more to it. Will Rogers' "Everything is funny as long as it is happening to somebody else," is a half-truth. To make us laugh, the sadism must be disguised, carried beyond reality into a fanciful world where nobody really gets hurt: if the man slipping on a banana peel actually injured his spine, nobody would find it comic—except perhaps the Marquis de Sade, whose works

163

are notably lacking in humor. The other half of the truth is Thomas Carlyle's "The essence of humor is sensibility; warm tender fellow-feeling with all forms of existence." Almost any situation can be treated as comedy—even the threat of nuclear annihilation, as Stanley Kubrick has shown—as long as the director makes clear by a stylized treatment that we are not in the real world. But if the treatment is too realistic, so that the comic situation is blurred by real emotions and the comic victims arouse our sympathy, the result is at best confusing, at worst unpleasant, and in either case unfunny. Only on the plane of fantasy can the sadism inherent in comedy be transmuted into Carlyle's "fellow-feeling," uniting butt and spectator in laughter at the godawful nature of things that defeats them both.

A good illustration of Rule 3 is the difference between Billy Wilder's *One, Two, Three* and two other recent films of his, *The Apartment* and *Kiss Me, Stupid.* The first was nothing great as comedy—a rapid-fire succession of gags sustained by James Cagney's vitality—but it was funny because it was deliberately artificial, playing around with the comic aspects of the cold war without pretending to strike below the surface to any human reality. I have analyzed *The Apartment* at length; here enough to note that its chief defect, trying to have it both ways by presenting a gamy situation as both comic and emotionally serious, also vitiates Mr. Wilder's new film, *Kiss Me, Stupid.* The situation is gamy indeed: an unsuccessful songwriter offers his wife for the night to a womanizing pop singer hoping he will plug his songs. But, this being a Wilder film, it's not as simple, or bold, as that: the songwriter hires a local tart to stand in for his wife; after the singer has amorously mauled the "wife" as the songwriter-"husband" looks on complaisantly, she finds herself attracted to the latter and he to her, so they throw out the singer, who goes to the local hot spot looking for a woman and—through complexities of plot too tedious to explain here—ends up sleeping with the wife, thinking she is the tart. What *she* thinks is extremely complex: hitherto a virtuous wife, she submits to the singer because she is angry at her husband (whom she has reason to believe has shacked up for the night with the tart, as is indeed the case), and also drunk, though not so drunk as, once she realizes who the singer is, not to combine business with pleasure by

164

bringing to his attention, before she gives in, one of hubby's songs. The finale, some days later, has the married couple viewing the singer on TV plugging the song. He says, "But, but how come?" or words to that effect, and she says, "Kiss me, stupid." Gamy? A whole game preserve. Leaving aside the laborious hammering home of the comic points (Rule 1) and the unattractiveness of the husband and his sidekick (Rule 2), *Kiss Me, Stupid* also violates Rule 3 by trying to engage our sympathies for the principals as human beings—the husband and the tart fall in love, for that night anyway, and virtuously unite to repel the singer's advances, while the wife has two excuses for cuckolding her husband: intoxication and a sense of duty. The only decent member of the quadrangle, oddly enough, is Dean Martin as the lecherous pop singer: his simple, direct sensuality blows like a fresh breeze through the foggy atmosphere of apologetic prurience in which the other three exist. Mr. Martin is also the only success as a comedian: he has an easy grace—a hillbilly Cary Grant—and the director has spared him those queasy, hypocritical "human feelings" about sex that make the other three angles so unamusing. Under Mr. Wilder's direction, Tartuffe would be not a comic monster but just another mixed-up human being like all of us, much to be said on both sides, nobody's all bad, and who are we to judge the poor fellow? Or to laugh at him?

The last part of *Bedtime Story* has Brando trying to con a girl into surrendering to him her virginity and her bankroll; he wins her sympathy by pretending to be a crippled veteran confined for life to a wheelchair. A comical cuss. In real life, the con man depends on the mark's being greedy, dishonest and foolish, and in con-game comedies this is the minimum, if we are to laugh. But the girl is presented as decent, generous and, except for her liking Brando, not foolish. It gets really hilarious at the end when that old cutup fakes recovering the use of his legs because of her inspiring love, heaves his bulk out of the wheelchair and, as she encourages him with proudly shining eyes, totters gamely toward her, saves himself from falling by wrapping his arms around her, and pushes her backward into the bedroom, closing the door behind them. The director passed up the final boff—we don't see him collapsing on top of her on the bed—but the joke's on her all right. The Marquis

165

would have been amused. Everything is taken back five minutes later, of course, the picture ending with Brando, regenerated and a heel no longer, married to the girl. I found this more depressing than the seduction, which at least was temporary; but now that nice girl will have to spend the rest of her life with Brando. Had *Bedtime Story* been done in the high style of the old screwball comedies, in which a heel is never resouled in the last act, the nastiness might have been disinfected. Though I wonder if Molière himself could have made comedy out of the wheelchair seduction. I also wonder how *Bedtime Story* went over in Veterans Hospitals, maybe on a double bill with another Brando picture, *The Men,* in which he is most affecting as a paraplegic war veteran. It must have helped him give an authentic performance when he played it for laughs in *Bedtime Story.*

A comparison of the old silent comedies with *Mad World* is interesting in terms of Rule 3. They presented not people but abstractions from people whose physical catastrophes were no more distressing to the spectator than the pulverizations and rebirths of animals in movie cartoons, since this is a magical world where nobody *really* gets hurt. But in Mr. Kramer's imitation, the old magical world has vanished: these comedians are flesh and blood and their sufferings are subject to the laws of the real world. The result is not amusing. An old man dying by the roadside after an automobile accident is not funny even if he is Jimmy Durante and even if we get many close-ups of his contorted face sweating with pain. A poor couple's pickup truck hurtling down a hillside out of control while the driver and his wife cling on desperately and their modest household goods spill out is not funny either, even if they are Negroes. A young married couple trapped in the burning cellar of a hardware store is not funny even if a stack of cans of paint is about to catch fire and incinerate them and even if they are named Sid Caesar and Edie Adams.

—June 1965

REPORT
FROM
THE
ACADEMY

SOME notes on a course in movie history and criticism I taught in the spring of 1966 at the University of Texas may be of interest, since the subject seems to be increasingly popular in Academe. According to Thomas Brandon, the doyen of 16-millimeter film distributors, almost two thousand film courses, of one kind or another, are now being given in our colleges and universities—which is a four-hundred percent increase in the last ten years. Mr. Brandon also estimates there are "approximately 3,500 film societies in existence across the country." These figures seemed to me high—also the press agent who sent out the release was named Jerry Sunshine, perfect in a way but not reassuring—so I queried Mr. Brandon, who has been thirty years in the business and should know, and he assured me he has the research to back them up. He said his definition of a "film course" excluded courses in history, oscillogy, etc., that make a tangential use of movies as what is known in the trade as "A.V.A.," or Audio-Visual Aids, and also that "a film society" is any group that rents films for noncommercial exhibition, from fifteen or twenty individuals who are curious about cinema and dissatisfied with what's on at the neighborhood theatre, through the campus film clubs with memberships in the hundreds, to the five thousand card-carrying members of the Dryden Theatre Film Society of Eastman House in Rochester, New York, whose director, James Card, has built up in recent years one of the three great American film collections, the other two being those of The Museum of Modern Art and of the Library of Congress.

Austin couldn't have been more different from what I'd expected, as a congenital Easterner, of Texas: an easygoing, pleasant, human-scale place where everybody was polite and friendly—one needs a decompression chamber to get back into the New York City atmosphere—even the cops, even my students. I met none of those outsize characters I'd read and heard about who brag about how big and rich and healthy Texas is compared to the mingy, impoverished and Commeuwnistically perverted rest of the country, and the universe. (The legislature was not in session, I should add.) Although that ranch on the Pedernales is only a short drive from Austin—"short" in Texas means anything under a hundred

168

miles—I can't recall anybody, town or gown, who reminded me of Mr. Johnson. Even the Texas Shriners, whose parading and cavorting my wife and I watched for two hours one morning, were more gentlemanly than similar groups I've observed in New York. True that we left town before that student (*not* in my class) killed fifteen people from the university tower—I might have been struck down trying to return a book to the library, of all absurd deaths. Also, one somehow got the impression that a revolver (pistol? handgun? what *is* the up-to-date term?) was standard equipment in automobile glove compartments along with road maps, sunglasses and Kleenex tissues; but everybody seemed so nice one didn't give it another uneasy thought.

I was not surprised that the enrollment for my film course was large, almost a hundred starters who shook down to about eighty-five, for I have done some talking on campuses about cinema and I know how central movies have become in undergraduate culture. Mr. Brandon is right in giving "primary credit" to "the youngsters themselves," and in stating that the faculties "up to now have done little to stimulate campus excitement in film as art." In my travels, I often felt like a belated Johnny Appleseed: the orchards were sprouting already, sometimes so vigorously that during the question period or at that mild academic festivity known as a "reception," scholarly infants turned up who knew more about many aspects of cinema than the lecturer. Not in Texas, however.

At the first meeting, I gave out a list of 121 films which seemed to me basic and asked each student to circle the ones he or she had seen. Two-thirds had seen less than twelve of the films, or ten percent, and one-third had seen less than six. The top fifth of the class—twenty out of a hundred—had seen from seventeen to thirty-five of the listed titles, and one sport had seen fifty-one, or almost half. Nobody had seen *Broken Blossoms, Intolerance,* (the college film society brought it there that spring), *Sous les Toits de Paris, Shoeshine, Il Posto, Los Olvidados, Variety, Arsenal, The Navigator,* or anything by Stroheim, Sternberg, or Pudovkin. *Ten Days That Shook the World, Metropolis, Olympia, Triumph of the Will, Le Million, Grand Illusion, The Rules of the Game, L'Age d'Or, Night and Fog* and *Paisan* each were seen by one student, often

169

that sport, out of a hundred respondents. *Dr. Strangelove* had been seen by 85, followed in order by *La Dolce Vita* (64), *8½* (60), *Divorce, Italian Style* (51), *Wild Strawberries* (47), and *The Silence* (46). Since most of the class were from Texas and practically all from the Southwest, it seems that in that region there are many fewer chances to see important films, especially from the past, than in the rest of the country. Despite the University's 25,000 students, for example, there is only one "art cinema" in Austin (it was showing *The Loved One* most of the time I was there). I should add that it was a very good class, with what I'm told was about the usual percentage of "A" and "B" students; lively, interested, most of them conscientious and all of them with those nice Southern manners. As for learning something about cinema, as I told them after the questionnaire, they had nowhere to go but up.

After each lecture I showed a feature film, about fifteen in all. By far the most popular was Carné's *Children of Paradise,* followed by *Citizen Kane* (which I showed at the first class as a compendium of technique), Keaton's *Sherlock, Jr.,* Lubitsch's *Trouble in Paradise,* Bergman's *The Naked Night,* and Kurosawa's Macbeth film, *Throne of Blood.* For me, the greatest disappointment was Fellini's *I Vitelloni,* whose big reputation I don't understand; it seemed dated and faded, much less interesting than an earlier naturalistic film I showed, Donskoi's *The Childhood of Maxim Gorky.* There were three sleepers, on the other hand for both me and the class: the Lubitsch film, which I hadn't expected to be as fresh as ever, perfectly stylized and paced and amusing after the rather slow beginning; *Point of Order,* the two-hour documentary Dan Talbot and Emile de Antonio quarried out of the TV coverage of the Army-McCarthy hearings, which was as funny and as dramatic as any feature film I showed; and that ancient of ancients, *The Cabinet of Dr. Caligari,* which I liked even more this fourth time around than I did in the twenties, a perfect work of art, everything consistent and working together, and so beautifully short, barely an hour. How good to see a film that one would like to be *longer!*

One other surprise was that it is possible to get almost any film one wants to show, so long as it is not a new one. The fees depend on the size of the audience and whether admission is charged; the films I showed cost from $20 to $75 each, the median being around

170

$40. There are a dozen or so agencies that rent out 16-millimeter films, as, in New York City, The Museum of Modern Art, Brandon Films, Continental 16, Janus, and Contemporary Films; in Chicago, the Audio Film Center; and in Dayton, Ohio, Twyman Films.

—November 1966

**THE
END**

T HIS is the last movie column I'll be doing for *Esquire*. It has become more and more difficult to write, and when I talked with the editors about the problem—which is also that it's become too easy, in a different sense, hence not stimulating, hence difficult —they suggested I might want to try instead a column on another interest of mine, politics, a proposal I accepted with thanks and alacrity.

I would like to attempt some explanation of this accumulating lethargy toward movie reviewing. The most obvious is subjective: this is the seventh year of the column and, for some reason, my attention span seems to be about six years, after which the eyes glaze and the mind wanders. My writing career, with the exception of *The New Yorker,* divides neatly into six-year periods: *Fortune* (1929–1936), *Partisan Review* (1938–1943), *Politics* (1944– 1949) and now *Esquire* (movies) from 1960 to date. This fateful symmetry, a limit so personal as to seem almost biological, may be the main factor, and perhaps I should leave it at that. But there were also always, or so it seemed to me, objective limits, mostly political, in the first three sexennials. And I think there is an objective reason for my feeling I've had it, for a while anyway, with movie reviewing, namely, that the postwar renaissance of cinema, which reached its height roughly between 1958 and 1964, has in the past two years gone into a decline that shows no sign of being reversed. Thus, looking over the past columns, I find I reviewed in 1960 *The 400 Blows* and *Hiroshima, Mon Amour;* in 1961, *L'Avventura, Breathless, Shoot the Piano Player* and *Viridiana;* in 1962, *La Notte, Jules and Jim* and *Last Year at Marienbad;* in 1963, *The Sound of Trumpets ("Il Posto");* in 1964, *8½, Dr. Strangelove, The Silence,* and *The Organizer;* in 1965, *A Hard Day's Night.* These were some of them masterpieces, all of them original and ambitious (and successful) works that it was exhilarating to see and challenging to write about. There were also, in those first four years, a considerable number of secondary works, not as important but still very interesting, such as *Shadows, I'm All Right, Jack, Pull My Daisy, The Lady with the Dog* (still the best postwar Soviet film), *Lawrence of Arabia* (best spectacular), *The Fiancées, Muriel, The Hidden Fortress,* and *Lolita.* In the last year and a half, however, I've seen no film in the first class and few in the second.

174

Both the postwar renaissance and its recent collapse may be to some extent traced to the same phenomenon: the culture boom, or explosion, something loud and indiscriminate whatever it's called. The post-1945 increase in American art-movie houses from fifteen to some eight hundred and in our university film clubs and courses, together with the vogue of cinema among young European intellectuals, has for the first time in movie history created an audience that is both sophisticated enough to appreciate (or, more accurately, to want, not quite the same thing) the most advanced kind of films and also large enough to make their production profitable at the box office. The trouble is this new audience *is* new, thus uncertain of its taste in movies (and even more in fine arts), thus prone to follow, often without much resistance, the lead of whatever critics or groups boldly assert they are avant-garde, such as our "underground" spielers and dealers (*ci-devant* "The New American Cinema"). This accounts for the *succès d'estime* of clinkers like the Mekas brothers' *Hallelujah the Hills!* and practically the whole *oeuvre* of Jean-Luc Godard after his first movie, *Breathless* (which didn't look as fresh when I saw it again last year as it had in 1961).

The new audience has also made plenty of mistakes on its own, falling for such "in" pastiches as *Tom Jones, The Pawnbroker, The Servant* and *He Who Must Die,* which use the postwar film vocabulary without understanding a word; pidgin cinemese. Nor has this audience, with its acceptance of received ideas and established reputations, once they have been passed on by the proper authorities, created a favorable atmosphere for art. Praise is agreeable always and to the most dedicated artist, but I should think it would be more helpful if it were informed, that is, cut by the tartness of criticism, even the acid of rejection. A depressing aspect of the last two years is the falling off of the recent work of almost all the major directors. One cause may be the adulation that bathes them continually, the enormous and respectful publicity that automatically greets each new film; I refer not to the humble efforts of press agents but to the unpaid touting by serious writers in serious little magazines, which today is far more effective. That kultur-bang. If the quarterlies come, can *Time* be far behind? A more important cause, however, may be the fact of life that few artists in any medium can produce steadily at their highest level; they have their ups and downs, like the rest of us, though you'd never guess it from the quarterlies. So, too, with movies in general, for art forms have their ups and downs, their periods of invention and of marking time, of Periclean expansion and Alexandrian stasis. These shifts used to take a long time—the Elizabethan impetus was not exhausted for a century—but things are speeded up now and perhaps the movies will revive in a few decades or years.

Meanwhile, I'll sit this one out. For criticism to be useful there must be some reasonable balance between original creation and the old stuff, the *déja vu,* the kitsch (which is now middlebrow or highbrow in form, even the lowbrows today are comfortable with Batman or Tarzan only when they are camped up). When kitsch becomes not predominant—it has been for two hundred years—but monopolistic, then one finds that as the years go by one has already reviewed, under another title, almost every new film one sees. While a good movie is *sui generis,* so that one has to respond to it specifically and individually, bad movies fall into categories and, once one has dealt with the category, it is tedious to keep repeating the demonstration. I seem to have been making the same essential criticisms, for example, of anything-goes unfunny comedies from *Zazie* in 1961 to *What's New, Pussycat?* last year and *Morgan!* last month. It gets tiresome. About all one can do with bad movies, after a while, is to treat them tangentially, as sociology or cultural history, but this isn't criticism, and it also gets tiresome, for here, too, there is repetition. I've said as much as I can, directly and tangentially, about those corny Biblical epics and also about the "underground" school, and I cannot face having to grapple with any more of the same. I have been accused of "not liking movies," which is nonsense: my difficulty is I like them too much so cannot bear to see the medium's wonderful, infinite possibilities not used to the utmost; I still think as I did in the twenties that the cinema is *the* great modern art—potentially.

While I like to carp and complain, even for me there is a limit. Much as I enjoyed savaging all those Roman-Christian epics—*Ben-Hur, King of Kings,* and *The Greatest Story Ever Told*—I've had enough. One of the advantages of giving up this department now is that I won't have to grapple with *The Bible.* Another is that I don't have to see any more movies by Joseph Losey, including *Modesty*

Blaise, or Tony Richardson, including *Mademoiselle,* or William Wyler, or Otto Preminger, or M. Godard, or several other directors whose work I doubt, from experience, will give me pleasure. I will also not have to see Charlton Heston parody one of my heroes, General ("Chinese") Gordon, in *Khartoum,* nor Mel Ferrer as the eponymous hero of Twentieth Century-Fox's (where could a corporate name like that occur except in Hollywood?) *El Greco.* Nor Warner Brothers' as yet untitled film, "an elaborate production based on the life and works of the great nineteenth-century Russian composer, Peter Ilyich Tachaikowsky," with Dimitri Tiomkin, "the distinguished Hollywood composer" as "executive producer . . . under Mr. Warner's personal supervision," making doubly sure the music will be high-class; this will be the first American-Soviet coproduction; hands across the Vulga. Nor will I have to comment on the inaugural address of Jack Valenti, who has transferred intact his gift for enthusiastic empathy from Lyndon Johnson to an even tougher assignment: the movie business. Refraining with difficulty from quoting here the whole twelve pages, I limit myself to the first page of the handout summary: "Hollywood, June 20: The new President of the Motion Picture Association of America, Inc., urged an all-industry audience today 'to build and create so that the people of our nation, and the world, will see in this industry a higher form of quality.' Addressing a star-studded luncheon he predicted that 'the greatness of the motion picture business is only now beginning to dawn' and described his convictions on how the industry should 'seize the future.' First priority will be given to 'refurbishing and illuminating the most precious commodity of this industry, its creative genius,' Valenti said. 'Let us live and so create that people will view this business and all who labor in it as men and women of taste and skill, of imagination and maturity, daring and discretion.' " You can say that last word again, Jack. Nor will I have to open the press releases that arrive daily from Embassy Pictures Corp., bearing such glad tidings as: "Joseph E. Levine has been decorated with the order of Commendatore of the Italian Republic," and "Joseph E. Levine has been named recipient of the 'Silver Plaque' [don't get the quotes, is it plated?] awarded by the Union of Italian Cinema Journalists" and "Martin Poll has been signed by Embassy Pictures to produce Joseph E. Levine's *The Ski*

177

Bum, the film version of Romain Gary's best-selling novel . . . the story of todays 'lost generation' of affluent, aimless world youth, told against a background of foreign intrigue, murder, smuggling and romance." (I suppose *somebody* must write these releases, but I shouldn't like to meet him, or it.) Nor will I have to worry about the Gallery of Modern Art's "Tribute to Joe Pasternak," which rolled on for two months this summer in its movie theatre and included four Deanna Durbin movies—*Three Smart Girls, One Hundred Men and a Girl, Mad About Music,* and *Three Smart Girls Grow Up*—plus many other works by Pasternak such as *The Courtship of Eddie's Father* (Shirley Jones, Glenn Ford) and *Girl Happy* (Elvis Presley and Mary Ann Mobley). Nor about The Museum of Modern Art's more modest tribute to Sam Spiegel, which lasted only three weeks. These celebrations of Hollywood producers by art museums are as if the A.S.P.C.A. protected the floggers instead of the horses.

Finally, and to make an end, by abandoning the column right now, I shall just miss The Fourth Annual Lincoln Center Film Festival.

—November 1966

178

PART FOUR

THE
RUSSIAN
CINEMA

EISENSTEIN
AND
PUDOVKIN
IN THE
TWENTIES

E VER since Eisenstein's *Potemkin* and Pudovkin's *Mother* were produced in 1926, the Union of Socialist Soviet Republics has been showing the rest of the world what can be done with the movies.* As Tolstoy and Dostoevsky took up the European novel and played upon it variations so fundamental that the instrument seemed to change its very nature in their hands, so Eisenstein and Pudovkin have taken up the cinema and developed it so far that it, too, seems almost a different vehicle from what existed before in this country and abroad. The rapidity of this development† is all the more remarkable when one considers the masterpieces that have already come out of Russia.

"Among all your arts the most important is that of the cinema." —*Lenin.* "Molding the feeling and intelligence of the masses is one of our political problems and for this end we find the movies most effective."—*Eisenstein.* Here we have a statement and an explanation. The statement is that the cinema is of the first importance to the Soviet. Explanation: because it is an incomparably "effective" means of influencing the masses and educating them in the doctrines of Communism. This social purpose has shaped, distorted perhaps, every movie that has been made in Russia. Therefore, whenever Russian movies are mentioned, some one is sure to cry "propaganda!" as if that settled the whole business. Presumably they would find the same taint in *Paradise Lost,* whose announced aim is "to justify the ways of God to man." The fact is that art is often aimed at the glorification of some social class. That the artists

---

* This article was written in 1931.

† The movies made in Russia before 1926 have almost no connection in technique and theory with those made afterwards. So embryonic was the Russian cinema in 1924 that an authority on it could write: "Some of its extreme supporters have a vision of a socialist mass film similar in construction to but different in meaning from *The Birth of a Nation* in which the people themselves could take a part." Needless to say, the "vision" of the "extreme supporters" was realized two years later in *Potemkin.* And the same writer dismisses the whole Russian cinema thusly: "Today it occupies a place in the universal film world best described as the lower depths. The Russian film industry needs technical experts, it needs photographers who can take a photo. . . ."

of the renaissance glorified the aristocracy and that the Soviet artists glorify the proletariat is not a very important distinction. The artist does not worry about the precise color of his social, moral, and religious views. He accepts those of his age and nation—or, if it suits his temper better, he revolts against them. But his primary interest is his art. He will take orders as to his views on Communism, Mormonism, or free trade, but he will not take orders as to the way he is to express these things in his art. The Hollywood director is subjected to just that sort of dictation: he must not bewilder his audience by telling his story in a subtle or original way. Every picture must be capable of being grasped by the 120,000,000 Lords and Masters of America, which means that every picture must come as close to mediocrity as is humanly possible. The Russian director has his orders plainly enough about the political tone of his pictures, but he is free to express this just as he pleases. He can be as bold and subtle and experimental as he wants as far as his technique is concerned; and this is the kind of freedom the artist must have.

This freedom, as contrasted with the intolerable bondage under which Hollywood groans,* is the condition that has allowed Russian directors to so far outstrip their Hollywood comrades in movie technique. That it exists in Russia and not over here is nothing to the credit of either Russian directors or Russian audiences. The average Russian audience is undoubtedly even less *intelligent* than the average American audience. If the Russians take a national interest in brilliantly (that is to say, boldly, subtly, and, to the average person, incomprehensibly) directed pictures, it is because of that very propaganda which bothers the aesthetes so much. This propaganda is the sugar coating on the bitter pill of art.† Since the Russian proletariat cannot get its political glorification without at the same time swallowing a certain amount of good art, it takes heart and gulps down both at once.‡ The point the aesthetes overlook is that the Russian cinema is primarily a manifestation of a great social renewal. The stimulus of a national awakening makes

* Hmmm . . .
† Double hmmmmm . . .
‡ Hmmmmm squared. (My style may not have improved after 37 years of practice, but at least I now see what was wrong then. Plenty.)

possible not only the enthusiasm of the people for movies experimental (hence difficult) in technique and serious (hence unattractive) in treatment, but also the creation of such movies by the directors. "New ideas can come only from new social forms," declares Eisenstein. "Russia has them and so Russia leads the world today. The Renaissance, for instance, could come about only when the old order was changed. So it is with film art, which comes about only after a big social change. At present America and Europe seem to be groping about for something they cannot find. That is why they are using our ideas." It might be maintained that no people has ever supported good art unless the entire nation was drunk. The merchants who paid for medieval cathedrals were drunk with what Lenin calls "the opium of the people." The Athenian citizenry who sat all day on stone benches to hear Aeschylus and Sophocles were obviously drunk—with national pride, most potent of liquors. The Russians of today are intoxicated with a great new social theory, whence their insane delight in good cinema. We Americans are only too sober.

Thus propaganda, instead of being the fatal weakness of the Soviet cinema, is, philosophically and historically considered, its greatest source of strength. Though it sometimes leads to inartistic exaggeration, it also provides that seriousness of purpose, that elevation in the treatment of a theme which is so marked in the movies of Russia and so lacking in those of this country. "Romantic entertainment does not enter our films," contemptuously declares Eisenstein. "We always have a message to bring out that will help build up our country under its new regime. . . . For a subject we always go to the heart of the masses, find out what they need, and then build a scenario around it." The Russian director has a message to give to the people, a message that they are eager to receive. He delivers it in his own way, dictates his own terms to his audience, which accepts his terms for the sake of his message. The teachings of Christ must have often been incomprehensible to the people; we know they were sometimes so to his disciples. But he continued to speak in parables, letting wisdom fall from his lips for the people to gather up as they might. "But without a parable spake he not unto them: and when they were alone, he expounded all things to his disciples." Prophets, artists, philosophers cannot afford

184

to compromise or condescend in their relations with the people. When the artist has no message, as today in America, he can preserve his integrity by keeping aloof from the people. But this course is not open to the movie director, whose work must be for the people as a whole. Since he has nothing to tell them (Henry Ford and Thomas Edison are the message-bearers, not King Vidor, not Josef von Sternberg), he must entertain them. If his work rarely comes out full and strong and living it is because his master, the mob, prefers the easily shallow, the safely dead. It is otherwise with the Russian director. His message makes him the master, the only tolerable position for a man of talent.*

There are several qualifications that must be noted here to the foregoing discussion. The distinction between the Russian and the American director cannot be wholly stated in terms of "master" and "servant" or of "bondage" and "freedom." It is true that the Russian director is not "free" so far as his social viewpoint goes, that he must express Communistic ideas in his pictures, but it is also true that he is eager to do so anyway. He is as much inspired by the vision of Communism as anyone. The American has greater freedom in that his pictures do not have to preach any particular doctrine, but this very freedom puts him at a disadvantage. Since the Communist ideology provides the Russian director with a point of view he knows his audience also holds, it makes communication between him and his audience much easier. The Christian religion has done the same thing for generations of artists. The American director, with no such definite system to show him the limits within which he must work, is as much at sea on this vital point as the other artists of this country. Nor are the shrewd pants-pressers who run our movies much better judges of what the public wants, as could be amply illustrated by box-office records. Another qualification must be made as to the "mastery" of the Russian director over his audience. Though it is accurate to term the American director the servant of his public, the Russian is so much in sympathy with the viewpoint of the people that no sharp distinction can be made as to which of the two parties is dominant. The relationship is that of colleagues rather than of ruler and ruled. There is one point that

* At last a statement I can wholly endorse, as of 1968.

185

needs more qualifying than any other, namely, the alleged "freedom" of the Russian director to mystify his audience with trick technique as contrasted to the compulsion put upon the American to keep his technique within the grasp of the crowd. The fact is that Russian movies are designed for the masses even more deliberately than our own. Their brilliant technique is simply what Eisenstein and the others have arrived at after a scientific study of audience reactions. From this aspect the technical superiority of Russian movies is due not to a disregard of the people but to a more intelligent and intensive study of them. Whereas Hollywood has merely tried to please the public's taste (a hopeless effort, for popular taste is notoriously unstable, and a useless one, for popular taste is always bad), the Russians have brushed this aside as unimportant, and have gone straight to the heart of the matter: not what *pleases* audiences, but what *affects* them, what moves and influences them whether they know it or not and whether they like it or not.

In considering the cinematic technique of the Russians the first thing that impresses the American observer is the artistic sophistication of the Russian directors. Most Hollywood directors are practical fellows who know pretty well how to knock together a movie but who are noticeably silent when it comes to aesthetic theory. The Russians, however, evidently have thought long and deeply about the nature of the cinema. It is the directors themselves who analyze their art, and it is they who lead in any discussion of its aesthetics. Over here the directors, perhaps wisely, leave theory to the intelligentsia. The causes of this striking difference are too complex to be analyzed here. One curious but possibly important factor may be mentioned: the shortage of camera film in Russia for many years after the revolution. This forced the directors to do a great deal of abstract thinking about their art before they ventured to use up any of the precious film. Many a Hollywood director would benefit from a strict rationing of film—though the masterful Von Stroheim works on precisely the opposite principle. Whatever the cause, the two great Russian directors are remarkably articulate about the cinema, so much that it will be possible to describe their achievements in technique largely through their own words.

186

The backbone of Russian movie technique is "montage," i.e., the arranging of the individual "shots" (a "shot" is the picture that is etched on the film every time the camera shutter opens) in a desired order. More fully: after the reels of film have been run through the camera, the director "mounts" the resulting shots. That is, he cuts them apart and arranges them in the order in which he wants them to be thrown on the screen when the film is projected. In emphasizing montage the Russians in effect declare that the important motion is not that which goes on before the camera but that which is created by one shot moving onto the screen as another moves off. "Cinematography is, first and foremost, montage," writes Eisenstein. And Pudovkin is equally emphatic:

> I claim that every object is a dead object even though it has moved before the camera. For movement before the camera is not movement before the screen. It is no more than raw material for the future building-up of the real movement, which is that obtained by the assemblage of the various strips of film. Only if the object be related to other objects, only if it be presented as part of a synthesis of different separate visual images, is it endowed with filmic life. . . . Every object must, by editing [i.e., *montage*], be brought upon the screen so that it shall have not *photographic* but *cinematographic* meaning. Editing is the basic creative force by power of which the soulless photographs are engineered into living, cinematographic form.

The movie camera feeds best on reality. The Russians have accepted this great truth as completely as the Germans have passed it by. "Away from realism to reality," cries Eisenstein. "From the studio setting and the professional actor to the original place and person. A thirty-year-old actor may be called upon to play an old man of sixty. He may have a few days' or a few hours' rehearsal. But an old man of sixty will have had sixty years' rehearsal." "I want to work only with real material—this is my principle," Pudovkin declares. "I maintain that to show, alongside real water and real trees and grass, a property beard pasted on the actor's face, wrinkles traced by means of paint, or stagey acting is impossible. It is opposed to the most elementary ideas of style." Where the

187

Germans with infinite labor and cunning paint lines on their actors' faces that *almost* look real and build palaces of lath and plaster that *almost* pass for solid stone, the Russians lazily and naively take their cameras to old men and photograph *real* wrinkles, set them up before palaces and photograph *real* stone. They have grasped the fact that the camera and the film it makes are the instruments of artifice in the movies as the brush and paints are in painting, and that what is before the camera is not another artifice but is the raw material of reality corresponding to the landscape that is before an artist. For an artist to view his landscape through colored glasses or for a director to work mostly inside the studio—this is, in Pudovkin's words, "opposed to the most elementary ideas of style."

It is understating it to call the Russians faithful to reality. They are intoxicated with it. Compared to the pictorial scope of the Russian cinema, our own movies are cramped and monotonous affairs. The Russians have let the camera loose into the open-air world of clouds, sunlight, rippling waters, mountains, palaces, fortresses, city streets, prairies. They have demonstrated the *extensive* powers of the camera, which can range over the world of matter with the tireless freedom known only to the machine. And on the other hand they have even more clearly demonstrated that the camera can, by means of the close-up, *intensify* its vision down to the minutest detail. They express a peasant's mode of life, for instance, largely by glimpses of such minutiae as the clay vessels from which he eats, the barbaric necklace his wife wears on feast days, the worn handles of his plow, the fences that lean crazily about his fields. In more complex social strata the realistic detail is even more abundant. A general is meticulously presented button by button from his oiled-flat hair to his shiny boots. Banquets, with their china, crystal, silver, and wine, are a favorite theme among Soviet directors. The Germans, too, are good at suggesting local color with such realistic detail. But there is a much more vital use of detail at which the Russians are unrivaled: the use of the close-up to emphasize the dramatic rhythm. A superb instance of this in *Ten Days That Shook the World* is the gigantic close-up of Kerensky's eye as he caps the decanter with the imperial crown. By bringing the camera lens within a few inches of the eye and the crown, the dramatic relationship of these two objects is powerfully

188

expressed. "The detail will always be a synonym of intensification," Pudovkin writes. "The camera, as it were, forces itself, ever striving, into the profoundest deeps of life; it strives thither to penetrate, whither the average spectator never reaches as he glances casually around him. In the discovered, deeply embedded detail there lies an element of perception, the creative element that characterizes as art the work of man. . . . In the disappearance of the general, obvious outline and the appearance on the screen of some deeply hidden detail, filmic representation attains the highest point of its power of external expression."

The two primary principles of montage and of actuality have radically affected the status of the actor in Russian films. Montage has obliterated the distinction between the performer and the setting in which he performs. Everything is reduced to camera fodder. "The man photographed," writes Pudovkin, "is only raw material for the future composition of his image in the film arranged in editing." And Eisenstein declares: "I do not believe in stars or the star system. My main characters (in *Old and New*) are a milkmaid, a bull, and a milk separator." This viewpoint is simply a recognition of the fact that film rhythms are created entirely by the director through montage, and that in montage animals, landscapes, even inanimate objects like separators are as much "actors" as are human beings. There is no reason why a director cannot, on occasion, get as striking cinematic effects from an alarm clock as he could from the most capable actor. If montage has lessened the importance of the actor, the doctrine of "actuality" has brought about an even more revolutionary change. This is the almost exclusive use, by Pudovkin and Eisenstein at least, of nonprofessional actors in their movies. The sailors in *Potemkin* are real sailors; the hero of *St. Petersburg* is an accountant in real life; the heroine of *Old and New* is really a milkmaid; and so on. . . .

But the Russians are by no means simple realists of the school of Zola. Their aesthetic combines naturalism and artificiality in the most confusing and interesting way. "The material of the film director," Pudovkin writes, "consists not of real processes happening in real space and real time but of those pieces of celluloid on which these processes have been recorded. Between the natural event and its appearance on the screen there is a marked difference. It is exactly this difference that makes film an art."

—*The Miscellany*, March 1931

Author's note: The above—from which I have excised several pages of quotation and exposition—is followed by eight pages comparing Eisenstein and Pudovkin in considerable detail. They are sound enough still but not so novel as they seemed to me then and so I have omitted them.

SOVIET
CINEMA,
1930–1940,
A HISTORY

WHEN Eisenstein's *Potemkin* was released in 1925, it made an international sensation. Even Hollywood was impressed by its power and originality; Douglas Fairbanks, Cecil B. De Mille, and other American movie celebrities made pilgrimages to the Soviet Union. In more intellectual circles, it was recognized at once that the cinema had at last spoken in its own language. The building up of a rhythmic structure in the cutting room ("montage"), the use of real settings and nonprofessional actors, the use of pictorial symbols corresponding to Wagner's musical "themes," the abandonment of the old literary theatrical unilinear narrative in favor of a many-threaded episodic development ("the compound plot"), the emphasis on the mass rather than the individual protagonist—these radical innovations freed the cinema from its bondage to the theatre and gave it for the first time its own aesthetic. It was soon evident that *Potemkin* was not a happy accident, but rather the first product of a new school of cinema.

Those were the years when one went to the "little" movie houses which showed Russian films as one might visit a cathedral or museum—reverently, expectantly. One joined a congregation of avant-garde illuminati, sharing an exhilarating consciousness of experiencing a new art form—many, including myself, felt it was *the* great modern art. In the darkened auditorium, one came into contact with the twentieth century.

The excitement of those years seems far away today. In the space of a few years, the great directors have been successfully discredited as "formalist" and "bourgeois," their concepts about the abstract use of sound denounced as heretical, and they themselves have publicly recanted and hailed as the highest summit of cinematic art a talkie—*Chapayev*—which might have come out of the Metro-Goldwyn-Mayer studios. The big film jobs have long been assigned to the members of the so-called Stalin School—second-rate talents who have been able to adapt themselves more successfully to the political requirements of the regime. Their films differ from those of Hollywood only in being technically less competent. Every one of the radical innovations which Eisenstein and his peers introduced, and which were the base of their entire theory of cinema, every one has been discarded—officially proscribed, indeed. Montage is hardly a memory, the professional actor has been reinstated, the

192

camera stays timidly inside the studio walls, the photographed play or novel has come back, and the slightest effort at experiment is a state offense. Any attempt to rebel against this degeneration is denounced as "formalism," an affair for the police. As for the mass-as-hero, most socially significant innovation of all, one has but to see a film like the recent *Peter the First* to understand who is The Hero in the Russia of Stalin.

In 1928, Eisenstein and Pudovkin issued a manifesto denouncing the realistic use of sound in the cinema and outlining a new "contrapuntal" approach, based on montage, which promised to revolutionize the sound film as their theories had already re-created the silent cinema. In 1928, Trotsky was exiled, the other makers of the 1917 Revolution were humbled, the Stalinist clique assumed full power, and the first Five Year Plan was launched. In 1930 the Plan was extended to the cinema, the production of sound movies was begun, and the bureaucracy swept all branches of the industry under the control of a single "All Union Soviet Film Trust." The severest critics of Stalinism could hardly have been prepared for the debacle that followed. Eisenstein and Pudovkin in 1928 predicted that the capitalist cinema would use sound "according to the laws of least resistance" and that the commercial sound film would enter into "a terrible . . . epoch of automatic utilization for 'high cultural dramas' and other photographic performances of a theatrical nature."[1] Their prophecy has come true, but for their own cinema as well.

The bureaucracy, however, worries not at all about this sort of degeneration. What they did not plan was a chronic crisis in production, which year after year fell far behind the "norms" of the Five Year Plan. This paralysis reached a climax last year, when just 25 full-length feature pictures were released, as against the 123 called for by the Plan.[2] Stalin followed his usual course: he dismissed as a "wrecker" Shumiatsky, the all-powerful chief of the movie trust, whom he had set up as dictator in 1930—and who had, of course, been faithfully carrying out his directives ever since.

Quantitatively and qualitatively, the Soviet cinema has been in a state of crisis ever since 1930. The roots of this condition go deeper than Boris Shumiatsky, deeper also than pure aesthetics. It is true that no art form can maintain itself at a high level indefinitely, and

193

that the causes of its decay are sometimes largely technical. But this decline has set in not after the possibilities of the new approach had been exhausted, but after only five years of growth and at the moment when the introduction of sound seemed to open up vast new fields for development. It came also as abruptly as an electric light is switched off. The clue to the decline of the Soviet cinema is to be found in politics and not in aesthetics.

Pre-Revolutionary Russian cinema was a poor relation of European industry. French capital financed the State railroads and the Putilov Steel Works, and French capital—the great firms of Gaumont and Pathé—controlled most of the Russian movie industry. The few films that were made in the small, antiquated Russian studios were provincial imitations of the European commercial product. When the Bolsheviks took power, *Kino-Gazetta,* trade paper of the Russian movie industry, issued an editorial warning against "the grave consequences that will result from the government's seizure of the cinema." "The art of the cinema will be destroyed," stated *Kino-Gazetta,* adding, somewhat obscurely, "Barter and speculation will replace pure art."[3] Most of the actors and directors emigrated with their employers. Unlike the theatre, where Stanislavsky and Meyerhold were in full career at the time of the Revolution, the cinema had to be built up on entirely new foundations. Protazanov is the only important Soviet director whose career bridges the Revolution. Before 1917, Eisenstein was a student of engineering, Pudovkin an industrial chemist, Dovzhenko a painter.

The cinema was at first put under the control of the Supreme Economic Council, which treated it neither as art nor propaganda but, with bureaucratic bluntness, as a branch of light industry. In the summer of 1919 the cinema was nationalized and transferred to the jurisdiction of the People's Commissariat of Education. In the years of War Communism, very little could be done, partly because the Allied blockade cut off imports of raw film, partly because the chiefs of the Revolution had more urgent matters on their minds. "At first, upon Lenin's advice, only topical news films were produced."[4] Later on, a few crude agitational features were made for the troops at the front. But once the Civil War was won, the Bol-

194

shevik leaders turned to the cinema for mass education and propaganda. In 1921 Lenin said, "The cinema is for us the most important of all the arts." "Here is an instrument we must secure at all costs," said Trotsky, who wrote a famous series of articles in *Pravda* proposing that for the Czar's great chain of State-owned vodka shops there be substituted a similar chain of State-owned movie theatres, and summoning Soviet artists to use the movies to break the hold of religion over the masses.[5] At the same time, the Rapallo Treaty and the Soviet-German trade agreement linked Russia once more with the rest of Europe, and made it possible to import some badly needed raw film. (Not until 1931 did the Soviet Union begin to manufacture its own film stock.) The New Economic Policy (NEP) caused exhibiting companies to spring up like mushrooms, trading in pre-Revolutionary films whose physical condition was as moth-eaten as their ideology. Most of them were shut down in 1923. The NEP men didn't venture to make any new movies. At first, the State looked abroad. In 1923, a group of foreign capitalists actually secured a joint monopoly (with Goskino, the State film trust) on all movie production. But the concessionaires failed to meet the terms, and the contract was voided. Later, Goskino negotiated with the Stinnes interests in Germany, without striking a bargain. At length, in 1924, in the seventh year of the Revolution, the Bolsheviks began systematically to attack the problem of the movies. Most of the existing producing companies were merged into a State trust called "Sovkino." With the slogan, "The Proletarianization of the Screen!" a drive was organized to form workers' film groups as a nucleus for a wide class-conscious audience. A central Council was set up, to which all scenarios had to be submitted in advance of filming, and which functioned as a censor and ideological guide.[6]

By 1924, the Soviet cinema was at last being integrated with Soviet society. It continued, however, to follow meekly in the wake of the European industry. Most of its feature pictures were Civil War melodramas: *The Red Devils* ("constructed on the model of the detective films of America; the action takes place during the battle of the Soviet cavalry against Makhno"), *In the Service of the People, The Commander of the Ivanov Brigade,* etc.[7] A few more ambitious productions, modeled on the "art" films of Germany,

195

were made under the supervision of Anatole Lunacharsky, Commissar of Education. Lunacharsky was cultivated, Europeanized, and tolerant of radical experiments in art. But he seems to have seen in the movies only a means of giving the workers Russian classics. Under his influence—often he wrote the scenarios himself—the Moscow Art Theatre acted out before the camera such works as Pushkin's *The Station-Master,* Tolstoy's *Polikushka,* and Gogol's *Taras Bulba.* These films were "artistically" set and lighted, but their only interest today is in the acting.

But even while Lunacharsky was laboriously reproducing literary works on the screen, new tendencies were developing. The "FEKS" group ("Factory of the Eccentric Actor") was organized in 1922, and in 1924 shifted its activities from the stage to the cinema.[8] "They base their technique on the grotesque but exact eccentrics of the circus, on the balance of acrobats. They repudiate all realism." (*Soviet Cinema,* Voks, Moscow, 1935) Kozintsev, L. Trauberg and Yutkevitch were members of the FEKS group. They believed that acting, lighting, and sets should be frankly artificial and symbolic. Their work has been called "expressionist melodrama." At the opposite extreme was Dziga Vertov, fanatic of the "documentary" film, whose program was: "Only documentary facts! No illusions! Down with the actor and scenery! Long live the film of actuality!"[9] During the Civil War, Vertov made newsreels with the partisan army of Kozhevnikov. He founded his "Kino-Eye" group in 1919. For a time, he was head of the cinema department of the All-Russian Central Executive Committee.[10] Years before any one else, Vertov proclaimed the theory, and acted on it, that the arranging of the individual shots in the cutting room ("montage") is the basic creative process in cinema. He was also the first to reject the professional actor. But he carried these theories, for whose discovery he must be given historical credit, to such doctrinaire extremes that in practice he tended to produce films that were either flat journalism or highly mannered *tours de force.* It remained for a less fanatical and broader talent, L. Kuleshov, to show the unlimited possibilities of montage. Kuleshov arrived at montage by a curious route: the shortage of film in the War years led him to experiment with making new movies by cutting up and rearranging parts of old ones. While he came to agree with Vertov on the basic importance of montage, Kuleshov opposed the "No illusions!" dogma and advocated the study of American films, especially the "Westerns" and the work of D. W. Griffith.[11] In 1920 he formed a group to work in the movies. Its most talented member was V. I. Pudovkin.

All of these tendencies were synthesized in the work of Sergei M. Eisenstein. From the FEKS group—Kozintsev and Trauberg later became his students—he took stylization and symbols, from Vertov a preference for nonprofessional actors and an aversion to studio sets, from Kuleshov montage. He began his career in the Meyerhold Theatre, which he left in 1921 to direct the Workers Proletcult Theatre, a "constructivist" group to the left of Meyerhold. His last theatrical production was a play by Tretiakov called *Gas Masks*. In his own words, "The cart dropped to pieces and its driver dropped into the cinema. This all happened because one day the director had the marvelous idea of producing this play about a gas factory— in a real gas factory. As we realized later, the real interiors of the factory had nothing to do with pure theatrical fiction. The plastic charm of reality in the factory became so strong that actuality . . . took things into its own hands, and finally had to leave an art where it could not command."[12] Eisenstein joined Kuleshov and Pudovkin in their experiments with the cinema. In 1924 he directed his first film, *The Strike*. And in 1925 he produced *The Armored Cruiser Potemkin*, which immediately made a world-wide sensation. The heroic, golden age of the Soviet cinema had begun.

In the five years 1925–1929 the Soviet Union produced a series of movies which were entirely different in technique. At the beginning of 1925 only fourteen percent of the films being exhibited in the Soviet Union were native products. A year later, fifty percent were Soviet-made.[13] Eisenstein in 1925 released *Potemkin,* in 1927 *October* (released in this country as *Ten Days That Shook the World*), in 1929 *The General Line (Old and New)*. Pudovkin in 1926 released *Mother,* in 1927 *St. Petersburg-Petrograd-Leningrad (The End of St. Petersburg),* in 1928 *The Heir of Ghengis Khan (Storm Over Asia)*. Kozintsev and Trauberg in 1927 released *The Union of the Great Cause,* in 1929 *The New Babylon*. Vertov in 1926 released *One Sixth of the Earth,* in 1928 *The Man with a*

197

Camera. A. Dovzhenko, the Ukrainian director, in 1927 released *Zvenigora*, in 1929 *Arsenal*. Besides the work of these masters, there were many single films of the greatest interest, such as Esther Shub's *The Downfall of the Romanov Dynasty*, Alexander Room's *Three in a Basement* (*Bed and Sofa*) and *The Ghost That Never Returns*, Victor Turin's *Turksib*, Ermlers' *Fragment of an Empire*, Protazanov's *The White Eagle* (*The Lash of the Czar*), and Ilya Trauberg's *The Blue Express* (*China Express*).

For most of this period, the NEP was in force, and the dominance of the Stalin group was still contested by the other Bolshevik leaders. In this temporary relaxation of political and economic pressure, with War Communism over and the Stalin dictatorship still to begin, the cinema had its brief but intense flowering. Even after the Stalin clique liquidated the opposition and seized complete control of the State apparatus in 1928, the effects were not immediately felt in the cinema. The great silent directors were in the middle of some of their most important films and their international prestige was so enormous that even the bureaucracy trod warily— at first. And so, although literature was handed over to RAPP (Russian Association of Proletarian Writers) in 1928, not until the spring of 1930 was any systematic attempt made to bring the cinema to heel.

If 1925–1929 was the Golden Age of the Russian cinema, 1930–1932 was its Iron Age. This was the period of "Military Stalinism," so to speak, when all the nation's resources, human and material, were conscripted to be hurled against the one great objective: fulfillment of the first Five Year Plan. There was forcible collectivization in agriculture and forcible proletarianization in the arts. The bureaucracy requisitioned propaganda to "sell" industrialization and collectivization to the masses. In two years this policy had laid waste the once-flourishing cinema industry as effectively as it laid waste the fertile Ukrainian farmlands.

In the spring of 1930 a *piatiletka*, or plan, was announced for theatre, cinema, sculpture, and painting. Five years of normal development in these arts were to be telescoped into the remaining three and a half years of the Plan. "It sounds crazy," wrote Walter Duranty, "but, as is often the case with the Russians, it is far less crazy than it sounds. What it really means is that there will be a considerable increase in State funds to support art—with the proviso, of course, that said art must follow Socialist lines."[14] According to the *piatiletka,* by the end of 1933 the annual production of feature films was to be increased to 350, which is more than all the studios of Hollywood combined produce in an average year. Mr. Duranty to the contrary, it *was* crazy.

The *piatiletka* for cinema was implemented by a decree bringing all branches of the movie industry—including equipment factories—under the centralized control of a new organization: Soyuzkino ("All-Union Soviet Film Trust"). At the head of Soyuzkino, Stalin placed Boris Shumiatsky, an energetic young bureaucrat. Shumiatsky's authority over mere directors like Eisenstein was, of course, absolute, nor was he backward about asserting it. But his chief concern was to rationalize the industry so that it could fulfill its fantastic production quotas. Even among their fellow bureaucrats, Shumiatsky and his aides were distinguished by the fervor with which they played at "American efficiency." In 1930 the chief of Amkino gave an American audience a glimpse of this dream world of "Fordism": "As in other big industries, the business is conducted by the Film Trust on a commercial basis. . . . The expenditure on negative film for the first negative is determined with a co-efficient 1–7, and on the second negative thirty percent less. . . . The norms for the personnel are fixed as follows: the director should produce in the second year of the Plan, at least one and one-half films, in the last year at least two films."[15] By now, Dovzhenko is eleven films behind his "norm," Pudovkin thirteen, and Eisenstein fifteen.

Within a year after Soyuzkino was formed, the movie industry had slumped both qualitatively and quantitatively. "A few years ago," Shumiatsky admitted in the fall of 1931, "we seemed to create many big pictures. Of late, it looks as though we were creating fewer. In reality, such isn't the case. The taste of our audience has developed very fast. Yesterday's films aren't up to today's cultural standards."[16] But the decline was not an optical illusion, and its cause was not an advance in cultural standards—which had, on the contrary, rapidly deteriorated.

For the past ten years the Soviet movie directors have been struggling to solve two major problems. One is technical—the use

199

of sound. The other is how to treat a new theme: the everyday life of the Soviet Union. These are difficult problems and, to the observer of 1930–32 it could not have been at all clear whether the failure to solve them was due to their inherent difficulties or to an unfavorable change in the social environment. But by now the historical drift is unmistakable. Not only have the Soviet directors failed to progress towards a solution, but in recent years a definite retrogression has been noticeable.

In their 1928 manifesto, Eisenstein and Pudovkin proclaimed that montage remained the basis of cinema form, and that realistic sound effects and the literal reproduction of speech were to be condemned because "the sound would destroy the montage. . . . Only the use of sound as counterpoint against visual cutting opens up new possibilities and will further perfect the art of editing. The first experiments with sound must be directed towards its pronounced non-coincidence with the visual image. Only such an approach will bring the desired effect and in time create a new orchestral counterpoint of sight images with sound images." In a talk at the Sorbonne in 1930 Eisenstein added: "I think the '100%-all-talking film' is silly. . . . But the sound film is something more interesting. The future belongs to it."[17] Dovzhenko stated: "The talking films still present a large number of deficiencies, and one of the most important and most menacing for the growth of true cinematographic culture is language—the spoken word."[18] These masters of the silent film, internationally famous and at the height of their careers, enjoyed such prestige that even the bureaucrats, at the time, accepted their ideas on sound. "Here in Russia," Solsky, head of the Moscow Sovkino, explained, "the talkies have practically no advocates. On the other hand, I believe that sound film not only has a great future but that it signifies a revolution of film and of art altogether."[19]

The years 1930–1932 should have witnessed the laying of the foundations for a great sound cinema along the aesthetic lines so universally agreed on. Instead, a strange lethargy seized on the leading directors. Eisenstein announced several grandiose projects, but finally went off to Paris—where he made a sound-short of little consequence—and thence to Hollywood and Mexico. Kovintsev and Trauberg made *Alone,* a conventional talkie. Vertov made

200

Enthusiasm: The Symphony of the Don Basin, which he described as "the first forward step of the camera eye from the optic capture of the visible world, to the optic-tonal capture of the visible and audible world. It is the ice-breaker-in-chief for the sound-news film."[20] But to the dispassionate spectator, *Enthusiasm* was just a silent film, with realistic "sound effects" and a canned musical accompaniment. Pudovkin was the only one to seriously attempt to use sound experimentally, but his *Life Is Beautiful* was a failure from both the aesthetic and the box-office viewpoint.*

Revolution and class war were the epic themes of the great silent film. The inauguration of the first Five Year Plan in 1928 called for new themes—industrialization and collectivization—which were harder to dramatize. The only completely successful industrialization movie was made in 1928: Victor Turin's *Turksib,* a documentary film on the building of the Turkestan-Siberian Railroad. Turin, who had spent some time in Hollywood, synthesized the technical proficiency of the American movies, the straight documentary subject matter of Vertov, and the dramatic showmanship of Eisenstein. But, although his film was the sensation of the 1929–30 season in Moscow and was widely shown abroad, he never made another movie. When last heard of (1935), he was working "in an administrative capacity."[21] The two most notable movies on collectivization were Eisenstein's *The General Line (Old and New)* and Dovzhenko's *Soil.* Neither was a complete success. A semi-official criticism is worth quoting: *"The General Line* took a romantic approach to collective farming and evaded the social and economic issues by artificially created trickery, such as the marriage of the bull. . . . For all its beauty, *Soil* evaded the main social issue of its theme, and the coming of the new order to the village was sensationalized by a murdering kulak rather than by the essential changes brought about by social consciousness."[21] Despite a certain lack of imagination—the critic seems to forget that

* The mounting pressure on living standards as the Five Year Plan neared its end is perhaps reflected in the successive titles of this film. In December 1930, it was called boldly, *We Live Well;* by February 1931, this had been hedged to, *It Is Necessary To Live Well;* and when the film was finally released in the summer of 1931, Pudovkin would commit himself to nothing more than *Life Is Beautiful.* Unlike consumers' goods, beauty costs nothing.

201

the movies cannot express a politico-social situation *directly,* but only in terms of its dramatic *equivalents*—this criticism has some justice. Brilliant as these films were, for the first time, one senses a slightly dilletantish split between form and content. *Soil* was an idyll—slow, poetic, timeless, ahistorical. The struggle between the kulaks and the collective farmers was a struggle between two elemental, mythical forces rather than a conflict of economic interests. And *The General Line* gave the impression at times that Eisenstein, perhaps a little bored with the theme, was diverting himself with technical fireworks. Such episodes as the bull's wedding and the milk separator sequence—witty and eloquent in themselves—were *tours de force* whose very power disintegrated the film as a whole.

To the Shumiatsky bureaucracy, the decline in aesthetic quality was less alarming than the failure to produce films of any wide popularity. At last, late in 1931, a hitherto unknown director, Nikolai Ekk, produced *Road to Life,* which was to this period as *Potemkin* was to the earlier and *Chapayev* to the succeeding period. (It may or may not be significant that this film was made for Mejrabpomfilm, owned by the Workers International Relief, and the one movie enterprise in the Union which was not controlled by Soyuzkino.) *Road to Life* owed its world-wide popularity to no aesthetic pioneering—it was a one-hundred-percent all-talking film —but to the gusto with which it treated an almost foolproof theme: the rehabilitation of a gang of *bezprezhorni,* or "wild boys." This theme also had the advantage, considerable in this "Iron Age," of being politically neutral. Everybody is in favor of reclaiming wayward boys—even the American Federation of Women's Clubs gave the film its official approval.[22]

The clue to the sudden sterility which struck the Soviet movie industry in 1930 is to be found neither in the problems of sound nor of new themes, but rather in the "forcible proletarianization" of arts and letters which was carried on by a set of ultraleftist political theologians and bureaucrats. The most notorious case was the dictatorship exercised over literature, with Stalin's blessing, by the RAPP, whose slogan was, "Art is a class weapon." For a time, the cinema had its own RAPP, in the Kino-Eye school of Vertov, whose documentary fanaticism seemed well adapted to turning out

202

propaganda for the Five Year Plan. Overnight Kino-Eye was inflated into a quasi-dictatorship over the entire industry. Vertov's contempt for the "bourgeois artificialities" of Eisenstein and Pudovkin was as violent as RAPP's for the "aestheticism" of the more talented Soviet writers. In 1921 the Kino-Eye group issued a manifesto demanding that only 25 percent of movies shown in Russia should be acted films, the rest to be documentaries. This was called "the Lenin Proportion," since Lenin had once expressed himself as especially interested in the newsreel.[23] Now this extraordinary demand was, for a time, actually honored: documentary films rose to seventy percent of the total output. The bad results of this line became evident sooner in the movies than in letters, and it was sooner abandoned. A critic friendly to Stalin has aptly described this Kino-Eye interlude as "another ideological expression of the severity of the first Five Year Plan."[24]

Nor were more direct expressions lacking. A theological censorship was alert to track down the slightest trace of "bourgeois" heresy. Every film was scrutinized closely from the standpoint of "100% class art." A movie called *Sniper,* for example, was criticised in the press because it "naively attempted to reconcile the bourgeois-Christian precepts of pacifism with Lenin's policy of turning imperialist wars into civil wars."[25] The greatest reputations were not spared. A dispatch from the Moscow correspondent of *La Revue de Cinéma* (July 1931) is illuminating: "According to certain rumors published abroad, Pudovkin, after the release of *Life Is Beautiful,* was deprived of his working card and expelled from the Party because of the 'petty-bourgeois idealism' of this film. We are authorized to expose these falsehoods, whose propagandist nature is clear when one realizes that a scenario is submitted, before it is filmed, to three different control bodies, whose function it is to pass on its educational, artistic and ideological value." It is hard to know which is the more shocking—the rumor or the argument against its validity. Eisenstein was also attacked. In a lengthy essay, the RAPPist Ivan Anisimov exposed the bourgeois nature of his work. And the 1932 edition of the Soviet Encyclopedia stated: "In his works, *October* and *The General Line,* Eisenstein despite his great ability, yet gave no deep analysis of the decisive stages of the Socialist Revolution and made a diversion to formal experiments. Eisenstein is a representative of the ideology of the revolutionary section of the petty bourgeois intelligentsia which is following in the path of the proletariat. . . ."[26] Just why a movie director should be expected to give a "deep analysis" of the 1917 Revolution is not clear.

But the *cause célèbre* was the attack on Dovzhenko's *Soil*. *Izvestia* began it with a three-column article denouncing the film as "counter-revolutionary," "defeatist," and "too realistic" in its portrayal of the peasantry. The article was all the more damaging because it was written by Demyan Byedny,* a writer of journalistic doggerel who lived in the Kremlin and was known to be close to Stalin.[29] Other journalists took up the cry, workers' clubs passed the usual "spontaneous" resolutions, and *Soil* was withdrawn for heavy censoring. The "realism" was deleted, as was the "counter-revolutionary scene," in which a collectivized tractor breaks down amid jeering kulaks. There were also cuts with a Will Haysian flavor: the removal of a scene in which a peasant girl tears off her clothes in despair after the death of her lover, and of a shot in which peasants, in an emergency, urinate to fill the radiator of their tractor. Dovzhenko had his defenders, but they operated on the same ultraleftist plane as the censors. One of them praised the last-

---

* The Stalin system can always be depended on to produce, ultimately, a rough sort of poetic justice. When Tairov a year or two ago produced Byedny's adaptation of the Borodin opera, *Bogatyrs,* the Central Art Commission closed down the show. Byedny had made three serious mistakes: (1) he had shown the Kiev robber bands as revolutionary elements, (2) he had represented the bogatyrs as ruling-class tyrants, (3) he had satirized the conversion of Russia to Christianity. This approach would have been good doctrine under the first Five Year Plan, but Byedny had underestimated the rightward swing of the second Plan. The correct line as of 1936 was that (1) the Kiev robbers were robbers and nothing but robbers, (2) the bogatyrs were legendary Russian heroes and hence to be forgiven their class origin, (3) the Christian Church had brought Western civilization to heathen Russia.[27] Byedny was one of the founders of *Pravda;* he had been writing political doggerel for Bolshevik papers since long before the Revolution; his verses had been flung broadcast from airplanes over the White lines during the Civil War, and were said to have caused many desertions; he was the most popular poet in the Union; he had received both the Order of Lenin and the Order of the Red Banner.[28] But all this availed him not—any more than Tairov's international fame in the theatre availed *him*. Both were disgraced. Byedny overnight lost his position of power, and perhaps even his suite in the Kremlin!

mentioned scene as "an interesting attempt to link up man organically with his machines."[30]

As the Five Year Plan approached its final year, the strain became intolerable. The industrial workers were on subsistence wages. Forced collectivization, jammed through under high pressure, was about to produce the terrible famine of 1932–33. The dictatorship of RAPP and the censorship were spreading a vast sterility throughout art and letters. Alarmed, the bureaucracy began to relax the pressure. In December of 1931, an official decree criticized ultraleftist tendencies in the cinema. And on April 23, 1932, the Central Committee decreed (1) the liquidation of RAPP, (2) the formation in its stead of a broad united-front organization to embrace "all writers supporting the platform of Soviet power and willing to take part in the work of Socialist construction," and (3) "a similar reorganization to be carried out in other branches of art."[31] The decree further stated that RAPP's ideology "has already become too narrow and is cramping the scope of serious artistic creativeness" and that RAPP "is in danger of becoming [!] an instrument for cultivating cliqueism . . . and for the alienation of important groups of writers and artists who sympathize with Socialism."[32] This was all very true, and had been equally true ever since Stalin in 1928 placed the knout in RAPP's grasp.

The Stalin line, in politics or in aesthetics, seems to have two unfailing characteristics: (1) when it changes, it does not merely shift direction, it reverses itself; (2) it always goes to extremes. It was not long, therefore, before a new dogma arose, a new revelation, to question which was heresy. This was partly a reaction against the old line: the "fellow-travelers" whom RAPP had rapped, now rapped the RAPPists.* But it was more than that. It

---

* The process had Stalin's blessing, of course. Stalin's classic tactic was to use one tendency to destroy another, and then to behead his executioner. Thus he used the Kino-Eye group to weaken the prestige of the Eisenstein-Pudovkin school and to line up the cinema one-hundred percent behind the Five Year Plan. Then, when the plan was finished and the great directors well bridled, Stalin threw his tools on the scrap heap. Vertov, Shub, Kaufman and the other Kino-Eye adherents have long since been cast into outer darkness as "formalistic."[33]

205

was a whole new aesthetic, the very own creation of the Stalin clique. One story is that it was christened during an interview which a delegation of writers had with Stalin late in 1932. "The writers promised the 'Leader of the Peoples' not to make any formalistic experiments, but to hold on high the flag of realism. 'Say rather, of socialist realism,' said Stalin. . . ."[34] It is difficult to discover precisely what he meant. The official definitions are: "critical assimilation of the art of past centuries" and "a culture that is national in form and socialist in content."[35] The *Literaturny Kritik* is equally vague: "The basis of such realism consists without any doubt in the recognition that art worthy of the name serves life and helps human beings who are constructing life to understand more clearly its ends, its possibilities and its vices."[36] Such definitions mean everything and nothing. But it is beside the point to analyze socialist realism as though it were a serious aesthetic philosophy. Socialist realism is nothing more complicated than Stalinist politics applied to art. In architecture, it means classical colonnades; in literature, the banal historical novels of an Alexis Tolstoy; in music, the "tuneful" marching songs of Dzerzhinsky; in painting, the academic French school of the last century, whose influence, outside the U.S.S.R., is today traceable chiefly in barroom art. In the cinema, it means Hollywood.

Socialist realism has, of course, its dialectical antithesis: "formalism." Roughly speaking, formalism is what is known elsewhere as "experimental," or simply "modern," art. The amount of energy and newsprint Soviet journalists have wasted in medieval debates as to what is and what is not "formalistic," is appalling. Stalin, who leaves theological hairsplitting to his underlings, bluntly cut to the heart of the matter when he admonished Shostakovitch to abandon his discordant modern technique in favor of melodies the toiling masses could whistle on their way to work. In a totalitarian state, art functions as an opiate, not a stimulant—or irritant. Leftism in art and leftism in politics are uncomfortably close relations.

The glorification of the masses, the expression of collective, socialist ideals—these tasks are no longer held to be "necessary" in Soviet art. A recent interview with a cinema executive gives a glimpse of the official "line": " 'How about propaganda?' I asked. 'Conscious agitational propaganda for communism or socialism is

206

out,' came the answer. 'There has been little or none of it in the last two years. It was bad art, for one thing and besides, the Russian people don't need it any more. They are thoroughly sold on this new economic and social order.' "[37]

The great directors throve little better under socialist realism than they had under RAPPism. Political censorship was relaxed in 1933 and 1934, but the new crusade against "formalism" began to gather headway. Dovzhenko's *Ivan* (1932) tried to show the adjustment of an individual worker to the Five Year Plan, but the only memorable sections are those showing the Dneiper River and the construction of the great dam—passages of poetical description, with only an incidental bearing on the theme. Kozintsev and Trauberg made *The Youth of Maxim* (1934), skillful enough and even moving, but a conventional talkie, with musical accompaniment. Eisenstein produced nothing at all. Pudovkin again attempted an experimental use of sound, but his *Deserter* (1933), while more successful than *Life Is Beautiful,* was on the whole a failure. It took him two years to finish it. In the discreet words of Paul Rotha: "Political events developed more rapidly than the film, and to save it from being out of date in its ideology [!], the scenario was changed during editing and whole sequences were suppressed. Technically, Pudovkin became absorbed in his complex montage methods and made several experiments with sound, but the social content of his theme escaped him."[38] In plainer language, Pudovkin had completed filming *Deserter* before the invention of socialist realism, and tried to patch it up in the cutting room to conform to the new dogma. The result was the usual one: he merely injured the film aesthetically, without making it acceptable politically. His theme remained a mass-revolutionary one, and he was unable to resist experiments with sound. Hence he was guilty, after April 23, 1932, of two heresies: "Leftism" and "Formalism." *Deserter* had to be taken off the screens of Moscow's two biggest movie theatres after eight days playing to half-filled houses. The press criticized it for dealing too much with politics![39]

Early in 1933 Ralph Bond called attention to the rise of a new school of Soviet cinema, "The Stalin School." "Stalin," he explained somewhat vaguely, "insisted on the creation of real people in Soviet art, and the directors have successfully followed this advice."[40] As the better-known directors failed to adjust themselves to the demands of the bureaucracy, the members of the Stalin School began to push them aside.

The founders of the Stalin School were F. M. Ermler and S. Yutkevitch. Both have long and undistinguished careers in the cinema. Yutkevitch was one of the founders of FEKS. Throughout the twenties he made routine documentary and educational films. In 1931 he produced an early talkie, *The Golden Mountains,* a tedious affair with long stretches of slow dialogue, whose chief virtue was its imitation of Pudovkin. But since it had an individual theme, it was, correctly enough, hailed by Professor Yesuitov, the Kremlin's voice on cinema aesthetics, as "a picture of great ideological significance." The *Soviet Culture Bulletin* added: "Its greatness lies in its profound and earnest social thematics."[41] Ermler made a number of obscure films in the twenties. His one success was *Fragment of an Empire,* significant because it centers about an individual, and because it casts a professional actor—Nikitin—in the leading role.

In 1932 Ermler and Yutkevitch collaborated on *Counterplan.* This was the showpiece of the celebration that fall of the fifteenth anniversary of the Revolution, as *October* had been the feature of the tenth and *Lenin in October* was to be the showpiece of the twentieth anniversary festival. (The progressive deterioration of the Soviet cinema may be roughly gauged by comparing these three films.) *Counterplan* took its text from one of Stalin's gnomic sayings, "The realization of our Plan depends on us, on living men."[42] The powers on high spared no effort or expense with the film: it was to show the world, and particularly the other Soviet directors, just what Stalin wanted in the cinema. Ermler studied at the Communist Academy for two years to prepare himself for his great task. Shostakovitch wrote the musical score. The theme was the foiling of an attempt at sabotage in a steel plant, obviously of the utmost political significance. But leaving aside politics, *Counterplan* was dull, a stage play acted out before the camera by professional "character actors." Its quality is suggested in this description from the *Soviet Culture Bulletin* (No. 10, 1932): "It freely combines elements of healthy romance with joyous comedy, dramatic intensity with lyric warmth . . . unimpeachable pictures of Leningrad's white nights. . . . Special mention should be made of the work of the painter-architect Dubrovsky-Eshke, who built within the studio a giant department of a metal factory with all of its machines and lathes." Eisenstein deserts the theatre for the cinema the better to capture the reality of a factory; Ermler-Yutkevitch bring the cinema back to the theatre by building a stage factory inside the studio. *"Counterplan,"* writes Professor Yesuitov, "was the first victory of socialist realism in the Soviet cinema."[43]

Despite the best efforts of the Stalin School, the cinema refused to thrive. Early in 1931 Vladimir A. Sutyrin, the youthful production chief of Soyuzkino, delivered a report to a conference of art workers. The cinema, he said, was in a "critical" situation; quantity and quality were both low. He suggested the remedies one might expect: bigger investments, more studios, rationalization, and "the formation of new cadres." The cinema was faced with "mounting difficulties," "its reputation abroad is at stake," he said, concluding with an urgent appeal for the "mobilization of all the resources and all the energies of the nation" to save the industry from collapse.[44] Shumiatsky was more sanguine. In fact, the worse the situation became, the bigger he talked. In the summer of 1931, when the cinema was almost at a standstill between the censorship, the bureaucracy, and the problems of sound, Shumiatsky announced that Soyuzkino planned to make five hundred full-length films in 1932, eighty of them in sound and twenty in color.[45] Two months later he was talking even more wildly: "By the end of 1932, we shall need 75,000 projection-machine operators. . . . We have today only three theatres in the whole Soviet Union equipped to show sound pictures. By the end of this year we shall have 100. Next year there will be 5,000"[46] But by the end of 1932 only 25,000 operators were needed, and there were 36 and not 5,000 sound theatres.[47] Lenin had a word for it: *komchvanstvo*—"Communist swagger."

Early in 1933, as the cinema continued to lag far behind its "norms," Shumiatsky announced a "complete reorganization" of Soyuzkino, which was put under the "immediate direction" of the Council of People's Commissars. But in spite of everything, when

209

the All-Union Conference for the 1934 thematic plan of the cinema met in the fall of 1933, Shumiatsky had to admit that only fifteen feature films were scheduled for release in 1934, and that during the last five years "at least half the films were bad. He also complained about the scarcity of directorial talent, putting the number of "first-rate directors" at fifty or sixty, surely a generous estimate. Yet when the Conference closed, neither Eisenstein nor Pudovkin had been assigned a theme. "I am now working on the script for *Moscow*," said Eisenstein. "I want very much to produce this during 1934, but the question does not depend solely on me." And when Pudovkin was asked what he was going to do in 1934, he answered, "As yet I don't know, but I'm beginning work with Vladimir Kirshon on *Aviation*." (Nothing came of either of these projects.) But Alexandrov, Eisenstein's assistant, who had found he could make slapstick comedies which pleased the bureaucracy if not the aesthetes, was in no doubt as to *his* plans. "I'm finishing *Jazz Comedy*," he replied briskly. "I shall deliver it in March. After that, I am writing with Kataev a comedy about a collective farm *Odarka* or *Four Bridegrooms*."[48]

By 1934 the sterility of the cinema was beginning to cause alarm even in official circles. The movie critic of the *Moscow News* wrote that the past year and a half "has been, not to mince words, perhaps the most arid period in the history of the Soviet film."[49] *Izvestia* surveyed the recent films and found them dull, inartistic, and overburdened with propaganda.[50] Dinamov, editor of *International Literature* and most official of official critics, wrote in a review of progress on the "art front": "Unfortunately, the cinema is greatly lagging behind the general program of Soviet art."[51]

But help was on the way. At the end of 1934, a film was released which was excellent alike as propaganda and entertainment: the fast-moving adventure story of Chapayev, the Red Commander. It had all the virtues—and no virtues beyond them—of the Hollywood "Western," with the White Guards cast as the cattle rustlers and the Red Partisans as the sheriff's posse. It was a hit at once. "Exceptionally interesting . . . a remarkable film," pronounced Marshal Voroshilov. "A new victory for Soviet art!" exclaimed Marshal Budyonny. The critics hastened to agree with these authorities, and, more important, so did the masses. *Chapayev* scored the greatest box-office success the Soviet Union has ever known, eclipsing even *Potemkin*. There was nothing accidental about this success. The bureaucracy lavished time and money on this supreme effort. The Vassilievs spent two and a half years on *Chapayev*— more than twice as long as Eisenstein had spent on *Potemkin* and *October* combined. The effort seems to have exhausted both the Vassilievs and the bureaucracy.

Ivor Montagu sees in *Chapayev* a sign of "an expanding delight in individualism and personalization in all art fields of the Soviet Union corresponding to the flowering of the individuality consequent on the raising of the level of living accompanying the second Five Year Plan. . . . No picture so simple, so innocent of a desire to prove points, or even of a feeling that they needed proving . . . could possibly have been produced anywhere but in a society that had long lost its doubts about itself."[52] "The Vassilievs," wrote Professor Yesuitov, "made a new synthesis of the creative aspirations of the Soviet cinematographic masters. This . . . has laid the foundation for a new epoch in the Soviet Cinema."[53]

On January 11, 1935, the Central Executive Committee of the U.S.S.R. announced a long list of awards to celebrate the fifteenth anniversary of the Soviet cinema. The Order of Lenin, the highest, went to eleven people, including Shumiatsky, Pudovkin, Dovzhenko, Kozintsev, L. Trauberg, Ermler, and the Vassilievs. The Order of the Red Star, two degrees lower, was given to Vertov. Eisenstein had to content himself with the title of "Honored Art Worker." It was clear which way the tide was setting.

In March, 1935, a "Film Festival" was held in Moscow. Its chief purpose was to stimulate sales of Soviet films abroad, which had fallen off since the advent of socialist realism. "Most of the festival visitors from abroad," reported the *New York Times,* "were business emissaries." Hollywood sent three current masterpieces: *Gentlemen Are Born, Our Daily Bread,* and *Cleopatra.* These were duly awarded various degrees of honorable mention by a jury composed of Eisenstein, Pudovkin, Dovzhenko and—Shumiatsky. After the festival—or wake—was over, Ermler and Shumiatsky led a delegation of film officials to Hollywood, where they spent six weeks learning how to make movies "in the American style."[54]

211

The festival itself was of slight importance compared to the closed conference which preceded it. Attended by the leading Soviet directors, cameramen, actors, scenarists, and film executives, it was held against a background of five years of sterility and failure. Morale was low, nerves were frayed, tempers short. Since it was out of the question to discuss frankly the political root of the trouble, scapegoats had to be found. As is the custom in the Russia of Stalin, the victims were made the whipping-boys. As Soviet engineers are punished when the bureaucracy's high-pressure methods and impossible production quotas cause breakdowns in industry, so Eisenstein and Pudovkin were publicly humiliated because their work had been sabotaged by the bureaucracy and its policies. The current success of *Chapayev* gave all the sharper edge to the attack.

A sympathetic observer gives us some interesting glimpses of this conference. Writing in *Cinema Quarterly* (Spring and Summer numbers, 1935), Marie Seton reported: "For four years there has been a crisis among the cinema artists. . . . They failed time and again to find and reveal the spirit of the time before that spirit had evolved into something different. [That is, they were unable to keep up with the rapid shifts in the Party line.] . . . For three days criticism raged fast and furious. . . . There was a deal of backbiting, particularly on the part of the second generation of directors, who often showed themselves intolerant, arrogant, and ungrateful toward the pioneers."

"I don't think that the Soviet cinema is only made up of heroes like Eisenstein and Dovzhenko," said Yutkevitch, declaring he spoke "for the great army of cinema workers." He also said that he liked American films "because they appeal to a great public, for, in the best meaning of the word, the cinema is a popular art." In conclusion, he made a "friendly criticism" of Eisenstein, "spoken as a practical man," for theorizing too much and producing too little. (As a practical man Yutkevitch should have realized that it was possible for Eisenstein to theorize about socialist realism but not to create under it.) Turning to Eisenstein, he said, "You are richer than all of us, but you are sitting on your own gold." Seton notes: "Eisenstein merely smiled."

Trauberg also called on his old master to stop theorizing and get down to work. He criticized *October* for the "stupid poetry" of its

212

palaces and statues. The truth is that Trauberg felt none too secure himself against the serious charge of "formalism." Although he and Kozintsev had renounced the stylized technique of *The New Babylon* in favor of socialist realism—as in the Maxim films untainted by formalism, or aesthetic interest—he considered it necessary to make a specific declaration: "He felt they had rid themselves of formalism, and thought the method of setting the individual against the social background of the period quite satisfactory."

The attack on the older generation went to such lengths as to alarm even the stage managers of the conference. At that time, the Kremlin's liaison officer in the cinema was Sergei Dinamov, then the editor of *International Literature*. Dinamov is—or rather was, since he has been deposed from his editorship and is now reported to be in jail—an energetic, humorless, zealous young literary functionary who had made his reputation as editor of the RAPP organ, *At Your Post*. It was his job to see that Good triumphed over Evil, but also that the mechanics of the victory were not too crudely exposed. He therefore felt it necessary to rebuke the overzealous partisans of socialist realism and to dole out a certain amount of diplomatic praise to the older generation—making it clear, of course, that they had much to learn, as well as unlearn. He also had to give "ideological directives" to the assembled cinema workers.

His main points may be summarized:

(1) Beauty is to be reinstated. (But it must be "true" and not "false" beauty.)

(2) The cinema must be "optimistic." (But beware of "an illusory optimism that rocks people to sleep."

(3) "One of the chief elements in Soviet film style is its true reflection of life."

(4) There must be more emotion. ("Without love and hatred there can be no art. . . . One cannot separate thought from passion. . . . What is wrong with Eisenstein's theory is that he separates thought from feeling.")

(5) There must be more heroes. ("I once gave an address at the Academy of Aviation. One of the commandants asked me a question: 'When will our artists show us the best people of the country?' I answered: 'When the artists themselves are the best people of the country.' ")

213

(6) The individual must replace the mass as hero. ("Learn from Shakespeare, in whose works the epoch becomes a man, the events of an epoch the acts of a man.")

(7) There must be more Passion. ("One must not be afraid of being passionate, for, after all, true Party art is truly passionate art.")

(8) The film must be built around the professional actor. ("The film without a hero was only an experiment. We need actors with great passions. Without actors we can do nothing. We cannot base our cinema on typage.")*

(9) "The important thing now is to think about the style of the Soviet cinema."[55]

Whatever the masters may have thought, they voiced complete agreement. At this conference, the same phenomenon could be observed which later was to mystify the world in the Moscow trials. The victims compete with the prosecutor in denouncing themselves, in repudiating the ideas and actions of their entire careers, and in paying homage to the very forces which are destroying them. The litany is familiar:

Dinamov: "The theory of a film without a plot is a very dangerous thing."

Eisenstein: "The intellectual cinema . . . is too vulgar to consider. *The General Line* was an intellectual film."

Dinamov: "The film without a hero was only an experiment."

Pudovkin: "In *Chapayev* we see how a real class character is made."

Dovzhenko: "*Chapayev* is tied up with the future of the cinema."

Eisenstein: "*Chapayev* is the answer to the very deep solving of Party problems in art."

Dinamov: "The voice of the hero must be the voice of the epoch, and the voice of the epoch must be the voice of the hero."[56]

The 1935 conference shattered the prestige, and the morale, of the three great masters of Soviet cinema. At the conference, Eisenstein announced that he was beginning work on a new film, *Bezhim*

* 'Typage' means the use of nonprofessional actors chosen for their symbolic value as mass types, as the sailors in *Potemkin,* the milkmaid heroine of *The General Line.*

214

Meadow, which was to be his answer to the "friendly critics" who urged him to implement theory with action. Two years later, the Central Administration of the cinema industry halted work on the film and, according to some reports, physically destroyed the almost completed negative.[57] The film was suppressed for the usual reasons: formalism and political leftism. By the end of 1937, however, Sumiatsky, who had led the attack on *Bezhim Meadow,* was in disgrace. It was announced that Eisenstein "has won a chance to come back" and that he was going to make a historical movie about the struggle between the Novgorod warriors and the German Baltic knights in the thirteenth century.[58] This time the Kremlin is taking no chances. To preserve him from the temptations of formalism, Eisenstein is being "assisted" by the reliable D. Vassiliev (who also assisted in making the politically and aesthetically impeccable *Lenin in October*) and has been given for actors such stars as Okhlopov and Cherkassov. And to make political "errors" impossible, he has been assigned a subject on which the views of the Kremlin are well known. This victory of the Novgorod nobles, led by Prince Alexander Nevsky, over their Teutonic competitors has been certified in recent history textbooks as the first victory of Democracy over Fascism. The official announcement of the film describes it as "dealing with the struggles of the Russian *people* [italics mine] against the German knights."[59] "The Kremlin," comments the *New York Herald Tribune,* "has decided that patriotism, far from being a bourgeois monopoly, has its function even in the workers' fatherland. *Alexander Nevsky* is being filmed to make the workers conscious of what they have to defend."[60] I suspect this is not its only function. The *Tribune* quotes an early chronicler on Nevsky's death: "The sun of the Russian land has set, my children. . . . Grant, merciful Lord, that he may see thy face again in the age to come, for he has labored for Novgorod and for the whole Russian land." I venture to predict that Eisenstein's new film will provide another cinematic avatar for Stalin. First it was Peter the Great, now it is Alexander Nevsky. When may we expect a re-take of *Czar Ivan the Terrible?**

* Author's footnote, 1968: *Nevsky* was, in fact, an avatar for Stalin; and Eisenstein did a "re-take" of *Ivan,* though with less successful results for himself. See later for details.

Pudovkin has been working for several years on *The Happiest,* a movie about the rivalry of two Soviet aviators in setting a round-the-world speed record. "We met Pudovkin in a cutting room in the Mosfilm studios, where he was editing a sequence of his second sound film, *The Happiest,*" a British group reports. "He was examining a strip of film which he had just had frame-cut for a speed effect. We chided him on indulging in the old tricks, and he apologized, saying that there was very little of this sort of thing in the new film, which has turned out to be a study of character revealed in dialogue and simple camera work—'no good for foreign audiences.' "[61]

Finally, there is Dovzhenko, who since 1930 has made four movies as against one apiece for Eisenstein and Pudovkin. Whether it is because his approach is emotional, instinctive, comparatively little guided by conscious theory, or whether it is because his films, unlike those of the cosmopolitan, internationally-minded Eisenstein and Pudovkin, are deeply rooted in the soil of his native Ukraine*— whatever the explanation, there is no question but that Dovzhenko has been able to adapt better than either of his colleagues. Since 1935 he has completed one film: *Aerograd* (American title: *Frontier*). This has some very beautiful landscapes—he borrowed Eisenstein's cameraman, Tisse—and some experimental use of sound, or rather of silence. But as a whole it is destroyed by the contradiction between the crudity of its theme—a melodramatic conspiracy between Japanese agents and religious fanatics to sabotage the Soviet Far Eastern government—and the epic grandeur with which this infantile plot is presented. There are several extremely fine effects, as the ski journey across the Siberian snow wastes, but the film as a whole seems mannered, overstrained, fragmentary. As in *Soil* and *Ivan,* Dovzhenko escapes from his political theme—which, perhaps, did not interest him very much—into pictorial lyricism. The leitmotif on the film is the question, repeated several times by the main character: "Is there anywhere in the world such beauty?"

* His first film, *Zvenigora,* was so impregnated with Ukrainian, folklore as to be at times unintelligible to non-Ukrainians. *Arsenal, Soil,* and his current film, *Schorss,* are all definitely at times mystically Ukrainian. Thus his work conforms to Stalin's well-known formula: "national in form, socialist in content."

216

Eisenstein is said to have been disappointed by *Aerograd,* and to have remarked: "The building up of the film on the pretext of the danger to the Far East represented by the religious community is rather ridiculous."[62]

When Stalin in 1934 gave Dovzhenko the Order of Lenin, he "suggested" to him that he make a film about Schorss, "the Chapayev of the Ukraine." "Dovzhenko was very keen about the idea and discussed it with the Ukrainian authorities," who were also "very keen" about it. Soyuzkino built him a special studio after his own designs, and thousands of Red Army troops were put at his disposal.[63] *Schorss* was scheduled for release last fall, but has been delayed. "One had the impression," reported the English technicians who talked to him last year, "that Dovzhenko fully realized the basic difficulty of the task which the Soviet state has set its artists in requiring them to deviate neither to the right nor to the left in following the path toward the ideals of the State."[64]

Three months before the 1935 cinema conference, on December 1, 1934, a young Communist named Nikolaiev assassinated Sergei Kirov, one of Stalin's chief lieutenants. "Nikolaiev's shot," we read in *The Letter of an Old Bolshevik,* "proved to be fatal not only to Kirov but also to the country as a whole and to the Communist Party."[65] In the three and a half years since Kirov's assassination, the Stalin regime has carried its Thermidorean reaction to almost incredible extremes. The recent laws making divorce and abortion difficult for the common people, the establishing of the death penalty for theft of State property, the restoration of uniforms for schoolboys and of Czarist military discipline and rankings in the army, the speed-up and enormous wage differentials of Stakhanovism, the annihilation, political or physical, of almost all the Old Bolshevik leaders—such symptoms of Thermidor have appeared throughout Soviet society.

In the cultural field, the screws were first applied with vigor on January 28, 1936, when *Pravda* launched its celebrated attack on the composer Shostakovitch. Since the liquidation of RAPP in 1932, Soviet arts and letters had enjoyed a period of comparative calm, freedom, and tolerance—"a general critical amnesty," in the words of Joshua Kunitz.[66] Webster defines "amnesty" as "the act of

217

a sovereign power, granting oblivion, or a general pardon, for a past offense"—and, indeed, oblivion is the most welcome gift the bureaucracy could make to any Soviet artist.

Pravda abused Shostakovitch's music as "un-Soviet, unwholesome, cheap, eccentric, tuneless, and leftist" and advised him to emulate Glinka and write tunes that could be whistled.[67] The attack was entirely unexpected—Shostakovitch for several years had been considered, inside as well as outside the Soviet Union, its greatest living composer—and evidently planned quite deliberately as the opening gun in a new offensive along the entire artistic front. At once a hurricane onslaught on leftism and formalism burst out in the press. *Pravda* denounced modern architecture as "monstrous trick architecture."[68] *Komsomolskaya Pravda* described Joyce's *Ulysses,* then running serially in another Soviet magazine, as "written in English that can hardly be understood by Englishmen. . . . Its style reminds one of the delirious babblings of a mad philosopher who has mixed all the known languages into one monstrous mess."[69]

Since 1936, in every cultural field, the socialist-realist line has been enforced more ruthlessly than the RAPP line ever was. The victims have included Tairov and Meyerhold in the theatre, even such harmless figures as Natalie Satz, creator and director of the well-known Moscow Children's Theatre. Pashukanis, for many years the all-powerful arbiter of Soviet legal theory, has been dethroned as "a counter-revolutionary and class enemy."* Pokrov-

---

* Pashukanis was disgraced because he held that law is a product of the bourgeois state and that, consequently, as the state withers away under socialism, so will its legal structure. But the 1936 constitution, which declared in its first article that socialism had been achieved, in later articles set forth an elaborate code of laws which Pashukanis himself had drawn up. Thus either Stalin or Pashukanis was at fault as a theoretician. It turned out that it was the latter. The dangerous political tendency of Pashukanis' theory became clear when he predicted that at the end of the second five year plan, in 1937, the withering away of the state would reach "a decisive stage." But when 1937 arrived, the state was obviously blooming more lustily than ever. Stalin had scored another theoretical victory over Pashukanis, who had failed to heed the Beloved Leader's words at the Sixteenth Party Congress: "Any dialectical thinker must understand that to eventually wither away, the state must first grow stronger." (See reference 68.)

218

sky, whose history of Russia Lenin recommended as a textbook, who in 1930 was described by the *Soviet Encyclopedia* as "the greatest Marxist historian not only in the USSR but also in the world," whose funeral in 1932 was attended by Stalin—Pokrovsky has now been posthumously purged, his work stamped "heresy," and his disciples described by *Pravda* as "Japanese-German-Trotskyist agents of Rightist dissenters." His chief sins seem to be his "ultra"-materialistic interpretation of history and his low estimate of such great national leaders as Peter the Great. In literature, by its nature the most dangerous sector of all, the toll has reached massacre proportions: the poets Byedny and Pasternak, the dramatists Kirshon and Afinogeniev, the novelist Pilnyak, and dozens of lesser writers have been denounced for formalism and sometimes even arrested for the corresponding political heresy, Trotskyism.[70] In the cinema, Shumiatsky called together the directors and scenario writers, warned them against formalism—"an abnormal outgrowth of form in a work of art to the detriment of its content"—scrapped "a great number" of completed films and had those in progress closely inspected for traces of the dread pox. As a result, in 1936 only 28 percent as many films were produced as were called for in the plan.[71]

In the last three years the Stalin School has perfected its monopoly on Soviet film production. All the major pictures, except for *Aerograd,* have come out of its workshop. These films cannot be classified on any aesthetic basis because all tendencies, from the expressionist melodrama of FEKS to Eisenstein's "Intellectual Cinema," have been swallowed up in the morass of socialist realism. As Eisenstein declared at the 1935 conference: "At the present stage, we craftsmen of the cinema have no difference of principles, no disputes about a whole series of program postulates such as we had in the past. There are, of course, individual shades of opinion within the comprehensive conception of the single style: socialist realism."[72]

Recent Soviet films, however, *can* be analyzed as to subject matter. There seem to be three major categories.

First, there are those on the classic Civil War or revolutionary themes. Almost all the more successful films are in this class:

219

Chapayev, The Last Night, Baltic Deputy, We Are from Kronstadt,
etc. These owe their relative superiority partly to having a theme
peculiarly well adapted to cinematic treatment, and partly to the
fact that they are living off the crumbs of the great silent-film
tradition.

Next, there are those films made direct to the order of the
Kremlin. In contrast to the generalized propaganda of the first type,
these are directed toward some limited political end of immediate
importance for the regime. They are likely to be heavy, lifeless, and
timid; their creators are paralyzed by the awareness of the immense
political significance of their work—and the penalties for failure.
The nature of the sermon they preach—at best reactionary, as in
Peter I, and often downright falsification, as in *Lenin in October*—
also has a corrupting effect on them as works of art.

Finally, there is the most significant category of all, the one
which has grown enormously in the last few years: films modeled
frankly on Hollywood and quite deliberately innocent of political
content. As the economic interests of the bureaucracy diverge more
and more from those of the masses, it becomes increasingly necessary to change the cinema from a stimulant into an opiate, from an
agitational-propagandist medium into an establishment for the manufacture of vicarious pleasures for the masses. The cinema of
escape has become an administrative necessity in Russia. The adventure film, defunct since the pre-1925 period, was revived in the
spring of 1935 with the release of Schneiderov's *Golden Lake,* and
there is by now even a Soviet Rin Tin Tin.[73] The screening of
literary classics has greatly increased in recent years. Stories by
Maupassant, Gogol, Pushkin, Ostrovsky, Dostoevsky and others
have been made into tediously theatrical movies. Last year it was reported that Soyuztorgkino might buy the screen rights to *Jane Eyre,
The Mill on the Floss, Pride and Prejudice,* and *Pickwick Papers.*[74]

But the great opiate is comedy. I must admit I have never found
Soviet movie comedies, even before 1930, especially comic. I
realize that authority is against me. "The achievements of the Soviet
cinema in the field of comedy," writes Shumiatsky, "are dealing a
blow of equal force both to the old banality of the film comedy and
to the ludicrous pedantry which would like to deprive the Soviet
cinema of the right to reflect our joys, our buoyancy, the robust
youth of the land of the Soviets."[75]

220

But Stalin has said, "Life is gayer, comrades!" And now that socialism has been achieved in Russia (see Article I of the Constitution), life *must* be gayer. The vogue of comedy dates from the beginning of the second five-year plan. In the fall of 1934, the State schools for training movie actors began to require of entrants a knowledge of singing and dancing. At the end of the year, the first all-slapstick comedy was released. That year G. V. Alexandrov, Eisenstein's collaborator on *Potemkin, October,* and *The General Line,* released his first musical comedy, *Jolly Fellows.* "The story is of a young shepherd who has unusual musical talent. He finds his way to the Big City and under the favorable conditions of Soviet life his talents come to fruition, and he develops into a great and popular artist [actually, a jazz band leader]. . . . It has ingenious stunts, lavish scenes, and so many laughs that at one time the producing unit seriously considered the advisability of cutting down on the humor."[76] Those who have seen *Jolly Fellows* agree it was as painful as it sounds from this description, but, with a certain amount of plugging from the Kremlin, it was a popular success. Alexandrov has become the leading exponent of musical comedy in the Hollywood manner. He was recently entrusted with the important task of making a documentary to illustrate Stalin's report to the Eighth Congress of the Soviets. It is not stated whether his experience in making comedies got him the job.

The Stalin School of comedy reached a new low in 1937 when it produced the first Soviet football comedy, Timoshenko's *The Goalkeeper of the Republic:* "a rollicking if by no means first-rate production, strongly reminiscent of American college comedies. . . . It is interesting for its carefree comedy, love emphasis, rapid tempo throughout, and exciting situations verging more than once on the highly improbable. . . . One of the most exciting moments of the picture occurs when the players arrive late at the stadium in a plane, bail out one after another, and descend to the field under fluttering white parachutes."[77] I still think Soviet comedies are terrible.

Four recent (1935–1938) films may fairly be taken as representative. I have chosen *Paris Commune* to represent the historical-revolutionary type largely because it offers an interesting comparison with a silent movie on the same subject. In the category of films

221

with an immediate political tendency, I have selected *Peter I* and *Lenin in October,* and in the category of apolitical escapist films, *The Rich Bride.* These three films have been officially recognized with awards and orders. The new chief of the cinema industry, Semyon Dukelsky, recently wrote of them: "These great victories were won as a result of constant attention to the Soviet cinema . . . on the part of the Party, the government and, personally, of Comrade Stalin."[78]

Paris Commune (Director: Gregory Roshal; Russian title: *People of the Eleventh Legion*). This picture was released on March 18, 1937, to celebrate the anniversary of the 1871 Commune. On the same date in 1929, Kozintsev and Trauberg released a film on the same theme: *The New Babylon.* These are both studio films, contriving their effects methodically out of plaster and klieg lights and highly trained actors, as against Eisenstein's method, which is to lie in wait for reality, surprising the moment when the face of an unknown in the crowd gives him what he wants, seizing the one detail and camera angle out of many which forces a ship, a statue, a palace to yield up its precise meaning for that instant of film. But there is, just the same, a difference. Kozintsev-Trauberg—I am speaking of the creators of *New Babylon,* not the manufacturers of the Maxim films—accept the responsibility imposed by their greater control over their material and press on to a new frontier which can be reached only by calculated, controlled artificiality. They carry the studio approach so far as to make it radical, experimental, positive—in short, an aesthetic *principle* from which effects can be obtained that can be had no other way. Roshal's exploitation of the studio is as opportunistic as theirs is principled. If he works with studio sets and professional actors, it is for the same reason Hollywood does: because it is easier. His use of the studio is banal, purely utilitarian, simply a crutch to help him to realism. *New Babylon* is stylized, *Paris Commune* merely conventional.

Politically, there is also a significant contrast. *New Babylon* is a revolutionary film. Its camera shuttles between the squalid misery of the masses and the vulgar luxury of their exploiters, weaving the two into a fabric of class conflict. *Paris Commune* is a Popular Front film. It contains no anticapitalist propaganda, little sense of

222

the existence of opposed classes. The bourgeoisie has dwindled to a pair of skulking, villainous factory owners, while the proletariat has been inflated into "The People," as represented by a few brave, noble and generous character actors and a mob of supers. These strictly nonpolitical heroes are fighting for nothing more specific than "democracy" and "a better life." One has the impression of the entire population of Paris, except for a few sneaking entrepreneurs, marching out to fight the protofascist troops of Thiers. *New Babylon* emphasized the class struggle inside Paris: the massacre of the Communards at the end is brutally portrayed. But the Second Republic which was founded on the corpses of the Communards is today the Popular Front ally of the Soviet Union. Roshal has therefore wisely limited himself to the parliamentary discussions among the Communards—which show the awful consequences of lack of "unity"—and the military operations against the Versailles troops. His film ends just before the final massacre.

The most striking common quality of recent Soviet films is a weakness, if not an absence, of structure. One episode follows another in chronological order, and that is about all. I suggest that this is one result of the socialist-realist dogma. As in all arts, form in cinema means the integration of the parts into a whole by means of such devices as rhythm, emphasis, balance, significant repetition, and variation. All of these are, of course, entirely artificial and even abstract methods, which inevitably involve a certain degree of stylization. But from stylization to "formalism" is only a step, and who can blame the contemporary Soviet director for not choosing to tread the edge of precipices? The effect of this taboo on formal devices is that Soviet films have become excessively slow, diffuse, and episodic. *Paris Commune* has a great deal of action but very little movement. A battle is followed by a debate, which gives way to a love scene, and then another battle, and so on. These episodes are not carried through to any fruition even in themselves: there is simply a dilettantish exploitation of their most obvious surface values, and then—cut to the next scene!

The Rich Bride (Director: Ivan Piriov; American title: *The Country Bride*). This film does for life on a collective farm what *Hit the Deck* did for life in the U.S. Navy. There is a comic old grandfather, gruff but with a Charles Winninger twinkle in his eye. There is a love duet, with boy and girl singing into each other's faces as they sit on a papier mâché tree trunk beside a studio brook, with stuffed birds, artificial daisies, and a property moon in the background. There is a leading comic who wears a tiny mustache and throws himself about with the painful verve of the pre-Chaplin school of comedy. There is a blonde heroine with mascara eyelashes, and a curly-haired leading man with very white teeth. And there is the conventional musical comedy chorus: a bevy of feminine harvest workers who run joyously up and down hill, flourishing scythes and rakes, shrieking with laughter. Everybody in the film, by the way, is excessively gay; there is continual chuckling, giggling, grinning, and laughing. The musical score is by Dunayevsky, said to be the most popular composer in the Union. He contributes several insipid love songs and "The March of the Tractor Men," in the old-fashioned oompa-Sousa manner. This old-fashioned quality is the most noticeable point about the film. It is the sort of thing Hollywood was doing in the early twenties.

The "trailer" advertising *The Rich Bride* gave a clinically accurate summary:

"The boy was a tractor driver—

"The girl was a farm worker—

"The place was a large collective farm—

"See what happened when a comedy of errors came between them!"

The Rich Bride has been awarded the Order of Lenin as "the best film on life in the Soviet Union today."[79]

Peter the First (Director: Vladimir Petrov; associate: Alexis Tolstoy). It is no secret that Stalin has come to think of himself as a modern Peter the Great, Westernizing Russia at whatever human cost. (That Holy Russia remained a "dark" nation despite all Peter's efforts to modernize it by autocratic fiat—this lesson in elementary Marxism evidently does not impress Stalin.) The first intimation came in 1931 when Stalin, during an interview with Emil Ludwig, expressed great admiration for Peter I. Ludwig said that his professors who had taught him Marxism placed small value

224

on heroic personalities in history. "They were vulgarizers of Marxism," replied Stalin. And so when Alexis Tolstoy wrote a historical novel about Peter I, it was hardly surprising that it sold millions of copies, that it was made into an equally "popular" play, and finally into a two-part movie on which no expense was spared. The first part was released in this country last winter. More than any other Soviet movie I have seen, *Peter I* makes clear what has happened in Russia. The spotlight is entirely on Peter, whose every eyebrow twitch is invested with deep significance. He is shown almost exclusively in his role as the destroyer of the boyars and priests (precursors of fascism, perhaps?), and there is only the merest suggestion that his policies also ground down the masses. The one clear statement of this, the brief shots of the workers toiling in the Petrograd marshes, is a perfunctory sign of the cross, a ritual gesture hastily performed, and then—back to the Great Leader! The film has been praised for its realistic treatment of Peter. It is true that he is presented as brutal, coarse, ruthless, an Asiatic despot with Potsdam trimmings. But these qualities are not presented satirically, nor even objectively, but with sympathy as the forgivable and inevitable excesses of a great national leader. The implication is that for such gigantic tasks, such heroic leaders as Peter are necessary and must be accepted, warts and all.

Judged purely as a movie, the first part of *Peter I* is rambling, dragged-out, awkwardly put together, badly photographed, and generally undistinguished, except for the excellent acting one still finds in Russian films. In technique, it is inferior to a similar film made in 1924, Taritsch's *Czar Ivan the Terrible*. Its director, Petrov, is a mediocrity whose cinematic values may be inferred from an article he recently wrote in *Moscow News* about the second part of his film. What seems to interest him most is that the shipyards of Odessa are working on twenty full-scale eighteenth-century battleships, every detail faithfully copied from old engravings, while Soviet garment workers are making five thousand absolutely authentic eighteenth-century military uniforms—all for the grand climax of his film, the battle of Poltava. This is to be re-enacted by countless hordes of extras in what the *News* proudly refers to as "the Cecil B. De Mille manner."[80] That in 1937 Soviet shipyards should be occupied with making such toys, by the way, is an ironic note on the economic as well as the aesthetic tendencies of the present regime.

Lenin in October (Director: M. Romm; associate director: D. Vassiliev). This is the Kremlin's official version of the October revolution and is reported to have been personally supervised by Stalin.[81]* Cinematically, there is little to say about it that has not been said already about *Paris Commune*. The sound track faithfully reproduces the speeches of the actors, the camera trots after them like a well-trained dog. It is all one-hundred percent socialist-realist, and it has nothing to do with cinema. Those who think of *Chapayev* as a major film will be disturbed by the connection of Vassiliev with so mediocre a production.

Politically, the film is more interesting. It presents Stalin as Lenin's closest collaborator in making the October revolution against the traitorous opposition of Trotsky, Kamenev and Zinoviev. It would be tedious to go into the numerous falsifications of history which this thesis involves. To mention two: the insurrection is Stalin's idea, not Lenin's, who begins his speech: "I agree with comrade Stalin that an immediate uprising is necessary. . . ." Lenin denounces the Trotsky-Zinoviev-Kamenev bloc (actually, of course, Trotsky stood with Lenin and Stalin in favor of insurrection) as "traitors" and "strikebreakers"—these men to whom a short time later he will entrust the Red Army and the Communist International. The *New Masses* has described *Lenin in October* as "history catching up with romance in the Russian revolution."

But more important than such falsifications of detail is the

* Those connected with the film seem to have been acutely conscious of its great political significance. *Moscow News* quotes Romm as saying he "felt awed by the tremendous responsibility" and continues, "Romm was hardly able to give any directions to the actors. He was trembling with excitement."[82] As for the unfortunate actor who had to impersonate Stalin—in the film, he seems hardly to breathe. Stiff in his military tunic, he ventures no mannerisms, no stage business beyond a noncommittal puffing on his big pipe. The other actors become noticeably constrained in their scenes with this human torpedo, charged with destruction. Even the ebullient Lenin quiets down when Stalin glides silently into the scene.

226

caricature of Lenin, who is pictured as a funny little man, full of endearing "human" mannerisms, bustling happily about the business of revolution, a Foxy Grandpa of the class struggle. In short, as Robert Forsythe enthusiastically put it in the *New Masses,* "A man who might easily have played third base for the Brooklyn Dodgers." Always in the background is Stalin—solid, silent, reassuring. Lenin's first words on arriving in Petrograd are, "Where is Stalin? Send him to me at once!" Whenever he gets into difficulties, he sends for Stalin. In Eugene Lyons' words: "Lenin is shown as the 'front,' a whimsical and much too human front. Behind him, doing the real work, giving the revolution its stamina, is Stalin. . . . The thought implicit in every foot of film is: what *would* nice old Lenin have done without Stalin?"[83] This comes out amusingly in the scene where Lenin—who is absent-minded, the lovable old fellow!—is going out without his overcoat, and Stalin, in a big-brotherly way, impresses on him the importance of dressing warmly in this uncertain fall weather. Romm missed a chance here for a theme song: "Button up your overcoat/when the winds blow free/ take good care of yourself/You belong to me!"

But *Lenin in October* has implications which go far beyond the question of whether Stalin or Trotsky or Lenin made the 1917 revolution. The very nature of that event itself is involved. Here it is depicted as an orderly coup d'état, engineered by two Great Leaders with some help from the sailors of the Baltic fleet. The workers appear only in one or two brief "mob scenes." When Lenin appears at the Winter Palace after its capture, the victorious proletariat is pushed back by sailors just as in bourgeois nations the police hold back crowds on similar occasions. One also recalls the ragged little soldier looking at Lenin and declaring in surprise, "Why, he's just like one of us!" . . . the young Bolshevik and his wife gazing, in cowlike adoration, at the sleeping figure of The Leader . . . the series of brief shots showing the progress of the revolution throughout the city, each one preceded by the caption: BY ORDER OF THE REVOLUTIONARY MILITARY COMMITTEE. Here is no confused, disorderly proletarian upsurge such as Eisenstein showed us in *October. This* revolution runs on schedule, taking its orders from above.

It is especially interesting to compare this film's treatment of the

227

storming of the Winter Palace with Eisenstein's. There is the same scrambling over the tall ironwork gates, the same panicky surrender of the Kerensky ministers, even—gruesome mockery—such direct imitations as the shot of the cruiser *Aurora* framed by the risen drawbridge, and the perfect circle of a stone ball on a parapet overlooking the placid, misty harbor. But in spirit, what a contrast! In *October,* the attack was made by a mob of civilians, sailors, soldiers, and leather-jacketted Bolsheviks. Here, wave on wave of blue-clad sailors sweep over the defenders, roll up the long marble staircases, irresistibly, in close, orderly ranks. The destruction that in *October* falls upon the Czarina's ikon-hung boudoir is answered here by a "bit" in which the leader of the Bolsheviks cautions the mob not to injure the statuary. In *October,* this leader is a wild-haired young intellectual, his pince-nez askew and his necktie under his ear, who excitedly brandishes a pistol as he receives the capitulation of the Kerensky cabinet. Here he is a common-sense-looking fellow, quite businesslike and stolid, who at the supreme moment of the enemy's surrender, strikes a comic, "human" note by pulling out a pocket comb and running it through his hair.* Both films end with a close-up of Lenin speaking at the Congress of the Soviets immediately after the fall of the Winter Palace. But there is one final touch in the 1937 version which is worth noting. As Lenin begins to speak, his face lit up with victory, his gestures expansive and triumphant, the figure of Stalin moves slowly across the background, behind the other figures on the platform, until he is standing directly behind Lenin as the film ends. The intention no doubt was to suggest the legitimacy of his succession, but the actual effect is almost sinister: the impassive face of Stalin looming up suddenly behind the smiling face of Lenin, radiant in his hour of triumph. Here is dramatic irony in the classical tradition: the audience sees the Nemesis which is still invisible to the hero.

Such is the Soviet cinema of today. But perhaps quality has been sacrificed to quantity? Perhaps the industry has been flooding the backward regions of Russia with films, of slight aesthetic interest

* This seems to be the type revolutionary in the cinema of socialist realism. We meet him again in *The Return of Maxim*—a matter-of-fact, practical sort who would make an excellent C.I.O. organizer.

228

but important as mass education? On the contrary, the paralysis which had seized on production in 1930 has, if anything, been intensified. In the fall of 1935, Shumiatsky returned from America full of grandiose dreams of a "Soviet Hollywood" on the shores of the Black Sea, where eight thousand film workers would turn out eight hundred feature pictures a year. Millions of rubles were spent on surveys, professors of meteorology took lengthy observations, American consultants were engaged to draw up blueprints, but at last report the project had been postponed "indefinitely" because of "practical difficulties."[84] Shumiatsky also talked a good deal about his plans to "Americanize" the industry: by the end of 1936, the three thousand existing sound theatres would be increased to twelve thousand, etc. Sovkino tried to exchange Soviet films for American equipment. But there was no longer any market for Soviet films in the United States.[85] For political reasons, the Kremlin insisted that films be made in the Hollywood manner. But this "Americanization" called for American equipment, which proved impossible to obtain because American audiences were not interested in imitations of Hollywood films.

Things got worse and worse. In 1935, 120 films were planned and 43 were actually produced. In 1936, 165 were planned, 46 produced, and only 33 released for public showing.[86] Surveying these, *Izvestia* called nine "successful," nineteen "average," and five "simple rubbish."[87]* At the same time, *Pravda* sharply criticized the industry for falling so far behind its Plan. Shumiatsky replied (1) that he would make 800 films in 1940, and (2) that the original 1937 Plan of 123 films was "unrealistic" and must be cut to 60. In the first six months of 1937 just four pictures were produced,

---

* That *Izvestia's* criteria were not exacting is indicated by its including among the nine "successful" films *Party Ticket* and Alexandrov's *Circus.* These apparently were not considered successful enough to export to this country, but one gets some idea of their quality from a recent article by H. V. Meyrowitz. *Party Ticket,* Mr. Meyrowitz thinks was the worst movie he saw during his stay in the Soviet Union, and he documents his opinion. As for *Circus,* he reports a conversation with one of the leading directors in the new Vertov school: "Esther Shub was sitting in front of me. I went to her after the performance . . . and I looked at her and said, 'Well?' and she looked at me with a very sad face and said, 'Well?' "[88]

and on June 1, 1937, only thirteen scenarios were in production.[89] In less complicated societies, Shumiatsky would have been dismissed for inefficiency. But in the Russia of Stalin such directness would be out of question. The frame-up system has reached the point of being automatic, so that guilty and innocent alike must be framed. In Shumiatsky's case, it is true, a frame-up was perhaps an administrative necessity. To have simply fired him as a bungler would have reflected on the regime which had kept him in office eight years.

The Shumiatsky frame-up showed imagination and humor. The basic charge was standard: he had "permitted savage veteran spies, Trotskyist and Bukharinist agents, and hirelings of Japanese and German fascism to perform their wrecking deeds in the Soviet cinema." But the specific incident the stage managers chose was something quite original. The Children's Film Trust had produced a version of Stevenson's *Treasure Island.* Early in 1938, *Soviet Art,* organ of the Central Art Committee, denounced this film as bourgeois (to get love interest, Jim Hawkins had been changed into Jenny Hawkins, with whom Dr. Livesey falls in love), and also as leftist (to get a class angle, the Irish revolutionary movement had been dragged in). If the producers had to do this, asked *Soviet Art,* why had they not at least read Karl Marx's 1869 letter on the Irish situation? A reference in the review to Shumiatsky as "the former chief" of the cinema industry was the first public intimation of his fall. He himself was not accused of wrecking but merely of "falling into the hands of wreckers who wormed their way into the administration of cinematography." He is today among the "missing."[90]

The Shumiatsky debacle stimulated much comment in the Soviet press as to what was wrong with the cinema. Four major weaknesses seemed to exist:

1. *The incompetence of the Shumiatsky administration, which oscillated between visions of the future and complete paralysis of decision in the present.* This is the reaction one might expect from executives who are called on to carry out impossibly ambitious plans and at the same time apply a political control which alienates the directors and scenarists they must depend on for production. The official excuse for the collapse is that Shumiatsky was given too much power. As an Amkino official put it, "Naturally, with

230

only one man looking after things, there was bound to be relaxation of vigilance in some directions and resulting mismanagement."[91]

2. *A failure to make use of available human material, which was largely due to the antagonism existing between the bureaucracy and the cinema workers.* We have seen how it was with the better known directors, who have remained idle often for years at a time. But this sort of thing was general. A census taken in 1937 of the 143 directors who had made one or more full-length pictures showed that 65 were directing pictures or preparing to do so, 45 were writing scenarios, and 33 were doing nothing. Out of 166 assistant directors, 67 were idle. The census was taken in perfect production weather.[92]

3. *Difficulty in getting usable scenarios.* "At present, there is a story crisis in the industry," the head of Sovkino said in 1930.[93] And in 1937 we read: "Dissection of the industry's troubles appears so far to have convinced a majority of the critics that the true villains of the situation are the scenarists, who write badly and slowly, and the executives. . . ." In 1935, the report continues, the Moscow studio paid 1,129,000 rubles for 38 completed scenarios. Of these only eight were judged "worthy of production," making the average cost of each usable scenario 141,125 rubles.[94] All this is interesting because, politically, the scenarist is in an even more perilous position than the director, since he must supply the ideological content of the film. It is not surprising that in recent years Soviet scenarists, in Ivor Montagu's phrase, have become "cautious."

4. *Production delays caused by changes in the political line, and wholesale scrapping of completed films for political reasons.* As examples of the first, Pudovkin's *Deserter* and Kozintsev-Trauberg's *The Youth of Maxim* may be mentioned. As for the second, see Yermolayev's recent article in *Pravda,* which states that thirty percent of the films produced in 1935 and 1936 (37 out of a total 126) were discarded as *brak* ("spoiled") at a loss of 15,000,000 rubles. In 1937 Soyuzkino lost 5,000,000 on two *brak* films alone: *Great Wings* and *Bezhin Meadow.*[95]

It is clear that these deficiencies cannot be charged merely to Shumiatsky's personal shortcomings. Their roots are political. The delegation of British film technicians which in the spring of 1937 made a friendly inspection tour of the Soviet movie industry understood this well enough: "We submit that the present policy of the Soviet state is bound to be antagonistic to the Soviet film industry."[96]

To the admonitions of friendly critics and the warnings of experience, the Kremlin has replied by replacing Shumiatsky with an agent of the Secret Police.

The psychological atmosphere of the interregnum after Shumiatsky's fall is symbolized by the fact that the New York office of Amkino stopped answering its phone. It was during this uneasy period that Stalin warned a gathering of film workers: "Soviet power expects successes from you!"[97] At length, on March 23, 1938, the Council of People's Commissars appointed a receiver for the bankrupt industry in the form of the All-Union Committee on Cinema. Precisely the same task faces the Committee in 1938 as faced Shumiatsky in 1930: to rationalize, plan, economize, and, above all, speed up production. So far there are no indications it will be any more successful, since, as is hardly surprising, there is no evidence that the Committee's political and aesthetic line differs in the slightest from that of "the former chief." . . . For 1938 the Committee has announced the modest total of 51 feature pictures. "The large number of films devoted to the problems of Soviet patriotism, defense and the struggle against Fascist agents is explained by the fact that these problems are of vital interest at the present time."[98] . . . Ermler's latest film, *The Great Citizen,* shows Kirov struggling against the Trotsky-Zinoviev gang (who try to restore capitalism) in the 1925–27 period. "The scenario for *The Great Citizen* was completed May, 1936, but filming did not begin until late in 1937, since the Trotskyist-Bukharinist wreckers in the management of the Leningrad Film Studios sought to prevent its production in every way."[99] Thus *Moscow News:* an imaginary group of Trotskyist-Bukharinists sabotage a fictional account of what they didn't do ten years ago. . . . Alexandrov has released a musical comedy about the new Moscow-Volga canal. It is called *Volga-Volga.*

But there is one significant point about the reorganization. The head of the new Committee on Cinema, and Shumiatsky's successor as movie czar, is Semyon Dukelsky, who has been described as "a tough-minded young man" who "came to the motion picture industry straight from the NKVD, or political police."[100] *Moscow News* further reports he was appointed "to introduce firm Bolshevik order" into the cinema.

The old-fashioned, unreconstructed liberals—as against the neo-Stalinist variety—explain the decline of Soviet cinema in terms of state control of the individual. The artist, they say, cannot create great works when art is made a state activity and is required to turn out "propaganda." This explanation is especially persuasive nowadays, when totalitarianism is getting such a bad press. And it is true that the policies of the Kremlin have been responsible for what has happened to the cinema since 1930. But from this historical fact it is not possible to deduce an abstract principle of aesthetics. It is not the mere *fact* of political control, but the *direction* of this control that has been damaging. In the twenties, the Soviet cinema drew its very breath of life from a close connection with the Soviet state and its propagandistic requirements. In the thirties, this integration has poisoned it. The Stalinists offer an explanation that seems, at first glance, to be more plausible: the Russian masses are backward, and so, in the world's premier democracy, democratic art must be simple and even, by our standards, a bit crude. But this explanation overlooks the fact that the masses were even more backward in 1925–1929, when the Russian cinema was the most aesthetically advanced in the world.

The great Bolsheviks had more understanding of avant-garde politics than of avant-garde art. "I have the courage to appear a 'barbarian,'" Lenin told Clara Zetkin. "I cannot appraise the works of expressionism, futurism, cubism and other 'isms' as the highest manifestations of artistic genius. I do not understand them. I take no joy in them."[101] They recognized the boundary line between art and politics, and they had no illusions about settling such issues by administrative decree. (Lenin is said to have attended a big show of constructivist art during the civil war. He looked around in ironical bewilderment, shrugged his shoulders and remarked, "I don't understand, but it's no business of mine. It's Lunacharsky's headache!") In their own field, artists were allowed almost complete autonomy. "Art has its own laws," wrote Trotsky.[102] "Every artist, and every one who regards himself as such, claims as his proper right the liberty to work freely according to his ideal, whether it is any good or not," said Lenin.[103] They realized that art cannot be produced to order, that the artist cannot function properly if he is stripped of his freedom, his independence, his dignity.

Such trifles mean nothing to Stalin, "the practical realist." The dangerous formulation of the RAPP—"Art is a class weapon"— has been officially repudiated, but in practice it is still observed. The result has been the terrible sterility already described in all fields of Soviet culture. More and more the Kremlin admonishes its artists to sing sweetly (or else!), and more and more, with the best will in the world, they remain silent. The old Bolsheviks had more conservative tastes in art than one might wish, but Stalin is a Philistine, so unconscious of his own limitations that he does not hesitate to interfere in the most intimate way in all fields of culture. He receives a delegation of writers and urges them to create according to the precepts of socialist realism, which he thoughtfully defines for them. He helps make a movie—and *Lenin in October* is the result. He receives Dzerzhinsky, composer of "tuneful" operas, to congratulate him and to warn him against the errors of Shostakovitch —and the Association of Soviet Composers passes a resolution: "The attention given to Soviet music by Comrade Stalin augurs very well indeed for its future expansion, etc., etc."[104]

It is not merely or even primarily a matter of Stalin's being a barbarian. It is true, most unhappily for Soviet art, that Stalin was almost the only important leader among the makers of the 1917 Revolution who had not spent any time in exile, and hence that he was comparatively narrow, uncultivated, and provincial. But if the Russia of Lenin and Trotsky permitted the development of avant-garde art, it was despite the leaders' personal lack of interest in it and because its political movement was forward, towards socialism, and so could not but open out a free field for advanced art.

Likewise, by its very nature, the Stalin regime must pursue a reactionary policy in art. Unable to conceive of such matters except on the lowest, most vulgar plane, it "integrates" art with the state by the bluntest sort of police measures. Its first recorded exploit in the cinema was a typical piece of petty vandalism perpetrated on

234

Eisenstein's great film of the October Revolution. According to Alfred H. Barr, Jr., *"October* was to have greeted the delegates to the tenth anniversary celebration of the October Revolution, but an absolute censorship of all the parts played by the recently exiled members of the opposition required laborious re-cutting. As a result, it was not completed until five months later."[105] One scene, however, in which the actor playing Trotsky had his back to the camera, was overlooked. When the film was first shown, Trotsky's figure was recognized—and applauded. At once, the lights were turned up in the theatre, and GPU men walked up and down the aisles looking for those who had clapped.[106] This excellent beginning has been steadily improved on, until today an agent of the Secret Police heads the cinema industry and every movie set is guarded by a soldier with rifle and fixed bayonet.[107]

A great deal has been written about propaganda in the Soviet cinema, most of it rather beside the point. There is propaganda—and propaganda. Those bourgeois critics who have dismissed Soviet films as "propaganda" really mean that it presents certain social values which they find strange—and hostile. If "propaganda" be used to describe such general expressions of *weltanschauung* as *Arsenal* or *Potemkin,* then the term must include also most other past and present artistic productions. Up to 1930, those in control of the Soviet state asked of the cinema only the most general sort of propaganda, celebrating the triumph of socialism, exposing the decadence of capitalism, giving the masses a sense of the heroism of *their* revolution. The present regime, however, has been more specific in its demands.

In the twenties, "propaganda" meant that Soviet directors made films expressing certain basic social values with which they were in ardent sympathy. The word, "sympathy," in fact, implies a detachment which was not the case: they were part of the society founded on those values, and this self-identification was a potent inspiration to them. In the thirties, they must become political hacks, lending their talents to whatever maneuver the Kremlin has put on the order of the day, obediently and fearfully treading the official line. One remembers the official astonishment at the success of *Chapayev,* which "was based on a theme that was generally considered to have become boring for Soviet audiences—the civil war."[108]

235

Here the Kremlin seems to have confused its own reactions with those of the masses.

During the first Five Year Plan, the movies were pressed into service to propagandize for the thesis that socialism can be built in one country. More recently, the movies have been called on to popularize an even bigger lie: that socialism *has* been built in one country. The crudity of these films, far from being an expression of a healthy new society, is as much a reflection of the reactionary nature of the regime as was the burning for political heresy, several years ago, of Eisenstein's film *Bezhin Lug*.[109]

Such evidence as I have been able to find as to the popular response to the cinema is not very satisfactory. The inarticulateness of the Soviet masses and the increasing difficulty of any spontaneous expression of their preferences make any final judgment difficult. But there are a few fragmentary indications. One recent visitor reports that movie audiences shout encouragement to the hero, groan at the villain, produce imitation kisses during the love scenes, and so on.[110] Another writes: "Strangely enough, though Soviet films were among the first to develop to a high degree complete naturalism in screen acting, Soviet audiences do not seem to mind seriously the type of film which features good old-fashioned theatricalism, with heaving bosoms, exaggerated gestures, artificial pauses, and everything heavily underscored."[111]

At the height of the great period of Soviet cinema, one finds the masses showing a preference for the Hollywood product. The popular success of the 1925 season in Moscow was not *Potemkin* but Douglas Fairbanks in *The Thief of Bagdad*. "American films," Paxton Hibben wrote in 1925, "dominate, inundate, glut, overwhelm the Russian motion picture houses today. Clara Kimball Young has a theatre solely devoted to her in Moscow."[112] Unable to afford enough American films to supply the demand, Soviet studios turned out imitation "Amerikansky Kartiny," with "American" lighting, camera tricks, and fast action. Charlie Chaplin and Mary Pickford had their Russian incarnations. Bolshevik Buster Keatons were chased by OGPU-Keystone cops around the Red Square. These films played to packed houses.[113] When Sovkino issued a report showing large profits for 1927, the bureaucrat

Yaroslavsky complained: "Neither *Mother* nor *Potemkin* was produced by Sovkino, which prefers quick profits on foreign bourgeois films to building up home products suitable for workers and peasants." He criticized Sovkino sharply for signalizing the tenth anniversary of 1917 with a showing of the Hollywood film, *Scaramouche,* with great profit. The difficulty, he admitted, was that audiences seemed to prefer "the comic, picturesque or adventurous pictures from America" to the aesthetically and politically superior Soviet productions.[114] So too with the popular response to the Russian films themselves. Pudovkin's *The End of St. Petersburg,* which at least had a hero and a plot, was more popular than Eisenstein's *October,* more interesting aesthetically but also more difficult.[115] Two years later, Pudovkin's *Storm Over Asia* was more enthusiastically received inside Russia, and for the same reasons, than Eisenstein's *The General Line.*[116] Probably the greatest box-office success among all Russian films has been *Chapayev,* which is well described as "a talking film of normal technique."

The Russian masses like the Hollywood type of film. Therefore, the world's premier democracy should give them such films, which it is now doing. So runs the simple reasoning of the Stalinists. All too simple. The matter is not as mechanical as that.

There is, for example, in Moscow the Museum of Western Art, which contains a famous collection of modern French paintings, from Cézanne to Picasso. There is also the Tretyakov Gallery, devoted mostly to the works of the Russian academicians of the last century. The Museum of Western Art is always empty, the Tretyakov always crowded. A recent special exhibition at the Tretyakov of canvasses by these academicians—Repin, Surikov, Kramskoi, Perov and other equally celebrated painters of battle scenes and winter sunsets—was visited by 700,000 people. A one-man show of Repin's work drew 8,000 on its opening day—as against 3,600 for a Rembrandt opening in the same gallery. *Moscow News* drew the moral: "In the Soviet Union, those masters of the brush, Rembrandt and Repin, have a mass following that cannot be dreamed of elsewhere in the world today." When Repin is bracketed with Rembrandt, strange things may be expected to happen in the art world. One reads of the housewife Nikolskaya, who wrote in the

237

visitors' book of one museum, apropos of certain "formalist" canvasses: "They are stupidities which it would be better not to show." A Moscow journal adds: "She was right, and they have long since been replaced by others of a much higher artistic value."

But two questions must be asked: (1) to what degree is this expression of popular taste spontaneous and to what degree is it stimulated by official policy? and (2) could this policy conceivably have guided mass taste into other channels?

In the example just given, these questions can be answered quite easily. The state has treated the Museum of Western Art as a veritable Cinderella, cutting its appropriation and selling abroad many of its masterpieces.* The Tretyakov, on the other hand, has had its budget steadily increased. If housewife Nikolskaya had asked for more, not less, abstract paintings, would her preferences have been taken so seriously?[117]

But, some will say, she "naturally" preferred realism to abstraction because she was a housewife. This leads to the second question: could any other orientation have been given to popular taste? In his *Seven Soviet Arts,* Kurt London gives a good answer:

"Artists like Kokoschka and Pechstein, Kubin and Picasso, Archipenko and Epstein, have each in their own sphere developed a great amount of revolutionary ideas and influences. Today their style is repudiated in the Soviet Union as 'formalistic,' as a manifestation of Western decadence, as individualism without any contact with the masses.

"These masses originally had, however, just as little connection with old art as with the new, because formerly the politico-economic systems of their countries offered them no opportunity of getting to know and understand it. Western art has for centuries lived without associations with the masses, particularly in the classical period which today occupies such a dominant position in the

---

* The story is told that the directress of this museum, on opening up one morning, noticed that a valuable Cézanne had been removed during the night and the other pictures rearranged so as to conceal the loss. She at once called the police, only to discover that the nocturnal raid had been carried out on orders from the Kremlin, which happened to need *valuta.* The authorities had apparently hoped that she would not notice the loss.

238

U.S.S.R. Thus the attitude of the masses both to the old and new art styles probably remains essentially dependent on the nature of the education afforded them by their respective states."

Why, after all, should ignorant peasants prefer Repin to Picasso, whose abstract technique is at least as relevant to their own primitive folk art as is the former's realistic style? No, if the masses crowd into the Tretyakov, it is largely because they have been conditioned to shun "formalism" and to admire "socialist realism." The regime has conducted this conditioning with its usual thoroughness, and for its own political ends.

The Eisenstein-Pudovkin school based their approach largely on the principle which London states above. Were they "Utopian visionaries"? The description I have given of the mass response to their films might seem to indicate they were. But the fact that it has been easy to popularize the conventional Hollywood type of film does not mean that it is impossible to interest the masses in something more advanced. "In Russia," wrote an English journalist recently, *"all* films are popular. A vast public, much of it still in the early stage of movie fascination, is hungry for films, and there are nowhere near enough efficient craftsmen to produce them. A failure in our sense of the word does not exist."[118] This would seem to be an ideal situation for raising the level of mass taste. The quotation from London given above indicates that "formalism" is not necessarily any bar to a popular response in the Soviet Union. There is also some interesting evidence that, in social content (as against aesthetic form), the Eisenstein-Pudovkin cinema was in some ways more appealing to the masses than the present realistic films.

Speaking at the 1935 conference, L. Trauberg, the director, made a comparison: "Chapayev is a hero, but he is not above the heads of the audience. He is their brother. But in *October* the people were very high up."[119] The pattern of development is clear. First the masses were exalted into the great symbolic hero of the Russian film; then they were reduced to their "proper" scale and portrayed, vodka, warts, lice and all, in the early social-realist films; and lately they have been crowded off the screen by the gigantic images of their Great Leaders. What has happened comes out clearly in a speech Eisenstein made at the 1935 conference. (That his intention was to justify, not expose, makes his words all the more revealing.) "It is not accidental," he said, "that precisely at this period, for the first time in our cinematography, there begin to appear the first finished images of personalities—not just any personalities, but of the finest personalities: the leading figures of leading Communists and Bolsheviks. Just as from the revolutionary movement of the masses emerged the sole revolutionary party, that of the Bolsheviks, which heads the unconscious elements of revolution and leads them towards conscious revolutionary aims, so the film images of the leading men of our time begin during the present period to crystallize out of the general-revolutionary mass-quality of the earlier type of film."[120]

The 1917 Revolution, sweeping aside the old order, opened a wide field to avant-garde art. In the first decade after 1917, the Soviet Union was the scene of a veritable renaissance of such tendencies: Mayakovsky and the LEF group in literature, Malievitch and Kandinsky in painting, the formalist and the constructivist schools of architecture, Eisenstein, Pudovkin, and Dovschenko in the cinema, Tairov and Meyerhold in the theatre. But it was not long before these groups found themselves opposed by more conventional artists, who now were emboldened to raise their heads again as it became evident that Holy Russia was still a vast and semiliterate land, Revolution or no Revolution. Finding no stable base in Russian society, the avant-garde in one field of art after another was ousted by the reactionaries, just as the Old Bolsheviks, whose advanced political theories similarly clashed with a backward society, were gradually reduced to impotence by the Stalin bureaucracy. The recent humbling of Meyerhold marks the end of the long struggle in the arts, as the execution of Bukharin means the end in politics.

In the cinema, by its nature the most popular of all modern arts, the struggle between those who fought to hold the gains of the Revolution, and those who based themselves on the backwardness of Russia, has been raised to its most dramatic intensity. Soviet directors of every school have had to accept as a basic factor the low cultural level of the masses. These masses have never been articulate enough to create their own cinema—the movies are hardly a folk art! All that has been done has been done from

240

outside, from above, by intellectuals and politicians, and the victory of the Stalin School is not due to its expressing any "natural," "spontaneous" mass urge, but to its alliance with a victorious political machine.

Since 1917, three major tendencies can be defined. Between 1917 and 1924, Lunacharsky, the Commissar of Education, attacked the problem honestly, but with none too much imagination. He used the film as a reproductive mechanism, to bring to the masses the great stage and literary classics. From 1925 through 1929 the Eisenstein-Pudovkin-Kuleshov approach was dominant. This took advantage of the very primitiveness of the people to create an art which struck out in new paths, unencumbered by traditional luggage. From 1930 up to the present, the Stalin bureaucracy has been dominant.

Lunacharsky's was the most direct approach to the problem. The moujik is "dark"? Then enlighten him! Benevolently, somewhat in the social-worker manner, he introduced the workers to their cultural heritage. The theatre and the cinema he seems to have looked on mostly as a relaxation for the toiling masses after a day spent in the unaesthetic factory. He encouraged the production of the Russian stage classics, and is said to have objected to the predominance of leftist propaganda on the Moscow stage in the early twenties.[121] But he shared the admirable tolerance of the other Bolshevik leaders toward the new trends in art. In 1924 he even ventured to experiment in the movies on his own hook, with the production of *Aelita*, a Martian fantasy with futurist sets by Meyerhold. But the radicalism in *Aelita*, as in the contemporary German film, *The Cabinet of Dr. Caligari*, was confined to the setting and costumes. Otherwise, the film was the usual photographic record of a stage play—in this case, a nonrealistic play. The experiment was not successful. Mme. Lunacharsky, herself a well-known actress, was probably thinking of *Aelita* when she said that they had made an attempt to break with realism and to give a revolutionary form ("including futurism and cubism") to the movies. "But we soon realized that this . . . was not adapted to the primitive, unsophisticated hosts of new movie patrons."[122] So they went back to realistic versions of Tolstoy and Chekhov, acted out before the camera by the Moscow Art players.

That same "primitive, unsophisticated" audience which had

frightened the Lunacharskys back to the safety of realism had a contrary effect on the rising new school of Eisenstein-Pudovkin-Kuleshov. On the basis of the discoveries of Freud and Pavlov (who placed at their disposal his laboratory for the study of reflex actions), they developed an art form which affected the audience at its most primitive level, striking through the layer of conscious culture down to the reflexes and the Freudian unconscious. Aesthetes and peasants respond with the same visceral reaction to stimuli like the well-known machine gun bit in *October* or the massacre on the steps in *Potemkin*. This psychological theory was the foundation for a technique which was purely cinematic, free from the literary-dramatic conventions of the usual film. They reasoned that the very cultural innocence of the Russian masses made it possible to approach them with such a technique. Since Soviet culture had to be built from the ground up—that is, from the level of actual literacy—why should it not be built along the same advanced lines as the new political structure? Thus the extremes met: the Left Bank, which had rejected the academic tradition, and the Russian village, which had never heard of it.

At first glance, the "Stalin School" seems merely to have returned to the Lunacharsky tradition. The literary classics are being exhumed again to stalk before the cameras, the Moscow Art players are back, even in the works of Eisenstein and Pudovkin, there is an end of montage, of the "mass film," the "intellectual cinema" and all such experimentation. But there is a difference. Once the cinema had progressed from Lunacharsky to Eisenstein, it became historically impossible for it *merely* to return to the more primitive level. Just as there is an important difference between the behavior of a real baby and the behavior of a dementia praecox patient who has regressed to an infantile state, so the Soviet cinema of today, far from being the healthy expression of a crude young society, actually is a pathological regression from a higher level of consciousness. It is not a repetition but a perversion of the old Lunacharsky tradition.

In an even more important way, the Lunacharsky cinema is set off from the "Stalin School." Lunacharsky himself was a man of cosmopolitan outlook, and the culture he tried to bring to the "dark" Russian masses was a European, not a Russian, culture. The films he supervised took the then new and progressive German realistic cinema as their model. So, too, with Pudovkin and Eisenstein, though their cinema based itself on another phase of European culture: the avant-garde tendencies of futurism, dadaism, expressionism, surrealism, etc. (There is a remarkable similarity in technique and psychological effect between Eisenstein's *October* and Cocteau's surrealist movie, *Blood of a Poet*.) When Eisenstein went abroad in 1930, the intelligentsia of Europe and America found that he talked their language.*

In their 1930 manifesto on the use of sound in cinema, Eisenstein and Pudovkin declared: "The contrapuntal method of constructing the talking film not only will not detract from the *international* [their emphasis] character of cinematography, but will enhance its significance and its cultural power to a degree inexperienced hitherto. Applying this method of construction, the film will not be confined within any national market, as . . . will be the case with the film 'theatre dramas.' "[123]

But it was precisely this *international* character of the Eisenstein cinema that most alarmed the Kremlin. If the masses are to accept the present totalitarian dictatorship as a fully realized socialist society, they must be cut off from contact with more advanced cultures. And so, in the last ten years, the Soviet Union has been slowly isolated. Its borders are the most hermetically sealed in the world, and against foreign book, newspapers, movies, ideas, even more rigidly than against persons. The mere arrival of a letter with a foreign stamp may be embarrassing to an artist or intellectual. The present Soviet cinema is part of a gigantic campaign to persuade the Russian masses that, under the wise guidance of Comrade

* At this period, Pudovkin, Dovzhenko, and Vertov also were allowed to travel abroad. These were triumphal tours, for their work had, in general, found its most understandingly appreciative audiences *outside* the Soviet Union. The situation was paradoxical. The 1917 Revolution had given Russian artists a chance to carry out their theories and develop their talents to a degree impossible elsewhere. For audiences who would fully understand their work, however, the Soviet directors had to look to those capitalist nations whose social backwardness made impossible a great cinema of their own, but whose cultural level was high enough to appreciate a great *imported* cinema.

243

Stalin, they have already scaled the topmost peaks of culture. This campaign is designed to reinforce, not to combat, those characteristic defects of backward cultures: provincial smugness, the ignorant acceptance of inferior, banal art forms as "healthy" and "normal," and a corresponding suspicion of more advanced forms. This is what, aesthetically, the theory of "Socialism in One Country" has meant.

The logic of the campaign has also led to the interdiction of all communication with the Soviet's own cultural past, so deeply influenced by European tendencies. It is dangerous for intellectuals to have statements they made in the twenties brought to light again today. Furthermore, each time the "line" changes, the preceding orientation becomes anathema, and another whole cultural period must be wiped off the slate. The sheer waste of this process is shocking: the social-realist cinema, for example, has made no use of the discoveries made by the Eisenstein school, which have been violently rejected as "formalistic" heresy—a matter for the police. Deprived of all fertilizing contact with its own past or with other cultures, Soviet culture has become sterile and debased. From the most international of all modern cultures, it has shrunk to the most meanly parochial.

But the process has had its compensations for the Kremlin, which finds such a culture much easier to manipulate for its own quite practical ends. It worries not at all that the final result has been the erosion of all specifically cultural values, leaving only the hard, naked substratum of political aims. These gentlemen of the Kremlin are practical men. And so they bear no malice toward the artists they have brought to heel at last, after so many years of struggle. Eisenstein's new film, *Alexander Nevsky,* properly chauvinistic in content and purged of all formalist tendencies, seems to have restored him to full official favor—just as Shostakovitch has returned to grace now that he has taken to writing 'tunes you can whistle." It is even reported that, after the preview of *Alexander Nevsky* in the Kremlin, Comrade Stalin himself congratulated Eisenstein and graciously forgave him his genius and extended the hand of Comradeship to him.[124]

—*Partisan Review,* July and August–September 1938;
Winter 1939

REFERENCES

1. *Close-Up*, October, 1928.
2. *N.Y. Herald Tribune*, January 10, 1938.
3. *Experimental Cinema*, No. 5, 1934, p. 44.
4. *Soviet Cinema*, edited by A. Arossev (Voks, Moscow, 1935), p. 289.
5. Ernestine Evans: "The Soviet Idea in the Kino" (*Asia*, August, 1926).
6. Much of the data on this early period comes from *L'Art dans la Russie Nouvelle: Le Cinéma* by R. Marchand and P. Weinstein (Les Éditions Rieder, Paris, 1927).
7. See reference 6.
8. *Soviet Cinema*, p. 96.
9. *Soviet Russia Today*, May, 1935.
10. *Soviet Cinema*, p. 98.
11. *Soviet Russia Today*, May, 1935.
12. S. M. Eisenstein: "Through Theatre to Cinema" (*Theatre Arts Monthly*, September, 1936).
13. *Soviet Cinema*, p. 290.
14. *N.Y. Times*, May 26, 1929.
15. L. I. Monosson: "The Soviet Cinematography" (*Journal of the Society of Motion Picture Engineers*, October, 1930).
16. *Moscow News*, August 3, 1931.
17. S. M. Eisenstein: "Les Principes du Nouveau Cinéma Russe" (*La Revue de Cinéma*, Paris, April, 1930).
18. *Close-Up*, October, 1930.
19. Rudolf Arnheim: *Film* (Faber & Faber, London, 1933), p. 232.
20. *Close-Up*, December, 1932.
21. *Art in the U.S.S.R.* (published by The Studio, London, 1935).
22. *Close-Up*, June, 1933.
23. *Experimental Cinema*, No. 5, 1934.
24. Speech by Ivor Montagu (in *Britain and the Soviets: Speeches at a Conference Held in London, December 7–8, 1935, by the Friends of the U.S.S.R.*)
25. *N. Y. Times*, February 7, 1932.
26. Kurt London: *Seven Soviet Arts* (Yale University Press, 1938), p. 289.
27. Kurt London: *Seven Soviet Arts*, p. 133.
28. *Moscow News*, December 20, 1932 and April 25, 1933.
29. *N.Y. Times*, April 10, 1930.
30. *Close-Up*, September, 1930 and *N.Y. Times*, April 10, 1930.
31. *Soviet Culture Bulletin*, No. 5, 1932.
32. *London Times*, April 27, 1932.
33. H. V. Meyrowitz: "U.S.S.R. Goes Hollywood" (*World Film News*, July, 1936).
34. London: *Seven Soviet Arts*, p. 139.
35. A. Arossev, President of the All-Union Society for Cultural Relations with Foreign Countries, in "Art in the U.S.S.R." (*The Studio*, 1935).

36. Georges Friedmann: "Revolt against Formalism in the Soviet Union" (*Science & Society*, Summer, 1938).
37. Fred Eastman: "Motion Pictures in Russia" (*The Christian Century*, September 9, 1936).
38. *Art in the U.S.S.R.* (*The Studio*, 1935).
39. Louis Fischer in *L'Europe Nouvelle*, January 13, 1934.
40. *Close-Up*, June, 1933.
41. *Soviet Culture Bulletin*, January, 1932.
42. *Moscow News*, November 20, 1932.
43. *Soviet Cinema*, p. 66.
44. *La Revue de Cinéma*, February, 1931.
45. *Moscow News*, August 23, 1931.
46. *N.Y. Times*, October 4, 1931.
47. *Soviet Cinema*, p. 292.
48. *Moscow News*, January 6, 1934.
49. *Moscow News*, March 24, 1934.
50. *N.Y. Times*, July 11, 1934.
51. *Moscow News*, May 26, 1934.
52. *Britain and the Soviets* (see reference 24), and *New Statesman*, February 2, 1935.
53. *Soviet Cinema*, p. 67.
54. *N.Y. Times*, March 31 and June 5, 1935.
55. Dinamov's speech was printed in *International Literature*, No. 2, 1935.
56. These quotations are from the account of the 1935 conference given in Paul Rotha's *Documentary Film* (Faber & Faber, London, 1936).
57. *Moscow News*, March 31, 1937.
58. *N.Y. Times*, December 30, 1937.
59. *Moscow News*, April 6, 1938.
60. *N.Y. Herald Tribune*, July 17, 1938.
61. "The Film in USSR—1937" (Report of the Association of Cine-Technicians Delegation to the USSR, May, 1937. Printed in the *Cine-Technician*, London, August, 1937. This Report is the most detailed and apparently objective survey of the recent Soviet cinema that I have been able to find.)
62. "U.S.S.R. Goes Hollywood" by H. V. Meyrowitz (*World Film News*, London, July, 1936).
63. "The Film in USSR—1937" (see reference 61).
64. Ibid.
65. From the Introduction to *Letter of an Old Bolshevik* (Rand School, New York, 1937).
66. "The Shostakovitch Affair" by Joshua Kunitz (*New Masses*, June 9, 1936).
67. *N.Y. Times*, February 14, 1936.
68. This account is taken from "Housecleaning in Soviet Law" by John N. Hazard (*The American Quarterly on the Soviet Union*, April, 1938).

69. *N.Y. Times,* April 17, 1937.
70. The fullest account I have seen of the literary purge is Joseph Barnes' article in the *N.Y. Herald Tribune* of May 12, 1937.
71. *N.Y. Herald Tribune,* January 10, 1938.
72. "Film Form, 1935—New Problems" by Sergei M. Eisenstein (*Life & Letters Today,* London, September, 1935).
73. *Moscow News,* May 9, 1935, and February 12, 1936.
74. *N.Y. Times,* February 21, 1937.
75. *Fifteen Years of Soviet Cinema* (Voks, Moscow, 1935), p. 27.
76. *N.Y. Times,* November 19, 1933.
77. See reference 74.
78. *Moscow News,* April 6, 1938.
79. Program note, Cameo Theatre, New York City, June 2, 1938.
80. *Moscow News,* September 22 and October 6, 1937.
81. See reference 71.
82. *Moscow News,* October 27, 1937.
83. *The New Leader,* May 21, 1938.
84. See reference 71.
85. *Business Week,* December 28, 1935.
86. See reference 71.
87. *N.Y. Herald Tribune,* August 29, 1937.
88. See reference 62.
89. See reference 87.
90. *N.Y. Times,* January 17, 1938.
91. *Motion Picture Herald,* January 15, 1938.
92. See reference 87.
93. *N.Y. Times,* June 1, 1930.
94. See reference 87.
95. See reference 71.
96. See reference 64.
97. *Moscow News,* April 6, 1938.
98. Ibid.
99. *Moscow News,* March 23, 1938.
100. See reference 60.
101. Kurt London: *Seven Soviet Arts* (Yale University Press, 1938), p. 66.
102. Max Eastman: *Artists in Uniform* (Knopf, 1934), p. 129.
103. London: *Seven Soviet Arts,* p. 66.
104. Ibid., p. 100.
105. Alfred H. Barr, Jr.: "Sergei Mikhailovitch Eisenstein" (*The Arts,* December, 1928).
106. Upton Sinclair: Personal letter to A. A. Leiva, June 1, 1933.
107. "The Film in USSR—1937" (*Cine-Technician,* London, August, 1937).
108. H. P. J. Marshall: "Fifteen Years of Soviet Cinema" (*Soviet Russia Today,* May, 1935).
109. For the *"Bezhin Lug* Affair," see particularly Eisenstein's "confession"

247

in *International Literature,* No. 8, 1937; Joshua Kunitz's article in *Moscow News,* March 31, 1937, and the amazing "explanation" in *Soviet Russia Today,* June, 1937.

110. R. Ford: "Moscow Goes to the Movies" (*Sight & Sound,* London, Spring, 1937).

111. *Moscow News,* March 3, 1934.

112. Paxton Hibben: "The Movies in Russia" (*Nation,* November 11, 1925).

113. *N.Y. Times,* November 7, 1926.

114. *N.Y. Times,* December 18, 1927.

115. Denis Marion: "La Ligne General" (*La Revue de Cinéma,* Paris, February 1, 1931).

116. See reference 105.

117. On this matter of the Tretyakov vs. the Museum of Western Art, see: *Research Bulletin on the Soviet Union* of the American-Russian Institute, July, 1936; *Moscow News,* November 25, 1936, and June 28, 1938; *Art & Culture in the Soviet Union,* Moscow, July, 1938.

118. Cedric Belfrage: "Russia's Hollywood" (*World Film News,* September, 1936).

119. Paul Rotha: *Documentary Film* (Faber & Faber, London, 1936).

120. S. M. Eisenstein: "Film Form, 1935—New Problems" (*Life & Letters Today,* September, 1935).

121. Joseph Wood Krutch: "Eisenstein and Lunacharsky" (*Nation,* June 27, 1928).

122. *N.Y. Times,* February 5, 1928.

123. S. M. Eisenstein and V. I. Pudovkin: "The Sound Film: A Statement" (*Close-Up,* October, 1928).

124. *N.Y. Times,* December 5, 1938.

248

THE
EISENSTEIN
TRAGEDY

W AS it only a dozen years ago that, with pious excitement, we went to "little" movie houses—the very term has disappeared—to see the new films from Russia? Is it so short a time since many of us were writing on the cinema as *the* great modern art form, the machine art whose technique was most in harmony with the dynamism of the machine age, the art that most powerfully affected such peculiarly modern areas as Freud's subconscious and Pavlov's reflexes, the only art that could sometimes bridge the gap between serious creation and mass taste, so that *Birth of a Nation,* Chaplin's comedies, *Potemkin* and a few other films might be said to have been the only works of our time that have been both popular and great? Our enthusiasm was not misplaced, our theories were not unfounded. And yet the wonderful possibilities that lay before the cinema ten years ago have withered into the slick banality of Hollywood and the crude banality of the post-1930 Soviet cinema. The potentialities, which really existed, which, for that matter, still exist and in even richer profusion, simply were not realized, and the cinema gave up its own idiom and technique to become once more what it was before Griffith: a mechanical device for recording stage plays. Like so much else in the last decade, it crept back into the womb, into unconsciousness. It has been many years now since, anywhere in the world, a film has been made which, aesthetically speaking, is cinema at all.

These depressing reflections are suggested by Eisenstein's new book, *The Film Sense,* which reads more like a conscientious and not too inspired Ph.D. thesis than like the work of the creator of *October* and *Potemkin.* The only valuable part of the book is the Appendices, which reprint some Eisenstein scenarios and articles and give a bibliography of his writings, films and unrealized projects.

I think *The Film Sense* may best be understood as an attempt by its author to adopt the protective coloration of official Stalinist culture. This explains the platitudes: the distinguishing mark of "an emotionally exciting work" is that it causes "inner creative excitement in the spectator" (page 35); "the technique of creation recreates a life process, conditioned only by those special circumstances required by art" (page 43); repetition "may well perform two functions"—(1) "to facilitate the creation of an organic

250

whole," (2) to develop "mounting intensity" (page 95), etc. It also accounts for the citations from Walt Whitman, Sir Joshua Reynolds, Lewis Carroll, Pliny the Elder and practically everybody else who strew the pages, apparently to show that Eisenstein has the authority of all past culture on his side. (Time was when that would have worried him!) And it also accounts for the ghastly "official" style in which the book seems to have been written—possibly Mr. Jay Leyda, the translator, is here partly responsible—so very different from the expressionist fireworks of Eisenstein's earlier writing. In fact, I would almost venture to say that Eisenstein has modeled his prose on Stalin's; there is the characteristic turgidity; the lingering over the obvious; even the familiar catechism form—isn't this a perfect echo: "What was the distortion in our attitude at that time to this indisputable phenomenon? The error lay . . . etc."

Above all, this hypothesis accounts for the remarkable change in Eisenstein's conception of montage. "There was a period in Soviet cinema," he begins his book, "when montage was proclaimed 'everything.' Now we are at the close of a period during which montage has been regarded as 'nothing.' Regarding montage as neither nothing nor everything, I consider it opportune at this juncture to recall that montage is just as indispensable a component of film production as any other element of film effectiveness." Thus montage, once the distinguishing principle of the Eisenstein school, has become simply one among many technical devices. Eisenstein has furthermore broadened his definition of montage until the term now merely describes any relation of elements in art. He has converted his old battle cry into a platitude. We are told that the "basic aim and function" of montage is "connected and sequential exposition of the theme, the material, the plot, the action . . . the simple matter of telling a connected story." This, he frankly remarks, is, of all aspects of montage, "the one really immune to challenge"—as indeed it is, since not even a Soviet commissar would deny the need for "a connected story." This is a complete reversal of Eisenstein's former theory. In his article, "The Cinematographic Principle and Japanese Culture," in *transition* for Spring–Summer, 1930, Eisenstein denounced the idea that montage is "a junction of elements" as "a most pernicous method of analysis." He continued: "By what then is characterized montage

. . . ? By collision. . . . By conflict. By collision. . . . From the collision of two given factors arises a concept. Linkage is, in my interpretation, only a possible *special* case. . . . Thus, montage is conflict. The basis of every art is always conflict."

Eisenstein gives no explanation for this reversal, in fact does not mention that a reversal has taken place. Soviet culture doesn't build on the past, any more than Stalinist politics do. The Party line, in art as in politics, changes overnight into a flat contradiction of yesterday's line, so that the present is related to the past only as good is to evil or black to white; the past is simply scrapped, buried, forgotten. Soviet artists have no tradition; they must wipe off the past, as one wipes off a blackboard, the day the line changes. They are unable to learn from the past, and their culture is shallow and undeveloped since it is constantly uprooted.

Eisenstein's change of mind about montage has nothing to do with aesthetic theory; it is simply an adaptation to the political pressures which have crushed all Soviet art in the last decade, and whose impact on the cinema I described in a series of articles in *Partisan Review* several years ago. The outlawry of "formalism," i.e., avant-garde experiment, in favor of "social realism" was partly an expression of the Philistine taste of the new-rich Stalinist bureaucracy, partly a move to harness art to the immediate service of mass propaganda (cf. Stalin's famous directive to Soviet composers to produce tunes the people can whistle on their way to work). In the triumph of the "linkage" over the "conflict" concept of montage these factors are involved—"linkage" is the Hollywood method, after all—and also another principle. The cinema is a dramatic art form, and dramatic structure depends largely on the tension created by conflict; but there cannot be conflict in a totalitarian state, since there is only one principle, one set of values authorized to be publicly expressed. I suggest, somewhat tentatively, that there is an intrinsically revolutionary quality to the conflict-montage of Eisenstein's *October* (1927), while the linkage-montage of *Alexander Nevsky* (1938), which robs it of any dramatic interest and makes it a static kind of masque or pageant, is in itself counterrevolutionary.

The grandeurs and the miseries of the modern artist find high expression in Eisenstein's career. In the decade following the October Revolution, his three great films—*Potemkin, October* and *Old and New*—were perhaps the supreme expression of the remarkable flowering of avant-garde art in the springtime of the new society. By 1929 the Stalinist bureaucracy had consolidated its hold on the State apparatus, and the great period of creativity in the arts was over. That year Eisenstein got permission to travel abroad. Whatever hopes he may have had of finding a more congenial milieu in the capitalist world—his difficulties with Stalin had begun as early as 1927, when he was forced to eliminate Trotsky's figure from all scenes of *October*—were frustrated with remarkable thoroughness. In Paris the police forbade the showing of *Old and New* to a private audience at the Sorbonne. He traveled on to Hollywood, where Paramount put him under a six-month contract with much publicity, and frustrated his attempts to make any movies. There followed the tragi-comedy of the Mexican film he made for a group of liberals headed by Upton Sinclair, which ended in Sinclair's asserting his property rights in the unedited film (which he later turned over to a Hollywood hack to chop into shorts) and Eisenstein returning empty-handed to Russia. The first indication many of us had as to what was going on in the Soviet cinema was the failure of Amkino to back up Eisenstein's efforts to get his Mexican film—said by many who saw the raw material to be potentially his greatest achievement—out of the hands of Sinclair.

I am told that when Eisenstein returned to Russia he was a beaten man, disillusioned with both the capitalist and the new Stalinist world. There followed a long and heartbreaking series of unrealized projects: a cinematization of Marx's *Capital;* of the careers of Ivar Kreuger and Sir Basil Zaharoff; of Vandercook's *Black Majesty;* the Hart-Kaufman comedy, *Once in a Lifetime;* Malraux's *La Condition Humaine;* a comedy called *MMM;* a big historical film covering four centuries of Moscow's history; above all, the humiliating treatment of the only project that got beyond the scenario stage, his half-completed film on peasant life, *Bezhin Meadow,* which was branded "formalist" and officially suppressed in 1937. The only projects Eisenstein has been able to realize since *Old and New* (1929) are *Alexander Nevsky* (1938) and the present book. Although in this book Eisenstein analyzes *Nevsky* as though it were a masterwork, devoting many pages to the technical strategy of a tiny section, the film has always seemed to me empty and boring. It is a slow-paced historical pageant, devoid of any content other than a poster-like kind of patriotism, and quite conventional in its cinematic technique. I think it may be referred to the same strategy of cultural camouflage that produced the book: a patriotic pageant is about as "safe" an art work as it is possible to create in Russia these days. Eisenstein's next film is also to be a historical one, based on Ivan the Terrible. It is immensely significant that the one project Eisenstein was able to complete in the last decade is *Nevsky*, while all the rest, dealing with themes in which there is contemporary life, came to nothing. Back to the womb.

Eisenstein's career has been a tragedy without a hero. He has forsworn his most cherished aesthetic theories when they met with official disfavor; viz., his abject behavior when his "formalist" heresy was attacked at the 1935 Film Conference; his confessional article, "The Mistakes of *Bezhin Meadow*" (*International Literature*, No. 8, 1937); his use of big-name "stars" in *Nevsky*, and his acceptance as collaborators in that film of D. Vassiliev, the leading "social realist" director, and Teleshiva of the Moscow Art Theatre. (In the twenties he wouldn't have wiped his feet on the Moscow Art Theatre.) He has also issued from time to time the kind of political statements required of Stalinist intellectuals, and with a grossness bordering on the cynical. Examples are "My Subject is Patriotism" (*International Literature*, No. 2, 1939) and the preface to the present volume, in which he envisions "the definitive rise of an art of the cinema" as a result of Anglo-Soviet-American victory in the present war, and in which he writes: "I have long been tied to America both by a deep love and by the great tradition of film-art. Now these feelings are heightened by the warm friendship in which our people are together delivering powerful blows to the scourge of darkness, blood and savagery, in the fight for the ideals of mankind, culture, humanity and light."* So excessive, indeed, has been Eisenstein's capitulation to the demands of the Stalinist bureaucracy that a friend of mine thinks he is satirizing Stalinist culture by

* "MOSCOW, Feb. 18 (UP): Sergei Eisenstein, one of the most prominent Soviet film directors, today launched a Soviet-German cultural cooperation program over the Comintern Radio Station. Broadcasting especially to Germany, Mr. Eisenstein said that friendly Russian-German relations established last year formed a solid base 'for increased cultural cooperation between the two great peoples.'" —*N.Y. Times*, Feb. 19, 1940.

wholly conforming to it. He cites the case of Ernst Jünger, who several years ago satirized the Nazi blood-and-race ideology by publishing, in Germany, a work carrying it to extreme conclusions. This theory is psychologically possible, from what I know of Eisenstein's personality. Two considerations, however, seem to make it unlikely: (1) Eisenstein's failure to produce anything of interest in the last decade (which argues that he made a sincere, opportunist effort to conform); (2) the fact that this mode of behavior, fantastic to our eyes, is the norm in the Soviet Union today, as was shown in the Moscow Trials and in the aesthetic capitulations of artists like Pudovkin and Shostakovich.

There is a modern sentimentality about the artist and intellectual which pictures him as a Prometheus defying the gods of totalitarianism in the name of Art and Culture. Such defiances are not unknown, but they are generally delivered from a safe distance—California is an ideal location. When, as in Russia, the artist-intellectual has remained within the totalitarian borders, he has reacted pretty much as Eisenstein has, submitting in aesthetic as well as political matters. About the only heroes in the tragedy of Stalinist culture were Mayakovsky and Yessenin, who instinctively chose suicide to creative death. The Nazi order is by now old and extensive enough for some further evidence to begin to appear. Braque has accepted a high artistic post in occupied France, and Vlaminck, de Segonzac and Derain are reported to have toured Germany on a "cultural mission." In an interview in the N.Y. *Herald Tribune* of August 16, Dr. John Altmann revealed that the greatest of German film directors, G. W. Pabst, famous for the anti-war films, *Westfront—1918,* and *Kameradschaft,* and for his wonderful cinematization of Brecht's *Dreigroschenoper,* edited the Nazi documentary terror film, *Victory in the West.* According to *Pic* for August 18, Pabst was secretly working for Abetz while he was in Paris before the war, ostensibly an artist-refugee from Nazism. Such reversals cannot but shock us, just as a book like *The Film Sense* is shocking coming from Eisenstein. But I think we had better get used to such shocks; there are probably more unheroic tragedies to come.

—*Partisan Review,* November–December 1942

There seems to be a natural hostility, incompatible with the best will on both sides, between modern totalitarianism and artistic creation. Capitalism perverts art or makes its practice more difficult, but totalitarianism simply liquidates it. In a predominantly private-capitalist society like our own, there are crannies in which the artist and intellectual can survive, as well as conflicting forces of which he can take advantage. Frick, the steelmaster, used to sit on a Renaissance throne underneath a Rembrandt reading the *Saturday Evening Post,* but the middle-class intellectuals, for all their economic impotence vis-à-vis Frick, were able to provide an audience for Joyce and James and Proust and Eliot. The "contradictions of capitalism," that bourgeois anarchy at which generations of Marxists railed, now turn out in our present ghastly period to have their advantages. For in the kind of society that has developed in Russia, there are no crannies, no contradictions, no conflicting forces—at least none of a growth sturdy enough to give shelter to the artist. There is only one culture, one conception of art, one criterion of taste and achievement; and if, as seems to be fatally the case, the one standard is that of Frick reading the *Satevepost* (without the Rembrandt), then the most dignified way out for the artist is Mayakovsky's.

The news comes, for example, that Eisenstein is again in trouble with the authorities—Part II of his new trilogy, *Ivan the Terrible,* has been found to be ideologically defective and will not be released. Although since 1929 Eisenstein has made every possible effort to adapt his genius to the base and vulgar uses required of it—and a few efforts one might think not possible, such as presenting the half-crazy, murderous Czar Ivan as a progressive Leader of the People—he has been in almost continual difficulties; in the last seventeen years he has completed only two films, both of them much inferior to the three he produced in the five years before 1929. Most of the other talented Soviet artists have also tried faithfully to follow "party directives," but have been little more successful than Eisenstein in avoiding constant harassment. One difficulty, perhaps the chief, is simply that they *are* men of talent—conscious, perceptive individuals who are mentally alive, who cannot help thinking freely, experimenting, seeing things in an original way, and so, despite their earnest wish not to, cannot help threaten-

256

ing Stalin's leaden dictatorship of mediocrity and lifeless conform-ism. One thinks of the writer in Henry James' *The Next Time,* who all his life tried to write something commonplace, cheap, vulgar that would sell but who kept producing one uncommercial master-piece after another. Or of the remark of the Prince—another leaden despot—in Stendhal's *Charterhouse of Parma:* "It seems that this is a man of intelligence who comes to us from Naples, and I do not like that tribe. An intelligent man follows in vain the best precepts, even in good faith; always in some way he is cousin to Voltaire and Rousseau."

Another difficulty is that serious artists, especially in a still primitive country like Russia, naturally are influenced by the ideas and techniques of more advanced countries. There is a spontaneous internationalism about good art. The current campaign against "alien" Western influences is the most extreme but by no means the first. As I noted in 1939:

> It was precisely this international character of the Eisenstein cinema that most alarmed the Kremlin. If the masses are to accept the present totalitarian dictatorship as a fully realized socialist society, they must be cut off from contact with more advanced cul-tures. And so, in the last ten years, the Soviet Union has been slowly isolated. . . . This campaign is designed to reinforce, not to combat, those characteristic defects of backward cultures: pro-vincial smugness, the ignorant acceptance of inferior, banal art forms as "healthy" and "normal," and a corresponding suspicion of more advanced forms. This is what, aesthetically, the theory of "Socialism In One Country," has meant.

There is an added motive today: to prepare for war against the West. In the "collective security" period and after Germany had attacked her in 1941, Russia looked on the Western powers as allies, potential and then actual. Her cultural policy, therefore, could not reach the degree of hermetism it is now attaining. Eisen-stein made *Nevsky* in 1938 and *Ivan* was projected and largely finished during the war period. For all their faults, they are sophisti-cated films, and extremely "formalistic" in the stylization of cos-tumes, acting, and setting and in the elaborate composition of each individual shot. They are not at all the sort of home-grown provin-

257

cial films—a blend of stodgy realism and naive melodrama—we generally get from Russia these days. When *Culture and Life,* therefore, criticizes *Ivan the Terrible* for its "failure to portray contemporary reality" and its "cold and passionless historicism" and calls for fewer films about literary and historical figures and more about "the simple Soviet people who are the real creators of history," one can assume that even a Soviet editor would not criticize a historical film for not dealing with contemporary life, and that what is meant is that the stylized, ornate technique is now considered "formalistic," "decadent," and "Western." It is also just possible that Eisenstein took advantage of the historical pageant to escape from that Contemporary Reality which both Russian artists and audiences seem to wish to forget. This suggests in turn another speculation: why is it that the dominant classes in America feed the masses dreams, romance, "escape" culture while their peers in Russia adopt just the opposite policy, although both have the same end in view?

—Politics, October 1946

"It exhibited ignorance of historical facts by portraying the progressive army of the *Oprichniki* [Ivan's equivalent of the OGPU] as a band of degenerates, similar to the American Ku Klux Klan, and Ivan, a man of strong will and character, as weak and spineless like Hamlet." Thus the Central Committee of the Communist Party of the Soviet Union explained its suppression of Eisenstein's *Ivan the Terrible, Part II,* in the course of its decree of September 4, 1946, which gave marching orders to the cinema. This was part of the great "culture purge" that began in 1946 and whose rationale received its supreme expression in the famous 10,000-word speech that August by Andrei Zhdanov, who up to his death in 1948 was second only to Stalin in the Soviet hierarchy. Declaring war on all contemporary non-Soviet culture as decadent, corrupt, antihuman, reptilian, cannibalistic, and generally not quite the thing, Zhdanov demanded that "our comrades, both as leaders in literary affairs and as writers, be guided by the vital force of the Soviet order—its politics." The Central Committee responded with

258

decrees that, in addition to the one on the cinema, criticized current practice and laid down detailed "directives" for reform in literature (August 14, 1946), in the theater (August 26, 1946), and in music (February 10, 1948). The Central Committee also, in its decree of August 4, 1948, officially repealed the Mendelian Law in genetics in favor of a new theory, by a home-grown biologist named Lysenko, which held that acquired characteristics can be inherited.*

The Central Committee's suppression of the second part of his *Ivan* trilogy must have been all the more upsetting to Eisenstein because up to then he seemed to have, at last, squared the circle and come to terms with the Soviet bureaucracy. After the premiere, in 1938, of *Alexander Nevsky,* Stalin clapped him on the back and declared, "Sergei Mikhailovitch, you're a good Bolshevik after all!"† And the following year, one Vsevolod Vishnevsky signalized Eisenstein's return to official favor with a biographical pamphlet which blamed his ten-year eclipse on certain unnamed "enemies and saboteurs" (as, for example, Boris Shumiatsky, installed by the Kremlin in 1930 as top boss of the cinema and given a free hand up

* For the text of these decrees, of Zhdanov's speech, and for much other fascinating and invaluable material on post-1945 Soviet culture, see *The Country of the Blind* by George F. Counts and Nucia Lodge (Houghton Mifflin, 1949). The effect of these "marching orders" from the political bureaucracy to those actually engaged in artistic and scientific work was, of course, not motion but paralysis. In 1947, for example, just six feature films—full length, nondocumentaries—were released in the U.S.S.R., and the average per year in the five-year period 1948–1952 was exactly ten. The surrealist nature of these statistics may be appreciated if one compares the nine movies made in the U.S.S.R. in 1951 with that year's production not only in the U.S.A. (432) but also in Japan (215), Mexico (102) and Egypt (96). Nor, on the basis of what one has seen of recent Soviet films, is there any reason to suppose that the U.S.S.R. has gone in for quality instead of quantity.

† So Marie Seton reports in her biography of Eisenstein (Wyn, 1952), a peculiar volume whose rich documentation on Eisenstein's career, feelings, and ideas conflicts constantly with her political line, which is favorable to the Stalin regime. Her data clash with her interpretation perhaps because of her close identification with her subject, and friend, who also, at least in public, always converted the thistles of political interference into the figs of socialist idealism.

to 1938 in reducing Eisenstein, Pudovkin, Dovzhenko, and the other great directors of the twenties to Hollywood-type hacks) who "prevented the realization of various projects and suggested to Eisenstein ideas which were invalid, confused his goals and offered useless material" until finally "the party and the government, and Stalin in particular, came to his aid." It would be painting an already refulgent lily to comment on this Tartuffian document, which continues: "We can only imagine what Eisenstein and other great artists could have created if not hampered by these obstacles."

Eisenstein's response to the Central Committee's rejection of *Ivan, II* was a confession of error that was a macabre echo of his apology, ten years earlier, when *Bezhin Meadow* was suppressed:

> I must admit that we artists . . . forgot for a time those great ideals which our art is summoned to serve . . . the honorable, militant and educational task . . . to build a communist society. . . . In the light of the resolutions of the Central Committee, all workers in art must . . . fully subordinate our creative work to the interest of the education of the Soviet people. From this aim we must take not one step aside nor deviate a single iota. We must master the Lenin-Stalin method of perceiving reality and history so completely and profoundly that we shall be able to overcome all remnants and survivals of former ideas which, though long banished from consciousness, strive stubbornly and cunningly to steal into our works whenever our creative vigilance relaxes for a single moment. This is a guarantee that our cinematography will be able to surmount all the ideological and artistic failures . . . and will again begin to create pictures of high quality, worthy of the Stalinist epoch.

Is all this perhaps irony? Did Eisenstein, by carrying the Stalin-Zhdanov line to its logical extreme, thus attempt to express his personal despair and cry a warning to the outside world? Was there perhaps some justice, from the Soviet point of view, in the Central Committee's reaction to *Ivan, II?* (Even *Ivan, I,* which was not banned, is full of a sinister, neurotic atmosphere quite discordant with the surface political "line.") What can Eisenstein mean by those "former ideas" which, though sternly repressed, "cunningly steal into our works whenever our creative vigilance relaxes for a

260

single moment"? What can they be but the artist's vision and energy which, whenever he is off guard, persist in shattering the crude, wooden formulas of "socialist realism" with effects that are subtle, original, living, hence unpredictable and hence politically anathema in a totalitarian state? Or, alternatively, was Eisenstein so neurotically dependent on identification with Soviet power that he never allowed its actual evil to come to consciousness, even when he was himself the victim? Eisenstein died in 1948, long before the post-Stalin "thaw" in Soviet culture. One can only speculate.

—*Problems of Communism,* January–February, 1955

Ivan the Terrible, Part II is the last work of the greatest talent the cinema has yet known. Griffith was the instinctive genius, creating a whole new art form *ex nihilo;* Eisenstein was the talented —and conscious—theorist who developed the filmic vocabulary Griffith had invented without quite knowing what he had done. *Ivan, II* is the late, final decadence of this talent and this consciousness. But the dying lion is still a lion.

Part I of *Ivan* was shown in 1945, but Part II was suppressed. Its current release is part of the post-Stalin "thaw." I applaud the decision of Khrushchev's bureaucrats but I think Stalin's were smarter. For *Ivan, II* is ambiguous, if not worse, as propaganda; and as art it is clearly Formalistic. Blocked since the early thirties by State decree from montage, Eisenstein smuggles formal beauty into his film by fantastic sets and costumes and by directing the acting in the most heavily stylized mode of grand opera. As Premier Khrushchev might, and perhaps has, put it: The Devil Creeps in by the Back Door.

The film shows the disintegration of Eisenstein's personality under the frustrations and pressures he had endured for fifteen years. His homosexuality, for instance, now has free play. Of the eleven leading roles, only one is female—the witchlike Efrosinia. There are an extraordinary number of young, febrile and—there's no other word—pretty males, whose medieval bobbed hair makes them look startlingly like girls. Ivan has a favorite, a flirtatious, bold-eyed young police agent, and many excuses are found for having

261

Ivan put his hands on the handsome young face. But Eisenstein was ashamed of his homosexual tendencies and their liberation meant despair, not joy. Has any orgy been less pleasurable than the womanless banquet scene at which Ivan soberly plots Vladimir's death? There is a wild (all male) dance, true, but the dancers fling themselves about not in sensuous abandon but in desperate frenzy. Everything in the film emphasizes this mephitic, airless, neurotic atmosphere. The Caligari-like sets are claustrophobic—the doorways so low that people have to stoop to go through them. There are almost no outdoor scenes; we are trapped in the oppressive gloom of Ivan's palace. The leading characters are men become beasts: Ivan is a lean, tired old wolf; the boyars are great fat bears billowing in furs; the two leaders of Ivan's Oprichina police are bulls with curls low on their brutal foreheads; the wicked Efrosinia is a beaked hawk.

Taken on the surface, *Ivan, II* is a parable justifying Stalin's policies. Ivan is the determined leader of the Russian people against their foreign and domestic enemies; his Oprichina is the GPU; the boyar nobles are the kulaks and other bourgeois elements, and they join with the church in working against Ivan-Stalin. Efrosinia, Ivan's aunt, who has poisoned his wife in *Ivan, I* and who now plots to kill him and put her son, Vladimir, on the throne—these treacherous kinsfolk are the Old Bolsheviks. Ivan-Stalin is reluctant to believe in Efrosinia's guilt—"Touch not the kinsmen of the Czar!" he orders the Oprichina-GPU—which is a bit of court flattery, since Stalin showed no such hesitation about condemning the Old Bolsheviks. Finally he acts when Efrosinia proclaims her jubilation over what she thinks is Ivan's murdered body. (It is actually that of her son, whom Ivan, in a Stalinesque bit of double-crossing, has persuaded to wear his robes, so that Vladimir receives the dagger meant for Ivan.) The film ends with Ivan on his throne proclaiming: "Now that we have put down internal treachery, our sword will be used only against foreign invaders."

But this surface reading is—superficial. Ivan is shown becoming a bloodthirsty beast, of course from the highest motives. "A monarch should follow the right if possible, but he should follow the evil path if necessary," says one of his advisers.

The crucial scene comes after Ivan has appealed for friendship to

262

Philip, head of the Moscow church, saying pathetically, "I am alone." Philip—who alone of the leading characters looks like a man and not like a beast—agrees on condition he will be consulted before Ivan executes any more of Philip's boyar friends and kinsmen. Ivan accepts this not unreasonable condition for friendship. But Malyuta, the chief of his Oprichina, has overheard the promise and there follows a curious scene in which Malyuta's great shaggy head is fondled by Ivan as he calls himself Ivan's hunting dog. "Trust nobody," he says. "You have power, use force!" He insists that Philip merely wants to gain time for his plots and he suggests that the thing to do is to execute Philip's kinsmen, the Volynetski. The next scene shows Malyuta beheading the three leading Volynetski. Ivan appears, views the bodies, and says, "That's not enough." Philip is then arrested and executed. It seems impossible that this rapid transition from vows of friendship to betrayal to butchery is not meant to suggest certain aspects of Stalin's statecraft.

There are two open homosexuals in the film, both villains. The minor one is the King of Poland, who is shown in his effete court camping around in a fantastically huge ruff—and, of course, plotting to lead a crusade of civilized Europe against barbarous Muscovy. The major one is the very odd character of Efrosinia's son, Vladimir, who is presented as drunken, cowardly and effeminate. He keeps telling his mother—a woman who makes Disney's witches look positively benevolent—that he doesn't *want* to replace Ivan, that he can't *stand* bloodshed, and that his only desire is to live in peace. These humane sentiments are accompanied by pouts and girlish eye-play. It is very confusing. But I think Vladimir is the key. He gets drunk at the banquet—the only one who showed that much spontaneity at that dreary carousal—and when Ivan craftily uses his old gambit, "I am alone and friendless," Vladimir is moved to say: "You have one friend—me." He shows his sincerity—a drunken one, true, but in *Ivan, II* any sincerity is welcome—by confiding that his mother is always after him to take away the throne from Ivan but that (pout) he doesn't *want* to. Ivan-Stalin at once begins to persuade Vladimir to dress up in his clothes, with the fatal results noted above.

Is it too much to speculate that Eisenstein identified himself with homosexual Vladimir, the helpless victim of palace intrigues who just wanted to live in peace (read: to make his films in peace) and thought all this political intrigue was nonsense? The late James Agee used to insist to me that in *Nevsky* and *Ivan, I* Eisenstein was satirizing Stalinism, on the principle of Swift's *Modest Proposal:* exaggeration that covertly suggests the opposite conclusion to the one overtly put forward. I didn't agree then but after *Ivan, II* I think Jim may have been right. Vladimir, for example, keeps falling asleep at crucial moments. This shows his frivolous nature, of course. But considered a little more deeply—or obliquely—may it not be intended to present him as the only sensible, decent person in that nightmare ambiance where the fight for power—or mere survival—makes men snarl and bite like animals? In Ivan's court, as in Stalin's, only the sleeping can be wise—or human.

—February 1960

From 1932 until his death in 1948, Eisenstein taught at the State Cinema Institute in Moscow. Vladimir Nizhny, one of his pupils, has now published a book, *Lessons with Eisenstein* (Hill and Wang, 1963) which gives a detailed and vivid impression of his pedagogical methods. Judging from this account of Eisenstein's discussions with his class on how to film four scenes—Vautrin's arrest in *Père Goriot,* Raskolnikov's murder of the pawnbroker in *Crime and Punishment,* and two episodes from the Haitian insurrection—Eisenstein was as great a teacher as he was a director. Nizhny studied under him in the forties and his book is based on detailed notes of what was said in class by the teacher and, hardly less important, by the pupils. For Eisenstein was a most unacademic type, a dialectician and conversationalist rather than a lecturer. One gets a charming impression of young artists working out their problems with, rather than under, their master. He is genial, impolite, undignified, making fun of them when they are slow or obtuse, but always ready to listen to any suggestion. He changes his mind, thinks out loud, cracks jokes, and keeps talking, talking, talking in a *gemütlich,* uncorseted yet serious way that is very pre-1917. One admires his resourcefulness, his wit, his patience, his

264

fertility of invention; also his ability to articulate why one solution to a filming problem is better than another. An intellectually exciting book—and Montagu's historical notes are copious and valuable.

That nothing came out of Eisenstein's fifteen years of teaching—no new school, no major directors—this was the last irony in the saddest artistic career of our times. All those dedicated students—a whole generation! All that experience and knowledge their teacher poured out year after year! All coming to nothing since the Party bosses didn't want an original or creative cinema—when a good bureaucrat hears those words he reaches for his . . . fountain pen—but rather the standard "socialist-realist" product manufactured by dependable hacks. As for Eisenstein and his young disciples, what better isolation ward than the State Cinema Institute? When the students emerged into the real world—or, more accurately, the Soviet bureaucracy's world, wildly surrealistic, but all the world there was—they either adapted or went under. As for their master, after the political fiasco of *Ivan, II,* he was no doubt glad to creep back to die quietly in the sheltering academic groves of the State Cinema Institute.

—December 1963

SOME POST-STALIN FILMS

THE CRANES ARE FLYING

This is the first Russian film to be released here under the 1958 cultural-exchange agreement. We sent them in return that soggy Bronx bagel, *Marty*. Although the Soviet critics liked *Marty*—after all, Socialist Realism it is yet—I think we got the better of the deal. *Cranes* is not a great film, but it is a good and a moving one. It is carried almost entirely by Tatyana Samoilova, a grandniece of Stanislavsky, who plays the young heroine, Veronica. Miss (or should one say Comrade?) Samoilova is . . . an actress. After Rita Hayworth, Ava Gardner, Sophia Loren and the other great stone faces of Western cinema, it is amazing to see what can be done with nothing more than two eyes, a nose, and a mouth. Her expression actually changes—she is fiery, contemptuous, girlishly pretty, noble, radiant, tired, ugly, or beautiful, all depending on circumstances; just like real women and just not like movie stars.

The chief defect is the plot. Veronica and Boris are young lovers—platonic, of course, this being the U.S.S.R. The war comes, Boris volunteers, and is killed. Although she gets no letters from him, Veronica is sure he is still alive. In an air raid she becomes panicky and is seduced by Boris' cousin, Mark, whom she then reluctantly marries. Later, she leaves Mark, who turns out to be a rotter, and the film ends with her finally accepting the fact of Boris' death and, if I may be short about it, turning her libido outward toward the Russian people. Leaving aside this factitious propaganda ending, the plot is weak because, although Veronica still loves Boris and believes him to be alive, she marries the repellent Mark. One might swallow the seduction, but why marry him? (Or is this part of Soviet Puritanism? If so, it is still absurd, like a ruined Victorian heroine.)

It may seem inconsistent of me to criticize the plot here and in other new films and at the same time admire Griffith's movies in which melodrama runs riot and motivation is, to say the least, casual. The difference is that current films are realistic narratives, while those of Griffith were not. The form of *The Birth of a Nation* is determined not by the story but by cinematic ideas; its characters are not individualized, they are more like mythological personages, abstract and simple, than like real people; the whole effect is closer to epic poetry than to a novel. Griffith's movies are of the same nature as Cocteau's *Blood of a Poet* or Dovzhenko's *Earth*. But almost all modern films are in the realistic genre of *Grand Illusion, The Informer,* and *The Maltese Falcon,* to name three of the greatest. And in this genre, plausibility of plot and character are important.

Cinematically, *Cranes* is interesting mostly in the way the director, M. Kalatozov, sneaks formalism in by the back door. *Ivan, II* did it by stylization of sets and costumes and *Cranes* does it by manipulation of the camera, which in moments of emotional intensity becomes the actor's eye and brain, as in the dizzily circling birch trees Boris sees as he dies or the blurred focus and jagged camera movements expressing Veronica's desperation during her flight. There are also two long sequences in which Veronica seeks Boris in vain through enormous crowds, the mood being established by having the camera focus on her as faces and bodies endlessly stream by her, engulfing and overwhelming her. It could have been done more effectively and economically by montage, but ever since Stalin banned it as formalistic, montage has been to the Soviet cinema what the bare female bosom is to Hollywood.

—March 1960

BALLAD OF A SOLDIER

The Russian New Wave, which made an initial splash with *The Cranes Are Flying,* has lost ground with Grigori Chukhrai's *Ballad of a Soldier.* If one wanted to be polite, one could call it idyllic and wholesome. I don't want to be polite and so I call it a contrived exercise in the *faux-naïf.* Most reviews I've seen have disagreed. *Time,* which could hardly have been politically prejudiced in its favor, calls it "the best Russian movie made since World War II—a vehemently original, beautiful, humorous, patriotic, sentimental journey through war-churned Russia." Granted "sentimental" and "patriotic," not granted the other adjectives. Originality is confined to an upside-down shot of a tank pursuing the hero; the beauty is of the Hollywood soft-focus luminosity kind; there is no vehemence at

269

all—shades of Eisenstein! It's all very noble and refined; the only not-nice persons shown in this sentimental journey through "war-churned Russia" are a venal guard on the train and a woman who has taken a lover while her husband is at the front. One concludes that the Russians are just about the *nicest* people in the world, enduring the horrors of war and invasion with the good-humored phlegm and consideration for others of Londoners queuing up for a bus. Somehow I don't think it was that way at all, nor do I accept the gentle, sensitive hero as a symbol of that Red Army which raped and looted from Budapest to Berlin with a ruthlessness not seen in Europe for centuries. This is public relations—"He was a Russian soldier," the commentator intones at the end—and that it has been accepted in the West as a charming idyll shows a natural craving for some kind of health and decency in movies on the part of the reviewers; their mistake is in not seeing that this kind of sentimentality is merely the reverse image of the exploitation of sex and sadism in the name of realism, and that it is also corrupt. One doesn't like to be sold a bill of goods even if it is tied up in pink ribbons.

—October 1961

THE LADY WITH A DOG

As a translation into cinema of Chekhov's story, Heifitz's film seemed to me exactly right, reproducing Chekhov's peculiar combination of pathos, comedy, and realism. The costumes and sets were unobtrusively of the period, and the acting was as natural and "undramatic" as Chekhov's prose.

The principals, Iya Savvina as the lady and Alexei Batalov as the lover, gave performances that were never a note too high—or too low. The minor parts were also well taken—always the sign of a good movie—such as Nina Alisova as the wife and Peter Krimov as the lady's husband, who in three minutes sketched in the character ("My husband may be a good honest man," the lady blurts out to her lover, "but he is a flunky in his soul!") with his discreet, gliding walk, his compulsive bowing, and his "modest, sugary smile." The

270

director is Josef Heifitz, whose *Baltic Deputy* (1937) I recall as one of the better "patriotic" movies of the Stalin period, which is not saying much. His *Lady with a Dog,* however, is something different from anything I've seen out of Soviet Russia: a film of unerring taste and sensibility which has no "social significance" whatever, beyond the depiction—following Chekhov—of the boredom and vulgarity of upper-class life under the Czar. But the point, as in Chekhov, is not social satire so much as a private, human drama. Perhaps under Khrushchev's (relatively) permissive aegis, the Soviet cinema is again beginning to send down artistic roots. This particular shoot is a delicate one; nothing much "happens" and the frustrated lovers remain so at the end. Those who complain that *The Lady with a Dog* is "slow" probably also find Chekhov slow. And life.

My one serious criticism is that, in the final scene, the lovers analyze their situation instead of existing within it. Exposition is the enemy of art. These last ten minutes are tedious because all has been "said" already, in action, and we learn nothing new from hearing the lovers put it into words. "Then they talked it all over," Chekhov writes, but he doesn't make the mistake of telling us what they said. The only word he reports is the man's thrice-repeated "How?" which is more moving than the extended dialogue we get in the film. If only the director had omitted the dialogue and cut to his final long shot, through a lighted window, of the lovers continuing (inaudibly) their desperate talking! A perfect visual equivalent of Chekhov's conclusion: "And to both of them it was clear that the end was still very far off and that their most difficult period was just beginning."

—February 1963

HAMLET

The new Soviet *Hamlet* is a successful though not a great movie. The chief trouble is that it is staged in the academic style as was Olivier's *Hamlet* (from which it has borrowed freely, as the device of having Hamlet's soliloquies take place in his head, or rather on

271

the sound track, a gimmick perhaps but not a bad one; but I wish those roaring seas around the castle hadn't also been borrowed). It opens with three riders, their long Sir-Henry-Irving–David-Belasco cloaks streaming behind them, furiously galloping up to the drawbridge of a picturesquely sinister castle as dark clouds scud across a stormy sky. One of them turns out to be Hamlet. The change in the play is all too typical; this is a Hamlet who rides and duels a lot more than he reflects; he is so much the man of action, indeed, that the long-debated mystery of the play—what keeps Hamlet so long from revenging his father's murder?—becomes more mysterious than ever, especially as the soliloquies in which he himself reflects on the reasons for his inability to act have been cut drastically ("To be or not to be" is reduced to half-a-dozen lines) or omitted completely. (In a *Hamlet* recently staged in Poland *all* the soliloquies were left out.) Innokenti Smoktunovski looks a little like Richard Burton and plays the part in the Burton style, only better, as a vigorous type who is much more at home with horses and women than with ideas. As the *Corriere della Sera* put it in a headline: "[The Venice Film Festival Closes with] *un 'Amleto' anti-amletico.*"

The translation is Pasternak's, the fruit of his long eclipse in the Stalin period when he translated poetry instead of writing it. The music is by Shostakovich and is as conventional as the *mise-en-scène:* quite good as movie-music rhetoric, but hollow and over-dramatic. The director is Grigori Kozintsev. Could this be *the* Kozintsev, I wondered, the founder, with Leonid Trauberg, in the early twenties of the super-experimental FEKS group (Factory of the Eccentric Actor) which applied slapstick, vaudeville and circus techniques to serious drama, often using acrobats in the lead parts, and who, again with Trauberg, made in the late twenties *The New Babylon,* an extraordinary movie about the Paris Commune that made brilliant use of surrealist stylization to express a social theme? Indeed it is *the* Kozintsev, still alive and if not kicking at least continuing to produce movies: he looked extraordinarily young, not a day over fifty when I saw him at the Venice Film Festival a few years ago. While his *Hamlet* "works" in its own terms, being coherent, well-acted, and handsomely photographed, there is something depressing about the founder of FEKS and the codirector of

272

The New Babylon now turning out such a conventional work—and taking eight years to do it. True, there are two flashes of the old FEKSian fire: the play within a play was excitingly stylized (but this seems to be foolproof; it was well done even in the Burton-Gielgud *Hamlet*) and, more original and important, the concept of Ophelia as an automaton, carried out with many fine touches such as the iron corset and brassiere her maids put on her after her father's death, which solves many problems in this difficult part. But such flashes are, after all, rather depressing, like the last flareups of a dying fire.

—December 1964

NINE DAYS OF ONE YEAR

"Comrades!" Soviet orators used to begin in the old days when those Five Year Plans were taken seriously, "Comrades! We must catch up with and overtake rottendecadentfascistic American capitalism!" They didn't make it in pig iron and *Nine Days of One Year* shows they haven't Caught Up With And Overtaken us in the production of kitsch, either, and for the same reason: we are constantly inventing more sophisticated methods of production. It is the ironical fate of a revolution whose leaders thought they were in the vanguard of history to have produced a culture that has chronically lagged several generations behind the worst (and the best) that capitalism can do. The paintings I saw at the Venice Biennale last fall were in the paleolithic or early *Satevepost* style of Leyendecker and Rockwell, except for a few that rose to the heights, now considered in the West well below sea level, of Meissonier, Rosa Bonheur, and Victorian storytelling pictures like Sir Luke Fildes' *The Doctor*. A Russian Andrew Wyeth would have the same revolutionary impact on Soviet art today that Manet had on French salon painting a century ago.

Nine Days of One Year is an ambitious panorama of life and love and death among Soviet atomic scientists, and I suspect it was intended as Sovkino's big export item for this season. If so, bureaucratic heads must be rolling, for it aroused the most intense apathy

273

over here and, a few weeks after its launching, slid gently under the waves. *Spurlos versenkt.* Its style shifts uneasily, one might say shiftily, between two archaic modes of American masscult. Sometimes it recalled *Yellow Jack, Men in White,* and such forgotten Epics of Science as Paul de Kruif's *Microbe Hunters.* And sometimes *John's Other Wife.*

The domestic kitsch may be represented by a scene at the conjugal breakfast table. Enter pretty young bride and her hubby, who is Wrapped Up In His Work. He: "What a nice bathrobe!" She: "I've been wearing it a month, darling." Cut. She is also unable to prepare oatmeal satisfactorily, or was it kasha? She (nervously): "How is the oatmeal [or kasha], darling?" He (without looking up from *Pravda,* or possibly *Izvestia*): "Good." Tears. Cut.

The dominant kitsch mode, however, is Heroes of Science. Dimitri, the work-enwrapped hubby, gets himself fatally irradiated, courageously according to the script, carelessly it seems to me, since he went back into a chamber despite frantically flashing danger signs. But it's hard to tell, really. For all the clipboards and wall-to-wall reactors and instrument panels, this atomic research institute is a very Russian affair—more Dostoevsky than Fermi—with scientists in long white coats rushing up and down the corridors shouting, when an experiment pans out, "Hurrah, neutrons!" (That's what the subtitle said.) They're keen enough, God knows, but in such an emotionally charged atmosphere it's hard to distinguish between bravery and sloppiness. The plot is clear, however: Dimitri is heroic, quietly heroic; his colleague and best friend, Ilya, is a basically decent fellow, but he has all kinds of half-baked ideas such as that mankind hasn't progressed, not even Soviet-Russian mankind, and that nuclear bombs may not be instruments for peace, not even S-R ones; Dimitri marries the girl, Lelya (he and Ilya are Rivals in Love, it's all clearly plotted), and ultimately converts his cynical sidekick to a more positive attitude—wipe that sneer off your face, Ilya!—by the (quiet) example of his own (quiet) heroism.

The fusion of domestic and scientific kitsch reaches a critical point and explodes with a roar, or whatever those nuclear piles do, when the dying Dimitri, after his great and fatal experiment has

274

failed, says to his wife, Lelya, in words that Greer Garson in *Madame Curie* might have uttered, quietly, to Walter Pidgeon: "I've now proved that one out of the hundred possible ways to produce neutrons doesn't work. That leaves ninety-nine still to be tried." To which she replies: "I love you." Hurrah, neutrons! There's nothing better in *Arrowsmith* (1925), by Sinclair Lewis with Paul de Kruif as research assistant, which *The Reader's Encyclopedia of American Literature* adequately summarizes as "A story of a young doctor and his struggle between his personal desires and his idealistic dedication to his scientific work. . . ."

But stay—*is* Dimitri in fact dying? The film ends with him about to undergo an operation that has been tried previously, with indifferent success, only on dogs. But in the bright lexicon of Soviet science, and Soviet kitsch, there is no such word as failure. The last shot is of a whimsical, stiff-upper-lip note from Dimitri to Lelya and Ilya (for export, they should have given Ilya a less sexually ambiguous name—it's the one avant-garde note in the film) asking them to get him some pants so he can sneak out with them, immediately after the operation, for a night on the town. The note is decorated with three little dancing stick figures. *Ben Casey* never touched this. You'd have to go back to *Young Dr. Kildare,* on radio, with Lionel Barrymore and Lew Ayres.

It would seem that, after the effort of producing, in the last twenty years, one fairly good movie, *The Cranes Are Flying,* and one very good minor film, a sensitive period rendering of Chekhov's story, *The Lady with a Dog,* the sick man of world cinema has fallen into another decline. (I must confess I missed *Song Over Moscow,* which the *New York Times* summarized as "a melodious, skittish operetta-type import from Russia," and *Time* as "a cinematic curio" with "an amateur-theatrical air"; although both agreed it was right good fun, I somehow don't think I would have enjoyed it.) The relapse is all the more disheartening because the quality of the acting is so good. Even the Sovkino bureaucrats have been unable to suppress a talent for dramatic impersonation which seems as indigenous to Russians as to Italians. But I felt the same sympathy for these gifted actors caught in the toils of Sovsoap opera as I did for John Gielgud trying to get humanity and coherence into the lead part in *Tiny Alice.* Especially for the three principals: Tamara Lavrova as Lelya, Alexei Batalov as Dimitri, and Innokenty Smoktunovsky as Ilya. Miss Lavrova, a graduate of the Bolshoi Theatre School, makes her film debut here, and at times she actually manages to suggest a woman. Mr. Batalov was superb as the lead in *The Lady with a Dog,* as was Mr. Smoktunovsky as Hamlet in the recent Kozintsev film. They both rise far above their material, especially Mr. Smoktunovsky, who might be advantageously substituted for Alain Delon, Anthony Perkins, Sean Connery and some of the other standbys in our movies. Those shadowy figures who arrange East-West "cultural exchanges" might give a thought to it. And also to importing Miss Lavrova—anything Claudia Cardinale can do she can do better. All this talent—Nikolai Polotnikov should also be mentioned, who makes Professor Sintsov a believable monomaniac and who unhappily disappears after the first reel—is wasted on this atomic version of *Grand Hotel.* Maybe it should be called *Grand Institute.* A good director might have saved a lot, but Mikhail Romm is not one. His best-known film, *Lenin in October* (1937), had the same great subject that Eisenstein had celebrated ten years earlier in *Ten Days That Shook the World,* and the contrast is a textbook illustration—one I have used myself, with parallel film clips—of the difference between talent and mediocrity. Here again he takes a big theme and reduces it to stodgy sentimentalism. In 1937 Romm may have been, understandably, intimidated by Stalin's cultural bureaucrats, but times have changed and in recent years his has been a courageously outspoken voice for artistic freedom. Which is admirable and heartwarming but doesn't make him, alas, any more inspired as a director.

—May 1965

276

PART FIVE

MOVIES
1960–1966

U.S.A.:
HOLLYWOOD

THE APARTMENT

It seems impossible that Billy Wilder, who made that tough, amusing farce, *Some Like It Hot,* should have next made *The Apartment.* But such surprises are so common in Hollywood as to suggest that "Billy Wilder"—and "John Huston," too—are actually syndicates.

The Apartment is without either style or taste, shifting gears between pathos and slapstick without any transition. Hydromatic. One moment Shirley MacLaine takes an overdose of sleeping pills, the next Jack Lemmon cheers her up by demonstrating his bachelor method of straining spaghetti through a tennis racket. (Later, a synthesis when he sentimentally plucks a strand of spaghetti from the strings.) We are asked to sympathize with these two "people"— the quotes are advised. The female, an elevator operator in a big insurance company, has yielded to a philandering vice-president because she (erroneously) believes he will divorce his wife and marry her. The male, a clerk in the same company, lets his superior use his bachelor apartment for sexual assignations, hoping for advancement by this pimping. Both the male and the female are presented as Little People, maybe not too bright, but thoroughly decent and wholesome. What can you do, after all, in a big insurance company? And where but in Hollywood would this situation be seen as comic material? The male duly falls in love with the female but he continues to let his bosses shack up in his apartment, including the vice-president and the female: he loves her but he respects her commitment to the v-p, and the v-p is, after all, a v-p. Finally in a big worm-turning scene which falls as flat as all the other climaxes, the male withdraws the key, the female hears of his heroic act (from the v-p) and runs through the streets to her (at last!) true love. The "credits," ironic word, state that Mr. Wilder and I. A. L. Diamond wrote the screenplay. Surely "Diamond" is a misprint for "Zircon."

It is interesting to compare a recent German film, *Rosemary,* with *The Apartment.* Both have the same theme, sex and big business, but in the former the logic is carried out and the girl is a tart and the pimp is a pimp, while in the latter it is fuzzed up with a queasy combination of slick cynicism and prurient sentimentality.

280

Rosemary is a moral film, *The Apartment* is immoral, that is, dishonest. Which won't prevent most of our movie audience summing up the former as "such an *unpleasant* film, so sordid," and the latter as "the one about that nice young couple."

—August 1960

The above review provoked more disagreement than any other I wrote for Esquire *except that of Tony Richardson's* Tom Jones, *another widely popular comedy I criticized on much the same grounds. To me,* The Apartment *illustrated Hollywood's lack of contact with reality. But a group of Hollywoodians—Cukor, Brooks, Wald, Taradash, and Zimmerman—whom David Susskind needled, on "Open End," with quotes from my review, thought I was the one with a defective sense of reality. So did several dozen readers who wrote in objecting to my review. I replied in a later issue:*

The most intelligent defense of *The Apartment* was made in a letter from Arthur Jordan Field, of Providence, Rhode Island, which begins: "I have followed your writhing through *Politics, Dissent, The New Yorker* and elsewhere, with varying responses." (I had hoped that "writhing" was a mistyping for "writing" but Mr. Field assures me it wasn't.) "But I'm afraid your latest effort to bring your free-floating critical technique to bear on the film world has been disastrous. . . . The diatribe against *The Apartment* can only be called wrong-headed."

To take up Mr. Field's points:

(1) "Shirley MacLaine does *not* yield to a philandering vice-president because 'she believes he will divorce his wife and marry her.' A clear and reasonable case is made for her being very much in love with him." *Actually, a case is made for* both *hypotheses and it is not at all clear which is supposed to be the correct one.*

(2) "Did you really feel the suicide and recovery scenes were implausible?" *Yes, what with that warm-hearted Paul Muni-type doctor and his w.-h. wife. Also I object to the injection into a hardhearted comedy of softhearted sentimentality. The confusion of genres is tricky business and I felt that Mr. Wilder was throwing in sob stuff in case the laughs weren't enough.*

281

(3) "Do you really feel that lending the apartment to company officials as a way of getting ahead in the corporate world was 'out of touch with human reality'?" *Yes, a person with Lemmon's other traits would not have played the pimp to ingratiate himself with his bosses. Nor can I imagine top executives having to borrow his ratty little apartment for their amours. In the non-Hollywood world there are other solutions open to the rich.*

(4) "You write that 'Both the male and the female are presented as Little People, maybe not too bright, but thoroughly decent and wholesome.' Actually they were neither perfectly decent nor entirely wholesome." *Yes and no. They are* presented *as decent, but their actions show they* are *otherwise. The characterizations conflict with the plot line and this indicates not human complexity but Hollywoodian irreality.*

(5) "I received no impression that Jack Lemmon 'respected' the girl's love for the vice-president, although he did accept it. There was certainly some unreal quality to his self-sacrificing, self-effacing behavior, but he was described as a 'shnook.' . . . Shnooks can be in love in their own way." *I would say that if a shnook normally behaves as Lemmon does when his girl is sleeping with his boss, then a shnook is someone who needs psychiatric help.*

(6) "You completely misrepresent the final scene. MacLaine does not run to Lemmon's apartment as to 'her (at last!) true love.' . . . Instead, she asks Lemmon whether he wants to finish a card game they had begun previously and when he says, 'I love you,' she replies, 'Shut up and deal.' What was impressive was Wilder's ability to *avoid* the typical Hollywood ending." *He avoided it only if one doesn't look too closely. The girl does run happily through the streets to the boy, and her "Shut up and deal!" is a declaration of love all the more sentimental for its stiff upper lip.*

I think Mr. Field has been taken in by Mr. Wilder's remarkable ability to have it both ways. An opportunistic ambivalence is the hallmark of his films. *The Apartment* is a transposition into comedy of another overrated film of Mr. Wilder's, *Sunset Boulevard:* for mercenary motives, a young man lends his room (in *Sunset,* his person) to lustful older people; he falls in love with a girl his age whose relations with the world of power are also suspect (in *Sunset,* the female scriptwriter is frankly out to make a career). Love makes him realize he is behaving badly—in the twenties one would have said that love "regenerated" him; the result is the loss of his job (in *Apartment*) or of his life (in *Sunset*). Although Mr. Wilder is considered a very cynical fellow in Hollywood, he seems to me not cynical enough; he uses bitter chocolate for his icing, but underneath is the stale old cake. Love Conquers All, ultimately. Under its influence, Jack Lemmon rises to heights for which his previous shnooky subservience has not prepared us. So with William Holden at the end of *Sunset:* he asks the girl out to the mansion of the aging star (Gloria Swanson) who is keeping him, reveals the real state of affairs and sends her back to her fiancé in a renunciatory gesture all too reminiscent of Sidney Carton's "This is a far, far better thing I do" scene at the guillotine in *A Tale of Two Cities*. He then packs his bags, virtuously taking only the clothes he arrived in, and walks out on Swanson, who shoots him. But he should have been either less of a heel at first or less of a hero at last. A genuinely cynical director like Lubitsch would have had him stay on with Swanson because he has come to prefer loveless luxury to impoverished love. A real sentimentalist, on the other hand, would have him marry the girl and begin a new, clean life. Mr. Wilder's ending tries to have it both ways, something as impossible in art as in life, though a feat achieved hourly in Hollywood, whose relation to either is distant.

—April 1961

THE UNFORGIVEN

How much strain can a director's reputation take? Of late years, John Huston seems to have been trying to find out. I think he has carried the experiment too far with *The Unforgiven*. Some B pictures are good fun in their modest little way, but there is nothing worse than a big Hollywood film that goes wrong. *The Unforgiven* is a work of profound phoniness, part adult Western—I prefer Tom Mix—part that *Oklahoma!* kind of folksy Americana. It is limp as drama, every situation is built up until it soggily collapses, even the final Indian attack is tedious: can this be the man who gave us *The Maltese Falcon* and *Beat the Devil?* Those Indians, by the way, are

283

as stupid as Mark Twain found Fenimore Cooper's. About forty of them, mounted and armed to the teeth, attack a ranch house defended by a man, a boy, and two women. Their method is to ride straight up to the barricaded windows and yell. Presently they are down to ten. Then some genius thinks of battering in the door.

The mood is established in the first three minutes by shots of Lillian Gish working a churn and of Audrey Hepburn running gaily over the prairie with wide skirts billowing. The latter pulls up, looks with starry eyes at a flight of wild geese high up in the Technicolor sky, and remarks to the former: "They're human too, maw. They jest fly a mite higher than us, that's all." Miss Gish is plucky, tart, downright, etc., one of those frail little pioneer women who Won the West. Plenty of moxie in that tiny frame. "If those big lumps want fresh bread, let 'em ride home and git it!" The talk is all that way or should one say thetaway? "A fur piece to go. . . . Howdy, mister. . . . Ain't a man can't be thrown, ain't a horse can't be rode. . . . Ef that don't beat *all!* . . . It's Injun work. . . . Wake up, Cash, we got company (cabin is surrounded by Injuns—this line is practically obligatory). . . . I'd take it most kindly, ma'am, ef'n yew. . . . I've got to know the why of it, Ben! . . . A man sets down roots, Cash, an' he don't like 'em cut off." Two hours of this can be most fatiguing.

Nor are the stars much help. Burt Lancaster is the big, strong, kind type, a young patriarch so to speak, wholly dependable, but jest a mite dull. The Indians are much more animated. Miss Hepburn essays the tomboy-cum-child-of-nature, but when she tries to be vital she becomes even more lifeless than usual. She is not an actress, she is a model, with her stiff meager body and her blank face full of Good Bone Structure. She has the model's narcissism, not the actress' extroversion. The door is giving way, the roof is burning, her maw has expired from an Injun bullet, she has been given the pistol with one shot in it for herself ("Is it pain to die, Ben?"), Lancaster is peering grimly through the smoke waiting for the final charge, and here is Audrey, somehow immaculate despite her carefully smudged face, showing us her Fine Bone Structure.

—June 1960

THE MISFITS

Like so many Hollywood films, this begins wonderfully and then
the life slowly leaks out. Begins well because all is fresh, no mistakes have been made, brisk technique is in command; but when it
has to grow up, it sogs. When these people, masterfully sketched in
as caricatures, try to become full-length portraits, one disbelieves
more and more. Hollywood can still sometimes do action—at least
John Huston can, but when he gets enmeshed in Arthur Miller's
script, he sinks into the bog of women's fiction. His reflexes are still
okay—the wild-horse-hunt at the end is excellent—but he's just not
up to a human situation. Which is a pity since the script that Mr.
Miller wrote for his recently divorced wife, Marilyn Monroe, was
an attempt to render her real, off-screen personality. That he sees
this pretty much as the rest of us off-screen people do is either a
tribute to her wholeness or a sign that Mr. Miller is not very perceptive. The flattering remarks the other characters direct to "Rosalyn," as she is called, are more embarrassing than revealing: "You
have the gift of life." "When you smile, it's like the sun coming up."
"How come you got so much trust in your eyes [or was it dust?]
like you was just born?" Montgomery Clift begins gay and strong
as a reckless young cowboy, but he is soon pushed back by Mr.
Miller's script—which has him psychologically crippled, like Hamlet, by his mother's having re-married—into his usual bewildered
style. Eli Wallach was bound by contract to deliver such Millerisms
as "We're all blind bombardiers. We kill people we don't know. I
bombed nine cities in the war. I can't make a landing and I can't
get up to God." Really. As for Clark Gable—who died soon after
making the film, some say because of his exertions in the horse-
hunting scenes—he does his wicked best, but the Millerite script
pushes him into psychological territory he's not equipped for; like a
wasp stuck on flypaper. At the end, when he is driving back in the
truck with Rosalyn after he has freed the wild stallion because of
her squeamishness, he says—the American male grateful for being
hobbled by the female—"God bless you, girl." Well, he gets it out,
as per contract. And *she* says: "When it's dark, how do you get
home?" And *he* says: "You pick out a star. . . ." Good-by, good-

by, Clark Gable, and I wish your last line had not been written by Arthur Miller.

—October 1961

WEST SIDE STORY

Although most of my colleagues thought this terrific and colossal, I didn't for the following reasons: (1) It's in the romantic-schmaltzy tradition of musical shows—*Oklahoma!, South Pacific*—rather than the good one, that of *Pal Joey* and *Kiss Me, Kate,* which debunks romance and is lively and disrespectful. (2) Bernstein's music is pastiche; one hears echoes of Rodgers, Kern, Porter, Romberg, even Stravinsky, for Mr. Bernstein is very *au courant,* a great hand at orchestration, but there's little to orchestrate; (3) Stephen Sondheim's lyrics didn't send me; the *Tonight* song came out like *White Christmas* and there were too many couplets like: *"Say it loud and there's music playing/Say it soft and it's almost like praying."* (4) Romanticizing those New York street gangs results in dishonesty: the candy-store proprietor overawes the Jets with his little-man decency and by sheer moral force expels them from his shop (in reality they would have slugged him); see also the scene when the Puerto Rican girl-member of the Sharks is roughed up by the Italian Jets without losing a single essential item of clothing, and the climactic fight in which the Queensberry rules are observed (the real gangs' idea of sportsmanship is ten to one, if you can manage it). (5) The artistic problem was to modulate between stylization and realism (that is, *South Pacific* realism); Jerome Robbins' choreography was as good as the critics said it was but I was bothered by its unresolved discord with the "real" story, which was treated naturalistically; thus the gangs dance out their antagonism in the opening ballet, which is wonderful as dance but which (of necessity) involves no body contact and no bloodshed: it is the mimic world. But then we are plunged into the real world, where lovers clinch awkwardly and enemies jostle clumsily, and the final fight, the one with body contact and blood, is partly stylized and partly realistic and one's suspicion is confirmed that they wanted to

286

have it both ways, an infallible sign of nonart. Mr. Robbins was dismissed as co-director halfway through the film; the charge was "perfectionism" which perhaps meant he wanted to have it only one way, *his* way. If so, I salute him.

—February 1962

LOLITA

Lolita is a good movie which might have been much better. For the title role, Stanley Kubrick discovered a teen-age television actress named Sue Lyon whose moods, accent, facial expressions, and body movements seem to me remarkably authentic—quite different from the clichés we usually get in such roles. The direction has Kubrick's virtues: a sense of form (opening and closing with the murder of Quilty, for instance, which is as comically horrible as it is in the book) and of tempo (so little waste motion that it seems *shorter* than its running time, most unusual in our films) and of what is a picture (how refreshing to have a sharp eye behind the camera and how lucky that Kubrick began as a still photographer). The script, credited to the author of the novel though I gather the director had some good ideas too, is tight and workmanlike. And there is Peter Sellers, as Quilty, who rips off two freestyle impersonations which are the best things he's done since *I'm All Right, Jack.*

Still, *Lolita* is a disappointment because we have a right to expect more from Kubrick. His film, while far above the Hollywood level, is still a conventional effort. What was needed was something much wilder and more original, something in the line of Vigo or Godard, which would find a cinematic equivalent for the exuberant, daredevil prose of the novel. I think there are two reasons for this failure to translate the spirit, as well as the literal story, of Mr. Nabokov's book into movie terms. One is the casting of James Mason as Humbert. The part demanded a protean, intellectual, obsessed personality—Olivier might have carried it off—and Mason was just not the type. He is what is called an "adequate" actor, which usually means "inadequate"—compare his and Ralph

287

Richardson's performances as the prosecutor in those two Oscar Wilde films; it was the craftsman vs. the artist—and his specialty has always been the stiff upper lip, whereas Humbert Humbert has a very loose upper lip; he is a volatile Central European, shameless and cynical, who would have thought his film shadow a hopeless square. Mason is indeed remarkably like Humbert's description of himself—"the writer's good looks—pseudo-Celtic, attractively simian, boyishly manly"—which is perhaps why Kubrick chose him; but he conveys no inner spirit to vivify this physique, and it is Humbert's garrulous self-exposure that makes the book interesting. Mason was conceivable as General Rommel and Captain Nemo, but these gentlemen were memorable for what they did rather than for what they thought or felt. Another casting mistake was Shelley Winters as Lolita's mother; Charlotte Haze was a genteel ladies'-club type; Miss Winters plays her so *fortissimo* that she becomes a brawling Bronx fishwife whom one cannot imagine having poor Charlotte's cultural pretensions—or getting Humbert to marry her, despite the nymphetic bait.

But the chief reason for the failure to recapture the quality of the novel is that Kubrick was evidently scared stiff of the Legion of Decency and such self-appointed guardians of our morals. Even the tiniest ads find space for the legends: "APPROVED BY THE PRODUCTION CODE ADMINISTRATION" and "NOT FOR PERSONS UNDER 18 YEARS OF AGE." These bows to Mrs. Grundy turn out to reflect accurately the nature of the film. The erotic and perverse flavor of the novel has been almost entirely expunged—I wonder why Mr. Nabokov agreed to this bowdlerization. This has been done partly by casting Miss Lyon, who was fourteen but looked seventeen, as the twelve-year-old Lolita—good as she is, her advanced age tones down Humbert's obsession from perversity into mere infatuation—but chiefly by omitting or blurring all the erotic parts of the book, one of whose charms was that it was romantically enthusiastic about physical desire as against the usual clinical or repellent treatment in current novels. Thus the first sexual encounter, at the Enchanted Hunters Motel, is one of the great passages in the book; libidinous feeling (and frustration) was lyrically, wittily described and in detail; when finally the encounter takes place on just the opposite terms Humbert imagined ("it was she who seduced me"), it is high comedy. But the movie gives only the most fugitive, embarrassed version of the scene. The book-Humbert had plied his prey with what he thought were sleeping pills but were in fact placebos, and she resists him not from chastity but "with the neutral plaintive murmur of a child demanding its natural rest." The movie-Humbert is too decent to resort to sleeping pills and, after a half hearted attempt to share Lolita's bed (the other Humbert just climbed in) he retreats to a folding couch, after protracted struggles to open it, which divert the audience with some good, clean, low comedy. Kubrick is too artful a director not to have realized this change of key was destructive to the mood of the scene—but of course this was just what he wanted. In the book Humbert is frustrated by Lolita; here he is frustrated by a sexless mechanism—a clear gain censorwise. The reverse seduction, the turning point of the book, is here attenuated to Lolita's whispering something in Humbert's ear; he looks surprised; cut.

I see no reason for going so far in bowdlerization. The book is not pornographic and—unlike Henry Miller's the *Tropic of Cancer* —was not challenged in the courts. Granted a book can "get away with" more than a movie, still I think this one could have come much closer to the erotic atmosphere of the book. The Legion of Decency would have tried to organize a boycott and the Production Code Administration's seal of approval would have been withheld, but movies have been commercially shown in this country which defied both these establishments. One can understand why Kubrick, as a businessman, didn't want to offend the bluenoses. But he is also an artist, and he missed a chance to challenge the worst aspect of our movie censorship: its disapproval of the erotic and its tolerance of the sadistic. Thus he dared to do Quilty's murder right out of the book, but he gives us no comparable love scene. In fact, sometimes one thinks that the only way to get real sex past the censors is to combine it with sadism; rape seems less objectionable to them than seduction, perhaps because it is less enjoyable.

—September 1962

DR. STRANGELOVE, OR HOW I LEARNED TO STOP WORRYING AND LOVE THE BOMB

With this *comédie noire* Stanley Kubrick clinches his title—one I conceded him years ago—to Best of Show among our younger directors and why stop there? Also Boldest. Of the great nightmare he has made a lafforama that leaves one with a painful grin on the face and a brassy taste in the mouth.

The story is from Peter George's *Red Alert* and is similar to that of another, better-known novel called *Fail-Safe,* so similar that the authors and publisher of the latter have settled out of court a plagiarism suit brought by Mr. George. A crazy American general sends a squadron of nuclear bombers to get in a first strike at Russia; after frantic efforts and unspeakable confusion, the American President manages to recall or have destroyed by the Russians all but one; this gets through and drops its bomb, which triggers off a nuclear death belt the Russians have secretly contrived; the picture ends with the world due to follow shortly. Very funny. What the autopsists call *risus sardonicus.*

It is amazing that the screenplay (by Kubrick, Mr. George, and Terry Southern—and from what I've read of Mr. Southern, I'd guess he is responsible for most of the dialogue and many of the more outrageous touches) should be faithful to this grim outline and more than faithful, you feel they really enjoyed their work.* It is amazing that Kubrick's direction should leave no satirical punch pulled: he gives us a *Walpurgisnacht* of folly and madness in which the principal actors are American generals, an American President and his Cabinet, and a German atomic wizard in their employ; and in which every sacred *idée reçue* of the cold war—from mother and ice cream to The International Communistic Conspiracy—is methodically raked over with a barrage of satire. It is even more amazing that Columbia Pictures Corp., a perfectly respectable American business enterprise, is distributing this preverted, to borrow from the script, travesty of the American Way of Life (and, of course, Death). As I write, the film has not been publicly shown. The repercussions may be interesting. Or, possibly, not: we have a way of defusing critics by agreeing with them—"I'm glad you asked that question."†

Dr. Strangelove is a machine constructed to deliver the maximum punch. The intercutting throughout of the American plane's progress with the "meanwhile back at the air base (or the Presi-

* See "Correction" at end.
† It was a big hit and there were no picket lines.

dent's war room)" sequences, for instance, is beautifully handled for suspense, and the plane's theme song, *When Johnny Comes Marching Home Again,* is exactly right in its cockiness and its outdatedness. But it is Kubrick's direction of the actors that I most admired: he has made them into *commedia dell'arte* grotesques, but grotesques that take off from a solid foundation of what one uneasily recognizes as our everyday American reality. Peter Sellers, as the President, is disturbingly right: a reasonable, decent little fellow who just wants to live and let live, but who is trapped in the madness of his military and scientific sorcerer's apprentices. As, his first call on the "red" or "hot" direct phone to the Soviet premier when he stalls, like a wife telling her husband she has wrecked the car, until he finally has to come out with it: "Well, Nikita, you know, the fact is, something very peculiar seems to have happened. . . ."

But the heart of the film is the military grotesques, and I wonder if Kubrick, even with Columbia Pictures behind him, will get away with it. (If he had only included J. Edgar Hoover!) The two lower-echelon types are stupid, illiterate cornballs. Colonel "Bat" Guano (Keenan Wynn) is convinced that the British Group Captain Mandrake—the only sensible military type we see—is either a spy ("What kind of fancy uniform is that?") or a "prevert" (this *must* be Terry Southern) and warns him, burp gun in hand, as Mandrake enters a phone booth to call the President: "If you try any preversions in there, I'll blow your head off!" The commander of the fatal plane, Major Kong (Slim Pickens), is a dim-witted Texan who rises to his big moment when the attack signal comes through: "Ah ain't much of a hand at makin' speeches, boys. . . ." He then exchanges his helmet for a cowboy's Stetson, and ends riding the bomb down like a bronco, flailing it with his hat and yelling "Yippee!" The two generals are stupid, illiterate, cornball and crazy. George C. Scott as General "Buck" Turgidson, liaison between the President and the military establishment, gives his best performance to date; he is really a "character" actor, and Kubrick pushes him all the way: such mugging—he has more facial muscles than Lon Chaney! But this is just technique, though always nice to see some in American movies. The great grotesque is Sterling Hayden as the loony general who launches the attack. He is a

291

certifiable madman—there might be some difficulty in committing Buck Turgidson—who orders the bombing as a last resort against "the Communist conspiracy to sap and impurify our vital body fluids" via the fluoridization of American water supplies.

I have never thought much of Mr. Hayden's acting, but he is very good here, so good as to be more than a grotesque: he is mad but human; one never knows quite what to expect next and so one has a certain empathy. This suggests one of my two criticisms: there are no overtones. All the characters, except Mr. Hayden, roll smoothly along their predestined satiric tracks. It will be objected that the style of the film is abstract satire and that human overtones are therefore not to be expected. Granted, but this brings me to my second objection: there is too much repetition. As, the scenes in the plane: one can have too much of twisting of knobs and readings of dials, even though the satiric point is the contrast between the precision of the means and the lunacy of the ends. There is also too much repetition of character: these are, rightly, comic-strip people, every man in his humor, but since humors are invariable and so incapable of development, there is a loss of interest if they are repeated too much. Yet they must be repeated—that's part of the joke, too. I recommend the study of Molière, who in *L'Avare, Le Misanthrope* and *Tartuffe* also manipulated fixed, static characters like General Turgidson, but who knew how to tread the narrow path between too much and not enough. Falstaff is the other kind of comic character, fluid and changing as life and so never wearying because each repetition is not quite the same. Hayden is no Falstaff, but the germ is there. And if Kubrick-Southern had been more of a Molière, their film would have been better. Though it's quite good enough for these times.

—February 1964

Correction: I am informed, by Reliable Sources, that I overestimated Terry Southern's contribution to the script of *Dr. Strangelove,* specifically that he came in only in the last few weeks, after it had been put into pretty much final shape by Kubrick and Peter George. He added some nice business and some fine touches, but his collaborators were more important than I'd thought. (Mr.

292

Southern's literary personality is so distinctive that his collaborators tend to be blanked out: *Candy* is treated by the reviewers as if it were his work alone although the title page clearly states that Mason Hoffenberg is its coauthor.) I was also wrong, as Mr. Brown of California noted in the May issue, about the movie script being faithful to Mr. George's original novel, *Red Alert*. I meant the movie was as uncompromising as the novel, which I hadn't read but had heard about, but I hadn't realized that Kubrick had converted a "serious" message-novel into a black comedy whose message was all the more really serious, as Lewis Mumford has pointed out, for being transposed into the mode of grotesque satire. My apologies to Mr. Kubrick.

—September 1964

PHAEDRA

Jules Dassin's reputation over here as a serious director has long baffled me. If he were French, one could lay it to *nouvelle-vague* snobbery, but he is in fact a New York boy. His *He Who Must Die* was considered one of the best foreign films of 1958 (I thought it a pretentious pastiche of Eisenstein-cum-socialist realism), and *Never On Sunday* was generally admired as a lighthearted comedy (I thought it leaden-footed and phony-folk). Now we have still another Dassin movie with a Greek background. *Phaedra* indeed! Euripides . . . Racine . . . Dassin—whither Western culture? In the Greek story, Phaedra falls in love with her stepson, Hippolytus, who rebuffs her; she denounces him to his father, Theseus, for having tried to seduce her; Hippolytus goes to his death and Phaedra kills herself. Melodramatic but logical. In the Dassin version, the melodrama is heightened and the logic is eliminated: Phaedra (Melina Mercouri) and Hippolytus (Anthony Perkins) fall madly in love and consummate their passion in a luxurious Paris flat; he asks her to leave his father for him; she refuses, for reasons I didn't quite catch, and goes back to her husband's luxurious country house in Greece; no sooner arrived there than she regrets her decision, but it is Too Late; Hippolytus-Perkins is now

293

through with *her;* alas and alas and etc. and etc., until finally their suicides put them, and the audience, out of their misery.

As is his habit, Mr. Dassin sacrifices background and character for dramatics. The husband (Raf Vallone, or Theseus) is alleged to be a shipping tycoon, but the Balzacian drama that this world might have afforded is reduced to a gala launching of a ship named *Phaedra*—the irony of it all—and a few long-distance phone calls conducted with the usual mastery of movie tycoons. His personality and his relations with his wife and son are barely sketched in, so one has no clue as to why they are both so willing to betray him, beyond that *coup de foudre* that is the last resource of cheap dramaturgy. Not enough, especially since Vallone, whose only definite trait in the film is virility, would seem much better able to satisfy the formidable sexuality of Mercouri—she has developed as terrifying a mane and set of teeth as Bardot, whose physical dimensions she far surpasses—than the wispy Perkins who becomes more fragile and epicenely contorted with each new film. He is so outmatched in every way, from breadth of shoulders to manliness of voice, that during the love scenes I had the unsettling feeling they were both in drag.

To be fair, there was one good sequence, a rendering of sexual intercourse that showed naked flesh through wavering water and rhythmically pulsing flames. Overblown but cinematically inventive. Mr. Dassin does have a flair for effect, as in the famous long, silent sequence of the bank burglary in *Rififi,* (even if Huston did it first in *Asphalt Jungle*). But he is lost when it comes to anything sustained and he is worse than lost, he is all too confident when it is a matter of inflating his melodramas with Social Symbolism. There was almost nothing but Social Symbolism in *He Who Must Die* and even in this sex drama he deploys black-garbed women of the people as an imbecilic Greek chorus, as when they marvel at the nocturnal launching: "They are powerful. They speak many languages. And they celebrate with fire in the sky." They come on again at the end as the wives and mothers of the sailors who have been lost on the *Phaedra,* which obligingly sinks at the very moment Mercouri is rushing to her husband's office to reveal her infidelity. (Even ships obey the iron laws of Dassinesque melodrama.) The women go through their paces, pushing back and forth and lamenting with picturesque vigor, but somehow one doesn't believe a word of it, and, what's more, one doesn't believe that Mr. Dassin does either.

—October 1962

THE TRIAL

" 'A novel by Kafka, that crazy, up-the-wall Czech genius!' said Orson Welles, reaching into the enormous box of Maria Guerrero cigars he habitually lugs around with him. 'Only people with nothing to lose could make such a film. The producers have no money, and I'm an outcast.'

"A gust of wicked laughter shook his Falstaffian frame, startling the waiter who was tenderly pouring us a fifty-year-old cognac. . . . He was in a mood for revelry, having completed here, after a year's travail, the toughest venture of his multifarious career—a screen version of Franz Kafka's nightmarish fantasy, *The Trial*. . . .

" 'You can start an argument in any crowd of Kafka fans,' I said, sniffling the cognac fumes, 'by asking them to explain the theme of the book. What do *you* think Kafka was saying?'

" 'The villain of the piece is Big Brotherism,' Welles replied. . . . 'K. typifies Organization Man. His crime is surrendering to the system that's destroying his individuality. Yet he tries to fight it. He represents the human condition today, half alive, half dead, conforming yet protesting. Like all of us.' "

When I read this in *The Saturday Evening Post* of December 8, 1963, I had misgivings; the banality of the interviewer—his piece was headed *Citizen Welles Rides Again*—seemed to find an echo in the interviewee. Anyone who could describe Kafka as "that crazy, up-the-wall Czech genius" is capable of anything, including the reduction of Kafka's dialectics to the clichés of Big Brotherism and Organization Man. And so it turned out: *The Trial* is a travesty of the original, and it substitutes nothing of its own; it is the emptiest, the most boring and pretentious film Welles has made.

After a century and a half of romanticism, culminating in such solipsistic excesses as action painting, it is easy to forget that a work

295

of art is impersonal fabrication as well as personal expression. If the latter is too prominent, the universal element—the form—is destroyed and the audience is involved only insofar as it is interested in the personality of the artist. Such "art" doesn't differ in principle from the narratives of patients on the analytic couch or the drawings of children and madmen (which may also have aesthetic qualities). The romantic movement, with its exaltation of the subjective over the objective, the artist over the work, has a lot to answer for. Including, I think, Orson Welles.

The entry "Steam Engine," in *The Columbia Encyclopedia,* begins: "—machine to convert heat energy into mechanical energy. Steam requires about 1600 times the amount of space as the water from which it is formed. The force of this expansion is the basis of all steam engines. The expanding steam issuing out of the boiler moves a piston within a cylinder [etc.]. . . ." That Orson Welles has a cinematic imagination with great expansive force has by now been amply demonstrated; it needs at least 1600 times the amount of space available in any subject. When it is confined within the unyielding framework of a realistic story, as in his masterpiece, *Citizen Kane,* and his near-masterpiece, *The Magnificent Ambersons,* it sets those pistons and cylinders in motion and does useful work. In *Kane,* Hearst's actual career and personality, plus Herman J. Mankiewicz' script (which played a larger part in the success of *Kane* than is generally recognized), provided this restraint, as did Tarkington's realistic novel in *Ambersons.* But when screenplay and setting are fantastic, Welles's romantic imagination dissipates its force in enormous clouds of steam. Or hot air.

In *Othello* (1952) Welles might have had something solid to push against, but he escaped, with a loud hiss, into cinematic camp. In *Mr. Arkadin* (1955) and *Touch of Evil* (1958) he let himself go, like an overweight matron indulging in desserts, in melodramas which seem to have been whipped up entirely for theatrical effect. There is almost no attempt at continuity or logic of either plot or characterization, and only a perfunctory stab at plausibility. Some of the individual scenes are masterfully rendered: the choreography of movement, the accentuation of what magician Welles wants us to see by lighting and camera angle, the flow of images freed by a virtuoso's touch from their routine movie duties to make the point

296

he wants to at the moment. But the scenes, brilliant as they often are in themselves, don't add up to a whole.

Looking at *Arkadin* is like hearing a singer with a magnificent range of expression giving his all to an opera composed by John Philip Sousa, libretto by Marie Corelli and Ian Fleming. Mr. Arkadin—played by Welles, another self-indulgence since he is an embarrassingly bad actor who always hams it up and is even worse when he underplays than when he overplays—is supposed to be one of those sinister international tycoons (one can't even define them without journalese) like Kreuger or Gulbenkian or Sir Basil Zaharoff, the "merchant of death." These gentlemen may have lived it up like Arkadin-Welles, but they must have devoted *some* time to business. We get exactly one glimpse of Mr. Arkadin's business life: he calls out to an aide, disentangling himself from bikini-clad sirens, "don't forget—exchange Mexican pesos for Chilean dollars —and *buy copper!*" The rest is Welles swelling around in a huge fake beard, a wig that shows a good half-inch of webbing in close-ups, an aquiline nose obviously made of putty, and a big black opera cape. A few "name" players have the time of their (but not our) lives in grotesque bit parts: Redgrave, Paxinou, Tamiroff— and the unhappily forgotten Mischa Auer as the proprietor of a flea circus. It is a fine moment when he rolls up his sleeve and says to his charges, with that leer no one else has approached, "Feeding time!"

Touch of Evil is better, if only because slightly more coherent, but I cannot take it seriously, as some of my younger friends do. Welles again over-underplays the lead, lurching around behind a swag belly, his cheeks stuffed with cotton like Lon Chaney and his features all sweaty and stubbly, mumbling and grumbling inaudibly. *The Maltese Falcon* is my idea of a crime picture: logical, realistic, sardonic, humorous, fast, unpretentious. *Evil* is fast, but none of the other terms apply. Welles never knows where to stop. Motivations are nonexistent; Welles makes anything happen if he thinks it will be effective. But if the plot is merely an excuse for fireworks, then each "effective" bit simply cancels out its predecessor. If *all* the cards are wild, you can't play poker. I'm told that in Paris they think *Arkadin* and *Evil* are Welles's masterpieces. *Tant pis*. The French seem to regard our movies as interesting

297

specimens of primitive handicraft, like birchbark canoes. But as a native, I find it dismaying that the creator of *Kane,* when left to his own devices, reminds me of a twelve-year-old who has been reading too many comic books.

That Welles should have attempted *The Trial* shows an extraordinary lack of self-knowledge. Few works could be less suited to his talents than Kafka's allegory of the relationship of man to a God who is omnipotent and incomprehensible, whose moral authority he recognizes while struggling against His concrete manifestations which are always either absurd or unjust or both. To explore this contradiction is the point of *The Trial,* whose drama is therefore all internal: such action as there is takes place merely to provide the characters with subjects for their endless casuistry about the "real" nature of this mysterious Authority. I doubt if any one could make a successful movie out of such material; certainly Welles cannot. He reduces it all to nightmare. The novel is tight, logical, classical; the film is diffuse, formless, romantic. Kafka tells his fantastic tale in the most prosaic, matter-of-fact terms, with a chastity of style that is exactly right; the most extreme violations of logic are presented in the most reasonable prose. "By an odd but obvious paradox," Camus writes of *The Trial,* "the more extraordinary the character's adventures are, the more noticeable will be the naturalness of the story. . . . Thus it is that Kafka expresses tragedy by the everyday and the absurd by the logical. An actor lends more force to a tragic character the more careful he is not to exaggerate it. If he is moderate, the horror he inspires will be immoderate." Cautionary words whose wisdom Mr. Welles's recent career demonstrates.

Welles's style has never been more baroque than in *The Trial,* his lighting and camera angles never more picturesquely exaggerated, his piling up of material detail (those toppling drifts of lawbooks, that forest of half-naked old men outside the court) never more excessive, his scale never more grandiose. But, as it is the loser of an argument who shouts, so this visual braggadocio is to conceal the fact that our director hasn't the foggiest notion of what *The Trial* is about. Expanding the normal-sized bank in which Kafka's hero worked into the Gare de Lyon—literally: Welles rented the

298

abandoned station—still doesn't put any meaning into the film. Those acres of desks are, of course, intended to suggest that Modern Man is Lost in the Conformist Mass—King Vidor did it better forty years ago in *The Crowd*—just as the last shot, when the smoke from an explosion takes on a mushroom form, is supposed to induce solemn reflections. The elaboration of scale and decor is as boring as in any Biblical spectacular and for the same reason: because it is used without mind or feeling, not to bring out meaning but to distract us from asking for it. Finally Welles has made his greatest casting mistake to date (and this includes Tim Holt in *Ambersons* and Robert Arden in *Arkadin*): Anthony Perkins. Kafka made Joseph K. a sober, solid citizen, a valued employee, since this makes his arrest and trial all the more absurd, in the existential sense. But Mr. Perkins is more like a sensitive adolescent in an Inge play than a stable young career man, and he expresses guilt the instant the detectives invade his bedroom; he flutters, he writhes, he teeters on the verge of hysteria. But if Joseph K. feels and acts guilty from the beginning, then the major dramatic point of the story is lost; there is no problem, no mystery, no tension, no movie. And in fact there isn't.

—June and July 1963

HUD

One of the advantages of this job is that I don't have to see many movies. The daily reviewers have to look at so many terrible films in the line of duty that, like front-line soldiers under bombardment, they welcome the slightest diminution of that awful racket. (Some of the weekly reviewers also seem to suffer from battle shock.) As a monthly reviewer, I am in the happy position of a staff officer far behind the lines, seeing at most a dozen films a month and those of my own choosing. My nerves are intact, my sensibilities unblunted, and when, as occasionally happens, I err, the fault is mine alone.

This is to explain, and excuse, the reaction of many of my colleagues to *Hud,* which they have hailed as realistic, honest, searching, probing and uncompromising—and so it is compared to most Hollywood movies. But Hollywood is no longer the world, and on the international scale *Hud* doesn't weigh much. The uncompromising realism is mostly in the veteran James Wong Howe's photography, which does give an unretouched picture of the arid, scrubby landscape of West Texas, its neon-squalid towns and its cheap clapboard houses, belligerently charmless inside and out. The director, Martin Ritt, must also be praised for attempting a contemporary Western that eschews glamor and heroics. (The ranchers wear, for instance, not the costly felt Stetsons of the traditional cowboy, but cheap straw hats like Ohio farmers, with the brims curled to imitate the real thing.) Another welcome novelty is the housekeeper, a woman long past her "prime," which in our youth-obsessed culture is about 23. In the Hollywood formula such women are either tough or silly or sodden. But this remarkable housekeeper, despite her advanced age, is still attractive and still has plenty of humor and spirit. Patricia Neal is splendid in the part, but she would have been more splendid had she not at times been a little *too* spunky. Since she is clearly a most intelligent actress, I blame this on Mr. Ritt's direction which doesn't err on the side of subtlety.

The rest is pretty much the old salad, with sincere dressing. The glamorously corrupt older brother (here an uncle) and the admiring kid brother (nephew) are right out of *All Fall Down,* to name the most recent stereotype, with Paul Newman as Warren Beatty and Brandon de Wilde as Brandon de Wilde. Newman's Hud is his best performance to date, a mild encomium. Bar his old tendency to emphasize a dramatic climax by simply raising his voice, he does seem more at ease before the camera; his woodenly handsome face is still as much his problem as his fortune; I don't know how he can get action into it, but mouthing his lines is not the way. Master de Wilde, who is getting to be quite a big boy now, is no better and no worse than he was in *All Fall Down.* He is identical. As is his part: both films begin with his extracting brother (uncle) from a squalid sexual imbroglio and both end with his walking out on the fallen idol into a New Life. Kabuki has nothing on Hollywood.

But the giveaway is Hud's father, the stern patriarch who loves The Good Earth, the stiff-necked anachronism in a degenerate age of pleasure-seeking, corner-cutting, greed for money, etc.—in

300

short, these present United States. How often has Hollywood (where these traits are perhaps even more pronounced than in the rest of the nation) preached this sermon, which combines maximum moral fervor with minimum practical damage; no one really wants to return to the soil and give up all those smart angles, so we can all agree to his vague jeremiad with a pious, "True, true, what a pity!" In Mr. Ritt's morality play, it is poor Hud who is forced by the script to openly practice the actual as against the mythical American Way of Life and it is he who must bear all our shame and guilt. When he asks his father why he has always despised him, he gets no more enlightening an answer than "Because you don't give a damn." Maybe a point, but it's not developed. Men of few words, these Texan patriarchs. Melvyn Douglas plays it up to the hilt in the best Hollywood-Kabuki tradition: brooding, bushy-browed, slow-spoken (if at all), a real down-to-earth old-timer, just like Ward Bond or Walter Brennan. He has many big moments—after all, his part has been taste-tested since 1910 and he introduces no new flavors—but perhaps the biggest comes when, leaning on a property fence and gloating over his broad acres, he tells Hud that oil prospectors have been after him, but that long as I'm above ground (son) there ain't goin' to be no holes punched in *this* land. Their entire herd of cattle has just been slaughtered by gov'ment agents because of hoof-and-mouth disease and Hud, greedy and corrupt as usual, suggests that those oil checks would come in mighty handy. But his old man takes the position that if God had wanted oil wells in the good earth, He would have put them there. At one point, Hud tries to have his father declared legally senile. Despicable. But understandable.

—September 1963

CLEOPATRA

Although I wasn't invited to the press showings, for understandable though not admirable reasons, I finally caught Joseph Mankiewicz' pop epic at a naborhood theatre at a merciful naborhood price ($1.25) and length (three hours). The spectacular scenes

301

were confused and oddly minuscule: the battle of Actium seemed to have been staged in a bathtub, and the great processions in Rome also looked miniaturized although they must have been enacted by actual full-size people—unless they've developed some very lifelike three-inch puppets out there. Nor was I prepared for the aggressive tastelessness of the sets, costumes and colors; *Ben-Hur* was prettier.

Still and all, there was Elizabeth Taylor. At first I was disappointed, a large statement considering my expectations. Then I realized what she was up to: Miss Taylor has attempted and, I think, achieved, nothing less than the unsexing and deglamorizing of the Queen of the Nile—Claudette Colbert couldn't quite make it, though it was a good try—and her reduction to a suburban matron of impeccable morals and peccable diction. A less-confident actress might have taken voice lessons, might even have dieted, but not Mrs. Richard Burton. Her matronly whine, as flat as her matronly figure was not, pulled us down to twentieth-century American terra firma on the rare occasions when Mr. Mankiewicz' script gave us the illusion we were in ancient Egypt or Rome. Hers was a camp performance as faultlessly off-key as that of Steve Reeves in *Hercules* and *Hercules Unchained*. No one who has ever been connected with *Cleopatra* seems to have any stomach for a *Cleopatra Unchained* and indeed the very notion is alarming—I'd back Miss Taylor against Mr. Reeves any day. But meanwhile we do have Moments, as when Lizpatra is dumped from that carpet at Mr. Harrison's feet, fully clad (just as well, considering a later glimpse of her rump as she is massaged) in a hostess-type wraparound bodice and skirt, all set to seduce the conqueror of the world with her Bronxville wiles. Mr. Harrison smiles tolerantly—his Caesar does a lot of tolerant smiling—and, one imagines, with some relief. She might have been wearing toreador pants.

—February 1965

THE BIRDS

The only point of interest about *The Birds* is that it's by Alfred Hitchcock.

302

Hitchcock's best films were distinguished by (1) technical brilliance, (2) persons and scenes that were superficially lifelike, (3) economy of means, (4) tight, logical plots. *The Birds* is a negative print of these qualities.

(1) I counted just two cinematic coups. One was the first bird attack: the heroine is rowing across a bay; suddenly a sea gull screeches down and rips her forehead open—the shock, the quick cutting, the changes in point of view, here we had the old master for a moment. The other was the gradual massing of the crows outside the school: the heroine is sitting on a bench, her back to a jungle gym on which one crow is perched; another settles down silently, then another, then a series of cuts between the unaware girl and the bars of the jungle gym which become blacker and blacker with dozens, scores, hundreds of ominously quiet crows. For the rest, Hitchcock's technical ingenuity is limited to multiple-exposure trick shots—371 is the figure he gives—that don't work very well.

(2) Everything looks fake, partly because of poor color, which makes the outdoor shots look like postcards and the interiors like ads in *Life*. The leads all act atrociously. This may be partly due to a script that gives them lines as unconvincing as their stock characters. But why must each play badly in a different style? Tippi Hedren, a glacial model in whom Hitchcock discovered talents that don't show up on the screen, plays in the stiffest tradition of junior-high dramatics. Rod Taylor is run-of-the-mill Hollywood—might do as the loyal sidekick in a B Western. Jessica Tandy overplays her role in *haut*-Broadway style. They can't make contact. Even the bit parts, once a Hitchcock specialty, have become labored, over-shrill, as in the lunchroom scenes.

(3) The old, or classic, Hitchcock followed Poe's recipe for the short tale: every sentence must contribute to the specific effect the writer wants to produce. This effect in Hitchcock's case as in Poe's—both are Pavlovian experimenters on the nerves of their audiences—is always the thrill, the Baudelairean *frisson*. In his better films the human aspect is sketched in only enough to engage the viewers' empathy and to lend plausibility to the unpleasant little surprises he has in store for them. But in *The Birds,* background has become foreground: we must sit through a half hour of pachydermous flirtation between Rod and Tippi before the sea gull attacks, and another fifteen minutes of tedium, mostly centering around

Rod's old girl friend, who plays badly in still a fourth style—method—before the birds get into action again. If one adds later interrelations between lovers, mother, girl friend and a particularly repulsive child actress, about two-thirds of the film is devoted to extraneous matters. Poe would have been appalled. Human situations, in short, are developed far beyond the modest needs of a thriller, so far indeed as to produce a kickback. Since, as Charles Higham observes in *Film Quarterly,* Hitchcock has never been good with this sort of material, his elaborate attempt to make us believe his puppets are people merely convinces us that they are phonier than his trained birds.

(4) As for that logic of plot and motivation which, as Poe and (the old) Hitchcock understood, is essential to enforcing belief in a fantastic story, consider:

¶ Tippi warns a teacher that crows are massing outside the schoolhouse; their jointly worked-out response to the threat is not to put the kids into the cellar but to march them outside to walk home. To no one's surprise but Hitchcock's, the birds come shrieking like Stukas down onto the helpless little column.

¶ As the final mass attack on the house begins, it turns out that Rod has forgotten to block up the chimney (although a destructive flood of sparrows had poured out of it only the day before) and also to put up the shutters. He repairs these negligences, though at the cost of some wounds recorded in interesting close-ups.

¶ Later there is a lull, after a specially determined onslaught (could gulls actually drive their beaks through a thick oak door?) and Tippi wanders upstairs for no special reason. Hearing noises in the attic, she opens the door and sees a great hole in the roof, with hundreds of birds sitting around. Her natural reaction is to enter the room, carefully closing the door behind her. She is at once pecked into insensibility (splendid color shots of her blood-streaming face and hands). Rod rescues her in the nick of time (more blood and grue) and she ends up on a sofa no worse for her experience than a stagy bandage on her stagy brow.

¶ Throughout the film everybody behaves with similar idiocy; we are supposed to believe, for instance, that a community of farmers and fishermen—tough, practical folk, one might assume—can devise no better defense, like maybe guns, than running around hysterically every time the birds make a pass. Tippi is an effete city type but still she might be supposed incapable of asking, after a flock of gulls have dive-bombed a picnic: "Mitch, this isn't usual, is it?" This helplessness is necessary, of course, so that Hitchcock can get plenty of those shock close-ups he seems to dote on in his old age, but it destroys that elementary logic a thriller must have to be thrilling. The only characters in the film who aren't birdbrains are the birds. How did those crows, for instance, pick just the right hour to congregate on the jungle gym? They must have known when school's out. We've lost an insult.

ADVANCED BIRD-WATCHING

The Birds had mostly a cool-to-frosty reception in the press. However, two of our *politique des auteurs* hierophants—one can't call them critics—have issued ex cathedra panegyrics that almost reconcile one to Bosley Crowther. No one can reach more inane conclusions than a thoroughgoing theorist. Thus Peter Bogdano-vich—whose recent Museum of Modern Art monograph on Hitchcock is useful for its data—winds up his introduction: "If he had never made another motion picture in his life, *The Birds* would place him securely among the giants of the cinema. And that is where he belongs." And thus Andrew Sarris concluded a long and uncritically enthusiastic review in *The Village Voice: "The Birds* finds Hitchcock at the summit of his artistic powers." It's not that one disagrees with such judgments, it's that there is no basis for discussion since they use methods of thought and rules of evidence not common in the outside world. Which leads us to the *politique des auteurs.*

This theory, first advanced by Truffaut in *Cahiers du Cinéma* when he was still a critic (I prefer him as a director), as interpreted by American enthusiasts like Sarris and Bogdanovich seems to be no more precise an instrument than a prejudice in favor of certain directors—Sarris calls them "Pantheon Directors."

"I can't imagine a bad Hawks movie!" a *p.d.a.* adherent once burst out to me. The general objection to this line is that even the greatest artists, being men and not gods, are fallible.

The specific objection is that this kind of grading is appropriate to eggs but not to works of art, where the criteria must be more

305

complex because the object judged is more complex. It comes down, ultimately, to value judgments ("taste," "opinion") which can never be settled as conclusively as the freshness of an egg. Which is not to say that one man's opinion is as good as the next one's. Before the ultimate is reached a critic goes through a process of defining, describing, reasoning, and persuading which is drawn from his own special experience and knowledge and which may or may not persuade his readers that his judgment is more accurate— "true" or "right" would be claiming too much—than other judgments, according to *their* experience and knowledge. Readers have their own ideas, too, if they're worth writing for.

So I'm not sympathetic to Mr. Sarris' attempt, in 51 pages of the Spring, 1963, *Film Culture,* to present a catalogue raisonné of the work of every American director of any importance, some hundred fifty of them, since D. W. Griffith. It is an extremely classified directory which begins with twelve "Pantheon Directors" (Ford, Hawks, Hitchcock, Renoir and Welles are the only ones still practicing) and then ranks the rest in hierarchical order under: Second Line, Third Line, Esoterica, Beyond the Fringe, Fallen Idols, Likable But Elusive, Minor Disappointments, Oddities and One Shots and—a bit desperately—Other Directors. Each butterfly is fixed on its pin in its proper place, easily accomplished once the buterflies are dead. I feel a sympathy for those hundred-fifty-odd directors such as I felt for the writers, from Homer to Tolstoy, conscripted by Dr. Mortimer J. Adler for his Great Books set. Many of them, I imagined, would have preferred not to be so canonized. And I imagine many directors, even those ranked in the top categories, may object to being pinned into the Sarris collection. One can't deny his labors have been heroic, but Procrustes rather than the fire-giving Prometheus is the hero.

Procrustes was a premature psychologist, fitting his guests to his bed by stretching the short and amputating the tall. His problem, like Mr. Sarris', was that almost no one fitted exactly. Why is Sidney Lumet Likable But Elusive, while John Frankenheimer is a Minor Disappointment? Why George Cukor in the Second Line and George Stevens in the Third? Etc., etc. The categories are obviously absurd, but even if they were more sensible (and fewer), matters would not be improved. It's at best a parlor game. (I speak

306

from experience since I unwittingly invented one called "Masscult & Midcult." It seemed a suggestive little formula at the time, but what a mess when oversystematic people use it to classify individual works! Its only future is as an updating of "Authors": Advance Three Spaces if you put *Our Town* in midcult; discarding Kipling as masscult, Go Back To Start.) Taken seriously, this kind of quality-grading simply makes it more difficult to evaluate works of art—as if it weren't hard enough already—by forcing them into Procrustean categories that always add or subtract something essential.

—October 1963

U.S.A.:
UNDERGROUND

PULL MY DAISY

This half-hour short is as refreshing as anything I've yet seen on this assignment. The amateur cast is mostly Allen Ginsberg, Gregory Corso, Larry Rivers, and Peter Orlovsky. The photography, at once realistic and poetic, is by Robert Frank, whose remarkable picture-book, *The Americans,* was lately published by Grove Press. The direction is by Frank plus Alfred Leslie, a leading abstract-expressionist painter. They have got a lot out of their amateur, and doubtless refractory, charges not by teaching them how to "act" but by eavesdropping on them; the effect is spontaneous and alive. But the surprise, for me, was the narration by Jack Kerouac, which kept things rolling along on a tide of laughter and poetry. The film opens with the title song, a neat little lyric sung with great style and *abandon* by Anita Ellis:

Pull my daisy
Tip my cup,
All my doors are open.
Cut my thoughts for coconuts,
All my eggs are broken.

Then Kerouac takes over, like a parody of the stage manager in *Our Town,* substituting a raucous city-streets accent for the latter's folksy twang. A better parallel is with a movie travelogue, for while the actors in *Our Town* do grab a few lines for themselves, here one sees the tireless lip movements of Corso, Ginsberg, et al., but only the voice of the kerouac is heard in the land. It is all paraphrase and commentary, a March of Time in which The Voice has got out of control. Kerouac shows an unexpected virtuosity at the great American art of kidding, and the two-ply comic effect comes off very well—the unheard actors busy with their own concerns while the heard commentator gives us a run-down, like a demented Bill Stern.

The scene is the squalid Greenwich Village flat of a railroad conductor who likes jazz and beatniks. The plot is simple. His much-put-upon wife is shown getting her little boy off to school ("He complains he has eaten ten thousand bowls of farina," notes The

Voice). This is accomplished and at once the beats file in. They sit, they talk, they smoke, they sit, they eat, they argue, they drink, they sit, they talk, they have a jam session, they sit, and finally they go. The only dramatic tension, aside from the wife's periodic efforts to kick them out, is provided by a solemn young square who arrives with his mother and sister for some serious discussion, of which he gets just as much as he provides himself. The message I take to be that a beat toils not neither does he spin or wash the dishes and that this is definitely okay. (I hear there's a Beats Anonymous—if you're tempted to take a job, you call up a member who comes around and talks you out of it.)

At this writing, Frank and Leslie are trying to get commercial booking for their film. It would seem perfect for the art houses, yet they report strong resistance even there. It can't be on moral grounds—there's no sex, no violence, it would damage the kiddies a lot less than *Ben-Hur*. Must be too beat, that that is too off-beat. Now if it had been in French . . .

—April 1960

SHADOWS

The great *succès d'estime* in London this fall is John Cassavetes' *Shadows,* which has received critical acclaim and is doing sensational business at the leading art cinema, the Academy Theatre. The excitement is justified. I found *Shadows* as refreshing as *Pull My Daisy. Shadows* is improvised, like *Daisy.* It differs in being feature length, in having a story, and in the excellence of the acting. Kerouac's narration swept along the stiff amateurs in *Daisy;* here we have professionals, young and unknown, but still professional; the girl, Lelia Goldoni, is especially good. The film, which cost $40,000, grew out of some Stanislavsky improvisations at the Variety Arts Studio of New York, of which Cassavetes was then director. He gave the actors a situation and they just kept talking, feeling it out, pushing at each other, kicking it around. Because the students were white and colored, Cassavetes devised a story of racial relations, or rather unrelations.

311

This method results in a lyrical realism, fresh and spontaneous. No Hollywood script writer of the slightest competence would have submitted a script like that of *Shadows*, in which nothing is "pointed up" and all is anticlimax. (Indeed, there was no script at all.) Nor would any Broadway playwright have produced such inchoate dialogue; the closest analogy is O'Neill's *Long Day's Journey Into Night*. The actors interrupt each other, talk at the same time, repeat themselves, fumble for words, don't finish sentences and are in general as clumsy and inarticulate as everybody is in real life. Everybody except actors.

The first version of *Shadows* was shown a year ago at Cinema 16. I didn't bother to see it because, from reports, it sounded arty and obscure, like Maya Deren's high-class doodling. I'm told that his friends convinced Cassavetes that unless he made clearer what was happening—unless, in fact, something *did* happen—his film would never get commercial booking. So he raised more money and remade the film drastically. He has been accused of selling out by some of the far-out critics, but I'm glad he did. Although obscurity is now equated with purity, I have a reactionary prejudice in favor of communication and I therefore favor a reasonable amount of selling out.

—March 1962

SOME ANIMADVERSIONS ON THE ART FILM

I have been looking through the old programs of Cinema 16, a New York film society with some four thousand members which is now in its fifteenth year.* I have been viewing some of its current offerings and I think it is time to cast a cold eye on what is known as "the art film." (By "art film" I do *not* mean the work of such directors as Bergman and Resnais but rather films made outside the normal commercial set-up.) Its ideals are high and it is dedicated to

* Cinema 16 died several years after this was written, no connection, I'm afraid. Amos Vogel, its founder and director, then joined forces, so to speak, with Richard Roud in running the annual Film Festivals at Lincoln Center, which have kept alive the Cinema 16 tradition. Nothing succeeds like failure.

truth—no escapism, no box office. I am in favor of high ideals, but why are they so seldom entertaining in art films? I am also in favor of Truth and Realism, but why are they here always depressing? Above all, why are most art films poor? Cinema 16 describes itself as "the Off-Broadway of the cinema" and "the Little Mag of the film world," adding that its "only ambition is to search out the creative, the artistic, the experimental; its only goal is to be the showcase for new directions in the cinema." Cinema 16 is not analogous to Off-Broadway and the little magazines because (1) their level has been higher than that of the commercial theatre and press; and (2) they have often first presented writers who later became famous (as Joyce and Eliot in *The Little Review* and O'Neill at the Provincetown Playhouse). Neither of these statements can be made about the art film, which has remained through the decades a stagnant little back eddy. It should also be noted that practically all the great films—Cocteau's *Blood of a Poet* and Vigo's *Zero de Conduite* may be exceptions—from *Birth of a Nation* to *Potemkin, Kane* and *L'Avventura* have been made in the ordinary course of commercial (or Communist) movie-making and so are not art films.

Cinema 16 must be given credit for first showing such films—all but one non-art—as Torre-Nilsson's *End of Innocence,* Eisenstein's *Strike,* Cassavetes' *Shadows,* and Resnais' *Night and Fog,* and for reviving such films—all non-art—as Renoir's *The Rules of the Game,* Lang's *M,* Dovzhenko's *Arsenal* and *Earth,* Donskoi's *The Childhood of Gorki,* Welles's *The Magnificent Ambersons* and Clair's *The Italian Straw Hat.* But these plums were sparsely distributed through a vast pudding of dullness, nor was I lucky as a Jack Horner. The dullness is spiced with Angst. The more distressing aspects of life are so frequently on view at Cinema 16 that I have often wondered just who its four thousand devotees are. Masochists? Psychiatric social workers on a busman's holiday? Whoever they are, they have taken a lot of punishment. Typical Cinema 16 documentary films of past seasons:

Images of Madness ("macabre journey through the universe of the mentally ill"). . . . *Frustration Play Techniques: Ego Blocking Games* ("special projective techniques developed at Sarah Lawrence College. . . . Hidden cameras record test situations in

313

which various children react differently to competition, frustration and prohibition"). . . . *Neurosis and Alcohol* ("cats are made neurotic and then subjected to alcohol"). . . . *The Invader* ("traces history of syphilis from fifteenth century"). . . . *The Praying Mantis* ("alien and horrifying universe . . . love and cruel death"). . . . *The Unknown Soldier* ("merciless inferno of blood and death"). . . . *Depressive States and Paranoid Conditions.* . . . *Maternal Deprivation* ("disturbed children at a French nursing home"). . . . *The World of the Microbes* ("in quest of the tubercle bacilli"). . . . *Psychotic Illnesses in Childhood.* . . . *May 2, 1960* ("Caryl Chessman's execution"). . . . *Abseits,* which is described as "water, wind, sunlight, and seagulls; the sounds and lonely grandeur of ebb tide on a North Sea beach." It's always ebb tide at Cinema 16.

This season (1961–62) Cinema 16 exhibited, in addition to shorts and revivals, four new feature-length movies: (1) *The Time of the Heathen,* (2) *The Sin of Jesus,* (3) *The Sun's Burial,* and (4) *Guns of the Trees.* Although they are of little or no interest as cinema, they are worth considering as typical specimens of the modern "art film." Each bears the stigmata of the genre.

(1) THE TIME OF THE HEATHEN

"Amidst solitude and desolation, a major new talent projects a psychological drama of guilt and violence," is Cinema 16's hard sell for this one. Well, as I have observed before, there is art-film cliché as well as Hollywood cliché and here Peter Kass, Ed Emshwiller and Peg Santvoord, with the loftiest intentions, have created a little anthology. The two protagonists are a seamy-faced wanderer who is not quite right in the head, and a Negro boy who is, one discovers without surprise halfway through the film, a deaf mute. There is the obligatory opening sequence of the man walking endlessly through a depressing landscape, the obligatory rape-murder scene, the obligatory chase through tangled woods (Griffith did it better in *Birth of a Nation*), the obligatory locations—ruined house, desolate beach. There is also a long color sequence of montages about the bombing of Hiroshima which, if compared with the similar montages in Resnais' film, will illustrate the difference between the artistic and the arty. This sequence is justified by the revelation that the psychotic wanderer has been reduced to his sad state by his guilt-feeling because he helped drop the bomb on Hiroshima. This is conveyed by a shot of the Distinguished Flying Cross falling out of his nerveless hand as he dies on the beach.

(2) THE SIN OF JESUS

In the January, 1949, issue of *Partisan Review* appeared a superb little tale by the late Russian writer, Isaac Babel, entitled *The Sin of Jesus.* Arina is a hefty servant girl in a hotel who has borne twins to her lover, the janitor's helper, and is pregnant by him again just when he has to go into the Czar's armies for four years. She knows she will be knocked up by the customers ("Whoever stops here, he's your master") and she prays for a husband to keep her out of temptation. Jesus appears to her and gives her an angel named Alfred. But things go wrong on the wedding night:

> They had drunk the vodka to the last drop, and now it took effect. As soon as they fell asleep, she went and rolled over on top of Alfred with her hot, six-months-big belly. Not enough for her to sleep with an angel, not enough that nobody beside her spat at the wall, snored and snorted—that wasn't enough for the clumsy ravening slut. No, she had to warm her belly, too, her burning belly big with Serega's lust. And so she smothered him in her fuddled sleep, smothered him in the midst of her rejoicing like a week-old babe, crushed him under her bloated weight, and he gave up the ghost, and his wings, wrapped in her sheet, wept pale tears.

Furious, Jesus denounces her swinish lust. But she turns on him and asks who made her that way if not he and his father. "There's no forgiveness for you, Jesus Christ," she says at the end, "no forgiveness at all, none."

It is a jaunty, slangy, humorous and poetic little parable, written with the directness and vitality of all Babel's work. I regret that the film which Robert Frank has made from it has none of these qualities, but rather their reverse. For I like Mr. Frank's photography and I liked *Pull My Daisy,* which he made with Alfred Leslie, and I should have liked to like *The Sin of Jesus.* But what can one do? It is so bad—pretentious, mawkish, arty—that at times it seems to be a parody of the kind of "serious" and "experimental" film that goes big at Cinema 16. Frank has refined the coarseness of Babel's tale and he has transposed its humorous vitality into the kind of high-minded pathos, solemnly symbolic, that is well-loved by those who live south of Washington Square. Instead of Babel's Arina, a brawling virago ("her huge red arms"), we get a distillation of the females in the Greenwich Village coffee bars: lank-haired, sad-eyed, scrawny, soulful, sensitive (though, alas, inexpressive), life's predestined victim. This dreary little-theatre type—Beatrice Lillie could play her—walks somnambulistically through a great deal of portentous photography, suffering copiously. ("He went away, he left me, I'm in trouble," she whines to Jesus.) And at the end, instead of Babel-Arina's flaming denunciation, Frank-Arina is merely pathetic. "Forgive you? I can't. I have no forgiveness," she murmurs bleakly. Mr. Frank has chosen for his locale a New Jersey chicken farm without realizing that chicken-farming is intrinsically comic. Cf. Sherwood Anderson's *The Triumph of the Egg*.

(3) THE SUN'S BURIAL

This was introduced by Cinema 16's publicity man with his usual restraint: "a paroxysm of violence and eroticism . . . the work of Japan's foremost New Wave director, Nagisa Ohshima . . . explodes with the anger and fury of their rebellion and reveals, beneath its squalor and brutality, a deep—and hopeless—humanism." I didn't catch the humanism or the eroticism—both concepts I'm sympathetic to—because I couldn't find anything underneath the squalor and brutality. It seemed to me a monotonous series of beatings up slung together without either motivation or cinematic form; the cutting was as arbitrary as in a "blue" movie, the only object being to get on to the next scene of mayhem; when two people met, one's only curiosity was as to which would smash the other to the ground first. Eroticism was represented by (a) the master of a brothel pushing the padded armrest of his crutch—he's crippled, natch—against the throat of a whore who had been so foolish as to get herself pregnant, slowly throttling her as everybody, including the neophyte boy who is presented as the innocent Candide of the film, passively listens to her strangled screams; and (b) two young toughs (one of them Candide) robbing a love-making couple in a park—Candide crashes a club down on the man's skull and his companion (he's *really* bad) rapes the girl after having stifled her screams by stuffing her mouth with a clod of grass (that's quite a close-up). There are several other scenes of deep (and hopeless) humanism. Candide, trying to go straight, is delivering a load of tripes on his bicycle; he is waylaid by the gang, who slug him to the ground, kick him senseless and then belabor him with assorted lights and livers. It all winds up—or so I've been told, I left shortly after the intestinal attack—with most of the cast, stunned or wounded by a grenade, dying in agony as they try to crawl out of the ensuing conflagration. *The Sun's Burial* is in color. Blood does make a nice red.

(4) GUNS OF THE TREES

Jonas Mekas is the film critic of *The Village Voice,* and the editor-publisher of a magazine called *Film Culture* which is, as Herbert Hoover once remarked of Prohibition, "an experiment noble in purpose." Sympathetic as I am to Mr. Mekas' purpose, which is to present with the utmost intransigence the true aims of cinema, I rate dedication lower than acumen and enthusiasm lower than talent. The proof of the pudding is in the eating and much of *Film Culture* and of Mr. Mekas' column strikes me as not very nutritious. Now we have his first movie, *Guns of the Trees.*

I found in my seat a leaflet by its creator which I read with nervous appreciation (will I dig it? am I square?) before the house lights went down. It was headed, with a jaunty echo of dry-cleaning establishments, "WHILE-U-WAIT," and its text raised considerable expectations:

> You may ask yourself, what is *Guns of the Trees* all about, what's the story.
> There is no story. Telling stories is for peaceful and content people. And at this juncture of my life I am neither content nor peaceful. I am deeply and totally discontent. Do I have to list the reasons why? Haven't you read your *Times* and your *Pravda* today? Why do you wonder, then, that poets are beginning to get uneasy?
> Yes, the artists are abandoning the beautiful, happy, entertaining, self-glorifying stories. They are beginning to express their anxiety in a more open and direct manner. They are searching for a freer form, one which permits them a larger scale of emo-

317

tional statements, explosions of truths, outcries of warnings. . . .
It's not through the mind and order that I create. I create through my ignorance and chaos. Order doesn't interest me. I know that through my chaos I have a chance of arriving somewhere, of catching some secret movements of the subconscious, of Life, of Man. . . .

Then the film began. George Jean Nathan once wrote a piece about the opening of the Paramount Theatre in New York circa 1926. He described in detail the platoons of epauletted, cloaked, shakoed ushers, the spotlights and the red carpets, the hand-painted oil paintings that lined the walls, the Baroque profusion of the gold-leafed interior, the stupendous obbligato on the mighty Wurlitzer organ, and then—I quote from memory—"the great golden curtains parted and we saw a movie in which a floozy seduced a bond salesman." Such, *toute proportion gardée,* was my reaction to *Guns of the Trees* after reading Mr. Mekas' eloquent leaflet.

I expected something profound and difficult. What I got was two contrasting love stories which were all too easily followed (once one got used to avant-garde cutting) since they represented Good and Bad, Creative and Destructive, Life and Death, or, exisentially speaking, Authentic and Inauthentic. The Creative, Authentic, etc., couple was colored, the Destructive, etc., couple was white. "The small people don't learn," says the Negro girl, who was embarrassingly smug, to the tense white girl, who later kills herself, "but people like you and me should learn from everything." This labored fable takes place in a welter of "avant-garde" effects that don't come off, as in the stylized mimes that open and close the film. The settings were grimly "realistic," in the mode that I remember from similar art-film efforts in the thirties: railroad yards, city dumps, crumbling walls and alleyways, frowzy parks, kitchens that could do with a little dishwashing. Shot 210 is described in the script as: "Somewhere in the Bronx. A field of broken glass, junk, sun— Gregory walks across the junkyard, slowly, looking down, black." Meanwhile, back at the dump. . . .

All that is spontaneous in *Pull My Daisy* is selfconscious here; Ginsberg is inferior to Kerouac as a narrator because he is really rhetorical while Kerouac is mock-rhetorical; here Ginsberg alternates with folk songs, the last refuge of the American left; he is too

318

pompous and they are too simple. All those MacLeishian questions: "What is man?" "Perhaps just to be." "Will it ever change?" No reply from Ben Carruthers' costar, Adolfas Mekas, Jonas' brother, who is perhaps the most stolid movie actor since Francis X. Bushman.

The symbol of police brutality is some cops timidly pushing around folk-singers in Washington Square; in the thirties the cops were, with not too much hyperbole, called "Cossacks" and they really roughed up Communist demonstrators in Union Square; a clear gain in civil liberties, but not much of a symbol of Power trampling underfoot those Flowers of Life.

Gregory (Francis X. Mekas) has a big scene with a social worker which runs: (Gregory speaking) "There is nothing wrong with Fidel Castro." "You compare yourself with Fidel Castro?" "No, I identify with him." "You realize Fidel Castro is a revolutionary. Are you revolting against something?" "Yes I am." "What are you revolting against?" (TV scripts run on this way but at least it's from hunger.) "Against dishonesty, corruption." "What do you want? To change the world? Is that your idea?" "I think everybody wants to change the world, no?" There then comes a blank white screen, which is Mr. Mekas' ingenious transition device, after which we hear the portentous tones of Mr. Ginsberg: "What do you think of America? You who run America, vote hypocrite, edit school books, make foreign wars, appoint aldermen and football coaches?

"You who therefore are America, the land that opens its mouth to speak with four hundred billion dollars of armaments and two cents' worth of measly foreign aid [anybody checked these figures?] all for bombs and horror, fraud, dope fiends, Syngman Rhee, Batista, Chiang Kai-shek, madmen, Franco—who else God knows. I refuse to read the paper."

Instead of transitional music, Mr. Mekas uses an electronic squeak of varying pitch. Very avant-garde but after a while it gets on one's nerves just like Hollywood's mood music. But he does score one coup: he has dug up from somewhere a line that still haunts me: "Where are the snows of yesteryear?" Now where could he have found *that*?

—April 1962

319

THE ABOVE-GROUND UNDERGROUND

According to *Variety*, there are now 550 "art" movie houses—there were just twelve in 1945—and the art circuit has become economically "interesting." (An art house may be defined as one that shows serious films when it can't get a Bardot.) The art circuit has hitherto shown foreign films almost exclusively, but now American films are beginning to be made for it. Two that are now doing well at the box office are *Private Property* and *The Savage Eye*.

The former was written and directed by a young man in a hurry named Leslie Stevens. I think it is more dangerous to cinematic standards than poor old *Ben-Hur* was, since nobody can mistake *Ben-Hur* for a work of art, while the art-theatre public, softened up by the Kazan-Williams kind of serious nonsense, may very well make this error about *Private Property*. In fact, they have made this error: the film, which cost $60,000 to make, is expected to gross a million, and Mr. Stevens now has a contract with Twentieth Century-Fox. *Private Property* combines commercial slickness with the pretensions of what might be called the lumpen-avant-garde, after Marx's lumpen-proletariat. On the one hand, the mood music bleats and moans, the script is what the press agents call "sex-ational," and the acting is undistinguished (except for that cool old pro, Jerome Cowan, who has a nice bit at the beginning). On the other, we have the usual lumpen-avant-garde characters: a sinister delinquent, an impotent moron, a stuffy business type and his sex-starved young wife; plus an orgy of camera angles and postgraduate lighting, the whole thing culminating in a knife fight in a swimming pool that is photographed underwater and that contrives to be as dull as the rest. (Who would have thought that rape and voyeurism could be made uninteresting?) There is, to confuse things still more, though it probably didn't hurt at the box office, a happy ending which consists of two mortal lines. The wife has just been seduced, raped and killed (that is, *almost*) by the two bums she has invited into her house for reasons inexplicable except that the script read that way. Her business-type husband, who has arrived Just In Time, asks: "Anna, are you all right?" "I wasn't," she replies in the understatement of 1960, "but I am now." The End.

320

The Savage Eye, which was edited, directed and produced by Ben Maddow, Sidney Meyers and Joseph Strick, was a hit at the Venice and Edinburgh festivals, perhaps for reasons having more to do with overseas notions of American life than with its aesthetic merits. Not that it's not an extremely interesting effort, far above the level of *Private Property.* Barbara Baxley, a TV actress new to me, is excellent in the lead and indeed the only important role. And the documentary shots of life, if one can call it that, in Los Angeles are extraordinary: the wrestling match, the strip tease, the revival meeting, the automobile accidents, the transvestites' ball, the beauty parlors, the bars and cars and cops and bums. It is a photographers' film and the credit for its virtues must go mainly to them—Jack Couffer, Helen Levitt, Haskell Wexler, Sy Wexler, Joel Coleman—and to the co-editing of Sidney Meyers, who directed *The Quiet One.*

The defects are in the script. The plot line on which the documentary sequences are hung is anemic and unconvincing: Los Angeles as seen by an embittered young divorcée. This stacks the deck to begin with, for life even in that air-conditioned nightmare (credit: Henry Miller) must have more bounce, humor, decency, and affection than she sees; one suspects the agony is being piled on, especially since Miss Baxley is a pretty and lively young woman who, one cannot help thinking, might command a far more attractive admirer than the porcine playboy the script dooms her to. (Her efforts to avoid his kiss at the New Year's party is one of the most revolting sequences I have seen in years.) The script is the work of Ben Maddow, who suffers from a compulsion toward "literary" writing—he also did the folksy-fakesy dialogue of *The Unforgiven* on which I have commented elsewhere. It is the style of pseudopoetic rhetoric invented by Norman Corwin and Archibald MacLeish: "Who cries out lonely on the naked mountain of love? . . . Searching the stone libraries for the green stone of illusion . . . the slime of loveless love."

The depressing thing about both *Private Property* and *The Savage Eye* is that the chief complaint I have been making about Hollywood movies, their inhumanity, applies also to these extra-Hollywood ventures. Both are deficient in feeling and sense, and

321

both use violence to mask this deficiency. Both also don't even carry out the logic of their inhumanity, both have upbeat endings. I have noted *Private Property*'s already. In *The Savage Eye,* the heroine, after smashing herself up in an auto accident, is brought back to life by blood transfusions, and she cries out to the anonymous donors: "Fluid into fluid, they've come to lift me/to touch,/ Lovers without names, and take me. . . . You, I love you, I love/ you too: poet and paranoid, ex-barber, ex-bartender;/hooker, boxer, homeless man, I love. . . ." Aside from the fact that it was done much better almost a century ago by Walt Whitman, this resolution strikes me as contrived and not felt. I have nothing at all against Love, it's a fine thing, but I do wonder why it is so often dragged into the last few minutes of our plays and movies. (Gore Vidal in *Partisan Review* and Robert Brustein in *The New Republic* have had some acute things to say on this subject.) Could it be that we Americans overvalue Love ritualistically because we undervalue it actually? Do we love everyone in general because we love no one in particular? At any rate, I object to Love as the *deus ex machina* lugged in at the end to resolve all the problems piled up by the preceding hours of conspicuously loveless human relations.

—October 1960

One of the less fortunate effects of the post-1945 upgrading of our culture is that the "art film" is beginning to influence Hollywood. One gets the worst of both—the pretensions of the one and the superficiality of the other. There was a lot of Art in that overrated melodrama, *The Hustler,* which was fine as long as it stuck to Jackie Gleason and the pool table, but sogged into sentimentality when it got into the love story, and there is even more Art in this new film by Jack Garfein. *Something Wild* was released by United Artists, but it would have fitted perfectly into Cinema 16's current season. A girl—stolidly played by Mr. Garfein's wife, Carroll Baker, who occasionally rises from the passive to the peevish—is raped in a New York park, runs away from her dismal home and falls in with a not-quite-right-in-the-head garage mechanic who keeps her captive in his (dismal) basement flat for what seems like

Ben-Hur's film time until they finally Get Through to each other and marry. (Cinema 16 at least would have had a downbeat ending.) All-too-faithfully transcribed from an all-too-earnest first novel—*Mary Ann* by Alex Karmel—this static tale would have defeated a better director than Mr. Garfein, who manages to be both tedious and overdramatic. Examples of the latter—the former let's take for granted—are the glittering cross that falls from her neck in the rape scene and her subsequent fainting in the subway under a whiskey ad that spells out with relentless irony over her lolling head: "SMOOTH . . . SOCIABLE . . . SENSIBLE." No less a composer than Aaron Copland did the score, but it turned out to be straight Hollywood schmaltz: sinister chords when something Bad is about to happen, soaring violins for Joy (not much of these), and an organ vibrating hammily at the happy ending. No less a cameraman than the veteran Eugene Shuftan (*Port of Shadows*) was also involved, with equally meager results: there were the usual sordid-shadowy scenes in the basement and the usual Art shots of the girl walking, walking through the city streets, like a Traffic Bureau documentary. The moral, which will be readily grasped by devotees of either TV or Cinema 16, is that much suffering is caused by the inability of people to communicate with each other. All too true. But two hours of noncommunicating can get rather boring.

—June 1962

THE COOL WORLD

Shirley Clarke's movie about a teen-age gang in Harlem seems to me a disaster in every way—as art, as realism, as Message.

It is confused, overstated, chaotically edited and, for all its handheld cameras and eavesdropping mikes, a conventional sob story. Those kids don't have a chance in the relentless grip of Miss Clarke's sympathy. The sound track is dolled up with jazz and rock 'n' roll mood music that rarely fits the mood and that is so loud it is hard to see the pictures. An unsuccessful attempt is made to combine documentary and melodrama, random shots of Harlem

323

street life being sandwiched between the fictional episodes. (The street shots are very good, perhaps because Baird Bryant was the director of photography; he also did splendidly in another off-Hollywood turkey, *Greenwich Village Story*.) Miss Clarke's strategy was to give an air of realism to her story by these factual interpolations, but they work the other way, showing up the phoniness of the fictional part. And, even worse, its dullness. Ordinary people going about their commonplace affairs prove to be more interesting to watch than the actors.

These are mostly amateurs: the Royal Pythons and their leader, Duke, and his-their girl, Luanne. The girl fails to achieve complete inexpressiveness, but the others come reasonably close. Amateurs can be effective, as Eisenstein showed, but they must be dominated by a director who uses them for his, not their, purposes—it is the painter who decides about a canvas, not the colors he puts on it. But here I felt the movie was directing the director; or, as the producer, Frederick Wiseman, stated about Duke and his gang: "They knew Harlem and the life of the teen-agers there. Shirley Clarke would often merely outline a scene and let them improvise on it. In a sense, they were really describing to us 'the cool world' of Harlem." This approach makes sense in a Flaherty documentary, but *The Cool World* is elaborately plotted and highly artificial. It is an error to assume that because somebody knows about a certain kind of life since he is living it, he will be able to express this knowledge in terms of art. On the contrary, professionals can improvise better than amateurs; it takes technique to "just be yourself." The Pythons do their best for Miss Clarke, beginning and ending each speech with "man," but it isn't enough. And what can the fifteen-year-old kid who plays Duke do but look puzzled (his other expression is sulky) when Luanne says, "Oh Christ, Duke, you're so *strange!*" Or when the blonde mistress of Priest, the gangster, burst out, "Oh God! I love him so. . . . Oh Duke, I'm so *lonely!*" What except back out of the scene quickly, and, I imagine, with considerable relief? Priest is played by Carl Lee, who also helped Miss Clarke write the screenplay and so is partly responsible for lines like the above—I also recall, "You're finished, Blood!" His acting style was as bad, and as incompatible with the rest of the cast, as when he played Cowboy in *The Connection:* a matinee idol,

324

narcissistically sinister, who relates not at all to the Pythons' amateurish "improvisations"; as if Lionel Atwill had wandered into a Method production. (As an actor, Mr. Lee is to his father, Canada, as Anthony Perkins is to his, Osgood.) There were two good performances in minor parts: Clarence Williams as the dope addict, Blood, and a ten-year-old who was lively and natural.

If Harlem were as this movie pretends it is, it wouldn't hold together for half an hour. Likewise with the Royal Pythons. The only characters who show any character or intelligence are Duke's mother and the junkie's brother, both of them bit parts. Duke, Priest and the Pythons are feckless, stupid, vain, shallow, brutal (though even here they are ineffectual), living only for the moment (and what a moment!) and for their fantasies of achieving power without effort or calculation: their behavior is disorganized and purposeless to the point where a decision to come in out of the rain would be a triumph of will and intellect. I cannot believe that Harlem, or even its teen-age gangs, are like this, and in fact the people we glimpse in the documentary scenes appear to be of a different breed from the cast—full of spirit, humor, purpose, common sense, and individuality. People, that is.

The ironic point about *The Cool World*—which, if by some mischance I were Governor Wallace of Alabama, I should distribute widely in segregated movie houses throughout the South—is that this racial libel was made with the best intentions. Indeed, that is the trouble. Miss Clarke accepts Harlem so uncritically that the only aspects of it she responds to as "authentic"—a century ago the word would have been "picturesque"—are the ones that appear to her to be most different from the white world. But if the Negroes were like her idea of them, they would be finished, kaput, if only because they are heavily outnumbered by the whites. And even if they were a majority, the mental and moral deficiencies she depicts so sympathetically would make it impossible for them to live with each other. The final turn of the screw is that these deficiencies are by no means lacking among the whites. I daresay that if our population today ran nine-to-one in the other racial direction, this patroness of the underdog would have remade *Tobacco Road* as a sympathetic plea for Understanding: *Uncle Jeeter's Cabin*.

It is interesting to compare *The Cool World* with Miss Clarke's film version of *The Connection,* which I liked. I've seen Jack Gelber's play (about another kind of underdog) and I haven't read Warren Miller's novel. Perhaps Miss Clarke is a translator rather than a creator and so is limited by the quality of the original work. Or perhaps she didn't do justice to the novel. In any case, the difference is that the junkies in her movie of *The Connection* are rendered as individuals, with peculiarities of their own, while the Negroes in *The Cool World* blur into an oppressed mass; also her point of view in the former is from the outside—detached and tough-minded and often humorous—while in the latter it is from the inside: protective, sentimental, humorless.

The Cool World begins well with a Black Muslim orator—played, I'm told, by a professional actor—ranting on a street corner: "The black man is the original man. The white man is the devil. White is the absence of color, and the white man is incomplete." But this is the last bit of realism, or coherence, we get. The next scene shows us a white schoolteacher taking a busload of Negro kids on a sight-seeing tour down Fifth Avenue to Wall Street; he does everything possible to antagonize them, heckling them about their manners as if he expected them to be Etonians, and he is devastated when they show little interest in the Plaza, the Empire State building, or even the statue of George Washington in front of the Sub-Treasury. I cannot believe a schoolteacher could be that naive and obtuse, or that he would distribute, hopefully, among his charges, a Stock Exchange leaflet headed "How to Own a Share of America!" Except for the purposes of racial melodrama.

I must be wrong, however. The experts are against me. "These Americans must see *The Cool World,* must see the roots of Negro desperation, and this is what your film unforgettably portrays," says Bayard Rustin, the director of the March on Washington. "Stark realism," says Whitney M. Young, the director of the National Urban League. While James Farmer, director of CORE, found the film "an overpowering experience. . . beautifully told," adding: "*The Cool World* is as shocking as the truth: It is the truth. And I sincerely hope the entire country will be your audience." Bosley Crowther, while worried about "a certain looseness and vagrancy in the style" and by "a too-free use of four-letter words," was impressed by "the sense of reality and the pounding vitality" of Miss Clarke's film: "It blisters the eyes and claws the senses with its vicious and hideous visual truths." *Newsweek* went all out on both fronts, art and realism. The *Time* reviewer, after making much the same criticisms I have made here, lost his nerve and concluded with one of his stylistic cadenzas: "Still and all, *The Cool World* has an impact and a fascination. Who will not remember the beautiful wild faces of the children, blooming like bright manna in the desolation? To see them is to die a little."

Well, I for one don't remember them with pleasure, even when backed up by a malapropos vulgarization of Madame de Sévigné's *"partir, c'est mourir un peu."* And I think a movie should be judged—still and all—on what appears on the screen and not on its avant-garde pretensions nor even its social point of view, however well-meaning.

—July 1964

HALLELUJAH THE HILLS

Jonas Mekas is the patron saint of the New American Cinema, from which I'm still hoping for something Cinematic, whether New or American. I write "saint" without irony: he is dedicated, selfless and courageous. He has recently invited martyrdom by exhibiting two sexually explicit, and perverse, movies, Smith's *Flaming Creatures* and Genêt's *Un Chant d'Amour;* the New York cops have accepted the invitation and have arrested him. The films seemed to me artistic rather than pornographic in intention, but intention is not execution and I don't see how one could honestly testify in court that either was of much artistic value. Like the Beat littérateurs, the movie-makers of the New American Cinema are moralists rather than artists. After the showing of *Flaming Creatures,* one of them denounced me as a stuffed shirt—another one thought my trouble was that nobody over forty could possibly understand it—because I insisted it was boring. "You'll see," he predicted. "In ten years there'll be fucking on the screen!" As I said, they're primarily interested in morals.

327

Now Adolfas Mekas, with brother Jonas as assistant director, has made a feature-length comedy that might be called Variations on Themes from Mack Sennett. Despite its avant-garde provenance, and despite a record number of "in" spoofs of and allusions to other movies, I didn't like it.

(1) The performers mugged it up amateurishly, their efforts at improvisation being especially painful since they had no technique, unlike Sennett's comedians who were either trained by him in a style as formalized as classical ballet or else, like Keaton and Chaplin, had learned their trade in such rigorously disciplined schools as the American vaudeville and English music hall. The male leads, Peter Beard and Marty Greenbaum, substituted vigor for skill, like musclebound wrestlers trying out for Balanchine. This must have been the director's fault, since Jerome Raphael, who was so good as Solly in *The Connection,* comes out here unintentionally oafish—and as nervously uncertain as the others.

(2) This kind of zany comedy, as Sennett knew very well, needs a strongly accented rhythm and a clear form precisely because it *is* so freewheeling. For the same reason, it needs a counterpoint of reality—what could be more prosaic than a policeman, the raw material of a Keystone cop? But here the opposite: formless, unrelieved fantasy. I left after the first hour, when I finally realized that literally anything could happen next, since there were no limitations, either realistic or artificial. Infinity in art is boring.

(3) I don't think it is necessarily funny for a comedian to trip himself and fall down, not even when he does it five times in rapid succession, not even when he does it in deep snow, not even when he is bare-assed. Nor do I think it a sure laugh if he squeezes his face out of shape against a windowpane, nor if he crams food overflowingly into his mouth at a Thanksgiving dinner (two comedians doing it are twice as unamusing). The food-cramming, I suppose, was suggested by Chaplin's force-feeding by the machine in *Modern Times,* but that was part of a satiric idea and was also executed with style, timing and other technical graces.

Except for Ed Emshwiller's superb photography, *Hallelujah the Hills* is worth noticing only because of its *succès d'estime.* Ever on the alert for the latest thing in the *faux bon,* the Lucepapers puffed it in *Time* and huffed it in that double issue of *Life* devoted to the movies, which was as appetizing as a double portion of cotton candy, though not as nutritious. It was invited to more international film festivals last year than any other American movie, and by now has opened in Paris, Milan, London, Amsterdam, etc. As an American culture export it has been received with the same mixture of romantic illusion and condescension as greeted Pocahontas and Buffalo Bill. "One of the most completely American films ever made, in its combination of anarchistic wackiness with a nostalgic sense of the lost frontier and the magic of youth" (*Sight and Sound,* London). "Imagine a combination of *Huckleberry Finn, Pull My Daisy,* the Marx Brothers, and the complete works of Douglas Fairbanks, Mary Pickford and D. W. Griffith, and you've got it . . . deliriously funny and ravishingly lyrical" (*The Guardian,* London). The Parisian press was, predictably, even sillier; the French adore their fantasy-image of us, compounded of Al Capone and the Cisco Kid, almost as much as they detest our reality. "Love and knowledge of the cinema enabled Mekas to go beyond everything that the art of the film has achieved until now" (*Le Figaro Littéraire*). "The young American cinema has never before shown us such spontaneity, such clarity, such health. . . . It is a film where the god Pan still lives. He wanders through the hills and, once again, everything sings" (*Arts*). ". . . a true joy for the spectator who can relax and curl up voluptuously in his theatre seat as if it were the couch of a hashish smoker" (*France-Observateur;* and maybe some pot *would* help; popcorn is definitely not enough). "*Hallelujah the Hills* has the charm of conserving its tonic effect when the immediate pleasure has passed; it attains in each of us some secret prolongation, beyond fantasy and simple amusement" (*Le Monde*). I offer this last, from a normally sober journal, as an all-purpose sentence for aspiring movie critics.

The note seems forced. These rhapsodies are in fact conditioned reflexes triggered by some chic stimuli the Mekas brothers have been lucky or shrewd enough to hit on: Experiment, Improvisation, Wild & Woolly America, the Cult of Cinema, and that Nostalgia for Slapstick which includes them all. At the preview, it was preceded by "a recently discovered Mack Sennett short" that I thought might have been left in oblivion. (Dare one say that a Sennett comedy

329

can be unfunny? Homer nodded, it was said, but that was before *auteur* criticism. Now it must be revised: Homer nods, but Hitchcock doesn't.) Still, hastily botched together as it was, I thought it more satisfying than the self-conscious pastiche that followed; it had at least the interest of a period piece. Louis Malle's *Zazie* (1962) was a similar pastiche. It was a far more skillful effort and it even had a few laughs, but it split on the same rock: History. I think it was Heraclitus who observed that you can't step in the same river twice.

—July 1964

ITALY

L'AVVENTURA

At the 1960 Cannes Festival, Fellini's *La Dolce Vita* took the Golden Palm while Michelangelo Antonioni's *L'Avventura* was dismissed with a Special Award by the critics' panel—A for effort. The Cannes consensus was that *L'Avventura* was obscure and tedious. An historic misjudgment, even for a film festival, but one understands how it happened. Compared to *Vita*, *L'Avventura* is in fact difficult (because its style is original) and slow-paced (because its concern is more with psychological nuances than with action). Nothing is "set up" for the viewer; meanings must be caught on the wing; it is hunting rather than the usual target-shooting.

The plot is simple because the point is not what people do but why and how they do it. A handsome, fortyish architect, Sandro (Gabriele Ferzetti), goes on a yachting trip with some friends, including Anna (Lea Massari), with whom he has been having a long, unhappy affair, and her best friend, Claudia (Monica Vitti). While the party is exploring a barren island, Anna disappears. Most of the film is about Sandro's and Claudia's search for Anna. Sandro is a modern-style Orpheus who doesn't really want his Eurydice back but thinks he ought to. During the search he and Claudia become lovers—they never find out what has become of Anna— and the cycle of unsatisfactory love begins again. This simple plot is enormously complex in its connotations. The destructive aimlessness of Sandro, for all his charm and professional success, is the point, and this point expands into a broader one—the unhappiness and rot of the upper-class milieu in which he exists. The sub-theme is the response of his two girls to this milieu and to Sandro as its symbol.

The structure is novelistic rather than theatrical, designed not so much to advance the plot as to bring out certain meanings. (One tends to forget how ruthlessly most movies are pruned for the benefit of the bud of plot, which doesn't flower anyway.) Sometimes the meaning is social as in the luxury-hotel scene at the end when the multilingual, well-dressed crowd is assimilated to the brutality and moral confusion of the street crowds we have seen earlier. Sometimes it is psychological, as in the brilliant scene of mutual seduction between the matron and the boy artist, irrelevant to the plot, but of first importance to the theme.

332

The sound track is a miracle. Instead of relying on "mood music," Antonioni uses everyday sounds, modulating and blending them to get his effects: the wash of waves, dogs barking, trains groaning and clicking along, the harsh confused sounds of a crowd, the panting breath of lovers. In the visit to the deserted town near Noto, silence prevails, punctuated finally by the slamming of the car doors as the baffled searchers drive away. The monotonous whine of the motor goes all through the boating sequence, emphasizing the bored, quarreling mood and rising to an ominous crescendo as the boat approaches the bleak cliffs of the island.

There are defects. The search on the island goes on too long: one barren rock is about the same as the next one even for symbolic purposes and when skin-divers and a helicopter are imported one wonders if one has strayed into a documentary. The minor parts are beautifully done, but the principals are uneven. Lea Massari as Anna is subtly expressive: frustrated tenderness turned into bitchiness. But she disappears too soon and Monica Vitti (Claudia) and Gabriele Ferzetti (Sandro) are as stolid as they are good-looking.

But it's still the best picture I've seen since *Hiroshima, Mon Amour.*

—April 1961

LA NOTTE

I found *La Notte* a come-down from *L'Avventura.* Not because Antonioni was "repeating himself"—though he was. Except for such protean innovators as Joyce and Picasso, most good artists "repeat" themselves in the sense that they have strongly marked personalities which express themselves in a preference for certain treatments of their material. The question is whether the treatment is adequate to the material, and I think his is. *La Notte* presents the same themes as *L'Avventura.* Major: a sexual relationship that has gone bad—in this case the pair are married, as if to demonstrate the prophetic truth of Anna's final words to Sandro before she disappears, "Why are you so sure that marriage would change anything?" The reason is also the same: the man is incapable of love and so is open to whatever sexual opportunities come along (which are all the more irresistible because he uses sex to escape his chronic feeling of emptiness). Minor: the corruption of art by the world; the sordid luxury of rich life, fatuous and joyless. But these are large enough themes to be repeated, with variations.

The trouble was that the variations didn't seem varied enough. I began to wonder why everyone was so unhappy, why so much angst? Lidia (Jeanne Moreau) and Giovanni (Marcello Mastroianni) hardly smile for two hours. Why are they so miserable, what's happened exactly to their marriage? The effect is brilliantly shown, but one gets no clue as to the cause. It occurred to me that the reasons for his characters' unhappiness have progressively become vaguer in Antonioni's films. Consider the male leads in *Le Amiche, L'Avventura* and *La Notte*. The first is an artist who is unhappy because he is not successful while his wife, also an artist, is; a solid reason that is demonstrated on the screen. The second is an architect who has sold out; also a solid reason for misery, but it is not demonstrated; it is assumed. The third, Giovanni, is a writer and there seems no reason for his angst; he has not sold out and his work is both popular and respected. Yet he is as woebegone as the other two. Equally puzzling is the angst of Valentina (Monica Vitti), the millionaire's daughter. *Why* does she feel "like a lost dog"? *Why* can't she "communicate"? Are we to assume that all who are either creative or rich are by definition unhappy? (But it was clever to make the pompous millionaire the only one in the cast who is happy and who communicates, or thinks he does.) I was also irritated in *La Notte* by another mannerism of *Antonioni's* —I was aware of it in earlier films but not irritated by it—namely, that his women are always betrayed by his men because the women are normal creatures who are frustrated by the inability of the men, neurotically withdrawn and passive, to give them the love they need. This reaches a climax here with the casting of Mastroianni as the husband writer. His unvarying expression of hangdog bewilderment is boring—no wonder his women are always in a highly nervous state. Nor could I believe in him as a writer. Real writers don't listen, they talk; and no writer has ever looked at a display of his books with apathy.

All these tendencies existed in the two earlier films—Gabriele Ferzetti was almost as passive as Mastroianni and the women were more active than Moreau—and yet I wasn't conscious of them as mannerisms. I think it may be that in *La Notte* the no-story-line approach, admirable as it is as a corrective to Hollywood, has been pushed too far. In *L'Avventura* at least one big thing happens: Anna disappears, and the search for her and the mystery about her give dramatic tension to the film. But here nothing happens, really; the husband and wife go through a day and a night and end as they began; each is tempted to infidelity but nothing comes of it—in the man's case for external reasons (the first time he is interrupted, the second time the girl is unwilling), and in the woman's because she withdraws at the last minute. (As usual, the man passively reacts while the woman exerts her will, making a moral choice.) I will be told that the very fact that nothing "happens" makes *La Notte* more profound than *L'Avventura,* that in real life it is the everyday texture of trivial, incomplete events that dominates, and I must agree that O'Neill's *Long Day's Journey Into Night* shows that this approach can produce drama. Here, for me, it didn't; it may be my fault, or it may be the director's.

Having said all of which, let me now say that *La Notte* has some very good things in it. The scene between Giovanni and the young nymphomaniac in the hospital is something that could only be done in this medium: the white walls, clinical, severely give an abstract counterpoint to the erotic movements; these five minutes are perfect cinema. Lidia's walk through Milan is an extended series of pictorial metaphors. She is conscious of males, smiles at the two joking bus conductors, intervenes in the teddy boys' fight (and runs away when the bare-chested victor swaggers toward her), makes her taxi driver fleetingly aware of her as a woman, etc. There are also aural and visual symbols: the crying child, the phallic posts, the ruined courtyard, the orgasmic roar of the rockets (cf. the nerve-racking noise of the traffic jam when she is quarreling in the car with her husband). The nightclub scene, when the couple try to take an interest in the inane acrobatics of the Negro girl performer—another metaphor, suggesting the combination of technical mastery and underlying triviality in the modern *dolce vita*—and fail because he is bored with his wife and she is resentful; the cutting between the performer's smiling face, triumphant in her skill, and the couple's antagonistic boredom makes the point economically. The party

335

which takes up the last half of the film has its *longueurs*. Parties are difficult to make dramatically interesting because they are centripetal, flying out from the center, and so it is hard to get much shape into them. With his usual instinct for form, Antonioni tries to make a virtue out of this by emphasizing the casual, kaleidoscopic shifts—one moment Giovanni and Valentina are playing a game alone, the next cut they have been joined by a crowd. He also makes a minor character—the handsome and foolish blonde—into a continuing symbol of the party's heartlessness. She is snubbed by Giovanni when she gushes about his work, her businessman protector brutally says to her, "Go away" (at this moment the hostess, as hard as she is genial, comes up, exclaims "Our Don Giovanni!" to the porcine businessman and takes him off to meet someone, ignoring the blonde who stands humiliated) and we glimpse her at the end sobbing hysterically in the garden and being consoled by a lesbian type.

La Notte ends with three superb scenes. There is the car in which the lovers are glimpsed through the rainswept windows, their dialogue indicated only by their gestures; the sound of the downpour and the darkness and light as the car passes streetlights enhance the mood. There is the trio between Lidia, Valentina, and Giovanni in which their shifting emotional relationships—for the rival women, as is usual in Antonioni, are attracted to each other and united in contempt for the man—are defined by some beautifully complicated film choreography. And finally there is the last scene between Lidia and Giovanni in the dawn on the millionaire's golf course, all done in that gray tonality Antonioni likes, as characteristic of his style as Matisse pink or Rembrandt brown. This begins with their facing each other in the formal pose of two ballet dancers as she tells him that the friend they visited in the hospital that morning has just died. It ends with his rolling on top of her and desperately making love as she protests but submits; the camera draws away from the clumsy, struggling couple and the film closes with an infinitely melancholy long shot of the cold dawn landscape. In between she reads him something she tells him a man once wrote about her; it is a long reverie, romantic and tender. "Who wrote that?" he asks when she has finished. "You did."

Whatever my reservations about the film as a whole, I think that scenes like these are as great as anything I have seen in the movies.

—May 1962

THE ECLIPSE

To the final work in what Antonioni calls his "trilogy" I address myself reluctantly and sorrowfully. For *The Eclipse* seems to me an almost complete failure: retrogression, not development. Antonioni seems to be turning inward, to be exaggerating his mannerisms and weaknesses.

The casting of the two principals, to begin with. Antonioni likes his women dominant, his men recessive. Ferzetti and Mastroianni were passive enough, but they preserved a certain male dignity. Now we have Alain Delon making a decorative hole in the movie as he did in *Rocco and His Brothers;* even if he were a competent actor, he wouldn't have been right. Playing opposite him is Antonioni's fatal "discovery": the handsome and inanimate Monica Vitti. I was right to complain that we lost the wrong actress—Lea Massari—at the beginning of *L'Avventura,* even though the reviewers praised Vitti and even though ten of the film's twenty-five festival awards went to her. She has not improved: she is still inexpressive—clumsy in motion and blank in repose. If Alain Delon is the continental Anthony Perkins, Monica Vitti has some resemblance to our Doris Day. It is especially embarrassing when she tries to "act," which is perhaps why Antonioni takes so many close-ups, more than I've seen since the days of Gloria Swanson and Mary Pickford. Miss Vitti seems to enjoy posing as much as her director enjoys recording her poses—sometimes one thinks one is leafing through a back issue of *Vogue*. This obsession has not been good for his art.

Antonioni's symbolism has never been more pretentious, and obvious. While Delon is trying to seduce Vitti, she opens a window and sees two nuns walking; lest we miss the point, the camera returns to them a moment later. There are too many arty shots, all

337

the worse when they Mean something, as Vitti glimpses a park grillwork that suggests her psychological imprisonment. The final abstract sequence, a daring idea and beautifully executed, is marred by the man reading a paper whose huge headlines read "GUERRA ATOMICA." It's even worse when the similes are extended into metaphors, as in the contrast between Civilized and Natural Man. Civilized Man is two long sequences showing the greed and frenzy of the Roman stock exchange; I got the point right away—the Russians did the same thing with the St. Petersburg bourse—but Antonioni repeated it for another fifteen minutes. Natural Man comes in when Vitti, appalled by the stock exchange, visits the apartment of a woman who has lived in Kenya. It is full of native drums, spears, etc., plus huge photographs ("Ah, Kilimanjaro—Ernest Hemingway!"), and she is fascinated by the woman's talk of the free, "natural" life of the natives. Suddenly she appears in blackface with copper rings around her neck, shaking a spear and doing a bottom-wagging tribal dance that was no more exhilarating than a later scene in which she capers around with her lover. Playfulness doesn't suit her.

Peter Schlemihl lost his shadow, but Antonioni is losing his substance. There is no content here beyond the most gaseous kind of smart philosophizing: Alienated from Materialistic Civilization, Modern Man cannot Love. Antonioni used to put some flesh on these dry bones, showing us specific people in specific situations—although, as I have noted, the misery keeps getting greater and the reasons for it vaguer. In *Eclipse* no reasons at all are given. It begins with Vitti leaving a man with whom she has had a long affair. She says she no longer loves him, but cannot say why and finally admits that she isn't sure what love is. She takes up with Delon for no clear reason and at the end seems to be about to leave him too, also for no clear reason. I write "seems" because on the one hand the lovers have arranged to meet again but on the other hand one gets the impression she will break the date. Or will she? If so, why? If not, why not? One is not sure that the director could answer these questions—or that he would consider them relevant. Antonioni has come to take the impossibility of love so much for granted that he no longer feels obliged to demonstrate it dramatically. Nor is Vittoria (Miss Vitti) any help. A plaintive *"non so"* is

338

her standard reply to all inquiries, and it is a relief when her lover finally snaps, "Can't you ever say anything but 'I don't know'?" She has some very deep lines. "There are days when everything is an object, including man." "I am in love with you but I don't love you"—which works equally well reversed, like some overcoats. Everything is vague about her—how she makes her living, who her friends are, what her tastes are, and above all what is eating her. She is a philosophical proposition walking around in skirts.

—May 1963

RED DESERT

Antonioni's first color film is the most beautiful and the most static he has made. The color is extraordinary, the real hero, plot, theme. He is said to have painted walls, buildings, and trees, if he didn't think they were the right shade, and to have worked on the master print as if he were making a lithograph. It seems doubtful that the dozens of other prints that will be needed for distribution can be brought to such technical perfection without bankrupting the producer. So perhaps Antonioni, who in *L'Avventura* first demonstrated that the movies can be anti-dramatic and novelistic to a hitherto unsuspected degree—I'm coming to regret some of the effect on movie-making of that influential masterpiece—perhaps he has made here his second innovation, a movie that must be printed by hand, so to speak, if it is to achieve its intended effect. For the color here is manipulated in the freest way to express the mood of scenes. Antonioni must have been seeing a lot of contemporary painting of the abstract schools; at least he has reproduced their color harmonies and dissonances in many scenes, as in the not-quite-orgy in the shack. How prints can be manufactured wholesale and yet retain the subtle and precise color effects of the "original" is a much greater problem than making a color reproduction of a Rothko or a de Kooning. That the most mechanized of the arts may become, in Antonioni's case at least, a handcraft is a good or perhaps a bad joke, but anyway an original one.

The story is a simple and, in terms of Antonioni's recent films, a familiar one: Giuliana (Monica Vitti) is a young married woman with a child; her husband is an engineer in a chemical plant in the industrial district of Ravenna; she is going through a nervous breakdown, the result of an automobile accident; another young engineer, Corrado (Richard Harris), an old friend of her husband, comes to work at the plant; he has an affair, if you can call it that, with Giuliana—at least they go around together, she depressed, he sympathetic, and finally sleep together; she leaves him but it may have done her some good: she seems slightly more cheerful in the closing scene.

Antonioni considers *Deserto Rosso* "very different from my previous films" because "it isn't about sentiments." "In this sense," he continues, "the conclusions made in my earlier pictures are taken for granted here. . . . The story I was dealing with presented different themes: the theme of neurosis, for instance. And perhaps the fact that I detached myself from themes as vague as that of sentiments has allowed me, this time, to give greater characterization to my personages. Monica Vitti has certainly felt closer to this type of woman than she did to that in *Eclipse*. In fact I think that with her modern and nervous acting she has rendered this character with extraordinary sincerity, and has given it an especially realistic physiognomy." But to me the film seems basically like *Eclipse:* the spotlight is concentrated on Vitti, who is as inexpressive as ever; she is once more in low spirits for no reason one can see—motivating them by an offstage car accident was a rather desperate effort, but, while it does explain her state literally, one still feels this is another installment of *The Miseries of Monica*. The industrial region she lives in seems to depress her, yet, compared to similar milieus in England and this country, it is positively beautiful, especially in Antonioni's lovely color. The chemical plant is presented as a symbol of the ugly inhumanity of modern mechanized life, but Antonioni's camera can't help making it look handsome.

The thinness of the subject matter—which is not thickened by Richard Harris' performance; even for an Antonioni hero, he is wooden, he looks as if he were stuffed—contrasts with the brilliance with which it is expressed to the eye. All through the film there are the most superb cinematic metaphors for Giuliana's neurosis: the factory dump, strewn with papers and ominous refuse like a battlefield, in which she wanders; the stertorous panting rhythm, like a laboring heart, of a smokestack which emits regular jets of flame and steam; the huge ships that keep appearing in extreme close-up like ominous monsters—there is one amazing scene when Giuliana, tense and hysterical, is standing by a window across which moves with extreme slowness an enormous black prow, blotting out the view inch by inch. But these images seem much too powerful for what they express, as the scene in the fog when Giuliana stands confronting four figures—her husband, her lover, and two friends—who are one by one blotted out by the thickening mist, as her neurosis separates her from them and erases them from her consciousness. Eisenstein never did anything more baroque, and yet all that is going on is that Giuliana wants to go back to get her handbag and they are offering to do so instead.

It is possible to see Antonioni's development in the opposite way from the way I do: not as an erosion of subject matter but as a progress toward pure cinema, much as painting went from representation to abstraction. But in that case, shouldn't he go all the way, like *Blood of a Poet* or *Zéro de Conduite*, instead of sticking to the narrative form? Although *Marienbad* does have a husband-wife-lover triangle, it goes much farther toward abstraction than Antonioni has. And the farther he goes in that direction without giving up the conventional kind of plot, as in his last two films, the more obtrusive is the discrepancy between the feebleness of what he has to say and the cinematic power with which he says it.

—December 1964

LA TERRA TREMA

Writing in the *Saturday Review* several years ago under the title, *Luchino Visconti: New Old Master,* Leon Minoff observed of *The Leopard,* then in production, that "for the first time Visconti has been given all the time (seven months) and all the money ($5,000,000) he needed to make a movie." *Rocco* had been his first box-office success—almost certainly because of the rape and

341

the later even more pruriently graphic murder of the rape victim—
and so he was able to raise the money and hire the star (Burt
Lancaster) to make a movie just the way he wanted to. That the
result was *The Leopard* I find depressing.

"*Ossessione* is credited with having pioneered back in 1942 the
whole direction of neo-realist film-making in Italy," according to
Mr. Minoff. Alberto Moravia, who has been reviewing films almost
as long as he has been writing novels, says he agrees, so I assume it
is true. But historical primacy isn't necessarily important to anyone
but the archivist—Porter used montage before Griffith, after all. I
wonder how good *Ossessione* really is, since most authorities,
including the two just mentioned, consider that Visconti's second
film, *La Terra Trema* (1947), is his masterpiece. And I *have* seen
that, twice.

Made in a Sicilian fishing town with amateur actors, *La Terra
Trema* at first glance seems to be the opposite of that Lancasterized
$5,000,000 color spectacle, *The Leopard*. But a second glance
detects similarities. Instead of the low-keyed documentary realism
I'd expected, something in the Flaherty manner, I saw a melodrama
whose photography was often in a "heroic" style—those skyline
shots of black-shawled women waiting on headlands for "their
men" to return from the cruel sea which almost everybody but me
seems to admire—that owed much to Eisenstein, just as the plot
and characterizations owed much to *Rigoletto*. There were many
beautiful pictures: the lights of the fishing boats twinkling in the pre-
dawn darkness or, perhaps the best thing in the film, the use of the
harbor front and the little streets and squares that run up from it as
a great multi-level stage. But what goes on on that superb stage?
Bergman and Welles have shown that a director can transcend his
theatrical training, but Visconti, who has directed many operas and
plays, is another Kazan. His simple fisherfolk suffer the conventional woes of the poor in grand opera: one daughter is seduced by
a cop, the hero loses his girl to the arrogant son of the local
wholesale buyer of fish, and there is the final scene when he and his
two young brothers, all in extreme tatters, have to Swallow Their
Pride in order To Keep Body And Soul Together and ask for a job
on one of the wholesaler's boats, amid a chorus of jeers and
laughter reminiscent of *East Lynne*. This one-way pathos—tragedy

342

is two ways, that is, there is a conflict—trundles along for three hours slowly, glumly, predictably. The good people are all very good, also poor and stupid; the bad people are all very bad, also clever and rich. Comparatively, that is: Visconti could have made a more interesting film had he subordinated his plot line to the camera, for what we *see* is that the rich are not very rich, dressing and behaving about the same as the poor they exploit, a tablecloth and a few bottles of wine being all that distinguish them; but this gray, realistic point would have clashed with the black-white "Marxist" propaganda he was after. Why, for example, does the proletarian hero take his fishing boat, which he has acquired by mortgaging his home in order to be independent of the wholesalers, out in a storm when no other boats venture forth? The commentary says it is because he is poor and cannot afford a day's idleness but this is nonsense since he could even less afford to wreck his boat, which he does.

As a parable of the class struggle, *La Terra Trema* has some curious aspects. After the hero loses his boat, the other poor fishermen don't help him but leave him to the mercy of the bosses. Maybe they resented his trying to become a bourgeois by owning his own boat, though I guess this is too subtle a notion to expect from Visconti. Perhaps the most sensible reading of *La Terra Trema* is as a monitory parable about bourgeois success, the opposite of what the director intended. The moral is don't go into business for yourself unless you are as smart as the competition. The hero definitely is not—no wonder he always looks so worried. He mortgages his house to buy the boat which he fecklessly loses in a storm, thus also losing his house; and it seems not even to have occurred to him that the local dealers, whom he constantly denounces as bloodsuckers, might not be keen to buy his fish; he should either have found another market out of town, or have given up the whole idea; instead he is surprised, and hurt, when he can't get a fair price from the local bloodsuckers. Despite his "Marxist" sympathies, Visconti, who is rich and of noble birth, obviously assumes that poverty means stupidity.

"I took the situation from their lives," Visconti says. "I told them, 'You are here, these are your conditions, this is your story, this happened to you. How do you react?' They talked their

language. They wrote the dialogue and I don't change a word."
Shirley Clarke said much the same about the Harlem kids who
appeared—you can't say they acted, really—in *The Cool World*,
and the results were much the same. Amateurs rarely make the best
scriptwriters or the best actors. Visconti's simple fisherfolk had
special difficulties: far from letting them speak for themselves or
showing any sensitivity to the real "conditions" of their lives, as de
Seta did, for example, in *Bandits of Orgosolo,* Visconti imposed a
stagy plot on them, photographed them far too picturesquely—
those black-robed women again, posing on windswept headlands—
and burdened them, as a final insult, with a dreadful commentary
(supported by moaning violins at the Big Moments) which hammers The Message home with all the finesse of a TV commercial:
"After twelve hours of backbreaking work, they return with hardly
enough to keep them from hunger. . . . The wholesalers buy for
nothing the fish they have caught with such pain. Theirs is a slavery
without escape." As Mary McCarthy remarked to me: "You come
out feeling not 'How terrible!' but 'How artistic.' He's more interested in showing you what a great director he is than in making you
feel their poverty."

—February 1966

ROCCO AND HIS BROTHERS

Rocco and His Brothers, directed by Luchino Visconti, is the
story of a peasant family that migrates to Milan from Lucania, in
the primitive, poverty-struck south of Italy—like Tennessee hillbillies moving to Detroit. The first hour is extremely good, in a style
that might be called "heightened realism"—the acting and photography are romantically exaggerated, but the aim is naturalistic,
something like *Greed*. One is involved, one is delighted by the
humor and tenderness and dignity and god-awfulness of people
living together: the quarrel at the betrothal party, the moving into
the dank basement flat, the scenes in the boxer's gym and the
laundry. But then the heightening goes too high. The last two hours
are dominated by two scenes of violence: the rape of a "decent

344

whore" (why are movie whores always decent?) by the brother she had rejected, a rape that is committed in the helpless presence of the brother (Rocco) she loves and that is followed by an interminable running fight between the two brothers; and later the murder, protracted and sadistic, of the whore by the first brother. These scenes reminded me unpleasantly of the shower-bath murder in *Psycho;* they seemed to correspond not to the requirements of the work of art, but to some neurotic need in the artist—or perhaps his sense of the exploitability of such a need in his audience.

Nor did I believe in Rocco, who is right out of Dostoevsky's *The Idiot,* another Prince Myshkin who returns good for evil. His reaction to the rape of his girl is to break off relations with her and insist she go back to his brother because the rape has shown she is more needed in that quarter. Not unnaturally, she feels this is monstrous and goes back to her ravisher only in order to humiliate him, the final upshot being her murder. *The Idiot* has much the same plot line, including the murder, but one believes it because Myshkin is made credible. But Visconti is no Dostoevsky. When Rocco tries to go beyond naturalism, it becomes not tragedy but grand opera.

—April 1961

THE LEOPARD

Luchino Visconti is generally considered one of the Italian big three, along with Fellini and Antonioni. But I wonder.

His latest is the most tedious spectacular I've endured since *Ben-Hur.* Why *The Leopard* is tedious is perplexing. It is remarkably faithful, in externals, to Lampedusa's fine novel. The color photography, the baroque decor, the period costumes are all superb. "He's the Tolstoy of interior decoration," some wit remarked. He is also the Zane Grey of interior cerebration. There seems to be nothing underneath this display, no thought, no feeling, no structure. Crustacean art, all shell.

To transpose a book into a movie means to destroy the *form* of the original in order to re-create the *effect* in another medium. But

Visconti has preserved the form without apparently suspecting it had any meaning. He "follows" the novel with doglike fidelity, the screenplay often literally reproducing Lampedusa's comments on the tragic dilemma of the Prince of Salina, caught between past and future in nineteenth-century Sicily. But putting an author's comments into direct discourse doesn't work; it sounds like a lecture on educational TV. Although Visconti is a Leftist sympathizer, he gives us less sense of the class struggle than Lampedusa, who was a conservative but also an intellectual, hence more inquisitive. Visconti's greatest stretch of historical imagination is ten minutes of Garibaldian insurrection ("To the port! Come on! Let's go!"), which show he is no Griffith. The dubbing, as in the above, is as bad as any I've heard, a large statement. "Would you excuse me? I should like to see if Angelica has arrived." "Of course, my dear Tancredi, of course." Or: "They laughed until their sides were bursting." Nobody talks this way except in a dubbing studio. The voices have no emotional connection with the faces on the screen, and they were in all kinds of drama-school dialects, including a butler and a statesman who for some reason affected an Oxford accent.

The visible cast was no better. Twisting and darting and pretty as a picture, Alain Delon as Tancredi creates the same vacuum he did in *Purple Noon* and *The Eclipse*. His butterfly quiverings destroy at every moment the image called for by the script, not to mention the novel, that of a cool, intelligent young man of action. As Angelica, Claudia Cardinale is half right—Lampedusa describes her as "lovely but vacuous"—the second half. As the Prince, Burt Lancaster is so uncertain that he sounds more dubbed than the others. He has the physique, the whiskers being a special triumph, but inside this magnificent husk, dressed to the nines in stock and tailcoat, what a shriveled kernel! The moral force, the intellectual passion, the authority as a man that make Lampedusa's Prince interesting are as lacking in this handsome clotheshorse as are the inner qualities of the novel in the pageant to which Visconti has reduced it. Crustacean art. And never more so than in the great ball at the end, lasting a full half-hour, which should have been the structural climax. But since Visconti has had nothing special in mind for the preceding two hours, all he can give us here—beside those long lines of elegantly dressed extras dancing endlessly up to the camera and then away from it—is a sentimental scene between the Prince and the young people, plus two political glimpses: Tancredi justifying the execution the next morning of some Garibaldian rebels; and the Prince snubbing a general who is boasting about his part in the final defeat of Garibaldi at Aspromonte. These scenes are perfunctory and confusing because Visconti, for all his "Marxism," hasn't bothered to establish in dramatic terms the break between the revolutionary Garibaldi and the bourgeois House of Savoy that is the crux of such action as the film has. Yawning through this interminable ball, I realized that Visconti is not interested in history or in people, but only in materialistic display. In this sense, he *is* a Marxist, though of the kind Marx himself used to call "vulgar."

—May 1964

SANDRA

This latest of Visconti's films took top prize, the Golden Lion, at last fall's Venice Film Festival, as did *La Terra Trema* in 1948 (those festivals!). But I'm sure it will never be selected as one of the ten best films of all time as was *Terra* in the 1962 *Sight & Sound* international poll of critics (those polls!). In a way, this is to its credit since an entertaining good bad movie is generally preferable to a pretentious bad good movie. Up to its last twenty minutes, *Sandra* is a romantic mystery story which is very much like Hitchcock's *Rebecca,* for all Visconti's portentous references to Electra and Orestes. (I propose a moratorium, in talking about movies on "saga," "epic" and above all "Greek tragedy, with all the inevitability of a.") The plot is essentially *Rebecca,* but with Claudia Cardinale in Laurence Olivier's role: a newly married couple arrive at the spooky ancestral home (of, here, the bride) fully equipped with a grim, closemouthed ("Were I but to speak") faithful retainer, a closet full of family skeletons, and a garden full of ghosts, especially on dark windy nights. After a number of disturbing intimations of something not quite right about the past, the

347

mystery is finally resolved and we all go home to the greater mysteries of real life.

So long as it is no more than a "Gothic romance," appropriately staged in Volterra, haunted by its Etruscan past and most sinister of Italian hill towns, *Sandra* holds up fairly well. That is, so long as we are not asked to accept it as anything more than what used to be called "good theatre." It is when Visconti, forced to explain things at the end, tries to make us believe his marionettes are people that his mastery of tone, atmosphere, surface effect, proves inadequate. Everybody begins to behave with a lunatic violence that seemed to me a device, no doubt more instinctive than calculated, to distract our attention from the absurdity and/or the ambiguity, in terms of real people, of the denouement. Did Electra-Cardinale sleep with her brother, does she still have a passion for him greater than for her stick of a husband, did their legal guardian betray their Jewish father to the Germans during the war? Hitchcock, in whose craftsman's head no dreams of Greek parallels danced, invented a plausible, unambiguous solution to the mystery. But here, after all the screaming and running around and beating-ups, even after the brother's suicide, I felt the director was as unable to explain the behavior of his marionettes as I was. But in general, *Sandra* was quite good fun and the Italian Elizabeth Taylor—Visconti isn't fortunate in choosing leads: Delon in *Rocco,* Lancaster in *Leopard* —was well up to her usual standard of performance.

—February 1966

LA DOLCE VITA

A three-hour panorama that combines art and box office, *La Dolce Vita* is doing record business at *two* first-run theatres here in London. It won the Golden Palm at Cannes last year, and its owners are reported to be holding out for a cool million for the American rights.* Fellini calls it "a fresco of modern Roman life"

* They got it, and also something more interesting: *La Dolce Vita* was the first foreign-language movie to run in American commercial theatres with subtitles. Up to then, only films on the art-house circuit, like Bergman's, had escaped dubbing. Fellini is said to have insisted on no dubbing as part of the deal.

348

and says his aim was "to put a thermometer to a sick world." But the calibrations are all in the high-fever zone and I suspect the doctor knew already just how sick the patient was.

For all its human insights—the hero's relations with his father and his mistress, for example, are sensitively realized—*La Dolce Vita* is a sensational film, using the word in the dictionary sense as well as the press agent's. That is, it goes in mostly for effects. Often quite good ones, like the bravura opening with the wide-armed statue of Christ darting and swooping over Rome and giving the city an ironical blessing as it is transported by helicopter to a new site. But still effects. The episode of the Hollywood movie star, for instance, *almost* comes off—it is surely the high point of Anita Ekberg's dramatic career—but it fails when Ekberg is required to progress from broad satire to a woman reacting to her husband, a demand she is pathetically unable to meet and one that would not have been put upon her by a director more sure of what he is after.

This indecision is what struck me most about the film, which is a Hogarthian rake's progress that culminates in an orgy as embarrassingly dull as screen orgies usually are. (I wonder what a real one is like.) There are seven or eight episodes, and structurally the trouble is they don't build. Most of them, furthermore, are too long. The miracle sequence makes its point brilliantly in the first ten minutes, but then goes on to repeat it in the second ten; the shameless prurience of the press photographers is established early, but they keep doing it all over again. Enough, one feels, and more than enough—and yet not enough in a deeper sense. The director is fumbling around, not quite sure of what he wants to say, and so he "covers" himself on the shotgun principle.

In Italy, *Dolce Vita* has been attacked and defended with equal immoderation, the Church denouncing it as immoral and the Left insisting it is a powerful social document. Both are wrong. It is a sermon against upper-class corruption, but one that exploits its gamy subject matter as much as it exposes it. Our own Cecil B. De Mille was expert at this. But of course what Federico Fellini has that De Mille didn't have is an interest in human beings—and a sophisticated technique.

—April 1961

JULIET OF THE SPIRITS

Among the many ways movie directors differ from other artists, two are striking—and depressing: they wear out faster, and the quality of their work fluctuates more rapidly and more violently.

"A movie director's artistic life is very short [Fellini observed to Lillian Ross—*The New Yorker,* October 30, 1965]. A painter, a musician, a philosopher can go on for twenty, thirty, forty, fifty years. But a movie director has ten years. . . . In our profession, you burn out easily. Why? Because success comes so fast. It corrupts you. The big danger is that success takes you out of life. You have money, so you buy a car, you don't go by bus. . . . You look at other people as if they were in a zoo. Success makes a separation between you and the world. If you are separated in this way, you die."

Fellini thinks he is an exception because "I do not have the feeling of success," and he may be right; it is too soon to tell since his first big success, *I Vitelloni,* was made only eleven years ago. But his new movie indicates a separation between himself and the real world which, let us hope, is temporary. And, coming right after the brilliant *8½,* it illustrates the second point above—the bewilderingly quick changes in quality.

In *8½* Fellini was Prospero, the mage who could make us believe in "the baseless fabric of this vision . . . this insubstantial pageant." But here he is the sorcerer's apprentice, unable to control the demonic spirits he has conjured up. Like the apprentice, his problem is not how to invoke his magical forces, quite the contrary. Assisted by his Ariel, Gianni di Venanzo, who shows himself as great a master of color photography as of black and white—the colors are delicate yet vivid, the purity of pastel united with the richness of oils—Fellini enchants our eyes with a profusion of images as beautiful as they are unexpected. The huge laboring back of an aquatic monster, festooned with trailing water weeds, proves to be a gardener cleaning out a pool; a caparisoned pagoda accompanied by chinoiserie figures becomes a party of bathers carrying a tent. There are some superb longer passages, such as Juliet's session with the hermaphrodite fakir, Bhisma; the memory flashbacks of the circus and the religious-school pageant, each of them harmonious, inventive, lovely. Too lovely, too picturesque compared to the childhood memories in *8½* which have a wildness and an emotional weight lacking in these pretty confections. Fellini's eye is as good as ever—a wedding breakfast glimpsed by Juliet is designed and colored like a Veronese banquet. It is the mind and the feeling, that fails.

Juliet of the Spirits is *8½* feminized: the same theme—a crisis in the life of the protagonist that forces him/her to come to terms with past and present—developed by the same mingling of reality and fantasy. The situation of a matron driven near madness when she finds her husband may leave her for a younger woman—this is not *per se* a less interesting subject than Guido-Mastroianni's problems of marital infidelity (the reverse of Juliet's) and creative block, but it is obviously less interesting to Fellini. "More than a confession— my testament," he said of *8½*. But *Juliet* is somebody else's testament, that of his wife, Giulietta Masina, who plays the lead. He does his best ("After *8½*, feeling it was time to make another film with Giulietta, I tried to get going . . ."), but he doesn't know or care as much about her problems as about his own, and the movie shows it. In *8½* the unreal is sharply counterpointed against the real, each contributing its full value to the whole composition. But here the dividing line is fuzzy, the contrast unclear. As an orator raises his voice and heightens his metaphors to conceal a weakness in his argument, Fellini tries to compensate for his failure to grasp his theme imaginatively by expanding fantasy until it merges with actuality and often obliterates it. Juliet and her husband (who is some kind of public-relations man) live in a neat little suburban house with servants, TV and all the comforts of a bourgeois home, but their friends dress and behave very much like the grotesque movie types that surrounded Guido. As for their next door neigh- bor, the nymphomaniac fantast Suzy (Sandra Milo surpasses her comic-sexy-fleshy performance in *8½*, Mae West, Italian style) who lives in a baroque-cum-art-nouveau dream palace full of refugees from an erotic nightmare and equipped with a tree house up to which she pulls handsome young men in a basket, a chute from her bedroom into a swimming pool for post-coital refreshment and other suburban amenities—as for Suzy, a neighbor more likely to lend a fix than a cup of sugar, she and her retinue and equipage are

351

as dreamlike as the visions that haunt Juliet. The only evidence to the contrary is that when they come to the bathing beach, Juliet's prosaic doctor also sees them. Viewers who missed this clue insist that Suzy & Co. are also part of Juliet's dream world.

This kind of confusion lessens the impact of Juliet's ingeniously pictured hallucinations and suggests that in the course of making the movie the director became as disoriented as his heroine. A new book, *Federico Fellini's "Juliet of the Spirits"* (Orion Press, $5.95) suggested to me that Fellini's directorial method may have been to blame. The book contains an interesting sixty-page interview plus the "screenplay" of the movie. The quotation marks are advised since it is only the roughest approximation of the finished movie, including scenes and dialogue and characters that don't appear on the screen and omitting crucial scenes that are in the movie. The interview explains these discrepancies:

"Often, while I shoot, I prefer to have the actors recite numbers rather than sentences written months before which I feel to be dated and out of place." [Sandra Milo, in the *New York Times* of November 28, 1965, quotes him as instructing her, during the filming of the tree-house sequence: "When the camera closes in, look down in the glass, smile to yourself and count one, two, three. We'll fill in the dialogue later." Griffith used his actors the same way, more as props than as sentient beings, not letting them see the script and often misleading them about the specific scene if he thought a simpler stimulus would get the effect he wanted.]

A film is the work of an author in collaboration with everyone, really everyone, from the Eternal Father to the lowest bit player. . . . How can you evaluate the imponderable—the right rain that suddenly begins to fall, a baby who really starts to cry, a visitor who arrives with a hat that is immediately utilized to define a character who up to that time was somewhat vague?

We need sorcerers in the cinema: the real work isn't making a choice of a character before or after, or deciding what he has to say. That decision will come, and it will be the right one, if you have been able to create a vital atmosphere in which something might be born. . . . If all has gone as it should, in spite of accidents and contradictions, if the oxygen begins to circulate, nothing more is needed. . . . Everything can be changed. . . . It is

352

pointless to remain faithful to steps you have made, to choices made day before yesterday, to something written five months before.

For a week or two, I have to see if the film has been born and where it's going. It is the film that directs me, not I the film.

Or, as Miss Milo puts it: "Fellini creates a unique atmosphere on the set. Even the crew becomes involved in the excitement and will do, or try to do, anything he asks, although nobody has any real idea what is going on. Still, nobody worries. They feel secure with him."

I wonder how secure they felt in this particular film, and I suspect Fellini may have been thinking of *Juliet* when he observed: "The director of a film is always in command of Christopher Columbus' crew, a crew that wants to turn back." His intuitive approach, depending on accident, improvisation and the creation of a "vital atmosphere," worked in *I Vitelloni* and *Cabiria,* whose raffish milieux Fellini knows by experience and understands emotionally, and in *8½,* which is about his specialty, himself. But the domestic pathos and bourgeois setting of *Juliet* are alien to him; his instincts are for the drama of high life or low life but they aren't reliable when it comes to the tedium of middle-class respectability. Since he cannot plan or calculate—in fact it's doubtful if he can be said to think in the ordinary sense of the term—he makes mistakes he doesn't make when his imagination is engaged.

A major mistake was casting Giulietta Masina in the lead. She is almost constantly onstage and it soon becomes clear not only that she is extremely limited as an actress but also that, whether from the passage of time or unsuitable makeup, costuming and direction by her husband or both, she is not attractive enough to engage our sympathies even on that level. (What a contrast in both respects was Mastroianni in *8½!*) She has only three expressions: a rather too childlike smile, a tight-lipped grimace of disappointment, and a wide-eyed blank stare that does duty for the rest. Also, and this must have been a fault of the direction, she seemed to make a point of never rising to any dramatic challenge, indeed to take a dreary pleasure in *not* responding. The general effect was the opposite of what the role demanded, more priggish than pathetic.

353

Fellini makes it pretty clear what happened, especially when he tries to gloss it over—diplomacy is as little his forte as hypocrisy:

"At the beginning, it was a serious problem to remove—not from her, from me—the smiles, the pallor, the winks of a lost puppy that she assumed in the roles of Gelsomina (in *La Strada*) and Cabiria, the roles that grew inside of me and finally were superimposed on her, in terms of cinema. The job of removing these without completely erasing them, that is, salvaging those features of Gelsomina and Cabiria that exist in Giulietta herself—this was painful. At a certain point, I thought I couldn't do it [and] I kept putting off the most vital and revealing scenes till the last. Then one fine day I made a discovery. Giulietta's resistance to the makeup, clothing, hairdo, earrings, her firm stands that other times seemed to me crimes against the character, intolerable interventions of femininity—this time they were functional."

A remarkably imperceptive account: those Harry Langdonesque fugitive smiles and winks from the *La Strada* days were not removed, and Mrs. Fellini's resistance may have been "functional," but it was not effective—or if it was, I hate to think what even less flattering makeup, hairdo, costumes, etc., Mr. Fellini originally pressed upon her. It's all very sad and one moral is that movie directors should really stop confusing their loved ones with their leading ladies. Giulietta Masina contributed exactly as much to *Juliet of the Spirits* as Anna Karina did to Godard's films or Monica Vitti to Antonioni's. One of the many chancy factors in this chancy medium is that a director's private feeling about an actress has no necessary relation to what his audiences see on the screen.

—March 1966

IL POSTO ("THE SOUND OF TRUMPETS")

For once, a festively decorated film—Critics' Prize, Venice; Grand Prize, London—proves worthy of those cardboard medals. Olmi's first feature film is even more of a triumph than De Seta's first, *Bandits of Orgosolo*, which it resembles in theme: how poverty presses human beings into inhuman shapes. That the people of

354

Bandits are primitive Sardinian shepherds while those of *Posto* are Milanese clerks turns out to be a minor difference.

A boy—you can hardly call him a man, he is so fragile, shy, round-eyed, inept—is about to take an examination for a clerical job with a big corporation. The pay isn't much, and will never be, but it's a lifetime job. The camera follows him as he walks through the streets of his working-class suburb, takes a train to the city and makes his timid way, past various official Cerberuses, to the lair in the glass-cement palace where the examination takes place for *Il Posto,* The Job. Another art-film documentary (the talkies have become the walkies) one might think, except that Olmi has something in mind as shown in the glimpses along the way of the vanity, cynicism, servility, good nature and other human qualities of the people the boy encounters. His point, which he sticks to with the perseverance of an artist and illustrates with an artist's versatility, is the frustration of human feelings by a social context—Antonioni's point transposed into a lower social key. Nothing much happens, as also with Antonioni: the boy is thrown together with the girl, who is also trying for *Il Posto;* he makes shy advances, she responds somewhat ("Domenico—that's an old-fashioned name—it suits you"); they both pass the examination and are assigned to different departments; he waits in the rain—one of the few lapses in directorial taste—only to see her go off gaily with a crowd from her new *Posto;* he gets drunk at an office party and acts freely with women for the first time, but she doesn't come; he is promoted from messenger after the suicide of one of the clerks and the film ends with a close-up of his face as he sits at the desk he will have for the rest of his life. The rhythmic thud of a mimeograph machine gets louder and louder, more and more menacing as "The End" appears on the screen. It sounds dreary, but it isn't because Olmi shows us his clerks and his doorkeepers and executives as individuals—the bit players seem to be people, not actors—and because he has a sense of style, every detail fitting harmoniously into the overall purpose. It is a quiet, uninsistent, unhurried style that takes a while to get on to; but once one has given up expecting the dramatic climaxes one is used to, one can see it's all exactly right.

—August 1963

THE FIANCÉS

Olmi's second feature film establishes him as the most currently interesting of the younger Italian directors. He resembles Antonioni in his austere, harmonious photography, his contempt for a plot line, and the subtlety with which he treats rather tenuous emotions. Their subject matter is inversely parallel: Olmi's theme is the miseries of the poor, Antonioni's the miseries of the rich.

I admired, as did most of my colleagues, Olmi's first film, *Il Posto*. It was a box-office failure. So is *The Fiancés*, despite the efforts of Janus Films, who let everybody in free on opening day in the hope that "hundreds of Olmi fans will be developed and that they will spread their enthusiasm throughout the New York area." It didn't work. *The Fiancés* lasted only two weeks and *Il Posto*, which was revived at the same time, didn't do much better. When the art-cinema public in a city like New York stays away from movies of this quality and stands in line four-deep month after month for *Tom Jones*, there's something wrong somewhere.

The Fiancés is a more difficult and ambitious film than that neat little triumph, *Il Posto*. The long opening sequence, mostly "under the titles," is one of the most original passages I've seen in some time. It's almost entirely soundless, to begin with. (Cf. the hard-sell mood music Hollywood puts under the titles—indeed, if one wants to experience the opposite in every way of a Hollywood movie, this is it.) A shabbily respectable community dance hall; subdued, lumpy couples and families trickle in while the porters are waxing the floor and sweeping up and setting out the chairs and tables; a blind musician is led to the battered upright piano; the first sounds we hear are four warming-up notes (under the credits for the producing company, Titanus Sicilia—an ironical parody of the orchestral frenzy that usually greets the company's name); silence again as the camera wanders around as at the beginning of *Marienbad*, taking long meaningful close-ups of people who will prove to be extras, a series of Cartier-Bresson snapshots set into motion; the camera finally comes to rest on a younger couple, respectable working class, sitting tensely at a table. They are the betrothed, *I Promessi Sposi*, and what a distance from Manzoni's nineteenth-century novel! The man asks the girl to dance; she refuses; more sitting; he gets up and dances with another woman; a seedy-flashy

356

type politely asks the girl to dance, she accepts, and now both the fiancés are apathetically revolving around the dance floor in the arms of others. Flashbacks begin to explain: they have been engaged for years but lack the money to get married; he is a welder and he has been offered a better-paying job "with a future" in Sicily; she doesn't want him to go, but he has decided to go nonetheless. The present is resumed: he takes a plane to Sicily, where he works, looks for a room, wanders aimlessly through a street festival, remembers episodes from his past with his fiancée, writes her, gets letters from her, feels lonelier than ever, calls her long distance; they are reconciled and the film ends with them still engaged and still unmarried.

This is all that "happens" and in this summary *The Fiancés* sounds like another of those dim, dull movies about Little People which are currently fashionable in advanced circles and which the retrograde moviegoer does well to avoid. Nor will I pretend there is not more than a bit of this in *The Fiancés*. I hope the protagonists of his next film will be a bit less acquiescent in their fate. The differences between Olmi's films and the standard products of the Little-Man-What-Now? school, however, are greater than the similarities. They are, in fact, decisive.

Olmi is a poet whose genre is the idyll: "a little picture . . . any simple description either in poetry or prose, of rustic life, pastoral scenes, or the like." Unlike some partisans of the underdog, he respects the limits of his genre, confining himself scrupulously to "the little picture" and "simple description" without any editorial nudging. The idyll has mutated since the Greeks. In *Winesburg, Ohio,* Sherwood Anderson wrote modern idylls, realistic compared to the artificialities of Theocritus, but sharing his nostalgia for a vanished age when life was more innocent and satisfying. Anderson's aim, however, was not the celebration of rustic simplicity but rather the contemplation of the destructive effects on simple people of an unsimple society. So Olmi. *Il Posto* was a melancholy idyll about death, the breaking in of a lively, innocent youth to the sophisticated routine of bureaucracy. In *The Fiancés* his theme is also idyllic, modern-style: the difficulty lovers have to keep on loving if they must "make their living"—their dying, rather—at the bottom of a money civilization.

Technically, Olmi seems to have made all the right choices.

His sound track is muted and often silent—one of the contrapuntal uses of sound Pudovkin and Eisenstein proposed in 1928, in vain for thirty years, turns out to be no sound at all. What sound there is, as in *Jules and Jim* or *8½*, is either dialogue, without musical "backing," or else banal tunes, the bouncier the better, played on a guitar, an accordion, a jangly piano, a jew's harp, an ocarina, or some other low instrument. For some reason these seem to fit movies better than full orchestras playing Tchaikowsky. His photography is so right that after the first ten minutes of delight, one takes it for granted. I did notice some close-ups of the girl—as beautiful as those Griffith did of Lillian Gish in *Birth of a Nation*—which placed her head at the extreme edge of the frame. Painters have been composing off-center for millennia, but I suddenly realized this can also be done in cinema: the "empty" wall that took up three-fourths of the screen was as expressive, and necessary, as the lovely head in the remaining quarter.

His actors were also right, especially the bit players and the extras. One of the striking things about Italian films today is the realism of minor performers. Either Italians are natural actors, able to project their personalities without theatrical cliché, or else Italian directors are clever at extracting imitations of life from their actors, professional or unprofessional. Probably both. In *The Fiancés,* as in the great Russian silent films, almost everybody is an extra. The acting credits list only the two *promessi sposi:* Carlo Cabrini (Giovanni) and Anna Canzi (Liliana). Miss Canzi was wonderfully expressive, but I thought Mr. Cabrini on the stolid side.

Two aspects of *The Fiancés* bothered me: the cutting and a tendency to shift into documentary. I realize these are also its most experimental qualities. But I must confess I lost track of the flashbacks so that throughout the whole film I kept expecting to be returned to the dance hall, thinking that was still the present; I may have been obtuse, or the director may not have indicated clearly enough that when Giovanni takes the plane to Sicily we have moved on into a new present. Time is becoming an increasingly tricky business in the modern movie. In the simple old days, when the hero, musing by the fire with his pipe and slippers, turned his thoughts backward, the signal was unmistakable: the present irised out and the past irised in or a veil began to thicken over the scene, or everything went shimmery. There were equally ingenious devices to indicate passage of time: calendar leaves turning over, a candle burning down, changing newspaper headlines. But now directors just cut to another tense without warning. An artistic gain but one has to be alert: a moment's inattention and one wakes up asking not "Where am I?" but "When am I?"

As for documentary, I think Olmi is strongly attracted to it and that sometimes he distorts the form of his narrative by taking too long over bits of reality extraneous to it.* The Sicilian sulphur works, for example, seduced him into a long series of industrial shots, interesting enough but many more than were needed to relate Giovanni to his new job. A more extreme instance is the barking dog that breaks up a church service, an episode connected with the story only by the accidental fact that Giovanni happened to wander in at that moment. But Olmi cannot show us everything his hero sees, unless we are to spend as much time in the theatre as Giovanni does in the "real life" his creator imagines for him. Mood can be suggested but if it is documented, it evaporates into confusion.

—May 1964

THE BANDITS OF ORGOSOLO

This, the first film of Vittorio De Seta, a young Italian director of whom I think we will hear more, is a story of shepherds and poverty in Sardinia that is beautifully severe in acting and photography and plot. The first half is superb. The action develops out of situation and character, as in life, and not the other way round, as in Hollywood; the brutal landscape, all volcanic rocks and stunted trees, is

* I learned later, from an article by Penelope Houston in the Spring, 1964, *Sight & Sound*, that Olmi had begun as a documentary film-maker, producing thirty between 1952 and 1959 for Edisonvolta, a large industrial company; also that he was much older than I'd thought: 32; I'd have guessed closer to 22; also that his first feature film was not *Il Posto* but *Il Tempo si e Fermato* (*Time Stood Still*), made two years earlier in 1959, which hasn't been shown here and which has won several prizes, including the recherche Golden Rhododendron, given for "the year's best film on a mountaineering subject."

359

sketched in as masterfully as the men who are part of it: grimy-faced, unshaven, dressed in tattered corduroys and sweaters, laconic; these are people who have learned to endure in silence and they express only the minimum necessary for practical life, which makes the moments of feeling all the more powerful—the man fumblingly patting the child's head, the older brother telling the younger how their father died. Nature is the major opponent, and the *carabinieri,* representing the State, the minor. In the middle section—the driving of the flock to new pastures—I think De Seta was seduced by photographic possibilities into drawing it out too long, as Antonioni was similarly seduced in the island scenes in *L'Avventura.* But for the most part he shows enormous talent—the opening shots of the deer hunt are a poem, and the final outcry of the man who has been robbed of his sheep by the protagonist (who has lost his own flock and has turned bandit) is a great coda: "What have I done to you? I am a man like you. How will I live?" As Flaherty did in *Nanook,* De Seta gets his effects simply by showing the austere reality of a style of life that is determined by the necessity of survival. This turns out to be more interesting than any amount of "dramatizing."

—August 1962

THE ORGANIZER

"Odd to see a typical labor film of the thirties made today," a friend said. But Mario Monicelli's movie, *The Organizer,* about the beginnings of the Italian labor movement, as exemplified by a strike in a Turin textile mill in the 1890's, is neither a typical labor film nor a typical historical movie. The latter views the past from the present, but here there is no such distancing; the past is the present, and the spectator feels as if the film had actually been made in 1895. The camera work has the bleak, grainy quality of photographs by Jacob Riis, the Brady of nineteenth-century industrialism, here made all the more real by the brutal noise and the haze of dirt from belt-driven machinery; the rough clothes of the men, women and children who work fourteen hours a day in the mill—

360

their strike is for a reduction to thirteen—seem not costumes but part of themselves like a second skin. *The Organizer* is a "labor film" in subject and in its sympathy for the workers, but they are neither sentimentalized as pathetic "little people" as in Hollywood films like *The Grapes of Wrath* nor heroically idealized as in *Strike, The End of St. Petersburg,* and other Russian films of the twenties. The only way it conforms to type is that the bosses are all villains; an artistic defect but perhaps not an historical one—there must have been something wrong with those early industrialists who confused morality with a fourteen-hour working day.

The Organizer moved and interested me more than anything since *8½*. As the *professore*—bearded, peering with myopic benevolence through his pince-nez—who arrives in town, on the lam from the police, to educate the raw workers (the very idea of a strike had not occurred to them before he descended among them from a passing freight train, literally a *deus ex machina*), Marcello Mastroianni is superb in still another new kind of role. (I once dismissed him here as another of those vacuous pretty boys European directors seem to favor as heroes; my only excuse is that I had not seen him in his best parts.) With delicacy and restraint he fills in the outlines of a rather complex man, who is personally gentle, humane and inept (his efforts to get enough to eat are touchingly ineffective, as when he marches into an expensive restaurant, draws a flute from his ragged overcoat and barely gets through the opening notes of *La ci darem la mano* before he is thrown out) but ruthlessly efficient as a professional troublemaker. The minor roles, as we have come to expect in Italian movies, are not only vigorously individualized but are also allowed by the director far more latitude of development than they are permitted in our movies. Monicelli has integrated the star into the drama, counterpointing him against the others instead of reducing them to background music. For considerable periods we don't see The Organizer at all, and when he does reappear—often materializing with a magical yet quite logical opportuneness, like a guardian angel—he is merely *primus inter pares,* first among equals, rather than the usual star-dictator.

In 1961 Monicelli made *Big Deal on Madonna Street,* the fastest and gayest Italian comedy of low life I've seen since Renato

Castellani's *Two Cents Worth of Hope* (1952). *Big Deal* is a parody of criminal-technology thrillers like *Rififi* and *The Asphalt Jungle:* the crooks, led by Vittorio Gassman with great dash and incompetence, make elaborate plans and do everything they should, only the plans don't work and they do everything wrong. It is interesting to see how, in *The Organizer,* Monicelli transposes the spirit and technique of *Big Deal* into serious drama. Though drama is hardly the word; if Monicelli has a "directorial trademark," it is anticlimax. Again and again he uses it to destroy the dramatic effects of a scene, to reduce it suddenly to the human scale—just the opposite of what an operatically minded director like Visconti does. The Sicilian workman, insulted by the boss, pulls out a clasp knife—and can't get it open. The Organizer arrives at the crucial meeting just in time to save the strike—pedaling like mad on a knife-grinder's bicycle with oil can bouncing around on the handlebars. A worker makes a passionate speech at another meeting; when he is done, they all look at one another—"I couldn't understand a word"; finally a woman explains, "He's from the Abruzzi, I know that language," and proudly gives a translation. A young striker, wanted by the police, boards a freight to get out of town. "Write to me, write to me!" his girl calls as she runs along waving goodbye. "But you can't read," he shouts back as the train rounds a curve.

Anticlimax is used in subtler ways also. After everybody has left the meeting at which Mastroianni has made his first triumphant appearance, persuading the workers to strike and explaining how they should go about it, he spies a sandwich left behind, unwraps it eagerly and has his mouth open for the first bite when the owner comes back for it. They stare at each other in silence, the man puzzled, Mastroianni with a curious mixture of humiliation and regret—he is, as usual, very hungry. Then he slowly wraps up the sandwich and hands it back. The most daring anticlimax is at the end, after the troops have fired on the strikers and the young son of the family with whom Mastroianni has been staying lies bleeding to death on the ground: Mastroianni runs back as the soldiers withdraw and, ignoring the boy and his weeping parents as they kneel beside him, paying no attention to their curses, searches anxiously on the ground for his glasses. Similarly, he shocks the mourners in

362

the house of a striker who has been accidentally killed during a demonstration by flourishing a newspaper and announcing that public opinion is shocked and that this may be the tactical turning point of the strike. He is a very well-organized organizer, professionally that is.

—October 1964

FRANCE

HIROSHIMA, MON AMOUR

Alain Resnais' first feature-length film is the most original, exciting, and important movie I've seen in years. The structure is, actually, cinematic: rhythm is built up by montage and the camera is used with a freedom we have grown unused to. The relation of words and images is perhaps its most novel, and interesting, aspect. The script, by the novelist Marguerite Duras, is brilliant in itself and is used by Resnais so as to suggest (at last!) a possible aesthetic for the sound film: the words either are commentary or, when they are dialogue, have a stylized simplicity and repetition which gives the effect of commentary. Instead of reducing the pictures to mere illustrations, the words keep their aesthetic distance, so that each element gets it full value.

Cinema is a contradictory art. Its microstructure is abstract: the individual "frames" are analogous to notes in music; the director builds, or should build, his film by arranging them rhythmically, harmoniously, and/or contrapuntally. But its macrostructure, its overall meaning, is novelistic: a story is told. In theatre this is also the case, but cinema is closer to the novel because its essence is time which can be treated in many ways (the physical limitations of theatre force it to condense time into a few typical or climactic moments) and because the accumulation of realistic detail is not only possible (it's not in theatre), but is also, as in the novel, an essential part of the medium.

For a movie is a series of photographs and the simplest photograph is a picture of *something*. Realistic detail is inescapable. Yet here, too, another contradiction. As Rudolf Arnheim has observed, a photograph is only superficially realistic, since the eye doesn't see a scene as the camera does: it doesn't cut it off at the edges, it doesn't focus on the foreground so definitely, and it sees things in three dimensions, while a photograph is flat. Furthermore, the composition of each shot, or photograph, in cinema is governed by the rules of art rather than of how it "really" looks.

This peculiar combination of the "real" and the "unreal" is pronounced in *Hiroshima, Mon Amour*. It is as stylized as *Potemkin,* as pure and powerful as cinema. But it is also a novelistic exploration of memory, a *recherche du temps perdu* comparable to

366

Proust. I have seen it twice and the second time it affected me even more strongly, because I saw much I had missed or misunderstood the first time (a rough test of a good movie). For the first time since Eisenstein, we have here a cinematic intelligence so quick, so subtle, so original, so at once passionate and sophisticated that it can be compared with Joyce, with Picasso, with Berg and Bartok and Stravinsky. The audience was extraordinarily quiet—no coughing, whispering, rustling of paper; a hypnotic trance. We were absorbed in the human experience flickering across the screen, attentive lest we miss a clue to the mystery. As in Henry James, the answer is arrived at by numerous approximations, little scenes (often only a few frames long) which cumulatively reveal the reality. It was oddly like a religious service, and if someone had made a wisecrack it would have seemed not an irritation but a blasphemy.*

A French actress of about thirty comes to Hiroshima to act in a peace-propaganda film; she becomes the mistress of a young Japanese architect; she tells him of her first love affair, at eighteen, with a German private stationed in her native town of Nevers during the Occupation, of how he is killed at the Liberation, how the townspeople shave her head, how her parents keep her in a cellar until her hair grows out again; in her new lover she sees her dead lover, whom she has forgotten as the actuality of the atomic bombing of Hiroshima has been forgotten; they part; "I'll forget you, I've forgotten you already!" she cries.

The opening sequence is powerful: the smooth naked flesh of the lovers, in extreme close-up, intercut with documentary shots of the effect of the atomic bomb on the flesh of the people of Hiroshima. (The counterpoint is announced with a great cinematic stroke—the lovers' bodies become rough under a fall of iridescent dust.) The woman keeps repeating, "This happened, I saw it" and the man contradicting: "It didn't happen, you didn't see it." For she has only

* As of 1968, this paragraph seems to me overstated, to say the least, but I have left it pretty much intact—I did delete a particularly fatuous putting down of Bergman as comparatively "arty" and "laborious"—because it shows something about the period. *Hiroshima* was the first major product I saw of the great new school of sound cinema that has developed in France and Italy in the last decade. My enthusiasm was excessive, but historically understandable.

367

seen the effects of the bomb emotionally and intellectually, she hasn't experienced them, and there is something inauthentic in her reactions. What is reality?

The opening is, indeed, *too* powerful; one remembers it more than is justified by its time (about ten minutes) or its aesthetic weight in the whole. For, although the horror of the bomb is rendered more imaginatively than in anything else I've seen, the main theme is something different. This note begins to sound in a first brief glimpse of her German lover dying in Nevers and it dominates the rest as she tells her Japanese lover bit by bit what Nevers means to her.

There is filmic time as well as "real" time; Eisenstein and Pudovkin knew it, but most modern film-makers don't. The Nevers sequences violate time as one does in thinking about a past experience; one begins *in medias res* with the strongest affective memory and then adds other bits to fill in the mosaic. Memory is the theme of *Hiroshima*. The remoteness of her memory of the German soldier is suggested by showing their meetings mostly in extreme long shots. But her time in the cellar, since it still affects her strongly, is shown in close-up. She can only keep aware of herself by drawing her nails over the walls until the blood runs; she sucks her bloody fingers; she sucks the saltpeter-salty walls.

The photographic counterpoint between the gray-black severity, stolid and stony, of ancient Nevers and the febrile, neon-lit transience of newly built Hiroshima is one of the dramatic tensions that gave life to the film. Hiroshima is never asleep, Nevers is never awake; yet there is death in both.

The woman says twice of her life in the cellar, "They were always playing the *Marseillaise*," and we see legs striding by in parade, but don't hear the music, an example of Resnais rejecting an easy ironic effect for a deeper one, for how *could* she hear that heroic tune, noble in other contexts but foolish here? Similarly, she tells him: "My mother tells me I am nineteen." "Do you spit in her face?" "Yes." But she is not shown doing so. As in Greek tragedy, the violence is offstage. Our present stage and movie practice is the opposite: everything is on stage including much that doesn't happen.

—September 1960

368

LAST YEAR AT MARIENBAD

In *Last Year at Marienbad,* Alain Resnais has taken the stylization of *Hiroshima, Mon Amour* a great deal farther. It is a charade, a masque, beautiful to the eyes—I can't remember a film of more sustained visual delight—and interesting to the mind, but curiously lacking in emotional affect. "For me," M. Resnais has said, "the film represents an attempt, still crude and primitive, to approach the complexity of thought and of its mechanisms. I have found that in each descent into the unconsciousness an emotion is born." For me, the emotions were stillborn; I couldn't find any human drama to hook them up to. Yet it is a fascinating film; I saw it three times in the same week and found it more interesting the third time than the first. It is the *Finnegans Wake* of the movies.

The setting is a vast baroque palace now converted into a luxury hotel. After a superb sequence of tracking shots roaming the walls, corridors and ceilings, the camera begins to pick up the handsomely dressed guests, who are as stiffly and emptily graceful as the plaster nymphs and cherubs, finally focusing down on three of them: A (Delphine Seyrig), X (Giorgio Albertazzi) and M (Sacha Pitoeff). For the rest of the film, X pursues A, insisting they had met last year at Marienbad (or perhaps at Friedrichsbad, he admits at one point), that they had been lovers there, and that she had agreed to meet him here a year later and go away with him. She denies they have ever met, he persists, she weakens, he suggests M is not really her husband, she temporizes (at times she tells him he is mad), nothing is clear, finally she apparently leaves the hotel with him. These ambiguities are made even more so by a constant—and unannounced—shifting between four tenses: past, present, future, and a conditional tense (it might have or it should have happened). Also by the most extraordinary bag of tricks that has ever been unpacked in a single film: quick cutting is constantly employed as are long tracking shots; overexposure is used to get a blinding white effect for scenes of violence or emotion; A appears, without transition, in different gowns (by Chanel); the same action is repeated four or five times in succession, as her sinking down on a bed or the remarkable sequence, in dazzling overexposure, when the camera rushes toward her over and over as she advances down a hall smiling ecstatically. The use of sound is equally original: almost all

369

the words are delivered offscreen, not only the commentary but also much of the dialogue. In 1928 Eisenstein and Pudovkin published a manifesto on the future sound film which advocated "an orchestral counterpoint of visual and aural images" and "the distinct non-synchronization" of sound and picture. This is the norm in *Marienbad*.

Other critics have thought *Marienbad* a masterpiece. I think they exaggerate, but it is certainly a work of art, that is, something all of a piece and consistent with its own assumptions. My difficulty is that these assumptions seem to me too narrow for a masterpiece; as a spectator, one feels like an animal that is being experimented on in a laboratory; the experimenters know what they are doing, but the animal doesn't and so it is hard for him (me) to become involved; no affect. One's mind and senses are stimulated but the emotional and intellectual meaning eludes one (me). Perhaps M. Resnais was too much influenced by his scriptwriter, Alain Robbe-Grillet, a leader of the French "objectivist" school of novelists. In a recent *Sight and Sound,* M. Robbe-Grillet describes a meeting of minds between him and the director which is rare in movie-making:

"I already knew his work, admiring in it an extremely firm and studied composition, with something uncompromising about it. I felt that it shared some of my own efforts toward a slightly ritualistic weight, a certain deliberation and a sense of 'theatre' and on occasion those fixed attitudes, that firmness of gesture, word and décor which make one think at the same time both of a piece of sculpture and of an opera. Finally, I found in it an endeavor to construct space and time in purely mental terms—those of dream, perhaps, or of memory, those of affective life—without overmuch concern for the traditional links of cause and effect or for a rigid time scheme for the narrative."

It is odd that M. Robbe-Grillet speaks of "affective life" since this is just what I don't find either in his own novels or in *Marienbad*. Perhaps the "objectivist" approach is *too* "uncompromising," perhaps the pure depiction of scenes and actions without any hint of the psychological processes in the characters that give them meaning is simply confusing. Perhaps, in short, the director and scenarist have, in pursuit of an aesthetic theory, gone beyond art, as I think Joyce did in *Finnegan,* for all the brilliance of individual

370

passages. The "ritualistic weight," "sense of theatre" and "firmness of gesture" were all accomplished by Carné in *Children of Paradise* without reducing the characters to A, X and M, while the playing around with dreams, time, and cause-effect were done in Cocteau's *Blood of a Poet* more effectively than here, possibly because it *was* playing around. Cocteau did not pretend to tell a story about people. It is the human aspect of *Marienbad* that is its weakness, as if Cocteau's method should be applied to a soap opera. Confusing—and inappropriate.

Everybody seems to have a different idea of the meaning of *Marienbad:* the hotel is actually a psychiatric sanitarium; the principals are dead; X is a lunatic, he is Life come to free the sleeping beauty from her baroque prison, he is Death come to claim her, etc. Its two creators warn us there is no symbolic meaning, that it is just what it appears to be, which doesn't help much. I suggest that it is to some extent a mystification. Bob Hope once gave a celebrated broadcast; he found on arriving at the studio that he had forgotten the opening script, in which he warms up the audience with jokes and patter, so he improvised three minutes of double-talk—the ostensible beginnings of jokes but no resolution—delivering it all in his customary rapid-fire style and taking care to use his typical climactic inflection when he came to the non-points of the un-jokes. Nobody noticed any difference; the audience laughed heartily.

We know that M. Resnais is a great student of Hollywood cinema, and I think it possible that among his aims in *Marienbad* was a kind of parody of the medium. Thus we have fragments of such conventional genres as high-life drama, romantic love, gambling, even a nuance of international espionage ("His passport was German. . . ."), but nothing ever develops. We have close-ups of significant-looking people, with snatches of portentous dialogue, but they turn out to be merely dress extras and nothing comes of it all—in Hollywood a close-up means business. There are echoes of directors like Von Sternberg (the feather costume worn by A, for instance) and at one point the shadowy bulk of Alfred Hitchcock can be spied in a corridor. The reflexes to which we have been conditioned by fifty years of cinema are constantly being stimulated, but we are as frustrated as Pavlov's dogs; the bell rings, but the food is not delivered. There is also the organ music—traditional

371

accompaniment of the silent film because of its shameless emotionality in expert hands—which swells to crescendoes that turn out to signify nothing at all. The effect is like climbing stairs and constantly stumbling over the final step that isn't there. *Marienbad* has more "to" it than this, but I think this is one of its important aspects and I shall not be abashed if M. Resnais denies it. He has an unconscious too.

—June 1962

BREATHLESS

I have always had a great faith in intellectuals, and so I was not surprised when Einstein predicted where that planet would be or when Trotsky organized the Red Army or when Eisenstein and Pudovkin created a great cinema on the basis of some extremely abstract ideas. But I must admit I was unprepared for the emergence from the chrysalis of *Cahiers du Cinéma,* an uncompromisingly highbrow, avant-garde and far-out Parisian magazine with the usual tiny circulation, of a whole school of critics-turned-creators which would revolutionize the French cinema. Alain Resnais (*Hiroshima, Mon Amour*) and François Truffaut (*The 400 Blows, Shoot the Piano Player*) were the first masters to emerge. Now they are joined by Jean-Luc Godard, who at thirty has become famous with his first feature-length movie, *Breathless (A Bout de Souffle).* He was helped, as should be the case with any new school in the arts, by two senior members who had been impressed by his short films: Truffaut, who wrote the original story, and Claude Chabrol, who supervised the production.

The story-line is familiar to the point of banality: a young bum (French, male) steals a car, kills a cop, shacks up with another young bum (American, female) in Paris, who finally betrays him to the police, who kill him. The point is there is no point—cf. Truffaut's *Shoot the Piano Player*—that things happen because other things have happened and not because of any human volition or cunning. The male steals the car because it was there and shoots the motorcycle cop (who was only after him for speeding) because

372

there chanced to be a gun in the car and pursues the female because he has a twitch for her which obsesses him because it is the only positive feeling he has. She turns him in because she finally decides she must extricate herself and can't think of any other way—though "decides" is wrong; her behavior, and his, is as planless as the reactions of paramecia who are bumped together or pulled apart by eddies in the culture fluid. And the police kill him because he fires at them with a gun that has been slipped into his hand by a well-meaning pal. It is all subhuman, without either will or feeling. There are interesting similarities to the current "objectivist" novels of Sarraute and Robbe-Grillet, which Miss Sarraute has described as concerned only with what "might be called 'tropisms,' after the biological term, because they are purely instinctive and are caused in us by other people or by the outer world and resemble the movements by which living organisms expand or contract under certain influences, such as light, heat and so on."

Yet the effect of *Breathless* is not depressing, as one might expect, but exhilarating. This is partly because movies are better at "objectifying" than words are. And partly because Godard has cast Jean-Paul Belmondo as the male and Jean Seberg as the female. Both are limited as actors—I predict that his aggressive ugliness and her torpid prettiness will become cinematic clichés—but they are just right here. A director should use his stars as ruthlessly as a painter his colors; he should be the subject, they the object. As Stroheim in *Greed* converted Zasu Pitts from her previous comedy gray into tragic black, so Godard has used Seberg's blank, vapid face—the kind that has launched a thousand bad movies—to get just the effect he wanted, which was that of a Bennington girl in Paris, seeking thrills and a career (both on a high, or Authentic, level) but childishly sucking her thumb in moments of crisis. A Daisy Miller of our time, the American Dream turning into nightmare.

What is especially interesting is the original style that Godard has devised to tell his story: jerky, discontinuous, staccato, perfectly adapted to render the convulsive style of this kind of life. There are no transitions, no developments; the montage often skips like a needle on a record. Again the resemblance to what the French objectivists are trying to do in the novel. "These movements glide quickly round the border of our consciousness," Miss Sarraute said recently of her "tropisms," on the B.B.C.'s Third Program. "They compose the small, rapid, and sometimes very complex dramas concealed beneath our actions, our gestures, the words we speak . . . such actions are extremely quick and precise. . . . I had to take many 'frames' to be able to catch these microscopic movements and then to show them as a slow-motion picture before the reader." But writing is not the art to do this; it does result in slow motion, in tedium; the movie camera is the right instrument, as *Breathless* shows. It catches "tropisms" on the wing; it doesn't describe, it states; and its motion is not at all slow. Godard uses his camera with the freedom of the gifted amateur who is innocent of all the conventions that the professionals have developed to take the edge off visual reality. In *Breathless* one sees the world not as it is—who knows what it "is" after all—but as an individual with a fresh eye sees it, which is the next best thing. Belmondo's drive from Marseilles in the stolen car, for instance, is a lyric of freedom, full of exuberance and humor. Its opposite, equally well done, is the long, aimless bedroom scene, in which it becomes evident, through many small touches of dialogue and expression, that each lover is so bound by childish ego as to be unable to make contact with the other, that they are emotionally impotent. This is the necessary prelude to the catastrophe.*

When one adds *Breathless* to *L'Avventura, Hiroshima, Mon Amour* and *Shadows,* I think it not premature to say that the sound film, after thirty years of fumbling around, is beginning to develop a style of its own. This new international school varies from improvisation to stylization—the difference is not as great as one might imagine—but it has three qualities in common: it subordinates plot to character; it uses images and sound to suggest a mood

---

* When I saw *Breathless* a second time, in 1966, this famous scene still seemed long and pointless but, alas, only that. Godard's style was new in 1961 but by 1966 it had been imitated so much by others, and by himself, that the originality was less apparent than the new conventions its success had established. The whole film had dimmed, and I was irritated—and bored—by the same artifices that had delighted me when Godard first invented them. Much the same thing happened, for me, when I reread the early Hemingway 35 years later (see my *Against the American Grain,* p. 175).

rather than tell a story; and it has restored montage and the camera to the dominance they had before they were dethroned by stage dialogue in 1930.

—July 1961

THE 400 BLOWS

François Truffaut's *The 400 Blows* seemed very good to me. Although it had admiring reviews, the house was thin the night I saw it. Perhaps the clumsy title, which in French slang means "hell-raising" but in English suggests nothing, was responsible. Or perhaps word got about that, French though it is, the film contains no sex. What it does contain is a subtly understated little story about a twelve-year-old boy who is unfortunate in his parents and his schoolmaster, who plays hookey, tries to steal a typewriter, and ends up in a reform school. The boy is superbly played by Jean-Pierre Leaud, and the film probably gains from the fact that he was discovered in a home for delinquents and that M. Truffaut had also done time in such places when he was a boy. Without ever being sentimental, the film draws a moving contrast between the purity, honesty, and sheer courage of the boy (even when he is being most delinquent, these qualities come through) and the corruption or obtuseness of the adults who control his life. All the parts, down to the thief to whom the boy and his school friend (another charming and believable child actor) try to sell the stolen typewriter, are well taken; they seem to be people, not character actors.

The 400 Blows is comparable in theme and quality to *Bicycle Thief* and *Forbidden Games*. It is perhaps closest of all, in feeling, to Jean Vigo's *Zéro de Conduite* (1933), though it is not as interesting cinematically. Both show how the adult world looks to the innocently cynical eye of a child, but *Zéro* did it by distortions and intensifications of what the child literally sees, a kind of poetic impressionism which rendered reality in completely subjective visual terms. But M. Truffaut, like other New Wave directors, merely uses camera tricks to enhance the story, a different, and lesser, thing. Still, they are very good tricks. Two sequences seemed

375

to me especially good. The long interview the boy has with the psychiatrist of the detention home, in which the camera is focused entirely on him (the psychiatrist is just the voice of adult incomprehension) and his moods are shown by a blurring and dissolving every now and then to come back into focus on a different aspect of his beautifully expressive face. The second is his escape at the end—the little figure trotting through interminable landscape to finally reach the seashore he has never seen but has dreamed of as meaning freedom, and then the last close-up, frozen in stop motion, of his face as he realizes there is nothing before him there either.

This is M. Truffaut's first film. I think he will go very far. And it is delightful to learn that up to now he has been, of all unlikely things, a film critic. One of such uncompromising severity, indeed, that he was banned from the Cannes Festival in 1958. He then married the daughter of M. Morganstern, the producer whose films he had attacked the most savagely; M. Morganstern at a family dinner inevitably said if-you-know-so-much-about-movies-let's-see-you-make-one; and the result was *The 400 Blows,* which won first prize for direction at the 1959 Cannes Festival. At least that's what the program notes say.

—March 1960

JULES AND JIM

François Truffaut is one of the handful of directors who have made contemporary cinema as original and exciting as it was in the twenties. Resnais, Kurosawa, Antonioni, Bergman, Welles, Jean-Luc Godard—these are his peers. He is about thirty and he has made three feature films: *The 400 Blows, Shoot the Piano Player,* and now *Jules and Jim.* The first is a minor classic, a study of childhood that is moving without ever being sentimental. *Shoot the Piano Player,* made from an American gangster thriller, to which it gives a comic twist, is more experimental and less successful, deliberately mixing up three genres which are usually kept apart: crime melodrama, romance, and slapstick comedy. I thought the mixture didn't jell, but it was an exhilarating try.

376

Now he has made his most important film to date, *Jules and Jim,* which has the emotional impact of *Blows* and the technical daring of *Piano Player*.

The story is a somber version of Noel Coward's *Design for Living*. It begins before the First World War and ends after Hitler's taking of power in 1933. Jules is German, Jim is French, and they are friends in the bohemian student world of pre-1914 Paris; they fall in love with Catherine; Jules marries her (mostly, so far as the film shows, because Jim was late for a date with her—ellipsis is one of Truffaut's favorite devices); the friends fight on opposite sides during the war; afterward, Jim comes to visit Jules and Catherine in their home in a German village and a *ménage à trois* develops which is complicated by Catherine's sometimes making it a *ménage à quatre;* everybody gets more and more tense and miserable; finally Jim decides to marry and to give up Catherine, at which point she kills herself and him.

The personal and the social-historical are interwoven throughout, an ambitious attempt. The first half-hour is *allegro:* the anarchistic freedom of prewar student life in Paris rendered by abrupt cutting, by streaking jump shots, and by photography which miraculously imitates the gray tone of old films—"I had Griffith in mind most of the time," Truffaut says. Then a montage of documentary shots of the First World War breaks in *fortissimo,* followed by a long *adagio* in which life becomes, as it did in the twenties, more problematic than pleasurable; and finally Hitler's coming to power, a sinister *vivace* that ends in disaster. This evolution, or rather devolution, of history is paralleled by a similar devolution of the personal relations of Jules, Jim and Catherine that also ends catastrophically.

So far, so great. But, as in *Marienbad,* I was constantly being buffeted, puzzled, and put off by what seemed to me perverse changes of the emotional mood. They were much less severe, since Truffaut is not as systematic as Resnais, following Robbe-Gillet's script, had to be, and also he is telling a temporally consecutive story, though in some ways this made the jolts all the more severe. There is an ambivalence about Truffaut's attitude toward his three lovers which often made it hard to see whether satire or sentiment was intended. The postwar *ménage à trois* is an instance. All the

377

conventional stimuli lead one to consider it a serious business—like Resnais, Truffaut is a great admirer of Hollywood and, like him, often uses its idiom in a peculiar way, half parody and half pastiche. The lovers' faces are shown in closeups, as lovely and expressive as Griffith's; the music is emotive and the outdoor shots lyrical; the love letters fly back and forth. But just as one settles into the warm bath of romance a cold shower descends: the letters are at cross-purposes and the marvelous shots from the airplane sweeping low over the countryside as Jim speeds back to his love turn out to be merely setting up an anticlimax, since she has again changed her mind. In the last fifteen minutes of the film, the conflicting shifts of mood became staccato, like a comic strip. First (wham!) Catherine pulls a pistol on Jim, who (bam!) escapes by jumping out of a window and (sock!) they are all three in a newsreel theatre looking at shots of Nazi book-burning, and then Catherine gets Jim into her car and (zowie!) drives it off the end of an incomplete bridge to fall into the river with a Mack Sennett splash, after which we see two coffins slowly moving into the flames of a crematorium (gulp!) and then a close-up of bones and ashes being pounded into a funeral urn. Now if these juxtapositions of comedy and tragedy are unintentional, then I think Truffaut is a little mad, and if he was making a metaphor about a world in which Nazi book-burnings—and death camps, as the bones and ashes suggest—can take place, then I think he miscalculated artistically, since he has not prepared us for such a transition between the romantic-ironic mood of the rest of the film and this brutal, abrupt ending.

I realize that not preparing the spectator is part of his aesthetic, and it often is much more effective than the overpreparation in most movies. But a good thing can be overdone. A central difficulty of *Jules and Jim* is the nature of Catherine. Is she a free spirit, generously giving herself to life as it corporealizes itself from time to time in men, courageously living by an ethic superior to the usual bourgeois one which demands some fidelity, or at least continuity, in sexual relations? Or is she a monster of selfish whim, without affective contact with others, and therefore ready to destroy her lover, and herself, when she is about to conclusively lose him?

The commentator who takes over much of the soundtrack some-

378

times suggests the former: "Catherine never does anything half-way. . . . Catherine is not beautiful or intelligent, but she is a true woman, a queen." And sometimes the latter: "She thinks that in a couple only one needs to be faithful—the other one." Jules, her sweet and patient husband (delicately played by Oskar Werner), is more consistent. "She thinks that whatever she does, God will forgive her in advance," he remarks early on, and his expression at the end after the double funeral is consistent with the commentator's last word: "Jules was overcome with relief." The balance would seem to dip toward the monsterette hypothesis. But Jeanne Moreau, in a great performance, makes Catherine so emotionally real that one begins to doubt the evidence not of one's senses but of one's mind. A recent issue of *Réalités* quotes the poet, Guillevic, apropos of her: "There are nice monsters—Who sit opposite you, their eyes swollen with tenderness/And on your hand/Place their velvet paw." This seems about right if one adds, out of fairness, that she is always completely sincere at each moment—it is that the moments are different from the men.

Recently I interviewed M. Truffaut, a small, quick, fragile, birdlike man with large, intelligent eyes who answers questions with a refreshing directness. I posed to him the problem of Catherine. He was amazed that it could arise: "She is a woman who wants to live like a man because that is her nature. The people in my film reject conventional morality, but they have their own kind, a higher one and an absolute one." (It is that "absolute" that bothers me.) He did not intend the exchange of letters and the cross-purposes in the postwar part to be comic: "The lovers were expressing their real feelings." The car tumbling into the river à la Mack Sennett didn't seem inappropriately funny to him nor did the cremation scene strike him as out of key: "The woman ends in water and fire just as she almost perishes in those elements at the start." He referred to Catherine's jumping into the Seine—characteristically, because Jules and Jim are making cynical remarks about women—and her setting her nightgown on fire, knowing Jim will at once extinguish it; these scenes, trivial and fugitive, don't seem to me to justify their *fortissimo* parallels at the end, and I don't think many viewers would make the water-fire connection that Truffaut does. I was also baffled by his pointing out that the shock of the cremation scene

379

was softened by the gay circus-like tune on the soundtrack—it had the opposite effect on me—and by his casual remark, when I pressed the contradictory moods (he preferred "dialectical") that "a scene or a sentence is often humorous precisely because it is pathetic." Yes, yes, but. He sees *Jules and Jim* as simply "a celebration of innocence and nobility." Yes, yes, but.

—September 1962

THE SOFT SKIN

Up to now François Truffaut has been unique because of the unvarying success with which he uses varying styles. Each of his three previous films—*The 400 Blows, Shoot the Piano Player,* and *Jules and Jim*—was a triumph, and each, in theme and style, a different kind of triumph. But now, in his fourth time at bat, Truffaut is out on a pop-fiction fly, and his b.a. has fallen from a perfect 1.000 to an imperfect (though still good) .750. Yet even in failure, he is original. Big directors usually fail in a big way, pretentiously, as Welles did with *The Trial* or Antonioni in *The Eclipse* and *Red Desert,* but *The Soft Skin* is a curiously unambitious failure. Why did he want to make it, one asks as The Eternal Triangle, like a suburban local, clicks along the familiar rails to the familiar terminus: the aging husband, the pretty airline hostess "young enough to be his daughter," the wife who shoots him when she discovers the affair. A twice-told tale in our own popular fiction and even more banal in its French counterparts. So why, M. Truffaut, why?

I suppose he would answer that a plot is just raw material and a director who knows his business can build a palace out of rubble as Griffith did when he made *The Birth of a Nation* from Thomas Dixon's *The Clansman,* or as he himself did when he transformed two not very distinguished novels into *Shoot the Piano Player* and *Jules and Jim.* But it takes a bit of doing, which he hasn't tried very hard to do. (It's especially puzzling that this time he was working from an original screenplay, of which he was coauthor.) The doing might have been done by stylization (jazzing up the plot with off-

380

key cross-riffs as in *Piano Player*) or by realism (developing the people beyond stereotypes as in *Blows*) or by a combination of both, as in *Jules and Jim.*

Realism, except for visual details which are often intrusive (as, the lingering close-ups of a car taking on gas at a filling station) because no connection is made with the particular situation, is of the most perfunctory sort. As the plot clicks along to its appointed conclusion, we learn little more about the triangle than we did at the beginning: that Pierre is an eminent literary journalist, as timidly confused emotionally as he is confident intellectually; that the girl, Nicole, is decent and generous; that Franca, the wife, is possessively domestic. An interesting trio, each angle well acted, especially Pierre (whom Jean Desailly makes believable as an intellectual, no mean feat on stage or screen), but I was curious to know more. Why, for example, is this apparently Pierre's first affair—judging from his schoolboy ineptness—although his career, and renown, must have offered him many previous opportunities and temptations? Why does Franca resort to murder rather than the divorce court? Granted her passionate domesticity, still it's 1965, not 1865. Such questions could have been answered by showing us what kind of individuals they are, but Truffaut seems to have assumed no such exposition was necessary. When no information was forthcoming, when each angle behaved strictly according to the geometry of pop fiction, I concluded that the demonstration was rigged so as to lead to the Q.E.D. implicit in the statement of the original hypothesis, or hypotenuse.

The alternative—stylization—flashed out brilliantly in the opening scenes but only fitfully afterward. I know of no director with an easier, more effortless style than Truffaut's. As Willie Mays or Shoeless Joe Jackson are called "natural ballplayers" in contrast to the studied technique of a Ty Cobb or a Stan Musial, so Truffaut is a "natural" director, like Fellini and unlike Antonioni. This is not a value judgment: Cobb was a better ballplayer than Shoeless Joe could have been even if his career had not been cut short by the "Black Sox" scandal, and virtuosity produced a greater movie in *Citizen Kane* than Truffaut has yet accomplished.

Truffaut has two particular virtues. He takes you right into the kitchen, communicating his delight in the very process of making a

movie, the pleasure, sensuous and intellectual, of making statements that couldn't be as well stated in any other medium. And he
has a peculiar knack for presenting a *mise-en-scène* that is neither
bigger than life (Welles, Resnais) nor smaller than life (Bresson,
Olmi) but exactly life-size. He feels uncomfortable with romantic
grandeur, as when he shoots it down to earth at the end of *Jules and
Jim*. But he also raises the commonplace to poetry, as in *400
Blows*.

The Soft Skin begins with Pierre's scramble to make the plane for
a lecture date in Lisbon. The confusion of getting home late from
the office, packing hastily (where's the *lecture?*), pecking a goodbye kiss at his wife while they decide whether the child should be
allowed to ride to the airport with him (oh, all right!) and the
mechanical order of phones, timetables, traffic, airport check-in
desks which is merely another kind of confusion—all this is rendered economically and yet completely, just life-size. We see next
the passengers crowding into the aisle as the plane lands; Pierre's
emerging into the sunlight, blinking owlishly, to be thrust into a
publicity photograph with Nicole; his descending the landing steps,
looking around vaguely until he is greeted by an eager Portuguese
cultural functionary of whom he cordially disembarrasses himself,
to their mutual relief; his ascent in the hotel elevator to the
luxurious suite that has been reserved for him, where he throws his
Unesco-type homburg on the bed and makes for the glittering
American-style bathroom. The lecture is omitted and we next see
him again in the elevator, with Nicole as a chance fellow passenger
at whom he glances shyly and whom he calls up from his room and,
with some difficulty, persuades to meet him for a drink the next
day, after which—a fine touch—he goes around turning on all the
lights. The stage has been set with cinematic swiftness: we understand Pierre's glimpse of an escape from the routine of his family
and public life. His despairing look as he first surveys the impersonal luxury of his hotel suite tells the story of his career—to the
tennis and the ski bum our foundationized culture has added the
lecture bum, so admired by everybody in general and so detached
from anybody in particular. But the drama that is played out on
this masterfully set stage comes to very little; I was still expecting it
to begin when suddenly it was all over. There are a few good things,

such as the satirical episode of Pierre's trip to Rheims to introduce a documentary film on Gide with a few well-chosen reminiscences ("He once told me an artist must always tell the truth"). He is lionized by the local intelligentsia so ardently that he cannot escape to the obscure hotel in which he has registered with Nicole, whom he has injudiciously taken along; the result is that both parties are furious. Or the scene described by John Simon in his *New Leader* review, "in which the hero toys with and undresses his mistress, who simulates sleep. The camera movements up and down the recumbent figure, the cross-cutting from avid yet slightly frightened face to rapt fingers gently exploring the texture of a thigh . . . the ability to suggest the extensiveness, manifoldness, delicacy of a girl's body and the awe rather than mere concupiscence it elicits— these reveal the master." As they do but, except for such interludes where his talent overmastered him, Truffaut sacrifices everything to the plot demands of The Eternal Triangle—eternal that is between 1860 and 1920. There is real, and contemporary, pathos in Pierre's problem as Nicole's lover, which might be summed up with a slight wrench of Marvell's couplet: "And ever at my back I hear/ Unesco's unwinged chariot hurrying near."

This would have been an interesting theme, and perhaps someday we will know why Truffaut chose instead to tinker with a dramatic machine, its only moving part coincidence ("Had I But Known"). As when Franca, having missed by a few minutes Pierre's repentant phone call, is set into clockwork motion with her gun through the streets of Paris toward the predestined End. A machine invented by Scribe and Sardou so long ago that the patents expired before he was born. Why, M. Truffault, why?

—May 1965

ZAZIE

I went to see *Zazie* with the liveliest expectations. People whose judgment I respect, Kenneth Tynan for one, had told me that it was funny and beautiful and original, combining slapstick and surrealism as only the cinema can do. Also that it was faithful to the

383

novel, *Zazie dans le Métro,* the latest extravaganza of the remarkable Raymond Queneau, whose parodic *Exercices de Style* seems to me perfect of its kind. Nor was I let down when I glanced over the foreword that Louis Malle had prepared for his film: ". . . A clutter of visual spoofs and absurdities follow each other at such a rapid clip that many are probably never spotted at all. But it doesn't matter whether the viewer misses out on a few gags—if the exuberance generates hilarity. The imbroglios and antics of Queneau's 'mad' people are spiked with take-offs on . . . *La Dolce Vita, Hiroshima, Mon Amour* and my own picture, *The Lovers.* . . . As seen through Zazie's penetrating outlook, the universe is in a constant flux, protagonists are torn in conflicting directions. Nothing is quite what it seems to be . . . Some of the more insane aspects of our civilization are magnified to nightmaresque dimensions. . . . The swift-moving pace is deliberately intended to re-echo the frenzied tempo of life today."

And in truth *Zazie* delivered all that Mr. Tynan and M. Malle promised, and more; perhaps the more was the trouble. The plot line is as simple in general as it is complex in detail. The eleven-year-old Zazie comes from the provinces for her first visit to Paris; her mother stashes her with her Uncle Gabriel (whose profession turns out to be female impersonating) for a few days while she (the mother) shacks up with a lover. Zazie is as tough as she is innocent—her foul language, bowdlerized by the translated captions, shocks even the raffish grownups she visits; she is in a very bad humor because her one interest in Paris, the Métro, is closed by a strike; after some fantastic adventures, Zazie is handed back to her mother at the station by Uncle Gabriel's wife and the film ends.

I don't understand why I didn't like *Zazie* more. It is in very pretty color; Catherine Demongeot is fine as Zazie, likewise Philippe Noiret as Uncle Gabriel, and indeed most of the others. M. Malle does everything that Mack Sennett did and more—slow motion, speeded-up motion, trick photography, stunts on the Eiffel Tower, an automobile chase through Paris which ends with a collision from which a chassis emerges with all hands speeding along unconcernedly on it; a man steps out of a window (to escape an enraged husband) and the next shot shows him dropping into a seat in a café underneath and impatiently calling for the waiter. It's all extremely high-spirited but, as with *The Joker,* after the first half-hour I began to wilt. Too much. Too crazy. No contrast. The old silent comedies M. Malle admires provided the necessary counterpoint of the normal. The chases and pie-throwings and trick effects erupted out of an everyday context. But in *Zazie* the fantastic is the norm and so the effect of each successive violation of reality becomes weaker until at the end what should have been the climactic explosion—a row in a night club, complete with pie-throwing (here it's sauerkraut) and total destruction—is merely tedious, and a little disgusting. M. Malle made the elementary mistake of trying to top excess by excess. The effect was more Teutonic than Gallic, or comic.

And can even the cleverest director now recapture the spirit of those old comedies? A man cannot become a child again, he can merely become childish (children are never childish). The Sennett-Chaplin-Keaton style is part of the childhood of the cinema. *Zazie* reproduces its externals faithfully, all too, but the innocence and spontaneity that made them charming—and funny—are lacking.

—February 1962

ENGLAND

SATURDAY NIGHT AND SUNDAY MORNING

The English are trying to have their own new wave but so far, except for *Room at the Top,* the results are unimpressive. The latest is *Saturday Night and Sunday Morning,* from a recent working-class novel by Alan Sillitoe. The photography is good clear documentary, the acting is excellent (especially Albert Finney and Rachel Roberts), the novel is rendered faithfully, but the movie is static. I think it must be Karel Reisz's direction. He has hitherto made only documentaries—I saw one, *We Are the Lambeth Boys,* that was so relaxed and underkeyed that it seemed to last as long as *Ben-Hur.* Although Mr. Reisz is not English, he shares the English delusion that life can be captured by detailed reporting. He spells everything out and holds each scene too long. In his *Lambeth Boys* one wriggled and foot-tapped as a bowling match or the ordering of food at a counter was rendered without excision—one felt one could have gotten that sandwich much quicker than the actors did. In *Saturday Night* it is more a matter of talk.

It is perhaps a mistake to let the author of the novel also write the screenplay. Writers hate to cut anything and Mr. Sillitoe has lovingly preserved as much of his novel as he could get away with. It was the director's job to see that he got away with the minimum, but this would mean, by cutting and visual effects, finding an equivalent for the original words and Mr. Reisz is not inventive. So one has many long dialogues, like the ones between the friends while they are fishing, in which the camera, like a faithful dog, peers alternately into the speakers' faces and tedium reaches such a point one cannot hear the lines. Too much is *said* in general and too little is *shown.* I saw *Saturday Night* the day after I had seen *Shadows* and it occurred to me that the problem of cinematic dialogue may be solved in opposite ways: either by spontaneous formlessness (*Shadows*) or by the most artificial intensification of form (*Hiroshima, Children of Paradise*). The kind of novelistic dialogue we get in *Saturday Night* is the routine middle way that is guaranteed to fail, since common sense never produces art.

Since I wrote the above, I have read the reviews in the London press over here.* They are all enthusiastic and even the more

* London, where I lived for part of 1960 and 1961.

388

sophisticated natives I've talked with, like Kenneth Tynan, are impressed with the film's "honesty" and "boldness." What to me was tedious to them was exciting simply because for the first time (they claim) working-class life has been shown in their movies not in terms of comedy or pathos, but straight. Unlike the young artist in *Sons and Lovers,* or the young clerk in *Room at the Top,* the hero of *Saturday Night* has no aspirations toward bourgeois status. I grant this is sociologically interesting as the latest crack in the British class system—what a lot of rifts that massive structure has survived since *Lucky Jim!*—but the Reisz-Sillitoe approach is so unimaginative that one gets only a superficial sense of working-class life. Novelty is not a substitute for art. The reaction here to *Saturday Night* reminds me of the early movie audiences who were thrilled by the fact that the pictures actually *moved.*

—February 1961

THE LONELINESS OF THE LONG DISTANCE RUNNER

If directors may be compared to horses, without offense to either party, I see Antonioni as a thoroughbred flat-racer, Truffaut as a steeplechase jumper soaring lightly over obstacles, Renoir as a Percheron that puts his great hooves down with delicacy, and Kazan as a show horse that turns out to be broken-winded. (Bergman is Black Beauty.) Tony Richardson I see as a hackney, by which I don't mean "hack," for he is ambitious and serious, but merely the dictionary definition: "a horse for ordinary driving and riding." To shift metaphorical gears, he is like the car of which dealers say, slapping a dusty fender, "This'll give you transportation." His new film, *The Loneliness of the Long Distance Runner,* is not bad: it has realism, pathos, an interesting performance by a new young actor (Tom Courtenay, who is no Albert Finney but will do) and a cinematic liveliness rare in British films about working-class life. Mr. Richardson appears to have been stimulated by the *nouvelle vague* into an unwontedly spirited gait. But he remains a hackney and his film offers simply transportation. A virtue—most movies don't get you anywhere—but a modest one.

389

The plot, taken from a story by Alan Sillitoe, who also did the screenplay, is similar to that of Truffaut's *400 Blows:* a slum kid, confused and embittered by a sordid home and a mother who has a lover, is caught stealing and is sent to a reform school. The theme is also similar: the rebellion, a touching mixture of cynicism and naïveté, of the kid against an adult world he sees, with reason, as hostile and hypocritical. Mr. Richardson's toughie is eighteen, as against M. Truffaut's twelve-year-old, but this turns out to be a distinction without a difference, since, as is well known, French and Italian babies are born ten years older than Anglo-Saxon ones. So the behavior of both heroes is equally childish. The French boy's inept attempt to return the stolen typewriter is paralleled by the English boy's stuffing the stolen money up a drainpipe whence, not to my surprise, it came cascading out at the feet of the detective who plottily arrived during a heavy rain.

The two films show the difference between an artist and an artisan. The defect of Richardson's is a radical one: he is unable to achieve unity—this, indeed, has become his directorial "trademark." Dissonance can be a kind of harmony, as the destruction of form can be a kind of form, but only if it is deliberate. Here the discords seem unintentional, as if the director were unable to control his material. An artist is an ascetic; he omits and simplifies, passing up chances for effects if they don't suit his purpose. But Richardson is a voluptuary of effects. In the beach scenes, we get close-ups of waves rippling over sands, wheeling gulls and other aspects of the seashore *pittoresque* which are as handsome as they are immaterial. Cf. the long shots of the deserted beaches at the end of *Blows,* which are also beautiful but which are related to the dramatic meaning. The boy, after his long run escaping to the sea, which he has never seen and which represents freedom to him, finds that this world is as empty and lonely as the one he has run away from. Once more, he has no place to go. Landscape here becomes another actor, as in the bleak dawn scene on the golf links that ends *La Notte.* But Richardson's landscape is like a pretty woman who "dresses up" a party but takes no part in the conversation.

Runner is overstated throughout, from the opening scene in the Borstal school; any staff that expended that much energy on meaningless shouting and hectoring would be exhausted in no time. The quiet, businesslike types in Truffaut's reform school are more real and also more sinister. Each film has a psychiatric interview that emphasizes the lack of contact between the boy and the interviewer. Truffaut had an inspiration: he doesn't show the interviewer; all we have is her voice, calm and self-assured; the camera is held on the boy's face as he tries, with touching honesty, to answer her questions, which are as professionally sophisticated as they are square in terms of the boy's actual problems. Another clever idea was to show the boy's face, through a series of stop-motion shots, dissolving and then recomposing itself into a different expression from one question to another, suggesting poignantly the innocent openness of his feelings. Richardson's version is not inspired, or clever: his camera just swings back and forth between the boy and the interviewer like a spectator at a tennis match.

Banality of form follows banality of function. Richardson shows his psychiatrist as well-meaning and directs his chief animus against an easier target, the hypocritical, bumbling, old-school-tie headmaster played by Michael Redgrave in the usual cliché terms, a performance that shows how hard it is for a good actor to rise above the level of a poor director. Truffaut presents his psychiatrists as the real villains precisely because they have a good conscience, being not only sincere but also scientifically up to date.

Finally, there is a revealing contrast in structure. Richardson's is fashionably "cinematic," cutting back and forth between past and present freely and often confusingly—a couple sitting behind me never did get oriented—while Truffaut's is tamely chronological. But the shifting between tenses in *Runner* is merely distracting, for all its display of virtuosity: just as one gets absorbed in the school, one is yanked back to the earlier home background, and vice versa. The clever M. Truffaut understands that while temporal acrobatics are appropriate for some movies—he uses them brilliantly in his next film, *Shoot the Piano Player*—they aren't for others. The kind of story told in *Blows,* and in *Runner,* is what the Germans call a *bildungsroman,* a novel about the development of a youth, as the original prototype, Goethe's *Wilhelm Meister.* This theme is best rendered in simple chronological order. The point is the cumulative effect of experience in the forming of a character and playing fast and loose with the time sequence blunts it.

—February 1963

391

TOM JONES

I went to this with the oddest mixture of anxiety and anticipation. On the one hand, it was the fall's biggest little-cinema hit, fervently praised by all the critics (except for Kauffmann of *The New Republic* and Simon of *The New Leader*) so that maybe I'd have to eat my many words about Tony Richardson's talents, or lack of them. On the other hand, I should not have minded such a meal since Mr. Richardson's triumph, while damaging to my specific judgment, would have reinforced my General Field Theory of Cinema: that the worst directors occasionally make good movies, and vice versa. So I went to *Tom Jones* quite willing to backwater, eat crow, and join in the chorus of "Bravo, Tony!" and "Jolly good show!" Also I had some nonprofessional hopes of being amused by a lusty gusty recreation of a lusty gusty novel from the l.g. eighteenth century. (I think the adjective "rumbustious" was also deployed.) For I like to be entertained, and I think that a movie that is not entertaining cannot be considered art, as was demonstrated by many of those aggressively "artistic" films shown at last fall's First New York Film Festival, including Jacques Baratier's *Dragées au Poivre* (*Sweet and Sour*), a new-wave comic extravaganza that has everything but humor. The question is what is entertaining ("to hold the attention agreeably")? For me, *Marienbad* is, Jerry Lewis isn't.

The most I can give *Tom Jones* is that, after a clotted, fumbling first half that teeters uncertainly between burlesque (the parody silent film under the titles—perhaps a little *too* cute) and social realism (the hunting scene with the gorily roweled flanks of the horses, the farmer holding his dead goose, the blood-flecked muzzle of the dying deer), Richardson decides on burlesque, so that what began as a halfhearted effort to reproduce the realistic satire of Fielding's novel becomes a pantomime that is often quite funny, as the famous scene in which the lovers-to-be gorge themselves at dinner, their busily working mouths and fingers suggesting the amorous greed to follow. Or moments like the can-you-tie-that? grimace, mugged directly at the audience, with which Mrs. Waters (Joyce Redman) greets the news that Tom, with whom she has just slept, is probably her son. All good clean fun that would be even

392

better if not cleaner if Mr. Richardson didn't overstress the comic note so often. But overstressing is his directorial trademark: here again we get the whole bag of tricks—including those ghastly "wipes" to get from one scene to another, also a narration in Michael McLaimmor's ripest tones—and they get in the way as much as ever. They overwhelm even Albert Finney, a splendid actor and also just right for Tom; his performance is so fragmented that almost any stout-thewed young man could have been substituted. Of Mr. Richardson's visual illiteracy I have said enough in previous columns; he is still analphabetic, unable to compose a scene clearly in front of the camera and so forced to overuse the close-up.

What's wrong with *Tom Jones,* whether as a version of the novel or as a film in itself, is epitomized by the casting of Hugh Griffith as Squire Western. It is hard to think of a role for which Mr. Griffith would not be Too Much, with his piercing glare, his insanely dominant nose, his beetling brows and cavernous mouth, his over-ripe Welsh diction. Perhaps God. He is all wrong as Squire Western, whom Fielding pictures—and the logic of the story demands— as the old-fashioned country squire: brutal, stolid, slow-witted, choleric, bovine. Griffith gets the choler but nothing else. He does Western in the camp tradition of Laughton's Henry the Eighth: wildly flamboyant, all broad gestures and flashing eyes and all giving the impression of an unstable neurotic who is overcompensating, as they say, in the lusty gusty direction. Fielding's squire had character; the Richardson-Griffith version has personality; not the same thing.

—February 1964

SPARROWS CAN'T SING

I went to Joan Littlewood's movie about low life in the East End of London with small expectations, anticipating the heavy breathing of the standard British socially conscious film. But she crossed me up. The pace is jaunty, nothing is underlined or lingered over, the touch is light. The plot is as slight as *Il Posto's* (or *L'Avven-*

tura's): a free-living young seaman (played *con brio* by James Booth) gets into port to find, with some difficulty, that his wife (a plump little blonde, with a two-foot Italian haystack hairdo, named Barbara Windsor who wonderfully manages to be sexy, funny, immoral, decent, real and grotesque all at the same time) has moved in with a bus driver. The poor fellow can't even find his old home, which has been bulldozed for a housing development—"They daren't go shopping around here," an old codger tells him with relish, "afraid they'll be tore down while they're out." It ends with a brawl at a pub, set off when the sailor and the bus driver finally confront each other, as in a Western; but it works out unexpectedly and inconclusively, as in life and not as in Westerns; the two males are held apart by the bystanders and never do tangle, and the last glimpse we have of the lovers is of him trying to beat her up but getting the worst of it; we gather they will be back together—for a time. Miss Littlewood, whose theatre in the East End is famous, is of the once new and now aging, if not aged, British school of working-class realism, but her spirit couldn't be more different from that of Lindsay Anderson, Karel Reisz, and Arnold Wesker. They are solemn about the class struggle; she giggles. They are tourists, she is a native and so takes the milieu for granted and records its humors with the easy disrespect Wilde's plays exhibit toward upper-class life.

Like *Il Posto,* which it resembles in no other way, *Sparrows* shows us the human grotesques that are molded by poverty. But with the opposite point: in *Posto* people are reduced to objects, to functions of the great corporation (though, since Olmi is an artist and not a propagandist, he doesn't overdo it: his people are deformed but still human) while in *Sparrows* the characters are liberated by poverty from convention and express themselves freely and eccentrically. *Posto* is Marxist (people are what social-economic pressures force them to be) while *Sparrows* is anarchist (there are lots of side exits from that one-way street of History). And what a clever symbol Miss Littlewood's is, the sparrow, that tough, lively, resourceful, tiny creature who is always able to *se débrouiller,* to Get Along, to Make Out in the most unfavorable environment! She has given us what William Empson calls a pastoral: a view of reality refracted through myth and tradition which is no more a Slice of Life than is Mr. Olmi's Milanese pastoral—the genre can be ominous, too—but which is nonetheless "real" for that reason. Indeed, all the more so.

—August 1963

THIS SPORTING LIFE

A decade or so ago Lindsay Anderson, then editor of *Sight and Sound,* published a famous manifesto, "Stand Up! Stand Up! Stand Up!," calling on everybody to stand up and be counted for a socially "committed" British cinema. His words suited the time and after the Free Cinema had produced some earnest, though to my taste not very enlivening, documentaries about lower-class British life (*We Are the Lambeth Boys, Together, Every Day Except Christmas,* etc.), Karel Reisz made the breakthrough into feature films with *Saturday Night and Sunday Morning,* which was to the British cinema what John Osborne's *Look Back in Anger* was to the London stage. I thought both film and play were overrated by the English, but then we have had serious social drama for decades, while to them it was all new and exciting. It was a creative movement for a while, but like most revolutions, it has been overdone: a low-life realistic stereotype has been established which is as boringly predictable as the high-life irrealism it replaced. *This Sporting Life,* directed by Anderson and produced by Reisz, in provenance is the climax of Free Cinema, in quality the anticlimax.

A doggedly grim story about a professional rugby player, *This Sporting Life* has one thing in common with *Tom Jones:* Anderson is as a-visual as Richardson and, like him, tries to conceal the fact by using cinematic "effects" where they are not needed or are positively destructive. I see no reason, for instance, except an effort at *nouvelle-vague* smartness, why the first part should be told in flashbacks from the dental chair in which the anesthetized Frank Machin (Richard Harris) is having his broken teeth repaired. And most clumsily contrived flashbacks—you keep landing back at that dental chair quite unexpectedly. Anderson's use of the camera is either too flatly, clutteredly realistic (the two scenes of players splashing around in the bath) or else too "indicative" (the death-bed scene, with the close-up of a spider on the wall above the dying

395

woman's head, the trickle of blood from her mouth as she dies being melodramatically echoed in Machin's squashing the spider).

Few Hollywood movies are as flimsily motivated as this allegedly realistic film. Machin suffers because he is unhappily in love and because he thinks he is being exploited by his employers. Both themes are puzzling. Why does he pursue his cold, angular landlady (Rachel Roberts manages to look surprisingly ugly) who is a middle-aged widow with two children, while he shows no interest in the hero-worshiping girls who pursue him? Can't he think of anything better to do with that white roadster than take his landlady and her kids to the park? Granted men fall for unsuitable women, but Proust shows you why Odette attracts Swann, and Maugham is explicit, in *Of Human Bondage,* about the masochism in Philip that responds to Millie's coldness and bitchiness. Anderson, however, is not explicit; in fact he seems to think no explanation is needed for a normal young man being obsessed by an aggressively unattractive older woman who sneers at him as "a great ape."

The class struggle is also unclear. Why is Anderson so sure that Machin is being put upon by the club owners? Before they hired him, he was a penniless drifter. They gave him money—beginning with a thousand pounds for signing the contract—and fame of a sort. True, rugby is a brutal game, and true, the owners don't get their teeth knocked out and Machin does; but neither are they local heroes. There is also that white roadster. Maybe he is exploited, but *This Sporting Life* makes a vaguer case for it than, say, Odets' *Golden Boy* or Hemingway's *Twenty Grand*. He suffers mostly, after all, from that miserable love affair, for which the club owners are in no way responsible. I suspect that Anderson and Reisz threw in the class struggle partly to pile on the agony: Free Cinema is decently depressing. And partly from sheer habit: Free Cinema is socially conscious.

—May 1964

KING AND COUNTRY

This film establishes Joseph Losey as a versatile director who commands a wide range of styles for wrecking a movie. In *The*

Servant he flattened a potential comedy-melodrama under unremittingly pretentious "effects," like dousing a hamburger with *sauce béarnaise* that is slightly off. Here he does the opposite, stifling a war movie by staging it as a photographed play that is denied all the resources of cinema except the close-up. "Completely different from *The Servant*," Richard Roud writes in the program of the Second New York Film Festival, *"King and Country* is as classical as the former was baroque." Well, that's one way to put it. Another way would be to describe *King and Country* as TV drama—I'm told that John Wilson's *Hamp,* on which it is based, was thought of originally for TV—rather than cinema. Except for three brief and stylistically jarring flashbacks to the outside world, Mr. Losey confines his camera to a few standard sets of trenches and dugouts—it's the First World War—that look as phony as the ones I saw on Broadway in *What Price Glory?* and *Journey's End.* This scenic poverty is matched by pernicious anemia of theme and plot. And banality. The theme is that war is hell and that courtmartials are unjust—*"Un desolato Film di Losey contro la Guerra"* was the accurate headline in one Italian paper when the film was shown at the Venice Festival. The plot is that Private Hamp is a common soldier in His Majesty's Forces—an all too common one, completely lacking in will, reason, individuality and other traits that are found to some extent in even the most deprived real person, though never in propagandist puppets. He has been through too much slaughter and after the butchery of the Passchendaele offensive has mindlessly started to walk back to London; he is caught, charged with desertion and, after a court-martial, executed. Although Tom Courtenay struggles manfully to get some feeling into the role of Hamp, the part gives no toehold for human expressiveness since Hamp has become a zombie—and the ruin of a zombie is an all-downhill affair, about as dramatic as the killing of a cornered rat. Sure enough, Mr. Losey has his soldiers trap a rat and execute him after a mock court-martial. One gets the point. And after ninety minutes of visual deprivation and sledge-hammer moralizing one remembers with affection Stanley Kubrick's treatment of the same war and the same theme in *Paths of Glory.*

—January 1965

397

THE PUMPKIN EATER

The "woman's novel" has been a staple of the publishing trade since those eighteenth-century sentimental romances parodied by the fifteen-year-old Jane Austen in *Love and Freindship* (*sic*) down to Faith Baldwin, Fannie Hurst and Daphne Du Maurier. The spotlight is on the heroine's feelings, which are always intense and complex; the males are seen only through her eyes, dimly, briefly, tending to be either louts or demigods according to her relations with them at the moment; simple organisms that require, and get, only the most cursory treatment. There has never been and never can be a good "woman's novel" for the same reason pornography cannot be art: because the view of life is too restricted, the aim too narrowly utilitarian. (Good female novelists like George Eliot and Jane Austen don't write woman's novels.)

It has often been observed that women don't enjoy pornography because their eroticism is more emotional and less sensual than men's, but I haven't seen it noted that precisely because of this difference the woman's novel performs for female readers the same humble task of erotic titillation that pornography does for men. If the pornographic hero is a sexual athlete, the heroine of the woman's novel is an athlete of the emotions whose feats of feeling are described in lubricious detail, while the males are reduced to objects of sentimental lust no more individualized as human beings than are the stripped beauties, of whom one learns nothing beyond their anatomy, who satisfy the physical lusts of the males in pornographic fiction. Because for some reason sentimental orgies are not considered immoral in our culture, the woman's novel has always circulated freely, without interference from the police, though it could be argued that its debauchery of sentiment is more damaging to morality than are the pornographer's boldest fantasies. As any one knows who has found the latter curiously boring after a few pages, the combinations and permutations of physical lust are severely limited by the not-at-all infinite capacities of the human body, while they are endless when it's a matter of feelings. Bodily impurity is superficial compared to the corruption and falsification of the psyche, and it affects a much smaller area of existence.

I haven't read Penelope Mortimer's novel, but if the movie is faithful, and I am told it is, Miss Mortimer has written a woman's novel to end all woman's novels, which of course it unhappily won't. The story is about a woman (Anne Bancroft) with a neurotic obsession that almost destroys her and her marriage. Her problem is an odd one: she is a compulsive breeder, she simply cannot resist one more child. When her latest husband (Peter Finch), a movie writer with the unimprovable woman's-novel name of Jake, who has manfully taken on her large and noisy brood by earlier mates— when Jake insists she stop procreating, she tricks him, gets herself pregnant again, and reels downhill to disaster like a Victorian drunkard. To the male mind, or anyway to this male mind, Miss Bancroft's weakness is irretrievably comic, and Jack Clayton, who once showed great directorial skill in his *Room at the Top* and whose later movie version of James's *The Turn of the Screw* was at least a respectable failure, hasn't improved matters by taking it as high tragedy. (Though since this is the dramatic crux of the book, he had no choice—except not to do the movie.) Nor is Anne Bancroft any help as the heroine: she is always intense, always serious, always emoting; she is one of those actresses who never let up, and before her agonized countenance had been on the screen ten minutes, in extreme close-up, I was silently begging her to stop acting just for a little breathing space; but she never did, nor did Mr. Clayton ever remove his camera to a decent distance from her all-too-expressive face. Poor Mr. Finch never had a chance to escape the nullity proper to the woman's-novel male. One learned far too much about her—so much and so intimately, indeed, that I felt embarrassed, as if I'd wandered into the Ladies' Room—and nothing about him.

Trapped in the claustral mazes of Miss Bancroft's emotions, which weren't interesting since they seemed related to nothing outside herself, I endured boredom that approached the absolute in spite of Mr. Clayton's desperate effort to liven things up by the most pretentious overdirecting I've seen since Jules Dassin's *Phaedra*. So many cinematic ideas, all bad, such as the hand ballet in arty close-up at the father's deathbed or the obtrusive symbolism of the antiseptic white light globe that slowly fills the screen in the sterilization episode. Nor did Harold Pinter's screenplay help, with its mannered repetitions, his gimmick for realistic dialogue: "I don't know what to do, I wish I knew what to do." "I'm so pleased you had that sensible operation, so sensible." "They came in the back gate. . . . Did you come in the back gate?" (He hadn't the heart for: "Yes, we came in the back gate.") The one spot of life was James Mason's performance as a lecherous philistine of surpassing nastiness. He redeems the honor of the male sex, betrayed by Finch's decent-understanding husband, by giving our sensitive heroine a very bad quarter of an hour indeed.

—January 1965

A HARD DAY'S NIGHT

The problem would seem insoluble: to make a good movie about the Beatles. They are cult-fetishes of adolescent hysteria, exploiting (and being exploited by) the mass market, related to their audience on about the same level as an African witch doctor to his clients, indeed on a lower one in some ways since the rhythmical beat that is their specialty is less sophisticated than the intricately varied rhythms of many tribal dances.

But the problem has been solved. *A Hard Day's Night* is not only a gay, spontaneous, inventive comedy but it is also as good cinema as I have seen for a long time. The Beatles themselves are partly responsible: they have somehow managed to retain their naturalness and individuality—one might even venture that much-abused word, charm—in the teeth of commercial success and teen-age adulation, perhaps because they really seem to enjoy their celebrity —the squealing mobs, the police escorts, the excitement, the money —accepting it all without hypocrisy, feeling so much at home in the predatory jungle of masscult that they can kid it, and themselves. But chief credit for the film's quality goes to its young director, Richard Lester, who has made *It's Trad, Dad,* a feature movie about jazz and pop singers and, with Peter Sellers and Spike Milligan, a short whose title exactly describes its content: *The Running, Jumping and Standing Still Film.* The same verve and originality, the same free use of the medium distinguishes *A Hard Day's Night,* which sometimes reminds one of silent slapstick (the beautiful long

400

shot, from high up, of the Beatles capering around a field, crossing and crisscrossing at top speed with perfect timing) and sometimes of the Marx brothers (the "clean old man" bit, Ringo's adventures as he strolls about town). There have been many efforts to recapture the spirit of those old comedies, but Mr. Lester's is the first I've seen that gets beyond self-conscious pastiche. Perhaps because he wasn't trying to recapture the past, but to present the Beatles, a very modern phenomenon. He has had the wit to give them their head, and to counterpose to their free exuberance the tense calculations of the entrepreneurial types who convert it into cash. The cross-purposes between a Beatle and the elegant clothes designer who wants to build a new line on this unlikely foundation, the nervous vigil of the television director waiting for Ringo to get back from his wanderings—these are as good satire and as cleverly cut cinema as is going. (The TV director is wonderfully played by Victor Spinetti, who starred in another British triumph of craft and spontaneity, Joan Littlewood's musical, *Oh What a Lovely War!*) The grand finale, when the Beatles put on their show, is unexpectedly moving and exhilarating because Mr. Lester manages to show the rapport the Beatles seem to have with their screaming fanatics, who are not so very much younger than they are, after all.

A Hard Day's Night is something that has become extremely rare since Chaplin and Griffith: a movie that is both a popular success— it grossed almost $6,000,000 in its first six weeks over here—and a *succès d'estime* with the critics. Credit should also go, by the way, to Alun Owen, who wrote the screenplay, and Gilbert Taylor, who directed the excellent photography.

—January 1965

THE KNACK

Richard Lester, the young Anglo-American director (born here, works there) whose *A Hard Day's Night* was the best comedy, perhaps the best movie, of 1964, displays here the same technical brio in every department, from cutting and photographic effects to witty scenario and clever use of actors. Yet for some reason *The*

401

Knack, although it won the Golden Palm at Cannes, was disappointing. Brilliant, yes; original, experimental, yes; but funny, no. It is about three people: a shy young man who doesn't have the knack of getting girls; a sleepily confident young man who lives in the former's house and does have the knack; and a provincial virgin who comes to London and, in the course of trying to find the YWCA, gets involved with them (and with a third young man whose precise role, or necessity, in the drama never became clear). She finally, and not unpredictably, turns down the young man with the knack for the young man without the knack. (Only an Ibsen could have wrenched it around the other way.)

I didn't see Ann Jellicoe's play, on which the film is based, but I gather it was, as plays usually are, limited in space to a few scenes and concentrated, in treatment, on the personal relations of the trio. Mr. Lester has taken this tight little kernel and exploded it, like puffed rice, into the most expansive kind of cinema. The characters run all over London in Mack Sennett chases, the longest being the transportation of a bed by various means of locomotion through miles and miles of streets. The time sequence is fractured by vivacious cutting, there is a Greek chorus of stodgy British types who comment on the antics of the young principals, also some wonderful fantasy sequences of erotic satire—those lines of adoring teen-age beauties wearing white "poor-boy" sweaters.

In short, Mr. Lester uses the devices he used to such splendid effect in *A Hard Day's Night.* Only here they don't work so well. *The Knack* seems overdirected. The play's melodic line of pathos and comedy is drowned out by the crash of the movie's drums and brasses. Mr. Lester's bravura approach was suitable for *A Hard Day's Night* because the Beatles are not people but simulacra created by the pop-culture market—and, with engaging frankness, by themselves. But here there are three individuals whose qualities, which are the point of the drama, are smothered when the director gives them the cinematic works. The final scenes, for instance, when the girl sees through the knack and flees to the knackless young man, are so over-movieized with dynamic cutting and close-up camera angles that it is hard to follow what happens, let alone the subtly developing shifts in the balance of sexual power. Ray Brooks is perfectly stylized as Tolen, the one with the knack, at once masterful with the girls and comic to the audience. Michael Crawford is appealing as the knackless Colin, though his acting style is perhaps too natural for this particular movie. Rita Tushingham, who in her two previous films, *A Taste of Honey* and *Girl with Green Eyes,* was an interesting *jolie laide* here has been reduced by extreme, harshly lit close-ups to a simple *laide*—the reverse of what Griffith did for Lillian Gish. I found her so distractingly unattractive as to make it hard to believe the two males would have competed for her. I see what Mr. Lester had in mind, the ugly duckling who turns out to swim better than all those white-sweatered chicks, but I think he overdid it.

—October 1965

HELP!

Cinema differs from other arts in the speed with which directorial talent often burns itself out. Consider the case of Richard Lester, the young American who has become one of the leading directors in England. Two years ago he gave us *A Hard Day's Night,* which succeeded in reviving a comic mode I'd thought long dead: slapstick satire. His next film, *The Knack,* seemed to me overdirected. It had some fine moments, but I began to wonder if Mr. Lester was as intelligent as he is obviously clever. *Help!* pushes this suspicion much farther. He has produced just the kind of elaborately unamusing comedy that Hollywood specializes in, a witless orgy of expensive production that strangles the Beatles, so fresh and spontaneous in *Night,* in a laboriously foolish plot line and smothers them under tons of handsomely colored feathers.

I saw both films on the same bill recently and while I was as much amused by *Night* the second time around as the first, I found *Help!* remarkably tedious considering that it spared no effort to be wildly comic every minute on the minute. Perhaps that was one trouble. *Night* had two real, solid targets to make fun of, both of them intimately known to the director and to the Beatles: show biz and the absurdities and pomposities of the adult world as represented by the clean old man, the police, and Victor Spinetti's superbly caricatured TV director. But the plot peg from which *Help!* dangles limply is just silly: the sinister-Orientals-trying-to-get-back-a-sacred-jewel business is too tired by now even to be kidded. The real-life milieu of *Night* repressed Lester's tendency to overdo cinematic tricks, allowed the Beatles to be themselves, and made possible a script with a cutting edge of wit. The cliché fantasy of *Help!* reduced the Beatles, and even Mr. Spinetti, to knockabout comedians, allowed the director too much freedom—indeed, forced him, in order to get any life or an imitation of liveliness into the proceedings, to string out and exaggerate the gags and to rush his camera all over the world from London to Switzerland to the West Indies (not to mention a tank battle on Salisbury Plain in the shadow of Stonehenge), desperately seeking picturesque settings which somehow turned out to be more monotonous than the drab English midland city to which the action of *Night* is confined.

The gags in *Night* were fast, almost thrown away at times, as Lennon's burlesque of the Queen cutting the ribbon ("I declare this bridge open") which comes on naturally when he grabs a pair of scissors from a tailor and which is all over in twenty seconds flat. At the same time, the Beatles were given time to fool around and establish their personalities, as in Ringo's wanderings around the town, a slow, poetic interlude whose casual humor was both charming in itself and also a welcome change of pace. In *Help!,* the opposite: the pace is frenetic throughout, which gives an effect of slowness, oddly, and which also suggests that the director realized the gags weren't much good and so needed to be pounded home. Even when he gets hold of a good one, he ruins it by elaboration: the first glimpse of the Beatles shows them walking along a shabby back street in London, bowing politely to two housewives who say, as each Beatle takes out a key and unlocks the door to one of a row of four modest little houses, "Now isn't that nice, success hasn't spoiled them"; the camera goes inside and we see that the four houses have been made into one, with a huge lavishly decorated living room. So funny so far. Then a rustic in gardener's clothes mows the luxuriously thick wall-to-wall carpet—with a pair of artificial dentures. Before using those teeth, or that gardener, Mr. Lester would have done well to have consulted the late Buster Keaton who, in an interview (*Sight and Sound,* Winter 1965–66) that should be required reading for all comedy makers, reminisced: "We learned in a hurry that we couldn't make a feature-length picture the way we had done the two-reelers; we couldn't use impossible gags like the kind of things that happen to cartoon characters [Mr. Lester shrinks a Beatle to five inches in one episode]. We had to eliminate all these things because we had to tell a very logical story that the audience would accept. So story construction became a very strong point with us."

Perhaps the trouble is simply that Mr. Lester got his basic training as a maker of TV commercials which are even shorter than two-reelers and which aim at maximum visual impact in minimum time, a hit-and-run technique which doesn't worry about logic or continuity. "The worst thing a director can do is to underestimate the speed of an audience," he told a reporter while he was making *Help!*. "Audiences of any age can grasp a sixty-second television commercial. Everybody in front of a telly is bombarded with quick cuts and sight gags. They have become used to taking in a lot quickly, and they react the way they are supposed to react." The lesson Keaton learned forty years ago when he began to make feature-length comedies like *The General* and *Sherlock, Jr.*, that a ninety-minute movie must be constructed differently from a twenty-minute one (or a sixty-second one), this is still news to Mr. Lester. Watching *Help!*, I felt I was being bombarded with two hours of TV commercials, some of them effective, most not, but each having the drawback that, not being subordinated to the whole, it tended to undermine the effect of its neighbors, like a roomful of brilliant conversationalists all talking at once. It is not a question of the speed of an audience's reactions—I agree that most directors underestimate it—but rather of how many disparate stimuli the audience can react to over a long period without getting dizzy—and bored. And the better the gags and visual effects, the more destructive they can be, as the handsome snow scenes in the Alps whose black-white brilliance throws out of key what comes before and after. "There is nothing worse with us than a misplaced gag," Keaton observed. "Someone may suggest a good gag or even an excellent one, but if it doesn't fit the story I'm doing and I try to drag it in, then it looks dragged in on the screen. So it's much better to save it until sometime when it does fit in with what I'm doing."

405

Common-sense aesthetics: if a detail clashes with the general composition, leave it out. But it takes an artist to be so sensible, and so ascetic.

—June 1966

MORGAN!

"Howlingly funny," said Mr. Crowther of the *Times,* "poignantly comic," said Mr. X of *Newsweek,* "hilarious," said Mr. Y of *Time,* "brilliantly cinematic," said Mr. Alpert of the *Saturday Review,* "something close to total success," said Mr. Gill of *The New Yorker.* It is only fair to add that some of these critics have reservations, Mr. Crowther's being, not unexpectedly, an elder-statesman kind (he found Morgan "a figure of fearful implications," concluding: "The only perilous thing about *Morgan!* is that it may cause us all to have a bit too much sympathy for beatniks and their childishness in a vicious world"), while Mr. Alpert's are almost total, his review being the most sensible of any I've seen except for John Simon's passionately reasoned diatribe in *The New Leader.* Still, the critics were, in general, enthusiastic, and even Mr. Alpert did concede the film was "brilliantly cinematic," which is like a diamond buyer being taken in by a zircon. *Morgan!* also made a stir at the Cannes festival, where its feminine lead, Vanessa Redgrave, took the "best actress" prize, and one hears about town that it is *the* film to see. I don't think it's *a* film to see, nor even that Miss Redgrave, handsome as she is, is much of an actress, not here anyway; she seemed stiff, mechanical, trying to make up for an uneasiness about the meaning of her part (with which I sympathize) by violent contortions of her lovely face and limbs, a nervous overemphasis which she shared with the film. Neither of them seemed very sure what they were about.

If *Morgan!* is supposed to be a comedy, and certain desperate attempts at slapstick suggest maybe it is, then I was not amused. Comedy, of all dramatic modes, as I've been observing here for several centuries apropos of such clinkers as *How to Murder Your Wife, Hallelujah the Hills!* (another of those exclamation points!),

It's a Mad (etc.) *World, Zazie, What's New, Pussycat?* and *The Loved One,* demands the utmost strictness, tightness, indeed austerity of form if it is to make us laugh; and slapstick, precisely because it is so freewheeling, demands even more rigor than other kinds of comedy, as Keaton and Chaplin well knew. *Morgan!* is as rigorous, formally, as *Help!*—a rule of thumb suggests itself: any dramatic production whose title ends with "!" must be viewed with suspicion, cf. *Oklahoma!.* If the intention was pathos, to move one by the plight of the (I shall not write "eponymous") hero, then it failed with me because Morgan seemed to me, for reasons I'll go into later, more madman than man. And if the director's aim was to satirize the bourgeois Establishment by contrasting it to an innocent spirit like Candide or Huckleberry Finn, then he failed again, indeed he convinced me, against sixty years of experience, that maybe there are worse styles of life than the bourgeois; namely, Morgan's. It will be said that Karel Reisz obviously had all three aims in view, and I will agree, but it takes a subtler touch than his to blend such different genres into a whole. Throughout his film a suspicion kept renewing itself in my mind that he was hopping nimbly, and sometimes not so nimbly, from comedy to pathos to satire, so that the general effect was a fast-moving, energetic confusion which conditioned the audience to forgive a comic scene that failed to come off because it was immediately overlaid by a whiff of pathos or a wink of satire, so okay it's not very *funny* maybe but it's not really a comedy, and then when one of the other two modes proved a dud, back to slapstick and you aren't taking it *seriously* are you, for God's sake? I don't say that discordant genres cannot be controlled so as to make a whole, merely that Mr. Reisz hasn't done it. The trouble with *Morgan!* is the worst kind there is: point-of-view trouble.

In the eighteenth century one of the fun things, if you were with it, was a visit to a lunatic asylum. In 1966 we go to see Mr. Reisz's movie. On balance, I think the difference is in favor of the eighteenth-century voyeurs. They laughed at madmen, a coarse and unfeeling reaction, but at least they had a healthy prejudice in favor of their own condition, sanity. But today we aren't so sure, we are much more refined and liberal, so we laugh not at but with Morgan—or, more accurately, we giggle along with him, uneasily.

407

Yes, yes, of course we know that he is, as Mr. Crowther so well puts it, "some kind of maladjusted nut," but isn't the conventional, bourgeois world he rejects rather odd, too? Yes, it is. But we give in too easily to "buts," there are always "buts" around, at some point one must draw a line and say but me no buts, this is this and that is that. This line has not been drawn in *Morgan!*.

Morgan is a young man of working-class parentage who, so far as is revealed in the film, is what they call a layabout and we call a bum, that is, he doesn't work, lives off others and has no particular talents or purposes—there is a quarter-hearted attempt to suggest he is, or was, a painter, but you have to be alert to catch it on the screen. He does have, however, two obsessions which make his otherwise repulsive personality of some interest and which also supply the entire dramatic power of the movie: he identifies himself, in fantasy, with apes, specifically gorillas, and with Marxism, specifically Trotsky. He yearns to be a gorilla for sensible reasons: gorillas are powerful yet gentle, pacifist vegetarians living freely in the jungle. How Marx and Trotsky, neither of whom were notably gentle or vegetarian, also got into his addled pate is not made clear, unless it was because Trotsky was a loser and was murdered by Stalin, with whom Morgan tends to identify the British upper classes; or because a gorilla obsession wouldn't have been very exciting at the box office but when you add Trotskyism you have something that is, you know, up-to-date, or fairly.

Such is Morgan. Before the credits go on he has, by some scriptorial magic, induced a young, rich and beautiful woman to marry him. As the film begins, she has had enough of him, she has denied him her person and her smart town house and is about to divorce him in order to marry a clever, agreeable, ambitious young art dealer whom I, personally, thought more admirable and attractive than her weedy, slack-jawed, demented husband. "Morgan is the consummate misfit," Brendan Gill wrote in *The New Yorker,* "an ugly, loving, irritable, ranting, unreasonable lout. . . . At the start of the movie I could scarcely bear to look at his coarse mug, much less listen to his horrible, whining Cockney voice, but by the end of the movie I was ready to champion him against all comers." (Such accurate data leading to such erroneous conclusions!) The plot line is Morgan's refusal to let her go, and his efforts to win her

408

back by a series of rather nasty practical jokes, not that all practical jokes aren't rather nasty, such as putting a skeleton in her bed (and then leaping on her when she starts up screaming), rigging up a loudspeaker system over which he broadcasts to interrupt her lovemaking with her fiancé, arranging a bomb to explode under her bed under similar circumstances (but which is accidentally triggered off, with "hilarious" results, when his mother-in-law, almost as odious and absurd a character as he, plumps down on the bed, is blown up and staggers out of the room, hat askew, face smudged, sputtering indignantly just like the old Keystone days), kidnapping his ex-wife (she has got her divorce) and trying to make a Welch lake into an African one with him as Tarzan (film clips of Johnny Weismuller) but failing because of her noncooperation, also the arrival of the police, and then, after a stretch in jail which pushes him over the edge, putting on a gorilla costume and breaking up the wedding party, after which he is cornered in the obligatory dump (symbol of our ugly, materialistic, death-infected society) and taken away in a straightjacket to what the eighteenth century would have called a lunatic asylum and we call a sanitarium. So he seems to end as what the subtitle calls "A Suitable Case for Treatment."

But stay! What is this vision materializing, in extreme close-up? I vow 'tis Vanessa Redgrave, no more his wife, true, yet pregnant and smiling. Our hero looks up from his occupationally therapeutic gardening at this vision of well-groomed, well-to-do beauty and asks, "Mine?" and she smiles, she smiles, she smiles, and after a while he gets it—'e's not tha quickest lad, oor Morgan—and he smiles, they both smile and Morgan is a man again and the camera pulls back and up and we see that the flower bed he's been working on is a huge hammer and sickle and it's a jolly cute ending which nobody can deny.

There must be something, some charm or charisma not manifested in what he says or does on the screen, that makes Morgan a positive hero instead of a slob, else why does his lovely, rich and apparently rational wife tergiversate about him throughout the film, despite his atrocious practical jokes, to the extent of letting him impregnate her? Is she as balmy as he? Or was she so bored by conventional existence in London that she welcomed Morgan's

409

obsessions as at least something different? Or is she supposed to see in him some life-enhancing quality that escaped me? The last seems the most likely answer—there is, after all, that exclamation point after Morgan's name. *Morgan! Oklahoma! Help!*

A positive hero, then, one who if he is a failure, a buffoon, and A Suitable Case for Treatment, stands as a symbol of some profound malaise in our society. That such cancerous depths exist is true, indeed a truism, but *Morgan!* doesn't explore them but rather exploits them, on the most frivolous level, for the consumption of that midcult audience which has grown so large, and so commercially interesting, in the last twenty years. Cinematically, *Morgan!* is a mess, a very up-to-date Carnaby Street mod mess like, say, *The Knack,* everybody (except the oldies) wearing "gear," loaded with gimmicks and hi-fi hilarity, busy every minute with sight gags, shock cutting, and frenzied action, its structure a loosely knit sequence of episodes that don't "build" because there isn't anyplace to go with a central character who is a loony—why shouldn't he do anything anytime? This frenetic style, at once violent and monotonous, is necessary to disguise the vacuum of meaning. Everything is reduced to what has become the easiest mode of midcult consumption, namely camp. I have long ago shed my illusions about Marx and Trotsky but they were serious men with serious ideas, and when Morgan demonstrates with an egg to a bewildered policeman how Trotsky's skull was caved in by the assassin's ax, I didn't think it funny, not even when the policeman, holding the crushed egg in his hand, said, "You could poach it." (One of the film's defects is that Mr. Reisz doesn't seem to have a sense of humor.) Nor was I entertained by the episode in Highgate cemetery when Morgan acts out his fantasies with the bust of Marx as his prop, beating his chest and, momentarily, turning Marx's great shaggy head into another gorilla. As for the last climactic sequence when Morgan has hallucinations in the junkyard, on which the director stinted no effort of cinematic imagination, I must admit it was very complicated.

One might call *Morgan!* a bit cynical in its exploitation of Marxism, gorillas, lunacy, and anything else that came to mind were it not for the impeccable record of Karel Reisz as an earnest and high-minded artisan, the doyen of the British "free cinema" school, the director of *Saturday Night and Sunday Morning,* which I didn't much like but which made the same breakthrough in the

British cinema in terms of social realism-cum-protest that John Osborne's *Look Back in Anger* (which I didn't much like either) had made several years earlier in the British theatre. (Myself, I would credit the breakthrough to Jack Clayton's *Room at the Top,* a year earlier and much better, but Mr. Reisz's film is always given the credit, perhaps because Mr. R. was the doyen of a "socially committed" group, whereas Mr. C. was just one more commercial director.) Now, with a neatness rare in cultural history, the director of *Saturday Night and Sunday Morning* has brought the cycle of social-protest films to an ambiguous but definite close with *Morgan!,* merging it into the swinging, hit-and-run, anything-goes school of what one might call Carnaby Street cinema, represented by movies like *Tom Jones, Darling, The Knack,* and *Help!.* English movies, like English styles in women's dresses and men's hair, are setting fashions now, and there is talk of a "renaissance" of British cinema, though a rebirth from what? The Summer, 1966, issue of *Sight and Sound* has a very trenchant and, for that all-too-bland journal, a refreshingly critical survey of this phenomenon by Philip French. "There is a feeling for the medium, a drive, a sense of style, a freewheeling vigor, for which there are few previous parallels," he writes, and I see what he means historically. He later qualifies: "The feeling for the medium is often only a concern for stylishness and fashion, the vigor a desperate energy that seeks to conceal a lack of content behind a battery of tricks." A concise evaluation of *Morgan!,* and if one wants an illuminating comparison, cf. a neglected French film of two years ago, Jessua's *Life Upsidedown,* also about a young man who gradually becomes "a case for treatment" but which manages to make one understand and sympathize with him, even to see how dull and pointless the life is he gradually withdraws from. Leaving aside odious comparisons as to talent, one difference may be that Mr. Reisz is "committed" to an antibourgeois viewpoint and so gives the best of it to his incipient Case for Treatment—police, lawyers, rich in-laws are all heavily caricatured—while M. Jessua is only committed to the observation of human behavior and so is able to reveal, existentially rather than polemically, the true horror of conventional life which is that it is so tedious. Almost as boring as Morgan's fantasy life, in fact.

—October 1966

SWEDEN

THROUGH A GLASS DARKLY

Though not as good as *Wild Strawberries* or *Naked Night,* this is Ingmar Bergman's best film in years. It is classically compact. The action takes place within twenty-four hours on a lonely Baltic island where four people are vacationing: a popular novelist who has failed as an artist and as a father (Gunnar Björnstrand); his adolescent son (Lars Passgård); his married daughter who is going insane (Harriet Andersson); and Max Von Sydow as her decent but unimaginative husband. All but the youth are regular members of the Bergman troupe and all are very good (Miss Andersson is superb). The first half hour, in which we gradually discover the realities behind what seems at first to be a remarkably attractive family party, is the kind of thing Bergman is very good at; I'm thinking of the picnic supper with its increasing tension (and the father's withdrawing on a pretext and howling out his pain), the amateur theatricals afterward, and the scene in bed between husband and wife ("You always do the right thing," she says bleakly, as they lie in each other's arms utterly out of contact, "and it is never any good"). The rest is less successful—too much talk, a Bergman fault (he is as much a stage as a movie director, after all) and also too much heavy dramatics (the seduction of the boy by his sister in the hold of the derelict boat with all that drumming rain seemed to me overdone as did, for all Miss Andersson's fire, some of the mad scenes).

The end is sheer disaster: after the woman has been removed, in a helicopter, to a mental hospital, the father—who, like the father in *Wild Strawberries,* failed his children because he is too cold and analytical—is so shaken by his daughter's collapse that he finally does Get Through to his son with a Message, which is that he has at last learned The Secret, which is Love. Furthermore: "God is love. That thought helps me in my emptiness." The last shot is of the ecstatic face of the son as he murmurs, "Father *talked* to me." All of this seems to me cant: that people should love each other and that much unhappiness is caused by their inability to communicate, these truisms have by now been thoroughly demonstrated on and off Broadway and in countless novels and movies, while as for "God is Love," this epigram may be copied off the wall of the nearest Protestant church. Perhaps "cant" is too strong, since (I'm

414

afraid) Mr. Bergman is sincere. Let's substitute "banality." "All these three films," he has stated apropos *Wild Strawberries, The Virgin Spring,* and *Through a Glass Darkly,* "are concerned with the problem of atonement. The problem of God is always before me, always present." These problems are in general meaningless to me: I don't feel guilty, I don't believe in God and am not much interested in whether I'm right or not. They sometimes become meaningful when someone like Dorothy Day, in her life, or T. S. Eliot, in his poetry, fills them with a personal, and so an original and interesting, content. This Mr. Bergman has never been able to do for me. "God is Love" indeed! I was told that at compulsory chapel in Phillips Exeter Academy. What does it *mean,* exactly? When Mr. Bergman can be explicit, in cinematic terms, I shall take his Message seriously. Meanwhile, I shall continue to enjoy the secular portions of his movies.

—August 1962

WINTER LIGHT

The new Bergman is acted with the competence we have come to expect from what might be called The Bergman Repertory Players; Gunnar Björnstrand as the pastor and Ingrid Thulin as his school-teacher-mistress were bleakly uncompromising in the lead parts, while Messrs. Knudsen and Thunberg were surprisingly three-dimensional in the bit parts of the church warden and the organist. Otherwise, all I can say for it is that it goes on for only eighty minutes. It begins with a complete church service lasting almost a quarter of an hour—hyms, organ solo, prayers, communion, sermon, the works—and it doesn't get any livelier. The pastor has lost his vocation: he cannot love his fellowmen and he isn't sure about God. He is unable to comfort a fisherman who has been driven to despair by the prospect of a nuclear holocaust; the fisherman commits suicide. He treats his mistress with psychological brutality, making her look to herself unattractive and sexually gluttonous— the scene in which he tells her off is really shocking, the one scene that rises to any dramatic intensity. The film ends with the pastor beginning another service in another rural church a few hours later,

415

this time with his dog-faithful mistress as the entire congregation, and the point seems to be that he will stagger on from sheer will, combined with mere inertia, preaching the Word of a God in Whom he has lost faith.

My quarrel is not with the grimness of Mr. Bergman's moral—whether man is "spiritually empty" or not seems to me about as important, and sensible, a question as what songs the sirens sang—but with his failure to express it cinematically. *Winter Light* is exposition rather than drama. We hear the characters, but we don't *see* them, except in lengthy close-ups as they are explaining their problems. Bergman has always had a weakness for philosophizing, but in his best films he has invented visual ways to convey his meaning. Here one gets the feeling he regards art as frivolous decoration that would detract from the message. At the preview I was given his "Introduction" to the film:

> My dear and greatly respected public: Though I cannot be with you this afternoon, I can assure you that my thoughts are with my movie . . . as it now meets with an audience. . . . Thoughts excited, anxious, and, above all, expectant. Perhaps you wonder why: a movie is only a play of shadows. . . . That is not true. . . . It is my hope that you will leave the theatre with a definite, felt experience, or a suddenly acquired thought. Or perhaps a question. Then my work and the work of my comrades need not have been in vain, and you will have given us the courage to proceed in our often difficult search for the hidden strengths of the spirit.

But, like any work of art, a movie *is* "a play of shadows," that is, a useless, artificial, nonmoral construction. In the strange realm of art, shadow is substance and the "search for the hidden strengths of the spirit" is frivolity.

—August 1963

THE SILENCE

Tennyson's "faultily faultless, icily regular, splendidly null" describes *The Silence,* the concluding film of Bergman's trilogy—the preceding two were *Through a Glass Darkly* and *Winter Light.*

After the famine of the latter, a diagram of a movie in which the only cinematic device Bergman allowed himself was the close-up, *The Silence* is rich: the silhouettes of tanks flashing rhythmically past a speeding train, the grotesquerie of a troupe of performing dwarfs (especially their last appearance, advancing in baroque costumes, with stately bows and flourishes, down the hotel corridor), Ingrid Thulin's face, photographed from above and upside down, in the throes of onanism or near-death (and the gong-like peals that well up on the sound track during the latter scene), her hooded lesbian spying on her younger sister (Gunnel Lindblom) washing herself, the agitated cutting as the latter wanders about the strange city in a state of frustrated sensuality, and the orchestration of photography, sound, acting and montage, each superb in itself, each subordinated to the general composition. Bergman has achieved a mastery of technique that makes most other directors seem clumsy and tongue-tied.

But what is he saying? For all its beauty, *The Silence* cannot be taken as "pure" cinema, a succession of images enjoyable in themselves, as in *Marienbad*, because it presents realistically drawn characters and because it obtrusively thrusts on us a system of symbolic meaning. But the characters and their motivations are not worked out enough for us to sympathize; the sisters' antagonism is merely "given" like an assumption in algebra—"let X equal 5"— without explanation or development, so that their actions seem increasingly arbitrary, and increasingly boring. Nor is the symbolic aspect any more satisfying. Not that it's obscure: beginning with its title, *The Silence* is clearly an allegory about noncommunication. Traveling back to their native Sweden, the sisters, accompanied by the younger one's small boy, stop over in a hotel in a country whose language is totally strange (since it was invented by Bergman) and whose inhabitants seem to know no other language. Their inability to communicate with anyone except through signs disorients all three, the sisters' antagonism becoming so exacerbated that the younger gives herself to a waiter, copulating wordlessly as the older looks on in horror and disgust, while the boy, neglected by his preoccupied mother and aunt, wanders aimlessly, and perilously, around the hotel corridors. Mother and son finally resume their trip, leaving behind the older sister in what may or may not be a

417

dying condition that may or may not have been brought on by exposure to the silence.

The trouble with the symbolism is partly that the theme of noncommunication has by now been worn threadbare, partly that it is heavy-handed (the one word the sisters recognize is "Bach," in an ad for a concert, thus demonstrating that Art is the Universal Language), but chiefly that it isn't carried out with either aesthetic consistency or intellectual clarity, constantly destroying, and being destroyed by the naturalistic detail in which it is expressed.

Bergman's tragicomedy is that he fancies himself, and never more than of late, as a philosopher, while in fact his great talents are for the concrete rather than the abstract, for realism, highly charged and poetic but still realism. Never more so than in his masterpiece, *The Naked Night* (1953), which presents alienation in terms of close observation of human behavior, the fantastic milieu of traveling actors and circus performers heightening rather than as in *The Magician*, subverting the underlying reality. The symbolism is implicit and not, as here, pasted on like a luggage label, to the wrong address. "When I was younger," he recently told an interviewer who pressed him about the meaning of *The Silence*, "I had illusions about how life should be. Now I see things as they are. No longer any questions of 'God, why?' or 'Mother, why?' One has to settle for suicide or acceptance. Either destroy oneself—which is romantic—or accept life. I choose now to accept it." The case is just the opposite. It was Bergman's earlier films that accepted life, coming to some sort of terms with it, however meager, like the old scholar in *Wild Strawberries* and the circus couple who are still traveling on together, despite their mutual (and unsuccessful) betrayals, at the end of *The Naked Night*. And it is in his recent films that he is obsessed by such large questions as "God, why?"—questions that his protagonists are unable to answer and so destroy themselves in madness (*Through a Glass Darkly*), despair at inability to love either God or man (*Winter Light*), or, here, death, psychological and physical. If this trilogy is Bergman's idea of accepting life, one wonders what he would give us if he rejected it.

—August 1964

418

JAPAN

THE HIDDEN FORTRESS

The Hidden Fortress is a potboiler by the prodigiously talented Akira Kurosawa—an adventure-story about medieval Japan that is partly an Eastern Western, partly a *kabuki* play, partly an exercise in heavily underlined realism that reminds one of the pre-1930 German cinema. The camera work is superb and the direction vigorous, and yet—like those old German films—one feels it goes on much too long. The realism and the *kabuki* stylization kill each other; the concluding ten minutes, when it all becomes quite frankly a fairy tale, are the best part. The film illustrates Kurosawa's two weaknesses: a tendency to overlabor and repeat (as in *Ikiru*—here an example is the obsession with making his characters scramble up steep, rocky slopes) and the mingling of incompatible genres; both are traits of a director who is unsure of his style. *Rashomon* and *The Men Who Tread on the Tiger's Tail* are the best Kurosawa I've seen, because they are all of a piece.

This uncertainty, this juxtaposition of incompatibles, is characteristic of Japanese films; behavior in them, for instance, is either very stiff, formalized, ceremonious—or just the opposite. It corresponds to the modern history of Japan: a clash between a feudal and a modern style of life in which the elements have not been synthesized into the middle-class pattern that the West has evolved over centuries, but continue to exist side by side.

This split emerges in *The Hidden Fortress,* a rendering of medieval Japanese life by a twentieth-century artist who appreciates the aristocrats aesthetically and yet feels a human sympathy for the peasants which would not have been felt by dramatists of the period. Kurosawa makes it a class matter: the two peasant soldiers are like Shakespeare's clowns—earthy, without inhibitions or dignity—while the princess and her general are frozen, withdrawn, contemptuous. But these are really, to a Westerner, two types of hysterical behavior, the open and the closed kind, as when the general's rigidity is shattered by strong feeling and he barks like a cougar. The line dividing the ceremonious from the primitive is much thinner in Japan than in the West.

—August 1961

THRONE OF BLOOD

Kurosawa's version of *Macbeth* omits the poetry, the psychology —and the tragedy. What's left is cops and robbers. And some marvelous photography. Kurosawa's pictorial style is at once virile and lovely, getting the most fantastically beautiful effects without any of the homosexual "camp" that often goes with them: those rearing, neighing horses; that grotesque medieval armor; the lone rider, with pennons flying, spurring up to the great barred castle gate; the softly waving plumes and fronds as Birnam Wood advances on the castle; the black bulk of the ruin in the long gray plain with which the film opens and closes. But the only content I could find was melodrama. Toshiro Mifune plays Macbeth; at first his style is exciting, but it soon becomes monotonous, all that snarling and baring of teeth, those vulpine laughs. Macbeth was more than a beast of prey in Shakespeare—and men are more interesting than animals; more complicated. I shall be told it's in the convention of the No theatre—the fright make-up of the witch and Lady Macbeth's death-white face and stylized gestures—but such exaggeration needs the severity of the classic No style to contain it and give it aesthetic point. In the romantic-realistic openness of *Throne of Blood,* it becomes merely sensational. And finally absurd, as in the last scene when his soldiers turn on Mifune-Macbeth and shoot him full of arrows as he reels and gibbers on the castle wall, the whack-thud of each arriving arrow being duly recorded on the sound track; he ends a porcupine, a pincushion, something out of Grand Guignol or grand opera but nothing out of grand cinema.

—March 1962

YOJIMBO

Kurosawa's latest Eastern Western is a comedown from *Seven Samurai* (1954) and even from *Hidden Fortress* (1958). It is nineteenth-century Japan, when law and order have broken down after the collapse of the Tokugawa Dynasty. A country town is being destroyed by the quarrels of two rival gangs; an unemployed samurai (Toshiro Mifune) wanders into town and resolves the problem by selling his lethally efficient services to each gang in turn—"Yojimbo" means "bodyguard." By the time he leaves, they are all dead, massacred either by each other or by Mifune's own relentless sword. "Now it will be quiet in this town," he says as he strides away from the smoking, corpse-strewn ruins. It is a dark, neurotic, claustrophobic film with none of the open-air romance of its two predecessors, to which it is related as *Psycho* is, in the Hitchcock canon, to *The 39 Steps* and *The Lady Vanishes.* As in *Psycho,* shock effects are substituted for cinematic vitality: the dog trotting along with something in his jaws that proves to be a human hand; the lengthy beating up of the hero by an acromegalic giant— an Oriental Jack Palance—in which each thud and crunch is recorded *con amore* the results later being shown in sickening make-up effects. Just like our own movies. The Japanese have long been noted for their clever mimicry of the West. *Yojimbo* is the cine-matic equivalent of their ten-cent ballpoint pens and their ninety-eight-cent mini-cameras. But one expects more of Kurosawa. I am told he is parodying our Westerns; if so, the joke is not funny. Some even suggest he is satirizing the notion of the U.S.A. and the U.S.S.R. achieving peace through competition in nuclear weapons. If so, he has miscalculated, dwelling so obsessively on mayhem that this, and not any moralizing, is the film's real content. Furthermore, a satire (or a parody) needs a norm to be successful. Mifune isn't it, even though he rescues the peasant's pretty wife (by treacher-ously carving up her six guards) and is on friendly terms with the peaceably-minded innkeeper and cooper. Tigerish as always, Mr. Mifune is just another wild beast let loose on the unhappy town. (I don't understand his reputation as an actor; he seems to me to be permanently stuck in his first role, that of the bandit in *Rashomon.*) And if Kurosawa's satiric intention was to show the good guy as no better than the bad guys, then one still requires a norm. The peasant is a coward and the two pacifists are helpless and slightly comic victims. The only personage one can respect, as a man at least, is the samurai, which leaves us where we were two sentences above.

—December 1962

422

THE
BIBLICAL
SPECTACULAR

BEN-HUR

Ben-Hur, as everyone knows, cost $15,000,000 to make, runs for almost four hours, has a cast variously estimated at 50,000 (by Metro-Goldwyn-Mayer) and at 10,400 (by *Time*), was directed by William Wyler, and has had the biggest advance sale ($500,000) in film history. But what no one knows who hasn't seen it is that it is lousy. The secret was well-kept by the New York newspaper critics: "a remarkably intelligent and engrossing human drama . . . real excitement . . . sober meaning . . . plain integrity" (*Times*), "squirms with energy . . . acting good to excellent" (*Tribune*), "a classic peak" (*Post*), "stupendous" (*News*), "extraordinary cinematic stature" (*Journal-American*), "massive splendor in overwhelming force roars from the screen" (*World-Telegram*). Even *Time,* which used to be sophisticated about films, went overboard: "The script is well-ordered and its lines sometimes sing with good rhetoric and quiet poetry. . . . Director Wyler's wit, intelligence, and formal instinct are almost everywhere in evidence and he has set a standard of excellence by which coming generations of screen spectacles can expect to be measured."

Against these bellows of approval, which might have been emitted by the M-G-M lion himself, I can only pipe that I found *Ben-Hur* bloody in every way—bloody bloody and bloody boring. Watching it was like waiting at a railroad crossing while an interminable freight train lumbers past, often stopping completely for a while. Because they had to spend that $15,000,000, every dramatic point is stated, restated, then hammered home with a dozen more inept speeches. The three main characters are played by Charlton Heston as Ben-Hur; Stephen Boyd, a stolid Western-type villain, as Messala; and a young Israeli actress, if one may use the term for courtesy, named Haya Harareet, who as Esther maintains an admirable composure through many harrowing situations. They are at no point in danger of lawsuits for impersonating real people. The tender passages between Heston and Miss Harareet make Joan Crawford's love scenes look animated. Misdirected by Wyler, Heston throws all his punches in the first ten minutes (three grimaces and two intonations) so that he has nothing left four

424

hours later when he has to react to the Crucifixion. (He does make it clear, I must admit, that he disapproves.)

But *Ben-Hur* is a "spectacle" and so, one gathers from the critics, must be judged by modest aesthetic standards. (Though, come to think of it, *Intolerance, The Birth of a Nation,* and *Potemkin* were also "spectacles.") The big spectacular moments—the seafight, the Roman triumph, the chariot race—failed because Wyler doesn't know how to handle crowds nor how to get a culminating rhythm by cutting. He tries to make up for this lack by huge sets and thousands of extras, but a Griffith can make a hundred into a crowd while a Wyler can reduce a thousand to a confused cocktail party. The sets, furthermore, are glossily new; the galleys look as if they were built yesterday, as indeed they were; the armor and helmets are shiny tin foil, and the columns of ancient Rome are of sleekest plastic. The chariot race, long on gore and short on excitement, takes place under three gigantic statues of a majestic phoniness (M-G-M claims they used one million pounds of plaster in the production; I believe it). The color photography was the glaring kind that makes the people stand out like waxworks, with no relation to the background. There was not even a decent, or indecent, Roman orgy, the only valid excuse for making a Biblical picture.

Instead of sex, *Ben-Hur* gives us sadism. As G. Legman demonstrated long ago in *Love and Death* (published by The Breaking Point Press), our mass culture compensates for its prudery about sex by the broadest license in portraying violence. *Ben-Hur* carries this principle to its extreme—De Mille, after all, gave us *both* orgies and bloodshed—omitting Roman eroticism but dwelling on Roman brutality with pornographic realism. We are treated to close-ups of the galled ankles of galley slaves, of their writhings under the lash of the overseers, of their gasping struggles as they drown. We are left in no doubt as to what a leper's face looks like on a Panavision Screen. We see exactly what happens when a man is run over in the chariot race, and we are treated to a good ten minutes of stimulating close-ups of Messala's bloody, crusted, broken face and torso while he is dying after being dragged face down in such an accident, all in full color and all suggesting a most insanitary butcher shop. (Any parent who takes a child to see *Ben-Hur* is

425

irresponsible.) The crucifixion opens with a shot of the nails being hammered into Christ's hands that is really quite graphic; it differs from similar shots in such Old Masters as Grünewald in lacking any sense of tragedy or religious awe, that is in being simply— graphic. (Christ wears a long auburn hair-do and is seen only from the back, a bit of reverence that reminds me of the modest gestures of a strip-tease.)

In short, here is a film that tries to debauch whatever taste, feeling or simple common sense Hollywood and television have left us. Here is blood blood blood—the brook running from the Cross is full of it. Here is a mad jumble of talents transmuted by Hollywood's alchemy into solid lead. Let us pass over the musical director, "the world-famous Dr. Miklos Rozsa," let us even pass over such extras, doubtless as eminent in the *haut monde* as Dr. Rozsa is in the musical world, as Prince Emanuele Ruspoli of Italy, Count Santiago Oneto of Spain, Princess Irina Wassilchikoff of Russia, let us even pass over the Baroness Lilian del Balzo of Hungary. Still, William Wyler has made some not-bad movies, and the script was worked on by, among others, Maxwell Anderson, Gore Vidal, Christopher Fry and S. N. Behrman. Quite a galaxy to produce this sputtering little Roman candle. Here is, finally, a falsification of the Bible in which not the Jews but the Romans are responsible for Christ's martyrdom. According to Matthew, Mark, Luke and John, it wasn't that way at all. *"Then said Pilate to the chief priests and the people, 'I find no fault in this man.' And they were the more fierce saying, 'He stirreth up the people. . . . Crucify him, crucify him!' "* But in this film, we see merely Pilate washing his hands and delivering Christ over to the brutal soldiery; ain't nobody here but just us Romans. (There *is* a brief shot of some high priests looking on at the crucifixion, but they look sad rather than jubilant.) But there are no ancient Romans around and there are many Jews and $15,000,000 is $15,000,000.

To conclude on a more positive and American note, let me admit, and indeed insist, that this *Ben-Hur* makes a real contribution to international amity. All the Romans are portrayed by English—or at least by British Commonwealth—actors, while all the Hebrews except Miss Harareet of Israel (using her for Esther was a really inspired bit of public relations) are Americans.

M-G-M attributes this to "Mr. Wyler's determination not to have a clash of accents," but I suggest that M-G-M, in a most tactful gesture, gave the colonial parts to the country that is now acquiring an empire and the imperial parts to the country that has recently lost one. Jolly decent, *I* say.

—March 1960

KING OF KINGS

Well, no one can say they didn't try. Mr. Samuel Bronston, the producer, discussed the script with the Pope. ("Now the way we see it here, your holiness, where He does the Sermon on the Mount we figure it needs action so we have Him walk around and answer questions from the audience like Jack Paar does only more reverential.") Mr. Nicholas Ray, the director, spent a year visiting "Europe's art museums, cathedrals and libraries." Twenty-four artists "hand painted"—nothing but the best—"the intricate mosaics" of Salome's dance hall, producing something like a credit manager's idea of total luxury. Mr. Philip Yordan, who wrote the screenplay, "availed himself of the counsel of religious advisers of all faiths, seeking as nearly a nondenominational viewpoint as possible." You can say that again. Dr. Miklos Rozsa, "world-famous composer" whose last *chef d'oeuvre* was the score for *Ben-Hur,* also did his homework, diligently haunting "Europe's cathedrals and cultural centers seeking themes of ecclesiastical inspiration." Mr. Joseph R. Vogel, president of M-G-M, and Mr. Sol C. Siegel, M-G-M's studio head, personally made a pilgrimage to Madrid to see the early rushes. It is not stated whether they also visited Europe's cathedrals and cultural centers, but their decision to buy a piece of *King of Kings* was wise. It is M-G-M's kind of picture.

I'd say *King of Kings* is slightly better than *Ben-Hur* and slightly worse than *Spartacus.* The genre is hopeless and that's that. On the evidence of such films, we are neither a Christian nor an artistic nation. The story of Christ, so moving and tender in the Gospels, is here drowned in the brutal sensationalism that is considered necessary to interest a mass audience: those Aztec massacres (Pompey's

427

slaughter of the high priests in the Temple, the butchery of the Jewish rebels in Pilate's courtyard) and that emphasis on blood (those close-ups of Jesus' half-naked torso writhing as he is scourged). This is counterbalanced by sentimentality, the other side of the sado-masochistic coin and equally titillating: Siobhan Mc-Kenna's Mary and Jeffrey Hunter's Jesus, both much too good to be true. Not that Hunter isn't better than I expected; at least he's restrained and dignified, and of course he—that is, He—has some quite good lines. His performance is a welcome relief from Hurd Hatfield's Pilate, right out of Grand Guignol, and Frank Thring's acting, which, one might say, out-Herods Herod. Miss McKenna's Mary reinforced my feeling that she has become hopelessly mannered; her trick of mouthing her words could be justified only if they were something to eat.

But there's really no point in going on about *King of Kings* this way, no point in objecting to the fake rocks and shrubbery and lighting in the Gethsemane scene or to the reduction of The Last Supper to a suburban cookout with picnic tables and bowls of tossed salad. Two nonartistic points, however, are worth making: (1) only those miracles are shown which can be explained naturally, post-Freud: the healing of the blind man and of the paralytic; (2) the responsibility for the crucifixion is again displaced from the Jews to the Romans, who are again made the fall goys.

On (1): considering the special resources of the cinema for showing real miracles—the loaves and fishes, the walking on the water—one must conclude they were omitted because it was felt they wouldn't go down with a modern audience. Probably not, but this merely shows we aren't a religious people. They couldn't avoid the Resurrection, but they contrive to suggest it might have been an hallucination. The creators of *King of Kings* yield to no one in their respect for religion, but they don't want to make fools of themselves.

On (2) I have more to say. When I reviewed *Ben-Hur* here two years ago and pointed out that the Gospels make the Jews chiefly responsible for the crucifixion and show Pilate as wanting to let Jesus go unpunished, this provoked a spate of angry letters. One Jewish periodical spoke of "ugly bigotry" and "literary refuse" and another, a normally sensible magazine called *Midstream*, asked

428

why I favored the inclusion of "a Christ-killer scene" merely "because the Gospels say there was one." *Midstream* also found something sinister in the fact that I was a member—along with Norman Thomas and David Riesman—of the advisory board of the now defunct *Jewish Newsletter,* which it described as "a little periodical which specialized in uncovering Zionist conspiracies" and which I should describe as a muckraking operation in the Lincoln Steffens tradition. Muckraking, for which I've always had a weakness, is a dangerous profession. If it's directed against O.K. targets like Tammany or Standard Oil or the Grand Mufti, then all Men of Good Will are on your side. But there are secular cows and sacred cows and Israel is now as much the latter as Soviet Russia was in the thirties.

When I made my gaffe two years ago, I took it for granted, as a WASP by upbringing, that the biblical account of the trial and crucifixion of Jesus was correct. Since then, I've learned, by the chancy methods that journalists learn things, that a good case can be made out that the Gospel writers, for propagandist reasons, played down the part of the Romans in the tragedy and played up that of the Jews. So I'm willing to agree that the matter is obscure and that the hundred or so readers who wrote in objecting to my remarks may have been right about the historical fact. But I'm not willing to admit, as most of them seemed to think was an obvious inference, that my error—if it was such—was evidence of racial prejudice. We live in a time when the pendulum of social justice has swung back too far, when certain racial groups are sacrosanct, so that when one states, depending on the New Testament, that certain Jews two thousand years ago wanted Jesus killed, one is accused of denouncing all Jews today as "Christ killers." I daresay that if one referred to what Sitting Bull did to General Custer, some Indian Protective League would jump into action. And in fact several letters have come in accusing me of being anti-Negro because I wrote that Harry Belafonte is not a genius and because I criticized the acting in *Come Back, Africa* and the music in *The Cry of Jazz.*

I won't insist I am not a racial bigot any more than I will insist I am not a liar. I will even admit that I think of Jews, Negroes, Ugro-Finns, Irishmen and other groups as no better than anyone else, and so feel free to joke, praise or criticize. Myself, I should consider it humiliating to be exempted, like a child or a lunatic, from the ordinary give and take of discussion, and I think the common "liberal" attitude today of so exempting Jews and Negroes is patronizing. When I was young, I never liked being patted on the head by my elders, since I felt this implied they were also my betters.

This said, let me continue my progress across thin ice by noting that the two Jews who, in the New Testament, play a specially evil role, namely Herod and Judas, are bowdlerized in *King of Kings*. Herod—that is, the Herod that ordered the massacre of the innocents and not Frank Thring's Herod Antipas, his son—is still a villain, but the commentary (which is intoned by no less an intoner than Orson Welles—how have the mighty fallen!) explains, if I got Mr. Welles's rich diction right, that he is an Arab whom the Romans made King of the Jews. Judas still betrays; not for thirty pieces of silver but because he is an optimist who sincerely believes Jesus will save himself from the cross by a miracle and thus confound the Romans. Was Herod in fact an Arab? And did Judas betray from overenthusiasm rather than venality? I'm just asking, fellows.

—March 1962

THE GREATEST STORY EVER TOLD

It seems to be impossible for this Christian civilization to make a decent movie about the life of its founder. From De Mille's sexy-sacred epics up to the film under consideration, George Stevens' *The Greatest Story Ever Told,* they have all been, as art or as religion, indecent. Yet the rules for success, deducing them inversely from the failures, are simple enough:

(1) Use the original script.

(2) Avoid well-known performers, especially in small parts.

(3) Try to realize that the past was once a present, as everyday and confused and banal as the present present, and that Jesus and the people of his time didn't know they were picturesque any more

430

than the builders of Chartres knew they were making Gothic architecture (though the builders of our collegiate Gothic did).

(4) Keep it small. In spirit: no dramatics, sparing use of emphatic close-ups and photography, no underlining of a story that still moves us precisely because it is not underlined; Jesus was a throw-it-away prophet, direct and unrhetorical even in a speech like the Sermon on the Mount. Also keep it small literally: no wide screen, no stereophonic sound, no swelling-sobbing mood music (maybe no music at all), no gigantic sets or vast landscapes or thousands of extras milling around with staves, palm branches and other picturesque impedimenta.

(5) The story of Jesus should be told with reverence for the text in the New Testament (taking into account historical corrections by recent scholarship), but with irreverence for the sensibilities of contemporary religious groups—Buddhist, Moslem, Taoist, Catholic or Jewish.

Of the three most recent stabs—*le mot juste,* I think—at the Christ story, Nicholas Ray's *King of Kings* is lowbrow kitsch, Pier Pasolini's *The Gospel According to St. Matthew* is highbrow kitsch, and the present work is the full middlebrow, or Hallmark Hall of Fame treatment. I must add, in fairness to Mr. Pasolini, that his was much the best try: it followed rules (1) and (2) completely, observed (3) intermittently, and systematically violated (4), which unfortunately is the most important. I must also add, in fairness to Mr. Stevens, that his movie was premiered "Under the Patronage of the President of the United States and Mrs. Johnson"; and, in fairness to myself, that even Bosley Crowther, normally a pushover for Biblical spectaculars, didn't like it.

For reasons which as usual escape me, George Stevens has long enjoyed a reputation in Hollywood as a dedicated artist. Dedicated he may be, but his films look to me overblown and pretentious, even *A Place in the Sun,* even *Shane.* Maybe it's because he takes so long—five years on *The Greatest Story.* Or perhaps it's because he takes himself very seriously—in Hollywood it's often all that is necessary. How can they tell out there, after all? Maybe the guy *is* an artist. Dismissing previous biblical films as "superficial," Mr. Stevens announced his treatment was going to be different. No clichés, he told a *New York Times* reporter, and furthermore: "The

431

basic theme of the story is one which, unfortunately, has not always been associated with it in the past. It relates to the universality of men and how they must learn to live together. I think it is a theme of great earnestness and utmost simplicity. And I think all the usual trappings connected with Biblical productions . . . are in alarming disagreement with this simple theme. We tried, without diverging from the traditional, to think out the story anew and present it as living literature." The safety clause about not "diverging from the traditional" seems to contradict the rest, but let's be realistic: it's a $20,000,000 property.

What I saw on that wide screen was something else again. Had I not just this moment thought up my five simple rules, I might have suspected Mr. Stevens had somehow got a peek and, reasoning that whatever I like the box office wouldn't, simply inverted them.

(1) The screenplay, by Mr. Stevens and James Lee Barrett, is "based on The Books of the Old and New Testaments, Other Ancient Writings, The Book *The Greatest Story Ever Told* by Fulton Oursler, and Other Writings by Henry Denker." Decent of them to list the New Testament and nice, if puzzling, to include the Old so nobody gets left out. The Other Ancient Writings are intriguing, as are the Other Writings, presumably non-Ancient, by Mr. Denker, an unknown writer to me. I have heard of the late Mr. Oursler but have not felt it necessary to read him. He is described in *The Reader's Encyclopedia of American Literature* as "a versatile writer . . . detective stories . . . plays and motion-picture scenarios, including *The Spider* (1927) . . . in 1944 became a senior editor of *Reader's Digest.* . . . His most famous books were those on the Bible and Christianity, particularly *The Greatest Story Ever Told* (1951). Oursler had a great gift for popularization." His religious career was eclectic: "In his early years Oursler was a Baptist, for a while he was an agnostic, in his later years a devout Catholic." Just the man for a biblical movie. There was one more litterateur involved. "Produced in Creative Association with Carl Sandburg," the titles proclaim—a job as vague as it was elevated. Mr. Sandburg seems to have been a kind of cinematic Holy Ghost. The script that emerged from this olio of writers and Other Writings teeters between the vapid and the punchy, every line destroying whatever illusion of history or religion the acting, photography

432

and direction have accidentally spared. "The party responsible is Jesus of Nazareth." "Don't lie there, Matthew, you'll catch a sickness," says Jesus, meaning a cold, but "sickness" is more Biblical. "Your majesty, if I may be so bold. . . ." "I have never liked you, Baptist," says José Ferrer (Herod Antipas) to Charlton Heston (John the Baptist) in his most sneering tone, which is plenty. Later they have a spirited exchange: "I've heard things about you, Baptist." "And I've heard many things about *you*, Herod [pause], all bad!" "How shall I be saved?" Herod asks, trying to change the subject—you can tell by Ferrer's expression he doesn't really mean it, just cynical and effete. His father, Herod the Great, alias Claude Rains, is even more cynical, in that world-weary style on which Mr. Rains took out a patent in 1927. But Baptist-Heston, who is neither cynical nor effete, replies with simple dignity: "By standing in the next line when you meet him—this side of Hell!" I prefer the original dialogue by Matthew, Mark, Luke and John.

(2) Max Von Sydow—who must have found George Stevens an interesting contrast to his usual director, Bergman—is a gentlemanly Christ, restrained, earnest and handsome in a Nordic way. I wonder why, incidentally, all movie Christs, from H. B. Warner on (with the exception of Pasolini's, who I'm told, is a Spanish Jew, though he looked just Spanish to me), have been non-Jewish; likewise most of the disciples, except of course Judas. I also wonder why those Jewish-chauvinist groups and magazines that gave me a hard time when, in my review of *Ben-Hur,* I complained the Crucifixion was blamed entirely on the Romans, have never made a fuss about this point. Why no protests against Mr. Stevens' casting the ostentatiously Irish Dorothy McGuire as Mary? I suppose it's a tricky business: the Semiticists don't want Jews to be villains in the Christ story, but they aren't keen either to claim the heroes for their side since, despite the recent scholarly researches—with which I largely agree—proving that the Romans were more and the orthodox Jewish authorities were less responsible for sending Jesus to the Cross than the New Testament alleges, still he did preach a new religion that was—and is—in important respects opposed to Judaism. Getting back to casting, Von Sydow is not bad as Jesus; for all his lack of Semitic expressiveness, he's at least dignified and he's not

so familiar as to make one think, "There's Max!" whenever he appears. But when Ed Wynn, wearing contact lenses, comes on as the blind Aram, a quaveringly ecstatic convert, I was wrenched back to the Texaco Fire Chief. I have noted the difficulty of suspending disbelief when Ferrer, Rains and Heston go through their familiar routines, also the difficulty of keeping Dorothy McGuire in focus as Mary, but I might add that Simon of Cyrene was all too obviously Sidney Poitier, ditto Van Heflin and Sal Mineo and John Wayne and Angela Lansbury in other "cameo" parts. The illusion-destroying effect was all the greater because they came on so suddenly and briefly. I never got used to them as, respectively, Bar Amand, Uriah, The Centurion, and Claudia; like some nutty relative bursting in dressed up as Napoleon. There was also that "Woman of No Name" who pushes through the crowd as Jesus is healing the sick and, after he has grappled with her, cries out in purest Bronx, "Oi'm cured! Oi'm cured!" and turns around to run toward the camera with arms waving in triumph—and damned if it isn't Shelley Winters. A shock like that can suspend belief for quite a while.

(3) Mr. Stevens says he tried to avoid "the clichés and the usual trappings connected with Biblical productions" and to "think the story out anew and present it as living literature." His effort was unsuccessful, one might say spectacularly so. He rushed to embrace every biblical-movie cliché and trapping in sight. Picturesque effects are unremitting, beginning with the star that guides the three wise men to the manger. It is a very large star, gleaming in the shape of a Hallmark cross in the dark-blue Panavision sky, and the wise men would have had to be extremely nearsighted to miss it. The manger is rather pictorial too, not to mention the lovely Miss McGuire ensconced there looking down with misty eyes on her miraculous babe. The wise men, like the other characters, have a tendency to get themselves photographed against the sky. I haven't seen so many skyline shots since Dassin's *He Who Must Die,* another Christ movie. It's in modern dress, but otherwise it's done in the same spirit.

(4) The scale is bigger than in any biblical film I've seen, which is a large statement. Not just Panavision but Ultra Panavision 70. Not just sound but stereophonic sound that comes at you from all

quarters. There are lots of squalling babies, to show that Life Goes On, and once the cry came so clearly from under my seat that I looked down to see if some careless mother . . . There are also lots of screaming gulls wheeling and gliding most pictorially to show that the lower orders also reproduce themselves—the M.P.A. Code should blacklist seagulls as local color, except in art films. The music roars and throbs and nudges continually, more Wagnerian than Christian. For the finale of Part One, Handel's *Hallelujah Chorus* was belted out with such deafening *brio* that, what with Lazarus rising from the dead and the extras running around like grand-opera peasants telling each other, needlessly since we and they had seen it happen, "Lazarus has risen! He's *alive!*" and Ed Wynn recovering his sight (*I think,* but there was so much confusion) and tottering up to Herod's palace to shout triumphantly up to the guards on the high Babylonian ramparts that Lazarus has risen . . . is *alive,* etc.—I then decided I had spent a reasonable amount of time, two hours, on *The Greatest Story* and that after this the Crucifixion could only be an anticlimax. So I left.

The landscape Mr. Stevens had chosen was a factor in my decision. With his customary thoroughness, he had, according to the *Times,* spent "months of research in the Holy Land." But he was disappointed: it looked worn, beat up, mingy, *small.* Not a worthy setting for the greatest story ever told. So he returned to the U.S.A. and shot the film in Utah, Nevada and California, where vistas are quite large. "Some of the landscapes around Jerusalem," he explained, "were exciting, but many had been worn down through the years by erosion and man, invaders and wars, to places of less spectacular aspect." Therefore, as one of his handouts puts it, our own West is a "far more authentic" locale for filming the life of Christ "than is the modern Holy Land." (The Forest Lawn cemetery in Los Angeles suggests in its literature that its replicas of Micheangelo's sculptures, carved by hand out of the same Carrara marble he used and by Italians just like him, are really closer to his conception than those chipped, stained, dilapidated "originals" in Florence.) So what we have is a biblical Western. Jesus and his disciples crawl like ants over the most stupendous kind of rocky terrain. The Sermon on the Mount is escalated to The Sermon on the Mountain, with Jesus on the pinnacle of a high mesa with scenery stretching for miles around him. He begins the Lord's Prayer in a meadow, then the bored camera moves off and we get some more mountain scenery and finally they camp by a broad river at the bottom of what looks like the Grand Canyon and, dramatically silhouetted against the sunset, with great black cliffs beetling over him and the wide river roiling turbulently as it catches the evening light, Jesus delivers the Lord's Prayer complete. The setting is impressive, a little too impressive. Custer's last stand or the battle of the Alamo might compete successfully with such natural grandeur. The Lord's Prayer gets lost in the scenery.

(5) All biblical movies are theologically circumspect, for obvious reasons, but this one overdoes it. The Romans are the bad goys again—though Pilate looks Jewish for some reason—and the Jews couldn't be more friendly to the founder of Christianity. Jesus-Sydow is walking with his disciples, and one says, "Look, some Pharisees!" (Like "Hey, Indians!") And there they are, those oft-denounced Pharisees: "Woe unto you. . . ." And they have come to warn him about certain plots against him. Nor is the Catholic audience slighted. When Jesus asks the disciples just who they think he is, exactly, Judas hems and haws ("Er, um, you're a great leader, a teacher"); the others are more enthusiastic but also vague; finally Peter gives the right answer: "You are the Son of God, the Messiah." Jesus is pleased: "Peter, you are the rock on which my church will be founded." As a lapsed Presbyterian, I object to this building up of Peter. He didn't show up so well at Gethsemane. Jesus said unto him, "Verily I say unto thee, that this day, even in this night, before the cock crow twice, thou shalt deny me thrice." And he did. Some rock. "Do you consider wealth a crime?" the rich Lazarus asks. "Not at all," smoothly replies Max Von Norman Vincent Peale, "but it may become a burden." One of the many things I admire about Jesus is his prejudice against the rich.

"The film moves to excite the imagination of the audience by rendering before it the beauty and the extraordinary nature of Him who represents many things, and one thing," states the vellum-paper program in that gnomic style of which Mr. Stevens is a master. "To recall, or is it to challenge, one's own image of Christ —an image derived from a word, a panel of stained glass, a Gothic-

436

lettered Christmas card, a burst of organ music, an inner exaltation, an experience."

You can get an image of Christ, it seems, from practically anything, including a Hallmark greeting card, except the writings of Matthew, Mark, Luke and John.

—July 1965

THE GOSPEL ACCORDING TO ST. MATTHEW

Pier Paolo Pasolini has had the original idea of making a movie about Christ by using the New Testament as his script, inventing no new episodes and putting not a word on the sound track that is not in the text of Matthew. I have never understood why the Hollywood mind, which exists in Rome as well as on our West Coast, in making "biblical" films always thinks it necessary to revise and rewrite the Gospel narrative, at great expense, when the original not only has been in the public domain for a long time but also tells the story better.

For the first half hour, I thought that Pasolini had also solved the problem of the historical film in general and of the biblical film in particular. The difficulty with almost all such films is that they look back at the past from the present, inflating it into the grandiose and the picturesque and insulating it in its own dreamworld—which, since it is jerry-built by architects who can only think in terms of the present, is banal and phony. What is needed is not to look back at the past—remember what happened to Lot's wife—but to think and feel oneself into it until it becomes not The Past but another kind of Present, one that chances to exist two hundred or two thousand years ago, one that we are now visiting by means of an aesthetic equivalent of H. G. Wells's time machine—the characters in that story were not looking back at the past, they were, for the moment, *in* it. Such a past will look very much like the present except for such details as costume and architecture (which are the main features of the Hollywoodian notion of the past); that is, it will be confused, often prosaic and grubby, and always, even at its most elevated moments, unpredictable. The Italian stage director,

437

Zeffirelli, whose Old Vic production of *Romeo and Juliet* fused past and present in just this way, has put it well: "If only I could be back in London, say, at ten-thirty a.m. on January 26, 1740! We have all felt this or something like it. Well, I would like to bring back that moment, with all its strangeness and awkwardness."

This was the feeling I got from the beginning of Pasolini's film: a direct, nonpicturesque treatment of the life of Jesus. St. Matthew begins his tale, for instance, after seventeen verses of genealogy:

> Now the birth of Jesus was in this wise: when his mother, Mary, was espoused to Joseph, before they came together, she was found with child of the Holy Ghost. Then Joseph her husband, being a just man, and not willing to make her a public example, was minded to put her away privily. But while he thought on these things, behold the angel of the Lord appeared to him in a dream saying, Joseph, thou son of David, fear not to take unto thee Mary thy wife, for that which is conceived in her is of the Holy Ghost. And she shall bring forth a son, and thou shalt call his name Jesus, for he shall save his people from their sins.

An awkward business for Joseph, finding his fiancée pregnant, and his relief must have been considerable when the angel explained about the Holy Ghost. (Awkward too for her son, according to a super-Freudian article I once read. "In this connection," observes the author *en passant,* "one is reminded of Christ's constant aggression against his own mother deriving from the fact that his unconscious did not believe her to be a virgin.") Pasolini confronts the awkwardness and sordidness boldly—as, for that matter, does Matthew if only one could read him without knowing in advance that Mary's pregnancy has a, to say the least, respectable provenance. His film opens with a very ordinary-looking middle-aged man, jowly and balding, tensely confronting his pretty young fiancée, who is visibly pregnant. They have had a row, he looks angry, she sad; he clenches his fist but does not strike her ("being a just man"): there is nothing more to be said; he strides away, leaving her staring down dejectedly, roams the fields in his humiliation, stretches down and goes to sleep; the angel appears, directly and simply, delivers her message and vanishes with the same undramatic abruptness; he smiles in relief, as who wouldn't, and goes back to Mary.

438

Throughout that first half-hour I was delighted with this kind of realism, by the authentic look of the landscape (Lucania, in Southern Italy, which looks much like photographs of the Holy Land) and of the people (mostly natives and all nonprofessionals, including the director's mother as the mother of Christ in the later scenes), by the interest of their faces, shown in extreme close-up, and by the visual echoes of Renaissance paintings: the helmets of the soldiers who massacre the innocents and the fantastic hats of the high priests were right out of the Uffizi, and the faces themselves for that matter: Mary was a Botticelli madonna, with her smooth full face and curiously curved lips; the angel was Mantegna, with her (I was told it was actually a boy) wild black locks and intense expression. The photography was also very good, as one has come to expect in Italian movies, both dramatic and harmonious.

But the second half-hour raised doubts which slowly became certainties. Those faces, at first so thrilling in their beauty or ugliness or ordinariness or brutality, became intolerable because they were always shown in extreme close-up. The close-up is the most powerful drug in the cinematic pharmacopia, but it must for that reason be used with moderation, else the effect becomes weaker each time until finally no amount of doubling and redoubling the dose stimulates the optic nerve. "Heightened realism," I had thought at first, and so it was, but as the film wore on the realism began to disappear and only the heightening remained. Nasty words like "arty" and "high camp" insinuated themselves into my thoughts until finally, after about an hour and a half, it seemed to me that *Il Vangelo Secondo Matteo* was performing on my higher faculties about the same degrading operation as *Ben-Hur* and *King of Kings* had attempted—though, of course, in a much more sophisticated and tasteful way, which somehow made it all the worse.

This feeling became a conviction during a twenty-minute passage in which Christ was shown, in extreme close-up, delivering the Sermon on the Mount plus other selected apothegms, His whole Message in fact, the only relief being that the background, insofar as it could be made out behind his enormous and tirelessly talking face, changed every minute or so. The effect was like a senator filibustering, or an Andy Warhol "movie": boredom, then irritation, then apathy. I don't like to be preached at for twenty minutes

439

head-on in a movie even by Jesus Christ, in whose Message I have the liveliest and most respectful interest. There was something very wrong about this passage, and about the whole film, once one had assimilated the novelty and truth of its beginning. Novelty and truth cannot simply be restated over and over, for in that case they cease to be novel—or true, since truth is various. This unfortunate passage, which should have been the climax of the film revealed instead a manneristic monotony, aesthetically, and, emotionally, a coldness that had bothered me long before. Perhaps Pasolini's conception of Jesus was at fault: his Jesus is an unsmiling fanatic, a reserved bureaucrat, combining the worst features of Trotsky and Stalin; his message of peace and goodwill and brotherhood is delivered with authoritarian firmness at best and at worst with something approaching an hysterical snarl; his attitude toward his disciples is distant, toward sympathetic outsiders, like the sick he heals, condescending, and toward hostile outsiders, contemptuous. Granted that the nineteenth-century idea of Jesus was often sentimental, I think that Pasolini's revised unstandard version has erred in the other direction. Or was it an error? Is there perhaps something rather odd about this retelling of the Gospel according to Matthew, so warmly human on the surface and so cold inside? It is true that the Patriarch of Venice has given the film his blessing and that the Office Catholique International du Cinéma—they're really up-to-date, compared to us Protestants!—has awarded it first prize for "the film which . . . makes the greatest contribution to spiritual progress and to the development of human values." But it is also true that Pasolini has up to now expressed in his novels and movies leftist views which have gotten him into trouble with the Catholic establishment (and much to his credit, I'd say). The present film is therefore rather puzzling. I don't think the director had his heart in his work, whatever the Patriarch of Venice may think.

—December 1964

440

PART SIX

TRIMS
AND
CLIPS

Since the only interesting things in *Come Dance With Me,* the latest Brigitte Bardot film, are two glimpses of that female mammary gland which obsesses Americans, and since they will undoubtedly be cut out by the censors, there is no reason to see the film, which is a Class C *roman policier* lacking either sex or drama for nine-tenths of its aimless meandering. Bardot has become a grotesque, a product of biological overspecialization like a borzoi; her face has been reduced to the sexual essentials and is, objectively considered, by now rather terrifying. A really innocent eye—of child or savage—would be scared to death by the close-ups: those huge staring eyes, the great thick-lipped toothy mouth, the cascades and whorls and fountains of yellow hair, like a witch-doctor's get-up. The mouth is alarming—"the better to eat you with, my dear"—and the whole face is brutal, but the hair is the thing. Sometimes it suggests a lion's mane, sometimes a baroque waterfall, sometimes the peruke of Louis XIV. The toucan has his bill and Bardot has her hair. Unhappily she has nothing else, dramatically speaking. Unlike her American opposite number, Miss Monroe, she has no lightness, no verve, no womanly softness, no change of pace, nothing but the petulant defiance of a depraved child. For once, We have scored over Them on the human level. Though one might say that the geneticists who produced Bardot were looking to the American market. (1960)

In the old days, *ante*-Hays Office, the movies were very sexy. Why the change? Possible explanations: (1) same kind of pressure-group tactics as put over Prohibition, with the Catholic hierarchy in the role of the Midwest reformers and alcohol-cranks; (2) accessibility of movies to children—note the even greater sexlessness of radio, which is even more accessible to all ages; (3) even for adults, the movies may be potentially too erotic for present-day society's good: the dark theatre, dreamlike atmosphere, sensual possibilities of lighting and angles that can make a bare shoulder suggest nudity. The camera is the great voyeur.

Whatever the reason, a sexually promiscuous people gets only the most asexual movies. There is less exposure of female bodies on the screen than in the average musical show.* A certain amount of psychological suggestion is permitted, also some sex, within strict limits, in the plot situation. But in general, the social historian would go far astray if he took the movies as an accurate reflection of American sexual mores.

The purity of Hollywood films is all the more remarkable if one contrasts the treatment of sex in American and in European movies. The Europeans treat sex as a natural part of everyday human existence—sometimes tragic, sometimes poignant, sometimes funny. Our films have a more adolescent approach, veering between the extremes of romanticism and sensuality, almost never *humanizing* the theme. Despite the Hays Office, our female stars depend much more on their physical charms than European stars do; they are younger, prettier, more voluptuous. (Rita Hayworth, Lana Turner, Betty Grable as against Garbo, Ingrid Bergman, Greer Garson.) So strong is the American urge to contemplate attractive female flesh—pin-up girls are peculiar to American armies—that sex is constantly being bootlegged, as in the "sweater girl" films which flourished until the Hays Office cracked down. And it is significant that the newspaper ads of movies, which are not controlled by the Hays Office, exploit the female body much more frankly than the films themselves dare to do. (1945)

* Sex is perhaps considered a luxury, which the $6.60 musical-comedy audience can "afford" but which would be too distracting and enervating for the masses who must do the work of the world—just as Prohibition was supposed to protect the workingman against the Curse of Drink, but no one worried about the coupon-clipper. Burlesque, where even more nudity is permitted than in Broadway musicals, might seem to disprove the rule, for it caters to an audience economically *below* the movie audience. But this is precisely the point: the lumpen-proletariat who patronize burlesque shows are as inconsequential, from the viewpoint of the social organism, as the top hats who go to musicals. The nonfunctional extremes can be permitted a sexual license which the working-class and middle-class millions must be denied. For these millions carry on their patient shoulders the real burden of society: the production and distribution of goods, the rearing of children.

There is nothing more vulgar than sophisticated kitsch. Compare Conan Doyle's workmanlike and unpretentious Sherlock Holmes stories with the bogus "intellectuality" of Dorothy M. Sayers, who, like many contemporary detective-story writers, is a novelist *manquée* who ruins her stuff with literary attitudinizing. Or consider the relationship of Hollywood and Broadway. In the twenties, the two were sharply differentiated, movies being produced for the masses of the hinterland, theatre for an upper-class New York audience. The theatre was High Culture, mostly of the Academic variety (Theatre Guild) but with some spark of Avant-garde fire (the "little" or "experimental" theatre movement). The movies were definitely Mass Culture, mostly very bad but with some leaven of Avant-gardism (Griffiths, Stroheim) and Folk Art (Chaplin and other comedians). With the sound film, Broadway and Hollywood drew closer together. Plays are now produced mainly to sell the movie rights, with many being directly financed by the film companies. The merger has standardized the theatre to such an extent that even the early Theatre Guild seems vital in retrospect, while hardly a trace of the "experimental" theatre is left. And what have the movies gained? They are more sophisticated, the acting is subtler, the sets in better taste. But they too have become standardized: they are never as awful as they often were in the old days, but they are never as good either. They are better entertainment and worse art. The cinema of the twenties occasionally gave us the fresh charm of Folk Art or the imaginative intensity of Avant-gardism. The coming of sound, and with it Broadway, degraded the camera to a recording instrument for an alien art form, the spoken play. The silent film had at least the theoretical *possibility,* even within the limits of Mass Culture, of being artistically significant. The sound film, within those limits, does not.

The whole field could be approached from the standpoint of the division of labor. The more advanced technologically, the greater the division. Cf. the great Blackett-Semple-Hummert factory—the word is accurate—for the mass production of radio "soap operas." Or the fact that in Hollywood a composer for the movies is not *permitted* to make his own orchestrations any more than a director can do his own cutting. Or the "editorial formula" which every big-circulation magazine tailors its fiction and articles to fit much as

445

automobile parts are machined in Detroit. *Time* and *Newsweek* have carried specialization to its extreme: their writers don't even sign their work, which in fact is not properly theirs, since the gathering of data is done by a specialized corps of researchers and correspondents and the final article is often as much the result of the editor's blue-penciling and rewriting as of the original author's efforts. The *"New Yorker* short story" is a definite genre—smooth, minor-key, casual, suggesting drama and sentiment without ever being crude enough to actually create it—which the editors have established by years of patient, skillful selection the same way a gardener develops a new kind of rose. They have, indeed, done their work all too well: would-be contributors now deluge them with lifeless imitations, and they have begun to beg writers not to follow the formula *quite* so closely.

Such art workers are as alienated from their brainwork as the industrial worker is from his handwork. The only great films to come out of Hollywood were made before industrial elephantiasis had reduced the director to one of a number of technicians all operating at about the same level of authority. Our two greatest directors Griffith and Stroheim, were artists, not specialists; they did everything themselves, dominated everything personally: the scenario, the actors, the camerawork, the cutting. Unity cannot be achieved by a production-line of specialists, however competent. There have been successful collective creations (Greek temples, Gothic churches, perhaps the *Iliad*) but their creators were part of a tradition which was strong enough to impose unity on their work. We have no such tradition today, and so art—as against kitsch— will result only when a single brain and sensibility is in full command. In the movies, only the director can even theoretically be in such a position; he was so in the pre-1930 cinema of this country, Germany, and the Soviet Union.

Griffith and Stroheim were both terrific egoists—crude, naive, and not without charlatanry—who survived until the industry became highly enough organized to resist their vigorous personalities. By about 1925, both were outside looking in; the manufacture of commodities so costly to make and so profitable to sell was too serious a matter to be entrusted to artists.

"One word of advice, Von," Griffith said to Stroheim, who had

446

been his assistant on *Intolerance,* when Stroheim came to him with the news that he had a chance to make a picture himself. "Make your pictures in your own way. Put your mark on them. Take a stand and stick to your guns. You'll make some enemies, but you'll make good pictures." Could that have been only thirty years ago? (1953)

Erwin Leiser, a Swedish director, has put together in *Mein Kampf* two hours of newsreels that show Nazism from Hitler's first speeches to those ghastly pictures taken in the liberated death camps. Mr. Leiser has treated the material with respect; his intentions are serious; all he lacks is imagination. His pedestrian compilation raises the question: can reality be captured by merely showing the actual? I think it cannot: the horror of the Warsaw ghetto and of the death camps is blunted by these pictures, as an atrocious crime is blurred by the matter-of-fact stolidity with which it is reported in the press. The first corpse is a terrible experience, the second less so, and finally one becomes either immune by repetition—as legend has King Mithridates immunizing himself by taking gradually increasing doses of poison—or, worse, morbidly fascinated by the spectacle. (Paul Goodman has some wise reflections on this point in his *Utopian Essays and Practical Proposals.* I might add that certain "girlie" magazines used to alternate cheesecake with photographs of lynchings, murders, even the death camps themselves.) For if one continued to respond to the brute, repeated sight of these sufferings and degradations—the mad-eyed starving Jewish children in Warsaw; those limp shiny naked bodies all lolling heads and waving arms and legs being bulldozed into a mass grave—if one kept on seeing these former people, both the dead and those who soon will be dead, as like one's self and so evocative of pity and terror, one would, I think, go mad. There is a merciful cutoff, like fainting under torture, and one either ceases to react or else one views it with detached prurience. Gaze not too long into the abyss, warned Nietzsche, lest the abyss gaze into thee.

The makers of *Mein Kampf* wanted to show, without reserve, the

447

Nazi horror. This is something that must be done. But their literal approach frustrates their intention. Alain Resnais' documentary on the death camps, *Night and Fog,* is a quarter as long as *Mein Kampf,* but it makes a stronger impression. Resnais and Jean Cayrol, who wrote the admirable script, included much gruesome material—too much for me, I had to close my eyes several times. But they know how to resensitize the spectator by a change of pace, by using such material only for the dramatic highlights of a composition that is predominantly muted grays and browns. Some things are too terrible to be looked on without the mediation of art; like wearing smoked glasses to look at the sun. Resnais and Cayrol have put an aesthetic distance between actuality and the spectator through such devices as the ironic essay on death-camp architecture: "A camp is built like a stadium or a big hotel. Men in the fields survey the land. You need contractors, estimates, competitive bids. A steam shovel hangs motionless from a rig. And no doubt a bribe or two. . . . Any style will do. It's left to the imagination. Swiss style, garage style, Japanese style, no style at all. Buildings resembling villas at the entrance to a camp. The architects calmly plan the gates through which no one will enter more than once." Their chief device is to alternate between present and past, using color shots of the weed-grown, pastoral ruins of the camps today to contrast with black-and-white shots from the terrible past.

Such devices assimilate these infernos to everyday experience; this doesn't make them less infernal—on the contrary—but it makes it possible to experience them emotionally.

Similarly, the moral horror of Nazism comes out less clearly in Mr. Leiser's nobly motivated film than in Leni Reifenstahl's evilly motivated *Triumph of the Will.* Miss Reifenstahl was Hitler's pet director and her purpose was to glorify him and his movement. But, since she is a prodigiously talented director, she can't help imposing on her material an aesthetic form that expresses, in spite of her intentions, the nature of the beast, as in those chilling shots of the Nazi leaders in oratorical frenzy. The equation works out differently, since we put a minus where she puts a plus, but since she is an artist she can't help clarifying.

In *Mein Kampf,* the impersonal, undiscriminating eye of the camera is substituted for the artist's consciousness. There is some-

448

thing revolting about this. What right has the camera to invade the privacy of the dead and the dying? People have a right to die without being photographed. What nature of men were those German cameramen who photographed the starving Jews of Warsaw? How could they have intruded? What are the moral limits of professional objectivity? And the British cameramen who photographed those corpses being bulldozed like road materials, were they not also morally obtuse, to say nothing of the military men—ours, note—who adopted such an efficient method of burial? The Greeks attached great importance to proper burial—cf. *The Iliad* and *Antigone*. They were not a very religious people, but they had a sense of human dignity. Does our insensibility to such matters reflect a tendency to treat people as objects? (1962)

Letter (Unanswered) to the General Manager of Loew's Theatres, 1540 Broadway, New York City

DEAR SIR:

National Velvet was shown at your Commodore Theatre (and doubtless at many other Loew's Theatres) last weekend. This is a film especially appealing to children; since *Lassie, Come Home,* nothing more definitely a picture for children has come out of Hollywood. Yet on the same bill—in fact, immediately following it—you showed an untitled Army Signal Corps film which is the most gruesome and sadistic film I have ever had the bad fortune to see.

The Army film is full of the most horrible newsreel shots of actual executions and atrocities by Japanese troops, of Chinese people being buried alive, of corpses being dumped into trucks, etc. The commentary repeats insanely, "Have you killed *your* Jap today?" The whole is supposed to have some connection with getting people to take jobs in war plants. The film is the product of a pathological mind and should not be shown even to adults.

But to show it on the same bill with a film which you must know will draw great numbers of children—this is criminal negligence and, in my opinion, should be punished legally as such. Don't you

449

people have the slightest knowledge of child psychology? Don't you feel any responsibility when you make up your programs?

I have a seven-year-old son who saw *National Velvet* at the Commodore; luckily I had seen the film there the day before and was able to warn his grandmother, who took him, to keep him outside during the atrocity film. But the theatre, she told me, was packed with kids whose parents hadn't been warned. What do you think the effect of seeing such a film was on *them?* Sights like those shown in that film can be a painful memory with a child for years, a source of anxiety and neurosis.

I suggest you consult some child psychologist in making up programs which may be expected to draw children. . . .

Sincerely,

FEB. 25, 1945.　　　　　　　　　　　　DWIGHT MACDONALD

The Best Remaining Seats: The Story of the Golden Age of the Movie Palace, by Ben M. Hall (Clarkson N. Potter, $15). In text and illustrations, this is a model of its kind—in fact, it's one of the most thoroughly *enjoyable* books I've read in some time. (For once, I agree with Bosley Crowther, who has written an appreciative Foreword.) As rural clergymen in nineteenth-century England used to write modest little works on the "antiquities" of their parishes, so Mr. Hall—a writer on *Time*—has given us an immodestly big work (11 by 9 inches) about *his* parish, which is the now-vanished world of the great movie "palaces," "temples," and "cathedrals." And as the charm, and value, of the clergymen's books came from the authors' affection for their subject, so here *The Best Remaining Seats* is a labor of love. The remarkable job of research, all from "original sources," and the prose in which Mr. Hall has conveyed it, an agreeable mixture of wit and scholarship— these cannot be bought by money, or even by the prospects of academic advancement. While hordes of graduate students are gleaning trivia in "fields" already plowed to exhaustion—*Melville's Symbolism: A Prolegomenon* or maybe *A Note on Race Relations in Cincinnati, 1901–1909,* to invent two studies that I hope are apocryphal—it is left to an amateur to preserve the fast-perishing ephemera of this neglected corner of our recent past.

450

The movie palace was the lengthened shadow of an extraordinary man named S. L. Rothapfel, who is still remembered as "Roxy." His palaces were mostly in New York City: his first effort, the Regent (1913), was followed by the Strand, the Rialto, the Rivoli, and the Capitol—theatres to which I was taken by my parents on special occasions, usually after a dinner at another midtown palace that specialized in spaghetti. Finally, there was the Roxy itself, "The Cathedral of the Motion Picture," which opened in 1927 with klieg lights, a Gloria Swanson picture (plus Miss Swanson) and a complete symphony orchestra under the personal direction of Erno Rapee.

Meanwhile all over the country other cathedrals were rising, their interiors achieving a grandeur of vulgarity which is perhaps unique in Western culture. "There were two major schools of movie-palace design," Mr. Hall writes, "the *standard* ('or hard-top'), which had its precedent in the opera house and vaudeville theatre, but which grew more exotic as the decade progressed . . . and the *atmospheric* ('or stars-and-clouds'), which borrowed from nature and the more flamboyant landscape gardeners of the past." Thomas W. Lamb was the leader of the standard school, which carried French and Italian baroque to its logical conclusion, not to mention what it did to the classic chastity of the Adam Brothers. John Eberson was the creator of the atmospheric, or *plein air,* school, in which the customers sat in a vast patio, replete with fantastic arches and cupolas and battlements of Spanish or Persian design, sometimes backed up by actual fountains and cages of real birds, while stars and clouds did their stuff in the fake sky. The chapters on the Roxy ushers, the Mighty Wurlitzer and other movie organs, and the standardization of "mood" music alone are worth the price of admission. The illustrations are copious, curious and splendidly reproduced on expensive, glossy paper. (1963)

Donskoy's Maxim Gorky trilogy (*The Childhood of Maxim,* 1938; *My Apprenticeship,* 1939; *My Universities,* 1940) is the most unrhetorical cinema I have ever seen, with one exception: Vigo's *Zéro de Conduite,* which the first two parts of Donskoy's

451

trilogy resemble in presenting life from the viewpoint of a child, with the baffling transitions, the obscure motivations, the poetic daze of adult life as it appears to a sensitive child, achieving a kind of direct realism which is so lacking in the literary-dramatic conventions we are used to that it has a surrealist effect. The great silent cinema of Eisenstein, Pudovkin, and Dovzhenko was rhetorical: a "grand style" developed by sophisticated artists who knew just what they were doing and analyzed it in books and articles. Donskoy breaks with this tradition; his work is low-keyed, unemphatic, emotional rather than intellectual, intimate and lyrical; he gives us not the masses, not History, but individuals—a whole gallery of grotesques, eccentrics, pungent characters like the grandfather and the bakery owner, noble people like the grandmother. The photography and montage are conventional and there are none of those dramatically composed single shots that burst on the eye so powerfully in *Potemkin* and *The End of St. Petersburg*. (When Donskoy does attempt the grandiose, as in the unfortunate last episode in the last film, where he tries to generalize the meaning of the trilogy, he fails, perhaps because he is an intuitive rather than a conscious artist.) The whole effect comes from simply keeping the camera on real people. How seldom does one see human beings on the screen, each behaving according to his personality, each being always unexpected—and presenting their slyness, greed, humor, violence, affection, rage, wonder, meanness, generosity without rhetorical emphasis and without explanation. Things are not "built up" any more than they are in real life; scenes are not resolved, they just stop, sometimes abruptly, sometimes ebbing away. Often nothing "happens" at all—as in the barge-unloading scene in Part 3 where, conditioned by Hollywood, I kept expecting a denouement but where, for all the dramatic tension, at the end we have simply witnessed—a barge being unloaded; though we have also experienced a poem about cooperative work. Donskoy carries out the logic of realism and, as always happens when the logic of any approach to life is carried out to the end, produces a profoundly artistic effect. Realism carried that far becomes formalism. Luckily, Stalin's cultural agents were not acute enough to realize this, which explains how Donskoy was able to make a great film, the only one to come out of Russia since 1930. They thought *Gorky* was a respectable exercise in socialist-realism. In this, as in other matters, they were wrong. (1957)

I think John Huston's *The Maltese Falcon* is the best crime picture ever made in Hollywood for the same reason I think *The Gunfighter* (the Gregory Peck, not the William S. Hart version) is the best Western: because each shows movie types behaving realistically instead of in the usual terms of romantic cliché.*

The Maltese Falcon—1941, Huston's first and, alas, best movie —is realistic about the three most important things in our society: money, sex, and death. Huston knows just what he is doing all the time; the mood he establishes is matter-of-fact and humorous, counterpointed against the melodramatic intrigue. (Two huge pistols become absurd in the hands of the ineffectual young punk.) The movement is brisk—how nice to be a little behind the director instead of, as normally, ten minutes ahead of him. The first time Bogart leans down toward Mary Astor the camera doesn't wait for the clinch; point made, they are lovers, on with the plot! Money is of frank concern to everybody, including the hero. Death is just one of those things—to the survivors. The day after his partner in the detective agency is killed, Bogart arrives at the office, impatiently endures his secretary's sniffling condolences, and interrupts to order the lettering on the door changed from "Spade & Archer" to

* *The Gunfighter* shows both the deadening effect of Hollywood and also the ability of an artist to survive. It was directed by Henry King, who in 1921 made another memorable film, *Tol'able David*. In 1925, he made *Stella Dallas*, a mother-love tear-jerker I still remember, for Belle Bennett's playing as much as for King's directing, and after that a long series of potboilers interrupted only by *The Gunfighter* in 1950. Such a biography—two fine works, thirty years apart, imbedded in forty years of junk—is possible only in a collective art like cinema, where the artist is less in control than in the older arts, the movie director being more like an orchestra conductor, a collective entrepreneur, than he is like the individual handcraftsmen of painting or writing. Extraneous factors play more of a part in the success of his works, hence great variation in quality is possible. In this respect, cinema is the art to which the *auteur* theory is least suitable.

453

"SAMUEL SPADE." Sex is simply sex; Huston's film is to Hollywood romance as *Don Quixote* was to the medieval tales of chivalry. Sam Spade has what is generally called a "continental" attitude toward women—he likes them but they aren't all *that* much. He rates his own skin first (realism about death), money second (in a capitalist economy, money is part of one's skin), and sexual love third. The great scene is at the end when he explains to his inamorata why he is going to turn her over to the cops for the murder of his partner. "But you *love* me!" she exclaims. "Sure I love you but that's beside the point," he replies and proceeds to draw up a balance sheet. On the one side, love. On the other: (1) he didn't care much for his partner, but in his business "when your partner is killed you have to do something about it"; (2) somebody has to take the rap and, since she in fact did shoot his partner, she is the logical choice; (3) how does he know she may not bump *him* off later on? "I'm not going to play the sucker for anyone," he concludes, picking up the phone to call the police while she looks on with horrified incredulity. The poor woman has obviously seen too many movies. (1960)

Recently I re-viewed, at the National Film Theatre in London, William Wellman's 1931 film, *The Public Enemy.* I had remembered it as good, but not as good as it now appears to be. The story is told in short tableaux which are developed only as much as is necessary to make the point. Like *The Birth of a Nation,* it is not the kind of continuous realistic narrative we have become accustomed to, but rather a discontinuous series of symbolic scenes, like metaphors in poetry, which in mosaic fashion build up the central theme. It is intellectually crude and cinematically sophisticated: one often finds one's self smiling at the naive heavy-handedness of the content while at the same time one is thrilled by the power and economy of the direction. The approach is direct and unpretentious, the pace is brisk, the whole thing lasts 84 minutes and it has more in it than a half-dozen of those lethargic three-hour epics we get nowadays.

It is, of course, James Cagney's picture. His performance is as

454

great as anything I've seen in movies: his balletlike control of his body, every movement at once precise and free; his extraordinary command of expression.

His Tom Powers has the heartlessness and grace and innocence of an animal, as incapable of hypocrisy as of feeling; the smiling, unreflective delight with which he commits mayhem and murder makes Humphrey Bogart look like a conscience-stricken Hamlet. (It is interesting that Cagney began his acting career as a female impersonator; extremes meet; there is something delicate, almost dainty in his ferocious virility.) He puts on the best drunk scene I remember; he is not just drunk in general, he is Tom Powers drunk. He expresses everything physically, as when, after successfully dating Jean Harlow, he does a little double-shuffle dance step before getting back into his sports car; or the animal grin as he ducks behind a wall with the machine-gun bullets chipping out the corner and his partner dying on the sidewalk, the reflex grimace of a fox who has escaped the hounds, and also the smile of I am Alive and He is Dead. Wellman uses Cagney with subtlety, keeping him in the background much of the time while secondary characters occupy the foreground. (This development of secondary characters is usually a sign of a good movie.) So it is all the more powerful when Cagney moves up into the foreground at the big moments; our taste for this extraordinary actor has not been blunted by seeing too much of him.

The Public Enemy differs in two important ways from the movies we get from Hollywood now.

(1) Its realism is blunt, direct, unsparing, as against the romanticized kind—at once souped up and slicked down—that Kazan gives us, for instance, in *On the Waterfront*. The only exception, and the film's chief weakness, is the good brother, who is much too handsome and noble. Beryl Mercer's mother and Jean Harlow's glamor girl are meant to be taken ironically, I think; each has played the role straight in many films, but here the mother is clearly a sap ("my baby" she calls the panther she has whelped) and Harlow's deep Mae-Western voice and ludicrously refined accent become satirical in this raffish context.

(2) There is none of the usual pornography of violence; the killings take place out of camera range, as in the shooting of Putty

455

Nose, where we hear the shots while the camera is on the horrified face of the accomplice (cf. the knifing in the Turkish bath in *Children of Paradise*). Cagney slaps a bartender, he pushes the celebrated grapefruit into Mae Clarke's face, and that's about all. But we get a better idea of his brutality in the efficient way he cuffs the bartender than we do from those leisurely beatings-up of present-day films. The part is greater than the whole. In art, at least. (1961)

The reissue of *Children of Paradise* has revived my faith in the cinema, somewhat tried by recent events. It looks even better now, in this longer version lasting almost three hours, than it did twelve years ago. It is, without qualifications, a masterpiece.

Marcel Carné, who directed it, and Jacques Prevert, the poet, who wrote the script, have made a number of other films, notably *Quai des Brumes, Le Jour Se Lève,* and *Bizarre Bizarre. Children of Paradise* was made in Paris during the German occupation, whence perhaps its "escapist" and "art for art's sake" quality— though why not escape if you can and what better sake than art's? It is a period piece, set in the Paris of the 1840's, the Paris of Dumas *père* and Balzac. The mood, perfectly sustained throughout, is romantic. The direction has feeling, taste, intelligence: old-fashioned virtues but this is an old-fashioned film. The acting is of a quality from some antediluvian age. It hardly seems possible that Arletty, Jean-Louis Barrault, Pierre Brasseur, Marcel Herrand and Louis Salou are practicing the same art as the Hollywooden mimes we are used to. Brasseur in particular is comparable to Olivier in range—he can modulate from soft, almost effeminate grace to incisive power. Prevert's script is simply a miracle; I think one might even *read* it with pleasure. The photography is dramatic yet harmonious, the sound track is subtle. Like the deacon's wonderful one-hoss shay, it is all of a piece and every piece of it is of the best workmanship. A rough definition of a masterpiece.

It even violates my own rules about cinema, another definition of a masterpiece (sometimes). The structure is not built by montage,

456

the camera is not mobile and is, furthermore, the servant, not the master of the action. The chief cinematic quality it has is the use of the close-up to point up visual details as the theatre cannot: Garance opening her bodice to her lover; the brief, stunning shot of Othello's blacked-up face in the play; the murder shown only by the spasm on the face of the accomplice. It's all highly artificial and stylized, an exercise in antiquarianism differing from similar efforts by Hollywood in being of the past psychologically as well as scenically. We hire historical experts to pass on every physical detail of *Solomon and Sheba* and then let Brynner and Lollobrigida do their stuff. Prevert's script is Balzacian, with its emphasis on will and passion and its bravura dialogue. What Balzac did for the Parisian journalistic world in *Les Illusions Perdues,* Carné and Prevert do for theatre and pantomime. These are notoriously artificial worlds, and Carné doesn't apologize for this, but rather emphasizes it, from the opening shot of a stage proscenium with the curtain rising (not on a play but on the movie itself) to the closing shot of the curtain descending; there are even two acts, with the curtain going up and down between them. The plot is also highly stylized. The four male principals are Baptiste the mime (Barrault), Lemaitre the actor (Brasseur), Lacenaire the criminal (Herrand) and the Comte de Montray (Salou). They revolve like satellites around the lovely moon of Garance (Arletty), at once worldly and remote, promiscuous and inviolable.

It is a ballet of passion, the dancers darting in and out of the figure as the plot and their own natures determine. The odd thing is that while Carné in a literal sense keeps reality at a distance, in a more profound sense he welcomes it. *Children of Paradise* is not "arty." It is not like those exercises in purity, sterile and monotonous, Dreyer's *Passion of Joan of Arc* (1929) and Bergman's *The Seventh Seal,* because it has characters instead of symbols. Each personage is at once consistent and unexpected, like real people, developing as one watches them, partly because their full being is not revealed at once and partly because they are changed by their fictive life in the film. Space forbids particularization but see William Hedges' article in the Summer, 1959, issue of the University of California's *Film Quarterly*.

Another definition of a masterpiece is: a work that imposes its

457

own reality. A corollary is that it refreshes rather than depletes, since a new vision is always exhilarating. A test of a movie for me is whether, when I emerge onto the street, I feel relieved at getting back into contact with reality, or whether, on the contrary, I look at the street in terms of the movie. After *Ben-Hur,* I felt as if I had been dragged around that racecourse with Messala and, compared to the dreary outrages on my sensibilities I had just been subjected to, the Broadway scene was the healing water of life. *Children of Paradise* is long, too, but after it I positively skipped out into Eighth Street. The projector was still whirring inside my head. I saw Garance in purple slacks, Lacenaire in a duffle coat. The Jumble Shop was a thieves' hangout and the costume-jewelry shops glowed with romance. (1960)

There is a scene in *The Birth of a Nation* in which a Negro carpetbagger asks Lillian Gish to marry him. It is introduced with a title: The Black's Mad Proposal. The scene simply illustrates this title. Extraordinarily crude. Yet here, *in petto,* is the basic aesthetic of the cinema. (Or *an* aesthetic, anyway.) A movie is, or should be, a series of such illustrations, each of them demonstrating some idea or situation. And the literary part, the words, should be kept at a distance from the pictures. Which is what, in its humble way, The Black's Mad Proposal does.

I don't know who first had the idea of pictorializing the "credits" or when the practice first began, but credits have been getting more and more important. Since they are overprinted with text, they must be simple and striking, and since they try to summarize the mood of the film, they must resort to stylization, which is at least a precondition of art. They are often the only satisfying part of a movie and I have no doubt there are by now sophisticated movie-goers who reach for their hats as soon as the credits are over. Paul Goodman once observed a similar oddity in radio: he argued that the singing commercial, detested by all right-thinking highbrows, was usually more interesting, in words and music, than the show that followed it. The reasons are the same as in the case of movie

458

credits. Lately a variation has been introduced: the action begins at once and often continues for some time before the credits come on. This precredit footage, also, is likely to be much better than the rest, for here we are in the magical world of art where meanings are not literal and not easily identified—Eden before Adam got around to naming the animals. (1964)

The most interesting thing about the movie version of William Inge's *The Dark at the Top of the Stairs* is that it is in color. There was a time when color was reserved for musicals and light comedies. But now it is often used for realistic drama, and I think this is a mistake. It is distracting because it emphasizes inessentials. In *Home from the Hill,* for instance, it amounted to a visual rape: a supermarket glowed like a Vermeer, overalled farmers sitting around in a town square looked like figures from the Sistine Chapel, shots of a barbecue reminded one of Rubens (or one of those full-color pornographic close-ups of roast beef in magazine ads). Here the color is milder, but still the family dinner table comes out like a setting for an orgy and a stained-glass chandelier takes the play away, visually speaking, from the actors. It is also a matter of the kind of color one gets in Hollywood films, a color so rich and intense that nothing looks shabby or everyday. The literal-minded argue that because one sees colors in real life, it is more realistic to show them on the screen, but I doubt this. The eye compensates for colors in some way; one is never conscious of them as one is in a movie.

In short, just as one doesn't see things flat and cut off by a quadrangle as on the movie screen, so one doesn't see colors as the camera does. And so "realism" isn't—really—the point at all. Color is an aesthetic convention, like the quadrangular screen. It is suitable for films of a spectacular and unrealistic nature—the paradox that color, which is intrinsic to our actual seeing, interferes with realism in the cinema is one that I cannot resolve, at least here—and even in such films it can be overdone. The best color I've seen has been in Soviet films—the most recent example is *And*

459

Quiet Flows the Don—which have a pale, pastel-like color as harmonious and unobtrusive as that of Corot. I'm told that the Russians have used this color because they couldn't afford anything more up-to-date, that it's an old German process they looted after the war. Most likely. And most likely also that when they have "caught up with and overtaken" capitalist industry they will be able to match the arsenic greens and cerulean blues and raw-beef reds of Hollywood.

The advent of color is one more illustration of the aesthetic damage done to the movies by technical progress. Similar progress has been made in black and white film, with similar results. When I last saw *The Birth of a Nation,* I was especially impressed by the beauty of the photography; this was partly a matter of Griffith's eye for both detail and overall composition, but I think it was also because of the harmonious gray tonality, so that each shot was seen as a whole, with everything related, the way a good painting looks. The kind of film now used is much more sensitive, and gives greater variations in tone, so that each object comes out in luminous, three-dimensional actuality. But for this very reason, the general effect is chaotic and inartistic, since every table, pot, and chair fights for supremacy. The same difference exists between Victorian photography and that of today; an averagely talented photographer of those days achieved unity more easily precisely because his film was inferior and hence *everything* didn't jump out at the eye. A Walker Evans solves the problem by careful, classical composition, a Cartier-Bresson by the opposite—catching the subject on the wing—a Robert Frank by emotional distortion and selectivity. But in Hollywood there are no such craftsmen and so the aesthetic ravages of superspeed panchromatic film (or whatever the stuff is called) are allowed to go on unchecked and in fact unrealized. (1960)

Wandering into a movie in Laredo, Texas, during a wait between bus connections, I was subjected to a half-hour patriotic travelogue, made for free by Hollywood to promote the sale of U. S. Savings

460

Bonds. It was titled *The Land We Love*. Like many gifts, it was on the economical side. Kitsch, camp, masscult—no term in my limited vocabulary but makes it sound better than it was. A kind of triumph: absolute cliché, absolute fakery, absolute boredom. Earnestly introduced by Hubert Humphrey looking us right in the eye—what *has* happened to that man?—with the Great Seal of the Vice-President of the United States leering over his shoulder, narrated by Raymond Massey, in that orotund diction than which no diction is orotunder, and photographed in the kind of color, alternately washed out and virulent, the *National Geographic* used thirty years ago ("Picturesque Patagonia, Realm of the Dreaming Past"), *The Land We Love* touched all the bases: Lincoln Memorial, winter at Valley Forge, free Americans voting freely with free American Negroes in line just like other folks, Plymouth Rock, Grand Canyon, Lincoln Memorial, free American father carving Thanksgiving turkey, statue of Hamilton balanced by statue of Jefferson, White House, Chicago skyscrapers ("Chicago, Chicago, that toddling town"), New York skyscrapers ("East Side, West Side"), Golden Gate Bridge ("California, here I come"), Lincoln Memorial, free Americans lining up to buy movie tickets (not free), Mount Rushmore, Mississippi riverboat (Mark Twain), Arlington, free trout fisherman, Statue of Liberty, quaint old New Orleans, quaint old Williamsburg, Liberty Bell ("Yankee Doodle"), New England church with steeple, dome of Capitol, Lincoln Memorial. I wonder how those bonds are selling. (1966)

Howth to wake into silverscreaming cinequanonsense the doublin mage's perplixacated maestropiece? To lustify that seemworld? Obliviously by giving a fairful earing to the joyceous blooms of vherbal slanguage mythed up with etymologicalities—and accompliced by flimflamfilm eyeings as well. In sport, Mary Ellen Bute's 97 minutes of vagariations on seems from *Finnegans Wake* is both punny and movieing. When I was invited to a press screening at The Museum of Modern Art, I couldn't imagine how a film version could avoid the pretentious, the vague and the arty. Miss Bute has

461

solved it by quarrying out of Joyce's logorrhean amplitude a plot line (often interrupted by cadenzas, but still a life line) that begins with Finnegan–H. C. Earwicker–Here Comes Everybody drowsing off in the conjugal bed; earthquake, tumultuous noise, the floor opens and, like Alice falling down the rabbit hole, he tumbles head over heels in his nightshirt through space while his wife, Anna Livia Plurabelle (All Ladies Plural?) peers down from the bed into the void. It ends with HCE and ALP waking up to a sunny Dublin morning; he goes off to work, she gets down to housekeeping. In between, dream episodes stumble over each other in a cinematic style alternating between the realistic and the fantastic, as good dreams do. Miss Bute has not said the last word on movieizing *Finnegans Wake*—her approach is fanciful rather than imaginative, in Coleridge's terms—but she has said the first word with style and eloquence. As have the 23 members of her all-Irish cast—the film was shot in Dublin—especially the four principals: Martin J. Kelley (Finnegan), Jane Reilly (Anna), Peter Haskell (Shem), Page Johnson (Shaun). As anyone knows who has tried to read *Finnegans Wake,* meanings that don't yield to visual inspection often become clear when pronounced aloud, with a light brogue. The diction of the cast—not a movie actor among them—brings out the meaning, beauty and comedy of the lines with a clarity surpassed only by Joyce himself in the single record we have of his readings from the work. (1965)

There are many styles for writing uncriticism, from High Academic ("The dichotomy between the vernacular ambience of Ebbets Field and the Sophoclean theme of hubris, one may hypothesize, is perhaps what endows Lardner's *You Know Me, Al,* with its essential formal tension"), to Low Journalese ("Make no mistake: *Lazarus and Messalina* is Sandro S. Perman's greatest. All I can say is *wow!*"). But the gremlin, or timelin, who does movies for *Time,* has invented a new one. Some specimens:

On *Yojimbo:* "Like a giant caldron the screen boils with life, and Kurosawa's telescopic lenses, spooning deep, lift the depths to the surface and hurl the whole mess in the spectator's face."

462

On *The Four Days of Naples:* "With the help of a telescopic lens it plunges the spectator like spaghetti into the boiling core of every battle—he goes in stiff with tension and comes out limp with fatigue."

On *Il Grido:* "*Il Grido* means *The Cry* and the cry comes from the heart. Antonioni opens the aorta of his talent and releases the cold gray mainstream of his feeling. . . ." A curious throwback to a *Time* review of Garcia Lorca I have preserved for sixteen years: "Among these lyrics are several as frighteningly alive as the jet from an artery."

On *Phaedra:* "When Vallone dispatches Mercouri to London to persuade Perkins to come to Greece for the summer, the iron gate of tragedy begins creakingly to close."

On *Night Is My Future:* "The Bergman who made this picture still had akvavit in his veins. Intellect, that glittering and treacherous Snow Queen, had not yet struck her icy sliver into his heart."

I think it was Wilde who said of another overemphatic stylist: "He writes at the top of his voice. It's so loud I can't hear him." (1963)

A recent issue of *Time* revealed that, for the past ten years, Those Reviews have been written by one Brad Darrach; it also printed his picture—he looks boyish and eager, as he should—and revealed that "Darrach's passion is writing, a craft at which he is so meticulous that if he had time he would probably want to cut his copy in stone." This might be a good idea; it would slow him down anyway; the trouble with Mr. Darrach is that he is so passionate and meticulous about words that he has no time to think. The occasion of his emergence from anonymity was a cover story he wrote, using the New York Film Festival as an excuse to celebrate the current renaissance in world cinema. The Festival itself he simply adored, praising "the karat of the films displayed" and describing as only he can describe its "half-dozen top-chop features."

Even for Brad Darrach, it was quite a production. We learn that *Knife in the Water* is "a Polish thriller as sharp as a knife and as smooth as water"; that *Rashomon* was a "cinematic thunderbolt that violently ripped open the dark heart of man" and that its creator, while "not everybody's meat," does "make telling use of telescopic lenses that drill deep into a scene, suck up all the action in sight and then spew it violently into the viewer's face" (the telescopic lens invariably sends him reeling into this metaphor, maybe something Freudian?); that Bergman is "a gangling, green-eyed snaggletoothed son of a Swedish parson" and also a great artist who, in *The Seventh Seal,* "plunges straight down into the abyss of God and wanders there among the gnarled and leering roots of living religion"; that Resnais "lacks humanity, lacks blood" (but "nevertheless his work is important"); while Truffaut is "as warm as Resnais is cold," makes films "about real people with real feelings" and "goes on growing"; that Visconti's films "are borne on a slow, irrefutable current doomward," or, to phrase it more meticulously, "On the tiny raft of hope his heroes glide toward the cataract of fate"; that Wajda is "the Polish Kurosawa" and Torre Nilsson "the Bergman of the Antipodes"; plus many other interesting and useful facts.

Mr. Darrach's steam-heated vaticinations, which, in our peculiar culture, were distributed to some two million adults, blow several gaskets in his finale: "A tremendous power, a great magic has been given to the men of the new cinema. What will they do with it? Will Resnais really be able to renovate the aesthetic of cinema? Will Bergman at last kindle the fire in the heart and light his gloomy world with love? Will Ray redeem his prodigious promise and become the Shakespeare of the screen?" Look for the answer on this station next week. And meantime a word from our sponsor: "Whatever happens . . . the world is on its way to a great cinema culture. The art of the future has become the art of the present." (1963)

In *The Elusive Corporal,* Jean Renoir gives us the World War II equivalent of his *Grand Illusion,* and how have the mighty fallen! The corporal (played with his usual insectlike precision by Jean-Pierre Cassel, of whom I for one have had more than enough) makes a number of attempts, the last successful, to escape from

464

various prisoner-of-war camps. The mood is comic and *gemütlich;* while it is good to have the German soldiery presented as people rather than as Nazi beasts, maybe Renoir overdoes it; nor do I believe the French even in 1940 were quite as cozily unheroic as here depicted. This reduction of the last war to a purely human scale falsifies it, resulting in such tasteless transitions as when Cassel's sufferings under the droning drill of the dentist are echoed by the whining motors of Luftwaffe planes bombing London. Aesthetically, the film is limp, meandering, confused. Renoir is an instinctive artist, with a groping, ruminating sensibility. In his two masterpieces, *Grand Illusion* and *The Rules of the Game,* this sensibility is confined within the hard boundaries of traditional social codes; the subtle interplay, for instance, in *Grand Illusion* between aristocrats, plebeians, Jews, intellectuals, etc. (also between wartime enemies, German and French), gives an automatic form and also calls into play Jean Renoir's ability to bring out the human realities suppressed by these abstract categories. He seems to need such hard social lines as a foil and when they are absent, as here, where everyone is classless and even denationalized—they are, in Nietzsche's phrase, "human, all too human"—he relaxes into sentimentality and a peculiar kind of aimlessness. (1963)

One of the tribal rites of the movie world is enactment of the film festival. Since it is a relatively inexpensive form of national advertising, there are now dozens of them from Berlin to Tokyo. The Irish town of Cork has just put one on; no doubt Bridgeport, Connecticut, soon will be in the running. The critics and cineasts for whom in theory the festivals are mounted find themselves submerged by starlets, businessmen and café-society types. Prizes are handed out lavishly, for obvious commercial reasons. Some day I hope to review a foreign movie that has *not* won any gold palms, silver lions, or bonze bears, not even a Special Award for Best Supporting Actress Over Sixty. I should look most kindly on such a film.

In 1959 I attended, at the invitation and expense of the Argentine government, its Second International Film Festival, which took place at a seaside resort called Mar del Plata. The American delegation was rather whimsically composed. It consisted of two representatives of the Motion Picture Producers Association; an editor of a movie trade paper; a Russian-born journalist who writes about movies for Italian papers; Linda Cristal, an Argentine-born Hollywood actress; the French poet, Saint-John Perse, and myself.

This Noah's Ark-load was met at the airport by large numbers of movie fans, reporters and photographers. Miss Cristal, a nice, sensible girl who also happens to be extremely pretty, was presented with three huge cellophane-wrapped bouquets and was extensively flash-bulbed. The president of the festival, Mr. Enzo Ardigo, was on hand, apologizing for his innocence of English, offering to carry our bags, warmly greeting Saint-John Perse as Sir John Percy. Later I learned that Mr. Ardigo, whose good will was matched only by his ignorance of cinema, is by profession a sports writer.

This note of benevolent confusion continued throughout the festival. The Polish delegation arrived two days late because it had been put on a plane that wound up in Calcutta. It was also rumored that the festival's safe had to be cut open by acetylene torch because someone had lost the combination and that the members of the jury almost missed the final grand dinner because someone else forgot to invite them. Although an illustrated magazine was published every day by the festival bureaucracy, it contained no practical information. With persistence one could get a schedule of films to be shown and even tickets to them. The latter involved a daily trip to a set of gloomy caverns lit by weak yellow light bulbs. In the Magnasco-like shadows, crowds of suppliants besieged a severe blonde who, after checking lists and conferring with mysterious officials secreted in an inner room, would either give out a ticket or, more frequently, refer the problem elsewhere. No one stood in line and the general effect was of panicky passengers rushing the last lifeboat. In dark corners little groups, heads together, carried on furtive negotiations. For every film one had to get a special ticket in this thieves' kitchen, and each time it was as if no one had ever gotten a ticket before. Fortunately, the quality of the films was such that, after five or six unhappy experiences, one had no ticket problems. The organizers of the festival were really not to blame for this; the major festivals—Cannes, Venice, Edinburgh, Berlin—get the best films; by the time it was Mar del Plata's turn, the pickings were slim.

466

Then there were the parties—and the crowds. The latter swarmed around us constantly, indefatigably, staring as if they hoped to read the riddle of existence in our faces. The starlets and the stars—Miss Cristal and a large expansive German named Curt Jurgens were the only two the festival boasted in the latter category—caused an enormous stir everywhere they went; one starlet, I noticed, had developed a shorthand autograph: two dashes and a dot. The spectators worked around the clock; emerging from a party at five a.m., we found the usual crowds pressing against the usual police lines.

The parties were numerous and elaborate, with expensive food and drinks and masses of well-groomed Argentines. The guests, once they had passed through the police lines, themselves became another crowd, looking around anxiously for The Important Ones —the flash bulbs were a clue. The most rudimentary conversation was difficult even if one could find a fellow delegate in the press of opulent supernumeraries. A waiter would be shoving a tray of cocktails at one, a celebrity would be posing amid the photographers' sheet-lightning, a band would be thundering in one's ear— Argentinian jazz is Wagnerian.

It was life at its most mass-ified. My letter of invitation had painted rather a different picture. I had been asked "to participate in a discussion on movie theories. Our invitation is inspired by the vivid interest we have in the great contribution that you could offer to this meeting, which we hope will be of great hierarchy." How great the hierarchy proved to be I don't know. The only meeting I was invited to spent two hours discussing a resolution that favored the wider international distribution of good movies. Nobody was actually opposed. The time was taken up with motions on procedure, that is, discussions of what to discuss. It was finally decided to leave the "implementation" up to a Permanent Commission. (1961)

The XIVe Festival International du Film at Cannes had better movies than the one I went to last year in the Argentine, but otherwise was not much different. There was the same peculiar

467

fusion of high life and mass culture, the same sense of Too Many People, of being lost in a super-production with a rather vague script. I've decided I don't enjoy film festivals; they probably work for stars (or starlets), for businessmen and for the public, but they make a critic feel disoriented. Confusion was less than at Mar del Plata—some genius had thought of giving one a pass to all the showings instead of requiring separate applications for each one—but still one was more likely to find the best trails through the festival jungle by consulting the journalistic underground in the Blue Bar, next to the Palais where the films were shown, than by struggling through the regular channels. For the press there was provided an impressive line-up of some twenty gleaming new type-writers in different scripts, but these were, naturally, strung down one side of the main lounge. I used one for several afternoons, tapping through animated conversations at my elbow (luckily I couldn't understand a word), through background music, and through the diversionary operation of a starlet who exercised her dachshund by throwing a ball the length of the room for him to scurry after with merry yips.

The mob scenes differed from Mar del Plata only in the smaller size of the public outside the police lines. (There is more to do in Cannes after dark, one assumes.) The other public, the one inside, distinguishable by the opulence of its tailoring and dressmaking, behaved as usual like so many bobby-soxers, applauding precisely the most pretentious and phony effects in the films shown in the Palais and pushing, cheering and clapping as the stars made their appointed orbits. The scene on the grand staircase of the Palais as Ingrid Bergman, Yves Montand, Anthony Perkins and Anatole Litvak arrived for the première of *Aimez Vous Brahms* (Englished as *Goodbye Again*), a bit of Saganesque nonsense they had con-spired to fabricate, was worthy of a Breughel: the press of fantastic hairdos and avid faces bathed in the apocalyptic brightness of the floodlights, the four great ones struggling to get through behind a skirmish line of white-gloved *flics,* the gowns and tuxedoes and hairdos surging toward the great ones as if to receive healing, benediction by touch, the jostling photographers, a predatory spe-cies right out of *La Dolce Vita,* all suddenly raising their cameras at the same time over their heads to snap-flash a hundred banal shots, like priests elevating the host, and such they are in this world—

468

their function is as much ritualistic as utilitarian. El Greco tableaux: the brilliantly lit rows of faces, rank on rank, calm or frenzied or adoring and all related to the sacred object in the foreground, which may be named Darrieux or Cardinale or even Perkins.

If the Blue Bar is the modest haunt of the cineasts and the staircase of the Palais the stage on which the rites of mass culture are celebrated, the terrace of the great white Carlton Hotel is the setting for more worldly activities. Here, for the price of a beer (75 cents) or a coffee (65 cents), you may see Lollobrigida having a tense argument with her husband; Richard Todd looking like a bewildered schoolboy; Sidney Poitier putting on a much livelier performance, ranging in a few seconds from the dignified to the impish, than (alas) he did in his Festival film, *Raisin in the Sun;* and the stout, middle-aged proprietor of a Nevada gambling club got up in a twenty-gallon hat and a dove-gray cowboy suit (picked out in multicolored rhinestones) and accompanied by a tall French blonde similarly hatted and caparisoned (except that her suit was blush pink); the rumor is that he changes blondes daily and that the suit goes with the job. Here you may also see, or sense, for they are not photogenic, the business contacts and deals that are the raison d'être of film festivals. What you won't see at the Carlton—back to the Blue Bar for that—is the beat contingent, led by Allen Ginsberg and Gregory Corso. I find it hard to take a line on the beats at Cannes. On the one hand, their presence was one more instance of their ambivalent lust for publicity from the philistine world they theoretically reject. On the other hand, they *are* ambivalent, a small but definite plus in this ambiance. Ginsberg was quite willing to be interviewed but he insisted—reasonably enough—on a free meal and drinks as the price. The lesser beats were more direct, lining up in their turtleneck sweaters outside the Palais as the elegant audience departed, holding out their hands and intoning: "Give us some money." Commercialism indeed, but direct and innocent, which is more than can be said for the operations of the more respectable participants in the Festival. There was also an element of parody in the beats' act. On the whole, they were a wholesome influence. (1961)

I Lost It At The Movies, by Pauline Kael; Atlantic-Little, Brown, $6. A reviewer has called this the best book of American movie criticism since *Agee on Film* (1958) and he may be right. At least I can't think of anything better in that interim. (Not that, as I'm sure the author would be the first to agree, there's been much competition.) It is exhilarating to come across film criticism that is both sophisticated and readable, lively without being nutty. A book, as they say, that it is hard to put down. In both senses. Miss Kael writes with wit, clarity and precision (the flip title is a lapse— and what *did* she lose at the movies?); she is sensible and she knows her subject thoroughly. She is good at generalizing: the two long essays that open the book are full of original and, in my view, accurate ideas on the aesthetics and sociology of today's movies and their audiences and critics. She is also good at particularizing, as in the reviews that make up the bulk of the book. I often disagreed strongly, but since she always gives specific reasons and examples for her opinions, I knew just where and why we parted company; as with any good critic, one learns from her misses as well as from her hits. And she is masterly in polemic, as Section IV, in which she disposes—patiently and reasonably—of, *seriatim,* Dr. Siegfried Kracauer's academic-extremist theories about *"the* essential nature of cinema" (as if "the" could apply to any art's nature, or essence), then of the unacademic-extremist and similarly constricting and falsifying theories, if one can dignify them by that term, of the *auteur* system-builders, and finally of two examples of the abuse of the medium for political propaganda: the rightist *Night People* and the leftist *Salt of the Earth.*

What I like especially about Miss Kael's book is that it is written from the outside. The trouble with most film criticism today is that it isn't criticism. It is, rather, appreciation, celebration, information, and it is written by intellectuals who have come to be "insiders" in the sense that they are able to discourse learnedly about almost any movie without thinking much about whether it's any good—the very question must strike them as a little naive, and irrelevant—because they see it as a greater, or lesser, manifestation of the mystery, the godhead of Cinema. Medieval theologians were concerned with celebrating the workings of God's universe, or at a pinch, explicating them so as to reconcile certain unfortunate deficiencies of this world, from a human standpoint, such as the Black Death or the Lisbon earthquake, with God's plan. It never occurred to them to question the plan itself, i.e., to criticize from a position outside the divine system. So with most of the writing in the more serious film magazines, whether the systematic, *auteur*-oriented ones like *Cahiers du Cinéma, Movie, Film Culture* and the New York *Film Bulletin,* or the broader, more eclectic quarterlies like *Sight and Sound* and our own *Film Quarterly.* Sectarian or not, their mood is one of celebration, not criticism, and their writers tend to ignore or explain away the artistic horrors in a scholarly way ("placing" them), and discanting at length on their meager positive aspects—there's *some* good in every man, or movie—as they piously avert their eyes, like the children of Noah, from the naked, scandalous actuality on the screen. The impresarios of last fall's Lincoln Center film festival, Richard Roud and Amos Vogel, are past masters at "insider" evaluation.

It is not a matter of knowledge. Miss Kael has seen as many movies, I daresay, as Mr. Roud and Mr. Vogel have—for some years she selected films, and wrote program notes about them, for an art movie house in Berkeley, California. But she has not become an insider. From her book, I imagine she would define, as I do, the critic's job as (1) to judge the quality of the film; (2) to state precisely, with examples, just why one thinks it good, bad, or indifferent; and (3) to relate it to other films and the history of the art. And I deduce, from her book, that she ranks these functions in that order. Certainly she never leaves one in doubt about her opinion of each film she reviews. Her likes and dislikes are as strong as they are unsystematic.

I have only two serious criticisms of Miss Kael's criticism: (1) she seems to me stronger on the intellectual than on the aesthetic side; (2) she is obsessed with other critics, using their opinions too often as a springboard for her own performance and almost always quoting them adversely, and often unfairly.

(1) She carries her sensible reaction against the cultist cant about foreign films, which accepts them indiscriminately if they seem to be "advanced," much too far: common sense often takes the place of imagination. She accepts *The Prize, The Pink Panther* and *Charade* because they are unpretentious, slickly manufactured

471

entertainments and she rejects an individualistic, powerfully realized film like *Viridiana* as "incomprehensible," which is the last
adjective I'd apply to it. All she can see in *Marienbad* is empty
mystification—mystifying it is, indeed, but not empty, unless one's
eye doesn't respond to an endlessly exciting series of technical
variations, each shot of great beauty and all related in a controlled
flow of images that don't tell a "story" very efficiently but do build
an abstract composition that affected me as music does. Sometimes
she seems to be perversely literal-minded, indeed philistine, as when
she observes, of the script of *Hiroshima, Mon Amour:* "I have
never understood why writers assume that repetition creates a lyric
mood or underlines meaning with profundity. My reaction is simply, Okay, I got it the first time, let's get on with it." To see repetition as merely time-wasting is to reject the most common technical
device in all arts. She goes on with a summary of the heroine's
previous traumatic experiences in Nevers, which she implies are
rather silly for reasons not stated, and asks "Was it possibly an
elaborate, masochistic fantasy for intellectuals?"

I now believe I overestimated *Hiroshima* somewhat—and Miss
Kael duly quotes an embarrassingly ardent passage from my review
to show it. My excuse is it was the first movie I'd seen in years that
used the medium with style and originality. But I still think the
Nevers flashbacks were as great cinema, in photography and montage and emotional effect, as anything I've seen, and I can't understand how Miss Kael could have been completely blind to their
quality whatever she thought about the falsity (which to me was
not apparent) of the heroine's sufferings. She seems, in fact, to have
reacted so strongly against the film as to have exactly reversed the
meaning of one scene.

> There is a crucial bit of dialogue: "They make movies to sell soap,
> why not a movie to sell peace?" . . . What makes the dialogue
> crucial is that the audience for *Hiroshima, Mon Amour* feels vir-
> tuous because they want to buy peace.

The question I want to ask is: Who's selling it? Not Resnais. It is the
woman (who has indeed come to Hiroshima to make a movie "to
sell peace"—its phoniness is made clear by shots of her in a stagey

472

Red Cross uniform) who asks the question. But her Japanese lover replies: "No, here in Hiroshima we do not joke about peace."

This is too long already to do more than mention Miss Kael's wholly contemptuous review of Fellini's *8½* as another example of her ascetic insensibility to the sensual pleasures of cinema—which is an art that appeals, after all, to the eye and the ear at least as much as to the mind—when she dislikes the literary content. Many other critics, as I noted in my review, valued the film much lower than I did, but she is one of the very few, among those who disliked the film as a whole, who didn't praise (or in her case apparently even notice) Fellini's virtuosity, his extraordinary command of the medium, and the distinction of di Venanzo's photography.

Coming to (2), Miss Kael is as ungenerous toward other critics as she is obsessed by them. She appears to consider them, almost without exception, as either rivals or butts or, usually, both. As if her security depended on eliminating all rivals to the throne. Certainly I am no exception. I was touched and pleased to read in the Acknowledgments: "And I wish to express my admiration and respect for Dwight Macdonald, who despite my hectoring him in print, has, personally, returned good for evil." Well, I suppose I'm at it again.

But I gather that Miss Kael's admiration and respect are for my moral rather than my mental qualities, since, of the thirteen references to me in the index, five are neutral while eight are hostile and, in most cases, unfair. I make my first appearance on page 20, classified with Richard Roud and the *Time* film critic as voguish, precious types who admire any nonsense so long as it is avant-garde and who revel in "experiences in pure form" and positively delight in a lack of content. "Dwight Macdonald calls *Marienbad* 'pure' cinema, a succession of images enjoyable in themselves," she quotes, accurately, from my review, but she omits the fact that I also criticized *Marienbad,* and denied it greatness despite the cinematic fascination it had for me, precisely because of its thinness and obscurity of content. This opening uppercut was especially jarring because it was so unexpected; up to page 20, I had been cozily thinking how much we agreed on so many points that many others don't agree on. I don't object to not being mentioned favorably, but I confess it's irritating to be often cited as an opponent, or a butt,

473

and never as an ally. I've written a good deal, for instance, against the *auteur* concept, but you'd never gather it from Miss Kael's lengthy survey. The cat that walks by herself.

On page 218, I am presented as a "square"—along with Stanley Kauffmann, another critic she might respect more than she seems to—who couldn't understand that *Jules and Jim* is an extraordinarily good film, when in fact I wrote a long and laudatory review. True, I did make some criticisms, a weakness of mine. On page 250 she welds me to my predecessor in this column, Kingsley Amis, as two blind mice who couldn't see the virtues of Satyajit Ray, although I began my first column with a fatherly lecture to Kingsley about his light-minded view of cinema in general and of *Pather Panchali* in particular. To think we Trotskyites used to protest against Stalinist "amalgams" in the innocent thirties—what amateurs they were! But words fail me (almost) when Miss Kael meditates on page 244: "Movies are, happily, a popular medium (which makes it difficult to understand why Dwight Macdonald with his dedication to high art sacrifices his time to them)." Considering that I've been writing about the movies as the most interesting "high art" of our century since the early thirties in little magazines like *The Miscellany, The Symposium,* and *Partisan Review,* this is a bit much. Nor has it ever bothered me that Griffith —or Dickens—were popular.

Maybe *I Lost It At The Movies* isn't as good a book as I thought it was when I began this review. And the hell with that "respect and admiration." (1965)

Cinema Eye, Cinema Ear: Some Key Film Makers of the Sixties, by John Russell Taylor; Hill and Wang, $5.95. Mr. Taylor, who writes on films for the London *Times* and *Sight and Sound,* is better at appreciating films than at criticizing them. His book is serious and, in general, intelligent, but it contrasts unfavorably with Pauline Kael's *I Lost It At The Movies.* Hers is sharp, direct, angular, disrespectful and often acidulous; his is smooth, urbane, reverential, often evasive and always mellifluous. She is a defiant outsider while he is safely ensconced inside the "in" citadel, as is shown by the directors he has selected to write about: Fellini, Antonioni, Buñuel, Bergman, Hitchcock, Bresson, Truffaut, Godard and Resnais. (His inclusion of Bergman, who hasn't been "in" for years, I think is due to cultural lag rather than daring.) For all Miss Kael's limitations—to be "in" is not, as she sometimes seems to assume, necessarily to be phony, and, except for his praise of recent work by Bresson, Godard and Hitchcock, I'd go along more with his taste in directors than hers—she is a critic, while Mr. Taylor is more of a fan.

It is amusing to observe his tactics when he has to deal with a product of one of his "key" directors (key to what? the kingdom of indom?) which he suspects may be terrible. Sometimes he takes evasive action on who-am-I-to-judge? lines. As with Resnais' *Muriel:* "Either you think it is a masterpiece or you cannot stomach it at all. My own feeling, I must confess, is closest [*sic*] to the latter position. . . . About such films there is really very little point in arguing." (I should think it is precisely such films that can best be argued about; but Mr. Taylor seems to think arguing a little vulgar, as perhaps it is.) Or on Fellini's disastrous episode in *Boccaccio '70:* "strange and not very successful . . . but at the same time one can see what Fellini is getting at." He can always see what a director is "getting at."

His other strategy, usually employed at the end of chapters on directors whose recent works have been disappointing, like Hitchcock and Antonioni, is to vanish like the cuttlefish in clouds of ink about The Future. Hitchcock: "After this peak [*Pyscho*] *The Birds* comes as something of a relaxation. . . . But what will come next from this most inventive, unpredictable of film makers is anyone's guess. Whatever it is, though, one can predict with reasonable safety that it will be brilliant of its kind." Like *Marnie*. His "in" approach is at its suavest in the conclusion of his chapter on Antonioni:

> Every film he makes is liable to elicit in advance almost as much dread as eagerness from even his most fervent admirers—a feeling intensified by the knowledge that his years as the height of fashion are bound to be paid for in the not too distant future by a violent reaction against his work. Will *Deserto Rosso,* his first film in color,

475

mark the beginning of a new Antonioni? And if it does, shall we like him as much as the old? That, alas, only time can tell.

That, alas, time has told: *Deserto Rosso* carries farther the attenuation of dramatic content that flawed *La Notte* and ruined *The Eclipse*. My faith—or anyway my hope and charity—survive, however, because it is always risky to write off a director of Antonioni's stature, and I have seen benign reversals, like Fellini coming up with *8½* after *La Dolce Vita*.* I don't subscribe to Mr. Taylor's *couturier* theory of cinema: that a *succès fou* is "bound to be paid for . . . by a violent reaction." This tells us more about ladies' hats than about art, for what is the whole "in" approach if not one of chic or, as our author dreadfully puts it, "the height of fashion"?

Perhaps I'm unfair. I may overrate Mr. Taylor's acumen and so think he is being disingenuous when he is merely being honest. A critic who thinks Hitchcock has made his best films since 1950 and who especially admires *Vertigo* ("perhaps the most haunting of all his works") and who calls Godard's *A Woman Is a Woman* "the most irresistible of his films" and his *My Life to Live* "a spiritual odyssey," must be credited with sincerity if only because the alternative is too depressing. Myself, I found *A Woman Is a Woman* resistible and *My Life to Live* tedious and yes I know that's the *point* and life is like that but I prefer to live mine outside the movie theatre and it's not as boring as M. Godard's film.

Mr. Taylor is one of those rare English journalists who writes badly. Can the most sincere of critics get away with calling anything "a spiritual odyssey"? I also think that, as a master of euphemism, he goes too far when he describes the scriptwriter in *8½*, whose contemptuous barbs drive Guido-Mastroianni to suicide, as "unhelpful." (1965)

* My faith in Antonioni was justified last year when he followed *Deserto Rosso* with the very different *Blow Up,* a fast, hard, varied entertainment which substituted satire for angst and was delightfully lacking in Monica Vitti.

Orange sunsets with black silhouettes against them; Confederate officers dashing, aristocratic, with yellow silk sashes; Union officers prosaic, bourgeois, no sashes; moonfaced black mammy—"yas'm," "sho sho," " 'tain't *fittin'!*"—devoted and comic (Hattie Mc-Daniel); high-spirited Southern belle tossing curls, pouting, often exclaiming "fiddle-dee-dee!" (Vivien Leigh); flighty, fluttery, feathery maiden aunt (Laura Hope Crews); burning of Atlanta in full color—horses plunging, horses neighing, hordes of costume extras rushing past camera, towers of flame, more silhouettes; Passion for The Soil symbolized by close-up of fist of squire of Tara (Thomas Mitchell) dribbling bits of it; noble, fair-haired, sad-eyed Southern gent (Leslie Howard) contrasted with cynical, dark-haired, bold-eyed adventurer (Clark Gable in terrific ascot ties); in short, all the humors and heartaches and glamour and stereotypes of women's-magazine fiction.

Such is *Gone With the Wind,* a reliable old property now in its fourth (or is it fifth?) international revival, a masterpiece of kitsch that is still entertaining after twenty years. It's corny and blowsy and phony, the slide trombone in the cinematic orchestra, and yet it is not boring. Why not?

(1) It keeps moving; if you don't like it, wait a minute. It has the brisk tempo that Hollywood movies used to have in the thirties. How lively and elliptical they were compared to the pedestrian languors of our films today; it now seems to take our directors twice as long to make their points. This is not because they have more to say; on the contrary, they hope, by laboring each scene, to disguise its emptiness, like a bore who tries to save a story by elaboration. (The clever bore cuts it short.) Victor Fleming was no great shakes as a director; I can't imagine even a French *cinéaste* pressing for a Fleming week at the *Cinémathèque.* But the late Margaret Mitchell crammed so much incident and characterization into her novel that Mr. Fleming was forced to step lively merely to keep ahead of the juggernaut of her invention. The quality of this invention is not fine, but there is considerable of it.

(2) GWTW is an unlikely mixture of romanticism and realism. It wallows in sentimentality, underlining every heartthrob with all the resources of music and photography, both exploited at their

477

most vulgar level. It has the courage of its bad taste. At the same time, it is quite tough-minded. Scarlett and Rhett are stock characters, but they are also individuals; she is selfish, greedy, unscrupulous, and these qualities are not glossed over any more than Rhett's cynicism and worldly callousness are—his contemptuous remarks about the high-minded gentleman played by Leslie Howard, the very pattern of a romantic hero, are refreshing. For all its heavy Victorian romanticism, GWTW is more realistic than any of our modern full-colored spectaculars. Its people—except for Melanie, a Dickensian heroine so good it is painful—don't fall into either the black or white moral slots, but are more in the gray range, like real people. In this respect, GWTW is also superior to the Tennessee Williams uncolored spectaculars—*Suddenly, Last Summer, The Fugitive Kind*—which divide the Saved from the Damned with Calvinistic rigor. In SLS and TFK one is told and told repeatedly and with great literary resource that Clift, Brando and Magnani are Saved while Hepburn and Jory are Damned. The dialogue in GWTW is less literary, but at least there is some doubt as to whether the heroine is a bitch—or rather, as to whether she is *only* a bitch. This makes it more interesting, more grown-up. Adult entertainment, that's what I like about *Gone With the Wind*. (1961)

Annals of Cinemectomy (Continued): I am informed that the last seven or eight minutes of Antonioni's *The Eclipse* have been cut from the prints shown in second-run theatres (even some in New York) so that the film now ends conventionally with the last scene in which the principals appear. The distributors probably thought the public would find this montage of atmospheric street shots puzzling and anticlimactic. They may be right, though audiences are often more sophisticated than our merchants of culture realize, but (a) how will people's taste improve if they are sheltered from aesthetic innovation? And (b) does even a businessman have a right to mutilate an artist's work? For mutilation it is, of the most serious kind. This final section, which naturally was hissed at

Cannes by the well-dressed barbarians who dominate there, is considered by many critics, myself included, the best thing in the movie. It is also essential to the whole composition, an abstract coda that restates in an original and powerful way the theme of isolation. But of course the stars don't appear in it—that's the whole point in fact—and so lop it off! (1964)

Movies: the History of an Art and an Institution, by Richard Schickel; Basic Books, $4.95. One of many lacunae in cinema literature, a body largely made of holes, is the lack of a general history. There are three good but limited works: Anderson-Richie's *The Japanese Film* (Grove, 1960), Siegfried Kracauer's *From Caligari to Hitler* (Princeton, 1947), and Lewis Jacobs' *The Rise of the American Film* (Harcourt, 1939). But the only two attempts at a general, international history I've found in English are the Bardèche-Brasillach *History of Motion Pictures,* which is both out-of-date (Norton, 1938) and mediocre, and Arthur Knight's *The Liveliest Art,* which is more current (Macmillan, 1957) and even more mediocre: an undiscriminating mess of tepid pottage that is useful mostly for its ten-page index of film titles.*

Mr. Schickel had a chance to fill the gap. It's too bad he's merely fallen into it. His work is ambitiously labeled "A Culture & Discovery Book," a series the publishers define, with professional optimism, as "combining sophistication of approach, individuality of style and simplicity of exposition." He achieves the last: "Unlike Mary Pickford . . . Chaplin was a screen artist of genuine distinction. There have been a thousand Pickfords through the years. There has been but one Chaplin." How true. The author's problem, with which he grapples manfully, is that while he knows, as a

* For the most complete, useful and up-to-date dictionary of films, directors, actors (including those bit players who made American movies what they were from 1920 to 1960) and technical terms see Leslie Halliwell's *The Filmgoer's Companion* (Hill & Wang, 1967, $12.50) an admirably comprehensive & concise reference work that never—well, hardly ever—fails to yield the data, including dates, one seeks.

479

sophisticated Culture & Discovery historian, that all that foreign stuff is Important, he also feels, as an American no-nonsense middlebrow, that Hollywood is no worse than a bad cold—sort of fun, really. *Cosa nostra.* He concedes not much can be said for Charlton Heston ("although he is a very useful performer," he adds, neglecting to define the utility to whom and for what), but he won't be hurried into extreme statements. "But if one is willing to approach [Rock] Hudson and [Tony] Curtis without preconceived attitudes, as do the youngsters who form the nucleus of their audience, there are pleasures to be gained from their presence," he writes. I'm willing enough but as an oldster with attitudes postconceived from long exposure to their performances I can't make it. I do agree, however, that "Curtis is a tremendously energetic performer."

Schickel's acceptance of Hollywood's amiable *cosa nostra* is the usual midcult blend of nostalgia and condescension. It gives way to uneasy suspicion when he has to cope with those unamiable, nonindigenous and often rather intellectual and even avant-garde movies everybody is always talking about. His eighth chapter, "A Regular Succession of Masterpieces," praises Antonioni at the expense of Fellini and Bergman ("In the end, Bergman is both boring and boorish," while Fellini's "bankruptcy" is "confirmed" by . . . "*8½*") and in terms ("Antonioni's characters live in a real world . . . no more tactile director now at work . . . gorgeously fluid sequence . . . achieves a reality, an intimacy with the environment which vaguer talents like Bergman and Fellini must envy") that made me wonder whether perhaps I have overestimated Antonioni. Earlier he does his duty, at length, by Eisenstein: "He was, very simply, a maker of epics. Not one of his films was a drama in which individual protagonists met in the classic situations of personal conflict." Like Milton or Dante. But after five pages of conscientious appreciation, full of Culture & Discovery, he comes down to earth: "Does all this mean that Eisenstein was the perfect film director? The answer is no. . . . For all their impressiveness as sights to behold, his films were curiously lacking in dramatic interest, suspense, in genuinely interesting character. Teeming with people, they were still often overly abstract works of art." Myself, I'm satisfied with the "impressiveness" of Eisenstein's films as "sights to behold"—I have a weakness for those pictures on the screen—and the last criticism I'd think of is a lack of "dramatic interest." I might have understood his charge of over-abstraction except that five pages later he writes: "The Buñuel films, perhaps because they are so abstract and general in theme, remain treats to see. *Caligari* and *Blood of a Poet* are difficult to view today. [Every time *I* see them, I'm struck with how exciting they still are, conceptually and technically.] There is nothing that dates as fast as yesterday's artistic radicalism." Like Giotto, Masaccio, Stendhal, Manet, Cézanne, and Joyce.

The last chapter ("Rain, Shine, or Kay Francis") comes down to terra firma again, namely Hollywood. After many pages of somewhat jittery euphoria—all those intellectuals breathing down his honest American neck—he concludes with the obligatory burst of optimism, or at least hope, a confused diapason in which the *vox humana* competes with less inspiriting chords: "When producers show a consistent ability to blend these elements ["technical skill," "ideology" and "building the feelings of felt reality about the ordinary life of our times"] then the American screen can lay claim to maturity. For the moment . . . it certainly cannot assert with any conviction that movies are better than ever. They are both better and worse. Like nearly everything at this midpoint of an agonizing century their future is ambiguous and the feelings of their friends ambivalent." Well, you can't say he's *wrong,* exactly.

There is one sentence in Mr. Schickel's book that I found both unambiguous and true:

"By and large, the world cinema has not been so fortunate in its historians." (1966)

The Films of Akira Kurosawa, by Donald Richie; University of California Press; $11. A big, handsomely designed book with many well-reproduced illustrations. Unlike many big, handsome movie books, it is even more impressive for its text than for its layout. Mr. Richie is the coauthor, with Joseph L. Anderson, of *The Japanese Film* (Grove Press, 1960; $2.95, paper), the definitive history. He

481

has lived in Japan for twenty years and has become to its cinema the kind of interpreter to the West that the translator, Arthur Waley, has been to its literature. His book on Kurosawa is comparable in scholarship, mastery of detail, interpretation and good writing to Richard Ellmann's biography of Joyce. I don't know any other study of a director's work that approaches its scope and intelligence. He devotes a chapter to each of Kurosawa's twenty-three movies to date, from *Sanshiro Sugata* (1943) to *Red Beard* (1965), "placing" each in the history of Japanese cinema and of Kurosawa's own development and analyzing each as to theme, story, acting, photography, music and directorial treatment. He goes into technique so extensively that I should think the book would be useful as a practical exposition of film-making regardless of one's special interest in Kurosawa.

A masterpiece of scholarship but not of criticism. Perhaps the very qualities that make it the former prevent it from being the latter, perhaps Mr. Richie knows too much, in a sense, is too deeply involved, too empathetic with Kurosawa's work—which he has seen in the making as well as on the screen—to be able to put enough distance between himself and his subject to make evaluation possible. There is almost no qualitative discrimination between the twenty-three films: all of them are valued on the same (high) level, which is untrue to life, artists being men, not gods, and therefore fallible.

His long—thirteen-page—appreciation of *Red Beard,* for example, failed to convince me it was any better than I thought when I saw it last fall at Lincoln Center. He meets the common objection that it is as sentimental as *Young Dr. Kildare* by arguing it is only as sentimental as Dickens or D. W. Griffith are at times, which may be true, but their better work, like Kurosawa's for that matter, had positive qualities I didn't find in *Red Beard.* Nor did his praise of the sound track convince me; granted that Kurosawa here "for the first time uses a stereophonic four-directional system," it nevertheless sounded like Hollywood "mood music." Critical anesthesia also mars the chapter on *They Who Step on the Tiger's Tail,* an almost perfect little (58-minute) work that is a favorite of mine. Almost perfect because the outrageous mugging of a low-comedy porter, more Ritz Brothers than Kabuki, clashes with the austere stylization of the rest of this legend of feudal loyalty. I learn from Mr. Richie that Kurosawa added this part to the traditional story because he wanted to include a popular comedian, apparently for the same box-office reasons we all condemn when we detect them in a Hollywood movie. ("We had to . . . make the picture lively," he quotes Kurosawa, without comment.) He comes close to criticism when he writes: "It is a straight film version of the historical anecdote (including additions from the No and the Kabuki versions) with but one change. But that change alters the entire meaning of the play. [It was] a bit like adding Jerry Lewis to the cast of *Hamlet.*" A page or two later, however, Mr. Richie reverts to empathy and scholarship, explaining at length how much livelier and, really, more *subtle* the simple old play became when Kurosawa jazzed it up with that popular comedian. Maybe Jerry Lewis could pep up *Hamlet,* too, one concludes.

The reader is warned not to take the bold-type subheads seriously, although they sound very businesslike and systematic: "TREATMENT," "THE STORY," "REALIZATION," "PRODUCTION," "EDITING," "MATERIALS," etc. They have little relation to the text and seem to have been stuck in by the layout designer wherever he thought the page needed some white space and a typographical accent—like, say, "CHARACTERIZATION," or maybe "CAMERA," depending on whichever fitted the space better. (1966)

Some circles in film criticism think it's square to consider subject matter. It's the technique that counts and the most hackneyed story can be transmuted into high art—in fact, the most circular and least square of film journals, *Cahiers du Cinéma,* often gives the impression that *only* a cheap thriller can yield high cinematic art. There's something in this emphasis on technique, which is at least more sensible than the opposite view that was held over here in the thirties when the proletarian novel, the "committed" artist and other absurdities of primitive Marxism were taken seriously (as they still are in England). But I wonder whether film-makers shouldn't begin to pay more attention to subject matter.

483

It's extraordinary what a narrow segment of human life is covered by our movies, and not only the Hollywood type but the best of the foreign ones too. It's all sex, violence, corruption, and all taken at their most pathological levels. Why do so few current films try to deal with two areas the novel has been at home with for a long time: history (beginning with Stendhal) and the prose of everyday life (beginning with Jane Austen)? History is reduced to costume drama. We have no lack of films about ancient Rome, but none about the New Deal; when Roosevelt is put on the screen, it is in *Sunrise at Campobello,* which has no politics in it, let alone history. One of the many originalities of *Citizen Kane* was that its subject was social—the effects of money and power—rather than personal. (Griffith and Eisenstein treated history in the epic style, like Homer; Welles brought in novelistic detail, like Tolstoy.) But no one has tried anything on that scale since, including Welles, who has narrowed his focus down to the usual sensational thriller from *The Stranger* (1946) and *The Lady from Shanghai* (1948) to *Touch of Evil* (1958).

As for everyday life, we get lots of "little man" pictures crammed with realistic detail—*Marty* is a sentimentalized and *The 400 Blows* an honest specimen—but, again, the personal is emphasized and the social excluded. Most of us spend half our life at work, for example, but this is the dark side of the moon as far as movies go; it is only our off-duty hours that are recorded on the silver screen. Marty's love life is thoroughly explored, but we get only a glimpse of him in the butcher shop. Zola's *L'Assommoir,* like his other novels, has a great deal about the working life of his proletarians but in *Gervaise,* the film René Clément made from it, this is reduced to a picturesque background for their after-hours of drinking and brawling and lovemaking. In *Rocco and His Brothers,* Visconti sketches in the laundry and the pugs' gym masterfully but skimpily; his real interest centers on the rape-mayhem-murder scenes which run on interminably. Myself, I wanted more laundering and less slugging.

I suggest that fights and killings are no longer exciting to watch for the same reason it's hard to pay attention to Beethoven's *Fifth;* we know every detail of the trip as a commuter knows every yard of the New Haven between Stamford and Grand Central. A bad man reaching for his six-shooter now affects me like a dentist reaching for his drill. Yet how interesting the professional life of a gunslinger might be on the screen, as against the usual theatrics. In fact, how interesting it is in Henry King's 1950 film, *The Gunfighter,* whose plot hinges on Gregory Peck's problems as an aging bad man. (The very notion that bad men grow old is as unusual in Hollywood as it is commonplace in the real world.) He is broke, homeless, tired, no pension or social security, and he is bored with killing. But his "rep" is so charismatic that every young punk in the dismal barrooms he frequents for lack of any better place to sit down aspires to hijack it by knocking him off, the only rule of succession recognized in the profession. A curious dilemma that must have vexed many a Western gunslinger in his sunset years, an occupational hazard like silicosis for a miner. Only Mr. King, among our filmic mythmakers, was clever enough to see it as dramatic material precisely because it was so unromantically undramatic in Hollywood terms. (1963)

INDEX

488

489

492